Unheard Voices
A Tranquebarian Stroll

Unheard Voices
A Tranquebarian Stroll

P. S. Ramanujam

University of Southern Denmark Studies in History and Social Sciences vol. 609

© P. S. Ramanujam and University Press of Southern Denmark, 2021
Printed by Specialtrykkeriet Arco A/S
Cover design: Dorthe Møller, Unisats Aps
ISBN 978-87-408-3328-7

Printed with support from:
Alfred Good's Fond
The Carlsberg Foundation
Farumgaard-Fonden
Den Hielmstierne-Rosencroneske Stiftelse
Konsul George Jorck og Hustru Emma Jorck's Fond
The Velux Foundations

University Press of Southern Denmark
www.universitypress.dk

Distribution in the United States and Canada:
Independent Publishers Group
www.ipgbook.com

Distribution in the United Kingdom and Ireland:
Gazelle Books
www.gazellebookservices.co.uk

Table of Contents

Preface 7

1. A Shipwreck and the Beginnings of a Colony 21
2. Jón Ólafsson's Saga 39
3. Inebriety, Intrigue and Slavery 55
4. Murders, Property Disputes and Caste Conflicts 67
5. Pluripotency, Power and Painting 85
6. A Stowaway from Tranquebar 113
7. A Forgotten Astronomer – A Forgotten Blessed Soul 127
8. Death, Despotism and Destruction 151
9. Pietism, Printing and Peccadillos 187
10. Philology comes to Town 217
11. Pride, Pomp and Circumstance 233
12. The Old Cemetery 257
13. A Musician and His Tragic Fate 273
14. Plunder in Porto Novo 279

Journey's End 355

Glossary of Indian terms 361
Bibliography of principal sources 363
List of Archival material from the National Archives 373
Notes 375
Index 409

Preface

The name 'Tranquebar' conjures an exotic, magical, and spicy connotation in most people. People tend to group all the 'bars' – Zanzibar, Nicobar, Malabar, and, of course, Tranquebar. The 'bar' is just a linguistic element and has no special significance in this context. Many are blissfully unaware of the existence of a sleepy little fishing village called Tranquebar on the south-eastern coast of India, but this was, in fact, the foremost institution representing 225 years of occupation by the Danes.

We have arrived in southern India – more specifically in Chennai, or Madras as it was called earlier, the capital city of the state of Tamilnadu. We are on our way to Tranquebar to explore the legacy left by the Danes. Denmark[1] occupied this area starting in 1620 and ending in 1845 with the sale of the colony to the British. Tharangampadi, or Tranquebar as it is more widely known, was the mainstay of the Danes in India.[2] How did the Danes get here? What were they doing here? What was life like during this period?

After getting used to the chaos and noise, the crowds and the hustle and bustle of the megacity of Chennai, we can start our exploration with a visit to the museum in Fort St. George displaying Danish silverware and cutlery. Later, we may take a slight detour to visit the Government Museum in Egmore to admire the fine Chola[3] bronzes, but also look at the cannons outside the building. They were made in the town of Frederiksværk in Denmark during the reign of Christian VII (1749-1808). And may be a tour to the Schmidt Memorial on Elliot's Beach in south Chennai? This is a memorial dedicated to the memory of Kaj Schmidt, a Dane, who drowned after saving the life of a British girl on 30 December 1930. Muthiah, a well-known historian of Chennai, says about the incident: 'That evening, the girl arrived at a grand ball being held in the city, as though nothing had happened.'[4]

We leave for Tranquebar the next day. A drive from Chennai to Tranquebar takes about 7 - 8 hours. It is only about 300 kms south of Chennai. We leave Chennai at about 8 in the morning. The first part of the route, up to Puduchery (earlier Pondichery), is good. Even though this is a national highway, you can expect some counter traffic on your side – we drive, *in principle*, on the left side. Cows and buffaloes, bicyclists and pedestrians can still find their way across to your side. We may even do some sightseeing on the way – why not stop at the remnants of the Dutch colonies of Alamparai or Sadraspatnam. Not at historic Mahabalipuram, though – it will require quite a few days. We reach the former French territory of Pondichery, or Pondy as it is fondly called, for lunch. After lunch, we drive through the narrow alleys of Cuddalore, another historic town. Then on to Chidambaram, an important temple town. Now the vista opens – pleasant rice fields full of greenery. The road, however, is narrow. Only the middle third is paved. Who has the right of way? That depends on who has the bigger vehicle. Finally, around 4 pm, we sight the tower of the Thirukadaiyur Temple – a place where Markandeya[5] was granted eternal life. A short distance afterwards, we see the entrance to Tranquebar.

16 April 2020 marked the 400th year of its Danish connection. On that day 400 years ago, Tranquebar was made available for Danish settlement by the Nayak of Tanjore; the Nayak signed an informal letter on a gold leaf. These days, the place is a peaceful town with no heavy traffic, and quiet by Indian standards. This place, which served as the administrative headquarters of the Danes for more than two centuries, deserves to be known to a broader public. Today, a casual visitor, not too interested in history, would be able to walk around the town and see the most important sights in about 2 hours. Ihle, a Christian Missionary from Denmark, visiting Tranquebar in 1888, noted (my translation from Danish), 'One does not need an hour to see the whole town, and in the countryside, there was only one place of interest – the cremation ground[6]… A whole month, we thought after spending eight days, will be almost unbearable' [Ihle]. Peder Hansen, the last governor of the Danish colony, remarked that the place was 'gloomier than a spruce forest' [Madsen].[7] For Peder Hansen and most of the other Danes living in Tranquebar, it might have been a gloomy place. For the later generations of visitors, tourists and historians, the site is exciting, brimming with history – a history told by the many archival and historical documents preserved in Denmark as well as India.

Denmark also had a colony at Serampore (Srirampur) in Bengal, and several trading posts, such as in Masulipatnam in Andhra Pradesh and

Calicut (Kozhikode) in Kerala. However, Tharangampadi, or Tranquebar as it is known, was the mainstay of the Danes in India between 1620 and 1845. During its heyday, the Danes controlled an area of approximately 50 square kilometres around the seat of power that was Tranquebar. In an area less than 1 square kilometre, Danes, French, English, Dutch, Germans, Portuguese, Armenians, Tamils, Telugus and Marathis coexisted in peace[8] [Ramanujam 2016]. This spatial and temporal confinement of the various cultures together with a large amount of archival information available in Denmark and India makes the history of Tranquebar unique.

In the National Archives in Copenhagen, Denmark (referred to as Rigsarkivet in Danish or RA for short), over 100 shelf-metres of documents in Danish exist – several of them have been read and cited elsewhere in the literature. There are also hundreds of documents in Tamil; few of these have been read and consulted. None of these is known to a broad audience either in India or in Denmark. There are also approximately a hundred Marathi (Modi) documents in Denmark. Several of these have been edited, translated, and analysed by Elisabeth Strandberg [Strandberg 1983]. The present book covers only the Danish period between 1620 and 1845, primarily because of the large amount of available archival information. At the Tamilnadu Archives in Chennai [Pandian], close to 300 bundles of documents from Tranquebar have not yet been studied in-depth.

Tranquebar was given to the Danes by the Nayak of Tanjore. We do not know how much 'tribute' was paid to the Nayak of Tanjore[9] between the years 1620 and 1644. Whatever it was, the amount was fixed at 2,000 Pardau in 1644 and remained unchanged until 1845.[10] Assuming that one Pardau was approximately equivalent to one Rigsdaler (rdl), the annual tribute to the Tanjore kings was 2,000 rdl from 1644 onwards. In Denmark, the salary of an ordinary worker was somewhat more than 1 rdl per day and that of a mason was about 2 rdl per day. To indicate the buying power in Denmark, for about ½ rdl one could buy 20 eggs; a couple of hens cost about 1 rdl, an ox 8-13 rdl, a cow 4-6 rdl, a pig 2 rdl and a lamb about 1 rdl. A thousand bricks cost 7-10 rdl [Thestrup 1999]. In Tranquebar, one could exchange 1 rdl for 10 fanoes. Jón Ólafsson, an Icelander stationed in Tranquebar in 1623, says that 1 fano had as much buying power in India as 1 rdl in Denmark. Remarkably, it is also possible to compare the monetary power in Tranquebar directly with that in Denmark. A document from the National Archives in Copenhagen[11] gives the salary of a bricklayer to be 1¾ fano per day in 1787 in Tranquebar whereas the corresponding salary in Denmark was 2 -2½ rdl [Thestrup]. Figuratively, in India, you could buy about 4,000 cows a year, or approximately 2 million bricks for the sum of 2,000 rdl. During the 225 years of rule, the Danes have left their mark in the form of several landmarks made of bricks – a fort from 1620, several houses and institutions, Lutheran churches and several churchyards, as well as names of streets, all of which tell many a story.

This book is about the historical significance of the town of Tharangampadi (pronounced Tharangambadi) or Tranquebar. It describes remarkable people and events in the town over the 225 years, as gleaned from the archives in Denmark. This book is not intended for serious political analysts, but rather a straightforward narrative of people, events, and life in general based on popular landmarks of the town. Historians may still find the citations from original documents at the end of the book useful for later analyses.

The book is arranged as a heritage tour of the town that was. We walk through five or six streets in the town, stopping at places where remarkable personalities had stayed between the years 1620 and 1845. In this way, a link can be established between the present and the past. Let us hear their stories from the documents of the National Archives of Denmark. The actual walk following our route through the town would take about an hour or two – but the fascinating stories of the people could fill several years. One event dominates the book – the plunder of Porto Novo in 1780 by Heider Ali's[12] troops. Most history books leave this unmentioned, or devote perhaps half a line to it. But as this event involves a Danish resident[13] of English origin, there are several documents concerning it in the National Archives. We hear the story from three different sources and, in the last chapter, from the person himself who was involved in the events.

I am indebted to several persons, who have made this work possible. I have corresponded with several, who had the patience to reply to me. I would like to acknowledge help and support from Kirsten Andersen, Torben Abd-el Dayem (posthumous), Helmer Aslaksen, Benjamin Asmussen, Lennart Bes, Lisbeth Cederberg, Jean Deloche, Esther Fihl, Erik Gøbel, Michael Helgert, Dennis Brauer Iversen, Niklas Thode Jensen, Viggo Knudsen, Søren Koustrup, Heike Liebau, Susanne Lindhard, Erik Hellerup Madsen, C. S. Mohanavelu, Andrew Murray, Ramachandran

Nagaswamy, P. S. Narasimhan, Kim Parfitt, Karl Peder Pedersen, P. S. Raghunandanan, V. J. Ramachandran (posthumous), Maria Refer, Simon Rastén, Christian Samraj, R. Sankar, Revathi and Vasudevan Srinivasan, P. R. Subramaniam, Ganesan Sundaram, Asger Svane-Knudsen, Venkat Vaidhyanathan, A. R. Venkatachalapathy and Bente Wolff. I also thank the reviewer of this manuscript before it went to publication. A very special thanks to Karin Knudsen, Tranquebar Association, for her untiring support and the many discussions and pictures during the entire project. The assistance of the staff of the National Archives in Copenhagen, the Royal Library in Copenhagen and the Public Library Service in Roskilde who dug up several of the reference books is gratefully acknowledged. The library service in Denmark, bibliotek.dk, has provided a fantastic service by getting all the literature that I requested. The free availability of books and articles in Google Books as well as the Digital Library of India, archive.org and academia.edu helped my work a great deal. I also thank Henriette Gavnholt Jacobsen, Handels- og Søfartsmuseet in Helsingør, Denmark for Ib Andersen's paintings and Christina Peters, bpk-Bildagentur, Berlin for permission to reproduce the portrait of Thomas Christian Walter. I thank the graphic designer of this book, Rikke Kvisgaard Laursen, for her excellent work.

This work is the result of more than 100 trips to the National Archives and the Royal Library in Copenhagen. All the transcriptions and translations in the book are mine unless specifically indicated. As anyone who has tried to do serious translation from one foreign language to another knows, one must be an expert in both languages to do justice. I must confess that I am not an expert in any language. I gratefully acknowledge the assistance of Karen Bek-Pedersen for her careful proofreading and copy editing and for her valuable comments. To avoid future misinterpretations, I have tried to give the original text in the Notes where possible. It is my intention to publish several original documents on my homepage, www.tharangampadi.dk; some of them can already be viewed.

All the photographs in the book are my own unless otherwise stated. As this is not an exhaustive work on Tranquebar, only monographs and publications relevant to the manuscript are listed in the Bibliography. For the sake of completeness, however, I have included a citation to the Tranquebar Initiative, which contains several references to the Danish rule from the last ten years or so, as well as to more recent details, where available.

'Many a mickle makes a muckle' is a Scottish saying. Publishing a book of this kind requires a lot of funding. I take this opportunity to express my gratitude to Alfred Good's Fond, Carlsbergfondet, Den Hielmstierne-Rosencroneske Stiftelse, Farumgaard-Fonden, Konsul George Jorck og Hustru Emma Jorck's Fond and Velux Fonden for their gracious support in the publication of this book.

Finally, I would also like to thank University Press of Southern Denmark and Michael Dam Petersen for their interest in publishing a book on the Danish Colony in India. Thank you, Michael, for your infinite patience.

Tranquebar
– a time capsule

14th century: Kulasekhara Pandian established the town of Shadanganpadi – later to become Tharangampadi.

1618: Christian IV (1577-1648) of Denmark sent an expedition consisting of four ships under the leadership of Ove Gedde (1594-1660) to Ceylon. Persuaded by a Dutch merchant, Marchelis de Boshouwer, Christian IV wanted to establish a treaty with the Emperor of Ceylon. The expedition left Denmark on 14 November 1618. Already during August 1618, Roelant Crappé, another Dutch merchant, left Copenhagen on the ship *Øresund* for East-India to pave the way for Ove Gedde's mission and was given the rights to trade and settle in Tranquebar.

1620: Roelant Crappé (as his name appears in the archival documents), having reached Ceylon (now Sri Lanka) during December 1619, captured small Portuguese vessels carrying areca nuts and rice. The Portuguese, however, lay in wait and wrecked *Øresund* outside the town of Caracal (Karaikal). Crappé was given asylum by Raghunatha Nayak. During April 1620, Raghunatha Nayak wrote a letter on a gold foil permitting Danes to settle at the newly established port of Tharangampadi (Chapter 1). Ove Gedde reached Ceylon on 18 May 1620 and found that Boshouwer had cheated him. Boshouwer and his son, Christian, had died on the way. Ove Gedde contacted Roelant Crappé, who invited him to visit the Nayak at Thanjavur (Tanjore). This resulted in a treaty between Raghunatha Nayak and Christian IV. One original of this treaty in Portuguese with Raghunatha Nayak's signature in Telugu is preserved at the

National Archives in Copenhagen. Roelant Crappé became the first administrator of Tranquebar and held this position from 1620 until 1636.

In **1623**, Jón Ólafsson from Iceland arrived in Tranquebar. He was a soldier at the Danish fort of 'Dansborg' for one year. He had ample opportunity to observe the daily life in India, and about forty years later wrote down his memoirs, giving fascinating details of his life in India. The descriptions of the last years of Ólafsson's life were completed by his son (Chapter 2).

1637-1643: Bernt Pessart was the Governor during this period. He was described as 'intelligent, but most unreliable'.

1643-1648: Willem Leyel was the new Governor. Two chaplains attained notoriety during this period for their irresponsible drunken behaviour. Both were sentenced to death by drowning. This sentence was carried out on Christen Petersen Storm, while the other chaplain, Niels Andersen Udbyneder, was sentenced to exile (Chapter 3).

1655-1669: The colony survived under the leadership of Eskild Andersen Kongsbakke. Kongsbakke came along as a constable with Willem Leyel. At times, Kongsbakke was the only Dane in the colony. He married a native lady. However, not much is known about his family.

1681: Satire was not appreciated in Denmark, and satire of the king, in particular, was punished with death. The Danish parson, Jacob Worm, was guilty of not only parodying well-established civil servants, but also of making indirect criticisms of the king, his mistress and their illegitimate children. He was tried by the police in Denmark and was sentenced to death, but because of his wife's indefatigable efforts, his sentence was commuted to exile in Tranquebar. Jacob Worm died at the end of 1691 or beginning of 1692 and was buried at the Atangarai (Nygade) Churchyard in Tranquebar (Chapter 12).

1705: The first Royal Protestant mission was established. The pietist king of Denmark, Frederik IV, was interested in sending missionaries to India and, as he could not find suitable persons in Denmark, he had to seek the help of Frankesche Stiftung in Halle, Germany.

1706: Bartholomäus Ziegenbalg (1682-1718) and Heinrich Plütschau (1677-1752) arrived in Tranquebar on 9 July 1706. Their successful Mission continues to this day. The first printing press in Tamilnadu was established by Ziegenbalg (Chapter 9).

1759-1790: Several members of Moravian Brethren came to Tranquebar. Their history can be seen at http://www.moravianchurcharchives.org/thismonth/10_07%20Tranquebar.pdf

1781-1845: Fighting between castes plagued the colony for several years. The disputes between the right hand castes, dominated by the Vellalar agricultural community, and the left hand Panchalar or Kammalar handicraft community consisted mainly of rights to carry out religious and wedding processions, status symbols etc. The Danish government did not want to get involved in this process. A 'Black Court' consisting of six Indian assessors (two Hindus, two Muslims and two Christians) was appointed to settle the disputes between the natives (Chapter 4). Since most of the Danes did not attain a sufficient fluency in Tamil, dubashes or interpreters were appointed. Gradually, the dubashes acquired more power. The Governor during this period, Peter Hermann Abbestée, was extremely lenient and allowed his subordinates (and their dubashes) to accumulate private wealth and power. Daniel Pulley was one of them (Chapter 8). Both Viraraghava Ayyangar and Gulam Muhammad served as intermediaries between the Raja of Tanjore and the Danish Government, as well as assessors at the Black Court. Their letters also document local histories, such as the invasion by Tippu Sultan, son of Heider Ali and an ally of the French in India.

1778-1807: Flourishing days for Danish overseas trade and commerce. In Tranquebar, this was also an action-packed period. Thomas Christian Walter, a baroque musician, leader of a concert ensemble in Copenhagen, found that his music did not interest people anymore and that his marriage was in shambles. He decided to become a civil servant in Tranquebar, and he rose quickly to the number two position in the cabinet after the Governor, which was that of the Chief of Finance. He died in Tranquebar at the age of only 39 – but the probate he left leaves no doubt regarding the wealth he possessed. It also throws light on the life of well-to-do civil servants in the colony (Chapter 11). Carl Ludvig Runge, a contemporary with Walter, was a sexton at the local Zion Church. He had the misfortune to threaten one of the missionaries in a fit of rage and was sent back to Denmark, leaving his very young children behind in Tranquebar. He never came to see them again (Chapter 13). The 1780s also saw the intensifying of the British-French wars (Mysore Wars) - Heider Ali, the de facto ruler of Karnataka, was everywhere. His son, Saeed Saheb, plundered Porto-Novo and took the Danish resident, Gowan Harrop, a hostage (Chapter 14).

1787-1791: Henning Munch Engelhart established an Astronomical observatory at the Zion Church in Tranquebar. Tragically, he died of malaria in 1791 while surveying the Nicobar Islands (Chapter 7).

1788-1806: Peter Anker, a Norwegian by birth, was appointed Governor of Tranquebar (Chapter 5). Peter Anker spent his early years in England and was thus favourable towards the English. One of his subordinates, Franz von Lichtenstein, was inclined towards France. This created a lot of tension in the colony. Daniel Pulley became unfriendly with Peter Anker as well as his dubash, Piragasam Pullei. One fascinating result was that an Indian from Tranquebar, Chinnayya Naik, landed in Copenhagen in 1795 to complain about Peter Anker to the King of Denmark. He was allowed to stay until his complaints were investigated. Unfortunately for him, Peter Anker's brother - Carsten Anker - was a Director in the Danish East India Company. Chinnayya Naik acquired expensive habits during his stay and borrowed heavily from the citizens of Copenhagen, promising to repay them in diamonds. He also married a Dane and had a daughter. Chinnayya Naik lost his case and was ordered to leave the country. He disappeared in South Africa on the way back to East India in 1803 (Chapter 6).

Peter Anker was also an artist and many of his paintings can be seen in Oslo (https://www.khm.uio.no/forskning/samlingene/etnografisk/artikler/bilder/ankers-malerier/). He later returned to Norway to his farm outside of Oslo where he died in 1832.

1808-1815: British occupation of Tranquebar.

1822: The philologist, Rasmus Rask, arrived in Tranquebar on his way to and back from Ceylon (Chapter 10). Dr. Rühde arrived in Tranquebar as a surgeon in 1804-1805 and worked there for 27 years. He died in 1832 and is buried in the Nygade (Atangarai) Churchyard. He wrote a very detailed article on the general health of the citizens of Tranquebar and surroundings (Chapter 12).

1845: Denmark loses its trade in India, and the English take over. The Danish government decided to sell the colony to the English in 1845. Peder Hansen was the Governor at the time. The colony was sold for 1,125,000 rdl. Peder Hansen had started writing the history of the colony.

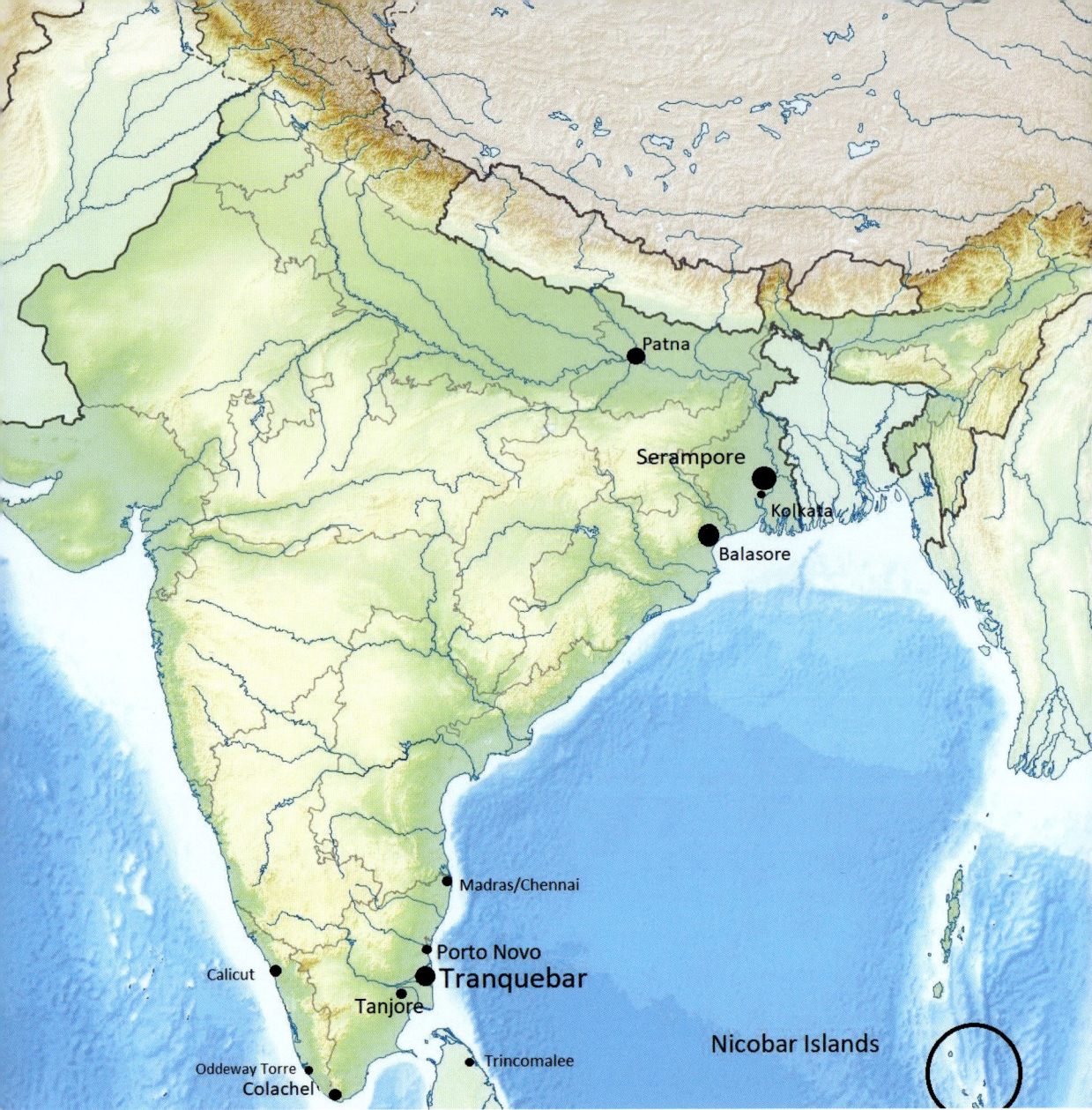

Map 1: Danish settlements in India. The Danes arrived in Tranquebar in 1620, and this was the headquarters for the next 225 years. Spices, such as pepper and cloves, were exported from here to Denmark. The second major settlement was Serampore, close to Calcutta (Kolkata), which was established in 1755. Fine muslins, gunpowder and opium were the prime exports from here. Other trading posts were established on both the west and east coasts of India, at Oddeway Torre (Eduva Thura, 1696), Balasore (Baleshwar, 1625) and Piply (Baliapal, 1625). Danish factories were founded in Calicut (Kozhikode, 1752), College (Colachel, 1755), Masulipatnam (1625) and Porto Novo (Parangipettai, 1669), Dannemarksnagore (1698), Patna (1732) and the Nicobar Islands (1754). Tanjore (Thanjavur) was the seat of the Nayaks and, later, Maratta kings (Topographic map of India, Wikimedia).

Map 2: Map of Tranquebar; a heritage walk around the town is indicated by the red line. The background map was made by a group of Danish architects in 1985. The numbers indicate the buildings and structures relating to persons described in the text. These numbers follow the chapters (Architectura 9, Arkitekturhistorisk Årsskrift, Selskabet for Arkitekturhistorie, København (1987) p. 74).

I

A Shipwreck and the Beginnings of a Colony

Late in the year 1619,[14] a Danish cutter, *Øresund*, was prowling the waters around Karaikal on the south-east coast of India when it was suddenly attacked by a fleet of six galleys under the command of Andre Botelho da Costa.[15] Its captain, Roelant Crappé,[16] and twelve of his crew escaped thanks to the assistance of a local fisherman. Salary entries from Leyel's period note: 'Cuti's mother, a woman whose husband saved the life of

Fig. 1.1: The new Masilanathar temple in Tranquebar. The first temple from 1305 named the town as Shadanganpadi, which over time evolved into Tharangampadi. The original temple, built a few hundred metres from the shore, has since been swallowed by the sea (photo: P. S. Ramanujam).

General Crappé when he lost his ship, *Øresund*, outside Carical' and record that she was paid 1 pardou every month for 25 years in gratitude as her husband saved Crappé's life.[17] The cutter was wrecked, and the rest of the crew captured and murdered by the Portuguese. Four heads were displayed on stakes to warn the enemies. Earlier, the cutter had captured several small Portuguese junks laden with rice and areca nuts on the east coast and auctioning goods with the permission of the King of Kandy. Roelant Crappé managed to reach the court of Raghunatha Nayak at Tanjore, to whom he must have expressed the wishes of his employer, Christian IV of Denmark, regarding trade relations in south-east Asia. A letter written by Raghunatha Nayak on 16 April 1620 on a gold-foil asserts: 'We order the creation of a port named Tharangampadi here and allow the export of pepper to that country (Denmark), as it is rare there'. Had it not been for Crappé and the brave, lonely fisherman from Karaikal, Tranquebar would not have made history. The unheard voice of a fisherman thus becomes all too important to neglect.

Today there is a town entrance, called 'Landporten', from the Danish period through which most of the traffic passes. We will come back here later. But let us walk down to the end of King Street – yes, that is what it is called even today – to the beach. There is a proper, paved road up to the parade ground, then a paved path on to the beach. We look to the left (towards north) where an old temple once stood and this is where the old history of the town began.[18] We shall start our stroll from this point.

A temple from the year 1305 devoted to the god Shiva stood close to the shore for several centuries. Known today as the Masilamaninathar (or Masilanathar) temple, it contained a stone inscription (now believed to be lost in the sea[19]) pointing to the origin of the name of the town. Maravarman Kulasekhara Pandyan, who was a devotee of the Hindu god, Shiva, named the place Shadanganpadi (Sanskrit: shad – six, angan – branches; Tamil: padi – town). According to Hindu philosophy, Shiva is the source of the six branches of the Vedas and the town was thus named after Him. Shadanganpadi eventually evolved into Tharangampadi – village of waves.[20] It has become a fashion to call the place the town of singing waves. No doubt, this arises because of the term 'padi'.[21] However, it should be mentioned that there are more than 200 places in Tamilnadu whose names end in 'padi',[22] and none else is associated with singing. It was here close to the temple that the Danes were allowed by the Nayak king of Thanjavur, Raghunatha, to establish a trading port, as confirmed by the gold foil letter given to Roelant Crappé.

By any means, this is a magnificent map of the town of Tranquebar (see next page) and all the more remarkable because the man who drew it had never been to Tranquebar.[23] The map is the work of Gregers Daa Trellund in 1733 from a sketch by an unknown person, probably from around 1690.[24] The perspective may be partly unrealistic, but the overall impression is majestic. There are some exquisite details on the map, such as the ox-driven oil press[25] at the corner of the Bazaar and Naichen (Naiken) Street at the top left, or the presence of a temple car on Kalnein Street, or the infamous wooden horse in the fort grounds. One of the largest structures, apart from the Danish fort, is the Masilanathar Temple at the corner of Setti Street and Frederik Street. Today, the old temple has been swallowed up by the sea. The new temple is less than ten years old.

In the 16th century, trade between East India and Europe was carried out almost exclusively by the Portuguese. Portuguese had also become the standard language of commerce. The Dutch were the ones to distribute the goods to northern Europe, and they collected the goods in Lisbon, Sevilla or other ports in Spain and Portugal. At the end of the year 1580, King Filip II of Spain forbade trade with Holland after Portugal and Spain merged. In 1588, Filip II captured all the Dutch ships in Spanish and Portuguese harbours. Later, the Dutch responded in kind. Even though the situation eased later, the Dutch continued to look for ways of establishing direct trade with India. In 1594, the Dutch opened their first trading company in India. During the 1590s, several small private trading companies were established. However, to combat the fighting among themselves and against pirates, the Dutch established an octroi for 'Vereinigte Ostindische Compagnie (VOC)' in 1602. The dividends were high, up to 75%. Danish sailors who visited India on Dutch ships brought news of the great treasures that could be won. Christian IV of Denmark was very interested in advancing the commercial and industrial potential of the country.

The history of Tranquebar starts in Denmark. Today, Christian IV is undoubtedly the best-known king to have ruled Denmark. He never hid his light under a bushel. In a perspective painting made by Johannes van Wijck in 1611, the merits of the city of Copenhagen are attributed to Christian IV. The picture has the title 'Copenhagen metropolis and port to the celebrated Denmark.'[26] Christian IV ascended the throne in 1596 at the age

Fig. 1.2: Map of Tranquebar drawn by Gregers Daa Trellund in 1733, it is an elaborated version based on a sketch from 1690. The map contains some exquisite details, such as an ox-drawn oil mill at the top left, a chariot of Gods on Kalnein Street (Pagodwognen) and a wooden horse used for punishment inside the compound of the fort. The mosque as well as 11 Hindu temples (four devoted to the God of Wisdom who has an elephant's head, Pulleyar) have been recorded on this map. Note the absence of the Zion Church and the New Jerusalem Church, which were built after the initial sketch map was drawn (photo: The Royal Library, Copenhagen).

of 11.²⁷ At the beginning of the 17th century, the kingdom of Denmark was vast – encompassing present day Denmark, Norway and a large part of what is now Sweden, as well as also controlling Slesvig and Holstein, now Northern Germany, as far south as the river Elbe. Having been in power for 20 years, this enterprising king wanted to expand the Danish export and import trade. He sent expeditions to Greenland and was interested in finding an alternative route to Asia through either the north-east passage north of Norway and Russia, or the north-west passage north of Canada through Hudson Bay.²⁸ The riches of the Orient were well known in the Occident. Since Vasco de Gama had arrived in India in 1498, Europe had already established trade links with India. According to an agreement between the Spanish and the Portuguese, the Spanish controlled all trade west of longitude 48° W, while the Portuguese were in charge east of there, thus controlling trade with India. Later, the Dutch also became pioneers in seafaring, becoming major players in the Oriental trade.²⁹

Two Dutch merchants – Jan de Willem and Hermann Rosenkrantz – first proposed the establishment of a Danish trading company to Christian IV in 1616.³⁰ Christian IV approved a charter for the Danish East India Company, assuring its management. He acquired shares in the company himself, which was to be run by a board of directors. In 1617, a Dutch merchant by the name of Marcelis Michielszoon de Boshouwer³¹ arrived in Denmark, claiming to be an ambassador of the Emperor of Ceylon. He displayed an impressive list of credentials said to be bestowed upon him by the Emperor:³² 'Prince of Migomme, Knight of the Order of the Golden Sun, President of the Wartime Council, Admiral and Naval Captain of the Kingdom of Ceylon'.³³ After the death of the Emperor, his son, Senerat Adassin, assumed the throne. Boshouwer now served the new king. In 1615, he left Ceylon at the behest of King Senarat, seeking military help to defeat the Portuguese. They were making life miserable on the eastern coasts of India and Ceylon. Hoping to get help, he visited Masulipatnam in India, Bantam in Java and then Holland. The Dutch, however, concentrated on strengthening their connections to Java and Sumatra and would not offer him any help. Later, having heard about Danish interests in the East, he arrived at the court of Christian IV. There were already many Dutch merchants and sailors employed in the Danish navy. Boshouwer was able to convince Christian IV that trading in Ceylon was very lucrative. He presented a document purportedly signed by the Emperor of Ceylon, giving him the Power of Attorney to negotiate on behalf of the Emperor. On 30 March 1618, Christian IV signed a treaty with Boshouwer, according to which Denmark would help the Emperor for seven years, providing him with a ship and 300 soldiers.[34] In return, the Danes could construct a fort, hold trading rights for 12 years and were promised a sum of 94,449 rdl. Christian IV eventually became the godfather for Boshouwer's son, who was naturally christened Christian.

An expedition to Ceylon set sail on 29 November 1618. The commander of the expedition was Ove Gedde. Ove Gedde, born in Tomarp (Kvidinge) in southern Sweden, was in possession of a solid judicial and military knowledge. At the young age of 24, he was appointed the commander of the fleet. The expedition consisted of four ships, two from the Royal Navy (*David* and *Elefanten* – warships) and two from the Danish East India Company (*Christian* and *København* – merchant ships).[35] The provisions aboard consisted of herring, cod, salmon, eel and dried fish in barrels, salted fish, pork, beef, meat without bones, 2 lasts[36] of grain, 4 lasts of peas, 46 lasts of bread, 16 lasts of butter, 10 ammes[37] of oil in case the butter ran out (or became rancid), 2 lasts of rusks, 13 lasts of beer, 1 barrel of fine beer, 84 ammes of sparkling wine, 4 ammes of strong sweet white wine, 72 ammes of French wine, 4 ammes of thin wine, 10 ammes of vinegar, 3 ammes of distilled spirits. Besides, there was rice, millet, wheat flour, salt, mustard and horseradish. There were also 650 pieces of cheese and about 160 kg of candles. There were 6 living lambs and 24 hens. Spices and condiments such as pepper, saffron, cloves, mace, ginger, nutmeg, capers, camomile, prunes, currants, almonds, candied lemon peels, candied ginger and about 240 litres of lemon juice to prevent scurvy were also on board. There was enough provision on *David* for 100 men for 15 months, and on *Copenhagen*, for 70 soldiers for 15 months. The ration on board was 3½ pounds[38] of bread and ¾ pound of butter per week, with meat rations consisting of ¼ pound of pork and ½ pound of beef three times a week, ¼ pound of dried fish four times a week, and about a litre of beer per day to start with [Abd-el Dayem 2006]. 'Among the stores were 283 carcasses of oxen which the King had bought from his wife's mother, Ellen Marsvin'.[39]

By the time they reached the Cape of Good Hope, Ove Gedde noted in his diary that 200 people on board the ships had died. Suddenly, having passed the Cape, the ship *David* with Boshouwer on board disappeared. It was not seen again until reaching Ceylon. During the voyage, relations between Gedde and Boshouwer were frosty, if not hostile. At the beginning of April 1620, the fleet reached the island of Socotra. On 16 May 1620, they sighted the enchanting island of Ceylon. To his chagrin, Gedde found during their first contact with the locals that the 'Emperor' turned out to be the Raja (king) of Kandy who had concluded a peace treaty with the Portuguese three years earlier. Gedde also found that both Boshouwer and his young son Christian had died en route, at Stephan von Hagens Bay[40]. During the ensuing discussions, it became clear that the king knew nothing about the treaty with the Danish king and that the document submitted to Christian IV by Boshouwer was a forgery. He did not recognise any of the content of the document; however, he promised to fulfil all the points in the treaty, except that he could not pay the amount demanded by the Danes.

While Ove Gedde was negotiating with the Raja of Kandy in early September 1620, Roelant Crappé from Tanjore contacted Gedde with the news that Raghunatha Nayak of Tanjore would be willing to establish trade with Denmark. Ove Gedde saw an opening and arrived at Tranquebar on 13 September 1620.

The much later funeral sermon for Ove Gedde by Michael Henrichsøn Tistorph is a surprising and fascinating source on his voyage to India.[41] It mentions that: '... on 25 Oct(ober) he came to Trangebari personally to travel to Tanjore, where the Court is held. On the 27th in the evening, he came to Actiur; on the 28th in the afternoon to Trimulavarde, then to Trissipal and Petti and on the 30th to Taaniur (Tanjore)[42], where the 'Type' nayak met him with a palanquin and 8 large elephants belonging to the King'. At Petti (Pettai), he was shown two chambers in the temple filled with pepper and 12-16 other chambers that were under heavy locks. Gedde was assured that all the storage chambers were full. After several misunderstandings due to cultural differences, Ove Gedde met Raghunatha Nayak on 2 November 1620; he noted in his diary for 13 November that it was Raghunatha Nayak's birthday [Schlegel].

At noon on 16 November, the Nayak showed Ove Gedde all the gold jewellery that he and his 365 wives used, precious stones, pearls and jewellery with diamonds, emeralds, sapphires and rubies. Raghunatha Nayak was willing to conclude a trade treaty with the Danes. Later that day, it was proposed to make two copies of a settlement in Portuguese, one for the Nayak and one for Ove Gedde. On 19 November, after several discus-

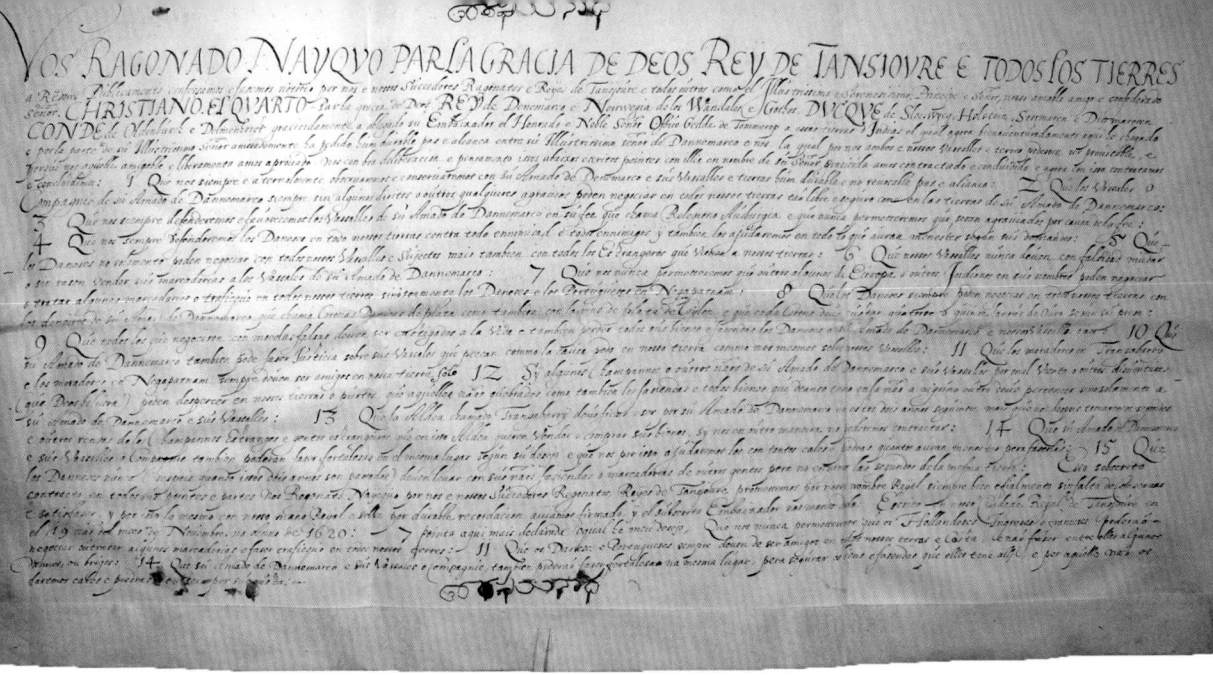

Fig. 1.3: The official treaty between Tanjore and Denmark, written in Portuguese on parchment. The document is signed only by Raghunatha Nayak, who was the king in Tanjore and to whom the land belonged, in Telugu. There is no counter-signature of Ove Gedde, who was the official negotiator for Denmark (Tyske Kancelli, Udenrigske Afdeling, E 1 Traktater (1454-1699)) (photo: P. S. Ramanujam).

sions, a new draft of the treaty was handed over to the court, signed by Ove Gedde and carrying his seal.[43] This treaty cannot be found. Raghunatha Nayak signed the final treaty on 19 November.[44] Contrary to all popular beliefs, it is not because of Ove Gedde that Denmark was allowed to trade in Tranquebar – the place was was given to Roelant Crappé acting on behalf of Denmark six months before the arrival of Ove Gedde. True, Ove Gedde concluded a treaty – but we only have the copy with Raghunatha Nayak's signature.

The funeral sermon continues: '... on 9 December (the king sent) a horse and 4 elephants so that he could travel around and look at the city. The town (had) deep and broad ramparts and double walls ... On the 16th, he was shown the king's treasury; and it was full of gold and silver and treasures'.

On 29 December, Ove Gedde noted in his diary, that "Pungel', the New Year of the blacks was celebrated'.[45, 46]

It is commonly believed that Ove Gedde started the construction of Fort Dansborg, as it stands today on the coast in December 1620.[47] How-

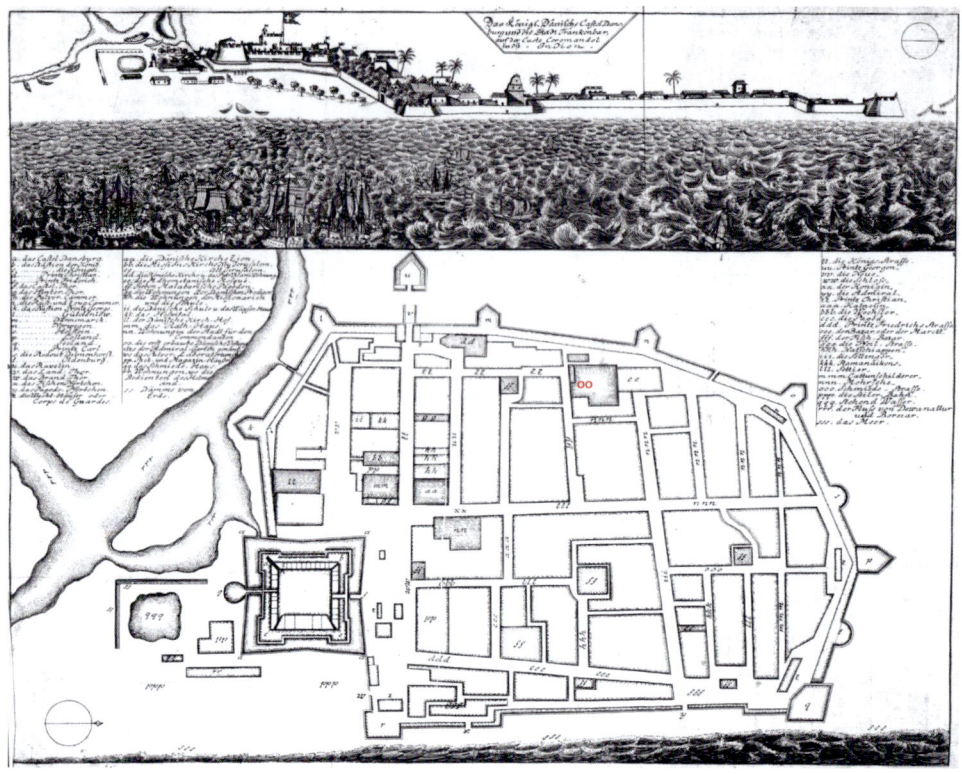

Fig. 1.4: Map of Tranquebar from 1730. The area marked 'oo' is, according to the missionaries, the place of the first Danish fort on Admiral Street. We do not know whether this is true – no archaeological excavations have been performed at this site. The missionaries settled in Tranquebar in 1706, establishing a Mission, a printing press as well as paper manufacture. During their stay in Tranquebar, they sent back several thousand pages with accounts of daily life in Tranquebar ('Die erste erbaute Dänische vestung', Ostindische Berichte, Teil 3, Cont. 29 (1730) page after 480).

ever, Henning Munch Engelhart casts doubt on this. Engelhart, the subject of a later chapter, served as an archivist at the fort in the 1780s, and he noted in his history of Danish East Indian establishments that the fort was 'the abandoned rampart at a place in the town called Admiral Garden, and on the street called Ove Giedde Street or Admiral Street'.[48] There could be

Raudra Chittirai 20

some truth in this since the missionaries reported to Halle in 1710 that a house located in Admiral Garden was once given to Ove Gedde.[49]

On 13 February, Ove Gedde returned to Ceylon, leaving Roelant Crappé in charge of the new trading post. On his way back to Denmark, he spent some time in Ceylon trying in vain to renegotiate a treaty. Leaving Ceylon on 9 May 1621, Ove Gedde arrived back in Copenhagen on 4 March 1622 with a cargo of pepper. He had been away for over 3 years.[50] Ove Gedde later became an admiral in the Danish Navy. He was imprisoned by the Swedes in 1658 and was released during the autumn of 1660. Shortly afterwards, on 19 December 1660, he died at the age of 66. He was buried in the Cathedral in Roskilde, Denmark, where his sarcophagus can still be seen.

Ove Gedde left three reports on his arrival back in Copenhagen in 1622. They have been transcribed by Schlegel[51] [Schlegel]: 'A record of everything that happened on this Indian travel, from the beginning on 14 November 1618 until 4 March 1622', 'A record of all that happened in Ceylon with the Emperor and in Coromandel with the Nayak of Tanjore from 18 May 1620 until 1 June 1621' and 'A record of all that happened between the Nayak of Tanjore and ourselves, as well as commerce in Coromandel'.

The gold leaf mentioned earlier is a marvellous document. Measuring approximately 400 mm by 25 mm, it contains about eight lines of miniature writing in Tamil.

Raghunatha signed his name in Telugu first, leaving someone else to fill in the text in Tamil. The letter was first correctly translated by Nagaswamy [Nagaswamy 1987, http://tamilartsacademy.com/articles/article23.xml].

Fig. 1.5: Letter on a golden foil signed by Raghunatha Nayak. This letter, dated 16 April 1620 (top left), was given to Roelant Crappé and asserts the creation of a port by the name of Tharangampadi and invites Danes to settle here. The name 'Tharangampadi' is mentioned in the third line. The letter assures a supply of pepper to Denmark, as this spice was rare. The golden foil is about 40 cm long and 25 mm wide, containing exquisite miniature Tamil inscription. Raghunathan signed his name in Telugu (bottom right). (RA, Tyske Kancelli, Udenrigske Afdeling, E 1 Traktater, Ostindien 1620 (Løbenr. 20). (Photo: P. S. Ramanujam).

Tharangampadi   Raghunatha

Fig. 1.6: Christian IV's letter to Rambadro Naico that was never sent. There have been doubts regarding the identity of the successor to Raghunatha Nayak. The Danish records are unambiguous that Raghunatha Nayak's eldest son, Rambadro Naico (Ramabhadra Nayak), became the successor. Rambadro Naico was the eldest son of Raghunatha Nayak and after Raghunatha's death, Christian IV of Denmark was motivated to send a friendly letter to the new king (Rigsarkivet, Den Ledreborgske Dokument Samling, (Løbenr. 89)). (Photo: P. S. Ramanujam).

The letter reads as follows:

> We, (the Royal Highness) Shrimad Raghunatha Nayak, send this message to the ambassador of the King of Denmark, on the 20th day of Chittirai in the year Raudra (corresponds to 16 April 1620 (auth)). We are prospering here. Kindly dispatch the news about the prosperity of Your Highness. We are

pleased to learn the news of that place brought to us by Captain Roelant Crappé and the General from Holland. Since we have agreed that we should not draw a distinction between Your Highness and Us and have agreed to live as one, we have honoured the Holland General and Captain Roelant Crape with palanquins and permitted the subjects of that country to come and settle here. We order the creation of a port named Tharangampadi here and allow the export of pepper to that country, as it is rare there. We have given an appropriate warning to the 'parangiyar' (firangi[52] – here Portuguese) against the trouble they caused to Roelant Crape, fined them 12,000 gold coins, and have issued orders to them not to interfere with your ships. We have sent back the General. Roelant Crape is residing here since we have ordered that this place should be made suitable for his residence. As it has been resolved that we should not entertain a distinction between our country and yours, we propose that people from your country come and settle in this place. Please arrange to frequently send us rare objects from that country. We are sending with these garments, two big silk garments, a hanging carpet, two upper garments, four painted carpets, two jamutad swords, a dagger with lion-handle, another dagger and four Singaram bows. Make sure that they arrive. Please give this message to the King of Denmark.

The missionary, C. T. Walther first translated this gold leaf into Danish and German in 1741. He made two horrendous mistakes in the translation. Firstly, he translated 'ulandisu chenneral' as 'Ove Gedde'. Secondly, he stated: 'since Captain Rulangkalappai had started trade in a Frankish[53] way, we forbade him specifically behaving like sailors and fined him 12,000 Pardao and ordered through the General that he should stay in this country, which has also happened'.

Why did Walther translate 'Ulandeesu chenneral' as Ove Gedde? And who in the years between Walther (1741) and Schlegel (1773) made the mistake of translating Raudra to 1621 (Raudra corresponds to the year 1620)?[54] Or was it Schlegel's mistake? The other name mentioned is 'ulandeesu chennaral', which refers to a General from Holland. The translation of 'ulandisu chenneral' as 'Ove Gedde' has caused misunderstandings until a few years ago [see Olsen (1967), Feldbæk and Justesen (1980), Fihl (1988), Diller (1999)]. Schlegel refers to Walther's translation of the gold leaf in his 'Samlung zur Dänischen Geschichte, Münzkenntniss, Ökonomie und Sprache' (Erster band). He could not get things to make sense. He says [my translation from German]:

> The date on this letter can be set to the year 1621 because by this time the treaty had already been ratified. Gedde was already in Ceylon in April 1621. I must leave it to the Malabaris to explain why he is called Ulandisa in this letter. Baldeus always calls the Danish commander 'Gule Gedde' [yellow Gedde – author];[55] I do not know whether this is just a mistake or whether it relates to the name Ulandisa. Roeland Crappe is known as Rulangalappai, which is merely a distortion of his name.[56]

This General from Holland mentioned earlier cannot be Roelant Crappé, as the letter clearly states that the General was sent back and Roelant Crappé was ordered to remain (Line 5 of the gold foil). Raghunatha Nayak could not have mistaken Denmark for Holland. He questioned Ove Gedde extensively about his country; whether it was far from Portugal, which of the kings was the most powerful – the Danish, English, Dutch or Portuguese?[57] Who, then, was the general from Holland accompanying Roelant Crappé? We do not know. It might have been Hermann Rosencrantz, as Engelhart has proposed.[58]

As mentioned, the first correct translation of the gold foil is Nagaswamy's from 1987 [Nagaswamy]. Surprisingly, there is one more translation of the gold leaf in the National Archives from 1791 (RA), which all historians seem to have overlooked and which is nearly correct.[59] This translation states the year of writing as Nala. Nala corresponds to the year 1616 and not 1620. However, 'Ulandisu chenneral' is here translated correctly as the Dutch General, and not as Ove Gedde. This translation also correctly states that there were two people present at Raghunatha's Court, and that the Europeans (Portuguese) were punished for harming Roelant Crappé instead of vice versa.

German missionaries wrote exalting accounts of Raghunatha Nayak's reign. Reports on how Raghunatha Nayak built several temples, gave them land and income, built houses for the temple Brahmins, established institutions with free meals for the thousands of travellers and choultries and planted several trees on both sides of the roads. Travellers who visited the shelters were given oil for washing themselves. Children accompanying the adults were given food, milk and fruit. Landowners should only hand in two fifths of their harvest. His rule was just.[60] Raghunatha Nayak was a great patron of literature and music and was an author himself. He may have found it difficult to negotiate with a man many years his junior. One might wonder what happened to the Nayak dynasty after Raghunatha Nayak. Most historians assume that Raghunatha Nayak ruled between 1600 and 1634. Vridhagirisan, an authority on the Nayaks of Tanjore, writes: 'Considering the duration of all the individual reigns of the Tanjore Nayaks, it becomes evident that Raghunatha, the most illustrious ruler of this family, had but a relatively short reign and his death will have to be placed about A. D. 1634' [Vridhagirisan 1942, p.213]. On the question of who succeeded Raghunatha Nayak, the Indian historians disagree. Vridhagirisan assumes that the successor to the throne was Vijayaraghava Nayak. He writes: 'Vijayaraghava's accession must have taken place in the year 1633 and that it was celebrated sometime before the death of Raghunatha'. There are many claims and counter-claims. Vridhagirisan mentions two sons of Raghunatha, namely Achyuta Vijayaraghava and Ramabhadra, and (Achyuta) Vijayaraghava would appear to be the eldest son according to the genealogy given in the Raghunathabhudayam of Ramabhadramba. At the same time, Vridhagirisan also cites a Jesuit letter: 'two brothers of the (Vijayaraghava) Nayaka, whom he (Vijayaraghava) had shut up in prison after pulling out their eyes to remove all possibility of succeeding him ... Ramabhadra could not have been on the direct line of succession ... it is not quite known for certain that Achyuta Vijayaraghava was also called Achyuta Ramabhadra' [Vridhagirisan, loc. cit. p.217].

The Danish records are unambiguous. Ove Gedde's diary for 4 November 1620 notes: 'I paid a visit to the eldest son of the Nayak and the heir apparent, who requested me to visit him often'. On 7 November: 'that same day, the Nayak requested me to visit his middle son, who had complained that I had not paid him a visit'. It is evident that Raghunatha Nayak had at least three sons. Citing a letter from Roelant Crappé written

Fig. 1.7: A view of Dansborg at sunset from the water tower. Ove Gedde started the construction of the fort in 1620. There were four bastions, one in each corner, which were later pulled down. The fort contained the governor's residence, soldiers' quarters, a kitchen, a church and a prison (photo: P. S. Ramanujam 2008).

on 17 September 1628 in Masulipatam (the original letter exists in the Archives), Schlegel writes: 'Ragnato Naiche (Raghunatha Nayak) died early on 25 November 1626 and was cremated on the same day with 119 of his wives. His eldest son, Rambadra, succeeded him to the throne and came with 100 men to the fortification of Dansburg' (in Tranquebar).[61]

Hidden in the National Archives in Copenhagen for almost 400 years, there is an innocuous letter from Christian IV written at his castle of Frederiksborg on 11 April 1631.[62] The letter affirms the affection of the king to the Nayak of Tanjore and expresses his wish for a continuation of the relationship between the two countries. The letter itself is not significant – but the addressee is: 'The mighty, Royal Prince Ramabadro Naico, King of Tanjore, our especially good friend'.⁶³ Evidently, after the death of Raghunatha Nayak in 1626, Ramabhadra Nayak succeeded his father until he was gruesomely relieved of his post by his younger brother, Achutha Vijaya Raghava Nayak.⁶⁴

Vijaya Raghava Nayak himself met with a tragic death in 1673 in a battle against Madurai Nayak. Madurai Nayak wanted a bride from Tanjore for his king, which was refused by Vijaya Raghava Nayak.⁶⁵ Venkata Krishnappa from Madurai and Vijaya Raghava Nayak met in a battle outside Tanjore. Earlier, Vijaya Raghava Nayak had imprisoned his own son, Mannarudeva, probably for falling in love with the daughter of an esteemed minister. Released from the prison, father and son now set out for the battle together. This was a battle for honour. The ladies of the Tanjore court should not fall into the hands of the Madurai soldiers. The ladies were locked in one room of the palace, which was then set on fire. There was only one survivor – a four-year old prince, Cenkamaladasa, who was sent away from the harem by his mother. Both Mannarudeva and Vijaya Raghava Nayak were killed in the battle, and this ended the Nayak dynasty in Tanjore. There are no Danish records of this event. However, a Dutch writer, Jacob van den Meersche, has documented the episode.⁶⁶ The Madurai dynasty did not last long. In 1674, Venkoji of the Maratha Bhonsle clan took over the reign. Even today, archaeologists are excavating a mound to the south of the main Tanjore Palace – who knows what they may find there?

Under what monetary conditions was Tranquebar given to the Danes? On 8 March 1832, 'Rajastry Sarbosy Maha Rajah' died and his son, 'Maharajah Sivasy Rajah Sattirapady' ascended the throne on the 24ᵗʰ of the same month, with the blessings of the British. The new Governor of Tranquebar, Konrad Emil Mourier, sent a shotgun for 130 Madras Rupies as a present. He also realised that correspondence with the British government in Madras regarding termination of the 'tribute' paid to Tanjore had been initiated, as the British controlled the Tanjore territory. In this connection, a thorough investigation of the origin of the tribute was carried out, citing all the previous treaties between Tranquebar and Tanjore.⁶⁷ There were several treaties written on silver 'olai's (palm leaves)– the 'olai' of Vijaya Raghava Nayak in 1644 stipulated that a tribute of 2,000 Pardau be paid annually.⁶⁸ (Unfortunately, the originals have disappeared, and only translations of these exist.)⁶⁹ This was confirmed by him in 1670 and was then increased to 5,000 Pardau in 1676 under Egosi Raja, with a 'gift' of three more villages – Thillaiyali, Erukatanchery and Poreiar. Every time more villages were given to the Danes, the 'tribute' increased; however, the basic 2,000 Pardau remained in force until 1845. The question of the tribute remained a thorn in the side of the Danish government. No proper agreement was made between Tranquebar and Tanjore as to the monetary tribute – it was not even known what the tribute was for. The last governor of Tranquebar, Peder Hansen, in 1830, tried to look for an argument based on Clause #13 in the original treaty of 19 November 1620 between Ove Gedde and Raghunatha Nayak: 'The village called Tranquebar shall be in the hands of the King of Denmark during the next two following years, but on condition that the proceeds from the foreign sampans and from foreigners who desire to sell or buy their goods in this village are collected by us, unless we make a separate arrangement'.[70] Governor Peter Anker was intrigued by this, which is perhaps the reason why he had the text from the gold foil from 1620 translated. This was also of great concern for the Danes in 1812 when Serfoji II ascended the throne.[71] A clue may be found in the reports that the missionaries sent to Halle in Germany; here, it says that the customs duty collected in the town belonged to the Nayak, whereas all the sea-customs belonged to the 'Admiral', meaning Ove Gedde.[72]

*

We now amble south for about five minutes and reach the entrance to the Dansborg fort. Built in 1620, this would serve as the Danish headquarters for the next 225 years.

2

Jón Ólafsson's Saga

Severely wounded onboard the ship that was to bring him back from India at the age of 31, Jón Ólafsson did not expect to survive. Before Jón Ólafsson left for India, a young man named Frederik had foretold him his life. Frederik predicted that Jón Ólafsson would meet with an accident while

Fig. 2.1: Map of Iceland with the location of Svarthamar, where Jón Ólafsson was born, marked with a red dot. Jón Olafsson was employed in the Danish army as a gunner (www.vidiani.com).

he was away, but God would save his life – however, the accident would be so severe that Jón Ólafsson would be reminded of it as long as he lived. Frederik also predicted that Ólafsson would be married twice in his own country, would not have any children from his first marriage, but would have 2 or 3 children from his second. Before leaving, Frederik said that he 'grieved over the many mishaps that lay before' Ólafsson.[73] Ólafsson lived to tell his story.

The southern side of the fort complex housed a kitchen and a jail, as well as storage space. Towards the northern and the western sides of the complex were small rooms, which formed the residential quarters of the soldiers during the Danish period. It was in one of these rooms that the Icelander Jón Ólafsson spent a year, in 1622.

Fort Dansborg was the first building constructed by the Danes in Tranquebar, and it belonged to the Danish Crown from 1620 until 1845. For the first many years, most administrative activities were confined to the fort. The construction of the Dannisborg (Dansborg) fort started during December 1620. By the time Ove Gedde left Tranquebar in February 1621, the structure had advanced so far that cannons could be placed on the ramparts.[74] The fort had a walled moat with four bastions at the corners. The entrance to the fort was across the moat via a bridge and an S-shaped access. The moat tended to clog up with sand blown in from the beach and, in the early years, this was removed manually. However, the moat was abandoned in 1788. A recent archaeological excavation revealed the presence of it.[75]

Let us enter the fort complex. This is not the original entrance to the fort; it was located further east. Inside the complex is a large ground, presumably used for parades, surrounded by buildings on all sides. The main building of the complex forms the eastern end of the fort. Inside this building were the administrative offices of the Danish East India Company, the Governor's residence and a church. This building now houses a museum. It was left to the Icelander Jón Ólafsson to describe the daily life in and around Tranquebar. His memoirs, written at the ripe old age of 67, contain impressive details that testify to his memory. During his stay, Jón witnessed marriages, funeral ceremonies and exorcisms, and he describes them in detail to the best of his ability. He proved to be an astute observer of the local customs and traditions. He noticed how the fields were sown and how the rice was harvested, how oil from dried coconut (copra) was

Fig. 2.2: Rooms where soldiers stayed in Dansborg. The room shown here is on the southern side of the fort. There were also rooms on the northern side, which have now been removed (photo: P. S. Ramanujam 2019).

extracted; he remarked on how people chewed sugar cane and how they ate mango, how they made use of palm leaves for writing, how arrack was made and how cotton was produced. Even after 35 years, he could remember words in Tamil such as nerpa (fire), tanari (water), cundovara (bring it), tingra (eat it) culcrani (drink it), pacra (see it), teyra (curd) etc. He observes that Portuguese is the language generally spoken around Tranquebar, even by the Indians. Jón Ólafsson stayed for a year as a soldier in the fort.[76]

Jón Ólafsson was born in 1593 on the farm of Svarthamar in Álftafjörð in Northwest Iceland to Ólaf Jónsson and Ólöf Thorsteinsdatter. Amazingly, the farm still exists. He was the second youngest of a flock of 14 children; however, all but three of them died early. He started to read and write at the age of 7. During the spring of 1615, when he was 22, an English ship was forced by storms to anchor close to his domicile. Jón Ólafsson, having an adventurous spirit, decided to travel by the ship to England after getting his mother's permission. From England, Jón Ólafsson sailed to Denmark to work as a groom, taking care of Christian IV's horses in Copenhagen. Later, he advanced to a job as a gunner in the service of the king. During this period, he became friendly with the master gunner, Adolf Frederik Grabow, who later became vice-president in the Danish East India Company. However, Jón Ólafsson claimed that, due to some misunderstanding, Grabow mistreated him and, in fact, imprisoned him. He was released on direct orders from the king but felt so mistreated that he wanted to leave the command of Grabow. At this time, an opportunity presented itself in the form of a voyage to Tranquebar. Jón Ólafsson could not travel on the first expedition, as his duties would not allow him to; but when the first ships returned from the expedition in 1622, he listened with great interest to the tales of the sailors, and his spirit of adventure was kindled once again. Jón Ólafsson registered as a sailor and a gunner and, after answering satisfactorily the questions posed during the interview, was conscripted on a monthly salary of 12 Gylden (increased to 13 Gylden in Tranquebar).[77]

Three days before the ship left, all those on the way to India were sworn in before the king, who in turn blessed the crew and wished them a happy voyage. The captain of the ship *Christianshavn* was Christopher Boye, who became a good friend of Jón Ólafsson. Christopher Boye was also on the first voyage to Tranquebar with Ove Gedde. There were 88 people on board the ship, most of whom were very unaccustomed to sailing. Jón Ólafsson was the ship's gunner. Christian IV wrote in his diary for 8 October 1622: 'The ship *Christianshavn* to East India'. The food onboard the ship consisted of bread, butter, meat, dried and salted fish, French and Spanish wine, as well as French and Dutch spirits. On Sundays, Tuesdays and Thursdays, which were meat-days, everyone got 2 pounds of meat for two meals, and on Mondays, Wednesdays, Fridays and Saturdays, which were fish-days, 2 pounds of fish. For every seven persons, there was 1 pound of butter; besides, on fish-days, there was porridge and on meat-days, peas or beans. On Saturdays, there were 3½ pounds of bread and 1 pound of butter each together with a pail of wine for lunch and dinner. The wine was to be consumed immediately and not hidden for later consumption. According to the ship's rules, it was forbidden to steal even half a can of water from others – the punishment was a death sentence. People were permitted to buy shirts, tobacco, cloves, nutmeg, cumin seeds and ginger as well as spirit and to carry these with them. Also, two persons were allowed to share a sheet with which to collect rainwater in emergencies.[78] Everyone was supposed to be obedient to the chaplain on board, and blasphemy was forbidden, the punishment being death by hanging.

During the summer of 1623, when one ship arrived in Tranquebar, cannon salutes from the fort as well as from anchored Danish ships greeted the *Christianshavn*. The day after the ship arrived, the captain went ashore to the accompaniment of a nine-gun salute. After about 10 days aboard the ship, the crew was allowed to disembark. Jón Ólafsson reports that, when they were about to go shore, they saw a colossal sea-snake the size of 900 ells or longer. (One ell is approximately 54 centimetres.)[79] Fearing this huge monster, they stayed two more days onboard and threw castoreum into the water to frighten the beast away. (Castoreum is a substance contained in two pear-shaped pouches near the groin of a beaver, of a bitter taste and slightly foetid odour and used in medicine.) Jón Ólafsson now became a soldier at the Dansborg fort and was the leader of a group of seven. Each group was given a room containing furniture, plates, cups and water-coolers (probably clay pots), which were buried up to the neck in the sand to keep the water fresh. On the third day after arrival, the group was informed of all the rules and regulations. There was a night watchman at each corner of the fort. A fifth watch was at the entrance to the fort. A watch lasted two hours, and a guard found neglecting his duty was doomed to lose his life. When a load of pepper arrived from the Raja of Tanjore, it was the soldiers' duty to remove all stones and straw from it, and they were given some wine in return. Elderly Indian women were employed to fetch water from far away, and each woman was assigned a room. An Indian named Atrumbus was assigned to wash the clothes for this group and, because of this work, he was called 'Maynath'. He delivered the washed clothes punctually every Saturday. On Saturdays, the soldiers received one fano extra to have their clothes cleaned. Inside the fort was a small church, and there was service every Wednesday and Sunday. Jón Ólafsson says that one Erik Smed oversaw all masonry. The actual work was done by the Indian masons, who were much faster and more knowledgeable in their work than Europeans.

On the southern side of the fort were the court and a secretariat. Other small buildings, as well as bedrooms, were located at the southern and

Fig. 2.3: Restaurant named after Jón Ólafsson in Súðavík, Iceland (photo: P. S. Ramanujam).

southwestern side of the fort. The kitchen and well were situated on the southern side. On the embankments around the fort, approximately 80 large and small cannons were placed. The meals provided were almost the same as during the voyage, except that one also received a portion of rice boiled in milk, fresh fish, pork, goat and different types of poultry.

Jón Ólafsson was told that the King of Tanjore, called Naike Ragnado,[80] worshipped a horned cow decorated with golden jewellery and precious stones. Every morning and evening, the king washed his hands in its 'water' and sprinkled it on his head.[81] The king had a son aged 17 or 18. The portraits of both father and son hung in the Danish church. Jón Ólafsson says that the prince wanted to convert to Christianity and follow its principles, but would not do so because of his father's wishes. In any case, prayers were said in the church for the king and the prince. Raghunatha Nayak's throne in the Tanjore palace was made of marble polished smooth as an egg. The palace priest (minister) sat opposite him on expensive gilded cushions. They sat with their legs crossed on gold embroidered pillows, which was only possible if the body were regularly massaged and anointed with oil and balm. Three boys stood around each of them; one of them carried betel leaf and paga[82] (areca nut) whose size, colour and hardness resembles that of a nutmeg. First, the nut was chewed and spat out; then the betel leaf coated with lime made from shells, called *bitilarech* or *bitalapaga*[83], was chewed and ingested. This made the king and prince feel more intoxicated than chewing tobacco; however, the betel was supposed also to be effective against dysentery. Another boy carried a golden vessel into which the king spat. The third carried a golden fan.

The priest or minister played an important role. When foreigners sought an audience, the priest determined the most auspicious time for the negotiations, even if they were to be held during the middle of the night. The king had 900 concubines of whom he gave away 300 to his son. These ladies had a majestic house of their own with windows of crystal glass. They had golden rings on their toes and fingers, in their ears and noses, they had ankle-rings and bangles of gold and golden crowns on their heads. Once a year at midsummer, they could partake in a procession with the king, to the accompaniment of 60 drums. When one of them died, a new woman took her place. When the king died, all of them were burnt with the king.

Ólafsson refers to the area where Tranquebar is situated as the 'Narsinga' kingdom and mentions how people are punished for various kinds of misdeeds with various 'fixed penalties'. He says: 'In the marketplace of this town [Tranquebar] are fruits, fowls, eggs, fresh fish of many varieties, also copper and brass work of many kinds, cotton, silk and many kinds of cloth, and every kind of fruit kernel, also gold and copper coins, all exhibited daily for sale'.[84] He describes how 'splendid' rice was harvested twice a year and how butter was produced from milk, how toddy was extracted from the palm trees, how palm leaves were utilized to inscribe books, how cotton was harvested, how elephant tusks were carved, how precious stones and gold were set in masterly ways, how printing was done on cotton and silk,[85] how swords and helmets and arrows were made from iron, how god-figures were immersed in the sea after festivals and how, once, a turtle carried nine people from the church. In each town around Tranquebar, there was a large temple surrounded by high walls. Inside the temple was a tall processional chariot with abominable and indescribable figures. In the temple, there were six figures of gods on each side in the form of oxen, boars, goats and buffaloes. (The milk from the buffaloes tasted just like goat's milk, remembered Jón Ólafsson.) Close to the centre of the back wall was a large altar, well adorned with golden jewellery, on which 'their' three main gods reside. These three figures were carried around in procession once a year, in the chariot mentioned above. All residents of the town took part in this 'stupid and useless task' of pulling the chariot around the town to the accompaniment of 30 or 40 drums and 3 trumpets on either side, surrounded by soldiers called Talliars.[86] Offerings were made from each house according to what people could afford. In the evening, when the chariot reached the door of the temple, the temple dancers performed dances in honour of the gods. 'Baldor', master of the dancing girls, rented them out for money to soldiers and unmarried men, and this money went to the temple;[87] the dancing girls were taken care of by the temple. A priest received the gods on their return to the temple, and the figures were then taken in to the accompaniment of ceremonies, drums, trumpets etc. The dress of the dancers resembled trousers with a lot of golden jewellery ornamented with pearls. The temple dancers performed every night between 9 and 12. One day, Jón Ólafsson and a friend of his, Peter Lollik, were able to bribe the priest into showing them the inside of a temple. Jón Ólafsson reports that there was nothing to see other than the six figures on either side, the three highest gods at the centre, the finely decorated altar and the dancers' costumes.

The locals celebrated their festivals at night to the accompaniment of dance and theatre, in which they dressed up in different costumes. Jón Ólafsson says that once they were able to watch such a drama from the fort when they were on night duty. It looked as if it were the history of the prophet Jonah from the Bible. One of the actors was dressed like a whale that devoured another actor.[88] Their high priest arrived in Tranquebar one winter. All the soldiers, priests and temple servants busied themselves in welcoming the high priest. After the high priest had crossed the river on an elephant, he was carried in a palanquin made of ivory and gold. He went into the temple and prayed for a long time. A tall mast was erected outside the temple and a seating arrangement was made on top of it. The high priest climbed up this mast around 9 in the evening, was quiet there until midnight and had discussions with the devil. The locals claimed that it was unnecessary to pray to God, because He was the King of Peace and Splendour and would not harm the people. However, it was necessary to pray to the devil and make sacrifices to him. The high priest had to consult the devil about the future, what the seasons might bring when ships would arrive from Denmark and about war and trade. After three hours, a massive fire was lit around the mast, and the high priest slid down into the fire. If the fire did not burn him, his prophecies would be fulfilled and, sure enough, the high priest emerged unscathed. The festivities continued with dance and music. Next morning, the high priest left for the town of Trichlagour (Thirukadaiyur, Tirukkadhavur?).

Then follows a description of how the Indians treat their dead and how they burn the bodies outside the city. Ólafsson had also heard about the *sati,* the practise of burning widows on the funeral pyres of their husband. He reports that the Danish officers tried to intervene and stop this practice. Jón Ólafsson was perhaps the first one to record what he thought of the locals. 'Many of the locals gathered around and looked at what the Danes did. On Sundays, some of them came inside the fort to witness the sermon in the church. They said that they would not give up their religion. They were blind in perpetual darkness (in not following the Christian belief), as might be expected. But in their way, they kept law and order, weights and measures and were righteous. They would never accept wine or other intoxicating drink, and when they saw a drunken man, they shook their heads, beat themselves on their chest, spat and shouted: 'he is 'buratze"(evil)' [Ólafsson].

The village of Tranquebar had border-stones located in three places. At each place, there was a rectangular polished stone and in it was a trough for charcoal. Anyone who carried anything of value past these stones had to pay customs. Even dried cow-dung was taxed. All produce, such as fresh fish, hens, goats, sheep, pigs, milk, rice and all kinds of fruit, was quite inexpensive.

The ship *Christianshavn*, on which Jón Ólafsson came to Tranquebar, set sail for Denmark during September 1623. (Christian IV noted in his diary: 'On 27 May, *Christianshavn* returned well loaded from East-India'). Jón Ólafsson sent a letter to his brother Halldór Ólafsson at Súdavik in Iceland through Peter van Bergen. That was probably the first letter from India to Iceland.

During the winter of 1624, 80 Danes were residing in the fort in all. About two thirds of them died that winter due to dysentery; Jón Ólafsson himself was sick for 11 weeks and 5 days, but he says that he was in bed only for two days. There was a separate burial ground outside the fort, with a fence and a secure lock. The chaplain was given the key when a burial was to take place. The deceased was accompanied to the grave to the sound of pipes and drums.

Two colleagues of Ólafsson, Stephen Andersen and Lars Simonsen, got very drunk that winter and started opposing their commander. The punishment for this offence was jerking. A ladder was placed against the end of a wooden beam projecting from the gable of a house. The criminal stood on the top of the ladder with his hands bound at his back. The rope went over a pulley fastened to the beam. On a given signal, the ladder was removed and the prisoner fell to the ground with the rope now pulling his hands above his head from behind his back. The hands were severed from the body due to the sudden thrust.[89] However, in the case of the two accused, all the merchants in the town together with three interpreters requested the commander that they be pardoned.

Ólafsson had a boy by the name of 'Sivile' to help him in his daily chores. After 12 weeks, Sivile left, having introduced another boy, 'Agamemnon' or 'Agamenon', as a servant. Agamemnon's brother, 'Catthay' (later Christian) had left for Denmark with the first ships. Agamemnon's mother begged Ólafsson to take care of her son, teach him the ways of a Christian and take him to Denmark, just like his brother. Every night, Agamemnon fell on his knees before Olafsson and asked him to bless him. His mother sent cakes to Ólafsson every Saturday. Once, when he was out with friends to relax, people shouted to them 'Pampe! Pampe!' (Snake! Snake!).[90] Ólafsson and others mistook this for 'bamboo'– but once when they realised the seriousness of the situation, they started hunting the snake and, after a long chase, Ólafsson cut the snake into two and jumped between the two parts of the body, so they could not join again (as he had been told). He was irritated that he was not allowed to cut the tongue of the snake since it could be sold for more than 100 rdl because of the number of diseases it was thought to be able to cure. The snake was more than 2 ells (about a meter) round, and about 8-9 ells long (about 5 metres). That night, everyone at the fort drank to Ólafsson's health.

One evening, Jón Ólafsson slapped a man named Peter Johansen in the face, as the latter spoke ill of Icelanders – and the punishment for this was a ride on the wooden horse. The wooden horse had a small and narrow back. The penalty of riding the wooden horse could vary from a number of hours to several days, and it functioned both as a psychological punishment because it incurred the wrath of pedestrians and a physical punishment, as it was extremely uncomfortable.

Jón Ólafsson provides an excellent description of an image of the local god, Ayyanar, made of pasteboard and leather and standing atop the figure of a horse. The figure standing on the horse 'had two faces, one in front and one behind with very fierce eyes'. He also vividly describes the local marriage customs, which entailed that all young daughters should be married between the ages of four and ten, their betrothal ceremonies, how every child bride remains at home with her parents until the age of 14 and then moves on to the bridegroom's house. He also witnessed the rites of exorcism in Tranquebar, which he expounds in incredible detail.

In October 1623, the King of Tanjore sent an officer, followed by 12 taliars to the accompaniment of war cries, as they usually did in this country. This officer demanded that the Danes deliver three carriages of lead. The president of the company replied that he would furnish as much lead as the king required, as soon as he was informed in writing what the king would pay per pound. The messenger became extremely angry at this arrogant reply and immediately left the place without even saying good-bye. When the king heard the message, he, in turn, grew irate and threatened to cancel the treaty and take the fort by force. The president and the governor replied that the king could do what he wanted. The king immediately called upon his commander, a man named Calicut, to march on the fort with an army of 40,000 people. The defenders of the fort also prepared themselves for the siege. All the cannons of the fort were in place, and ironspikes 9 inches long were strung together along with gunpowder to serve as deadly cannonballs. About 800 barrels of drinking water were stored inside the fort. Calicut had 1,000 elephants, 1,000 horses and 1,000 camels in his army. All the residents of the town supported the Danes, and even the Indian soldiers and taliars joined in the defence effort. A large portion of the fortress wall collapsed two nights before Christmas Eve, boding ill. However, a couple of months after the New Year, the Danish ship *St. Laurentius*, which had been sent to Tenassarim, came back. On sighting the ship, cannons were fired from the fort in salutation. Calicut sent his people to investigate the cause of the commotion, and when he noticed the Danish ship, he quietly withdrew from the place with his troops. Soon after, two more ships *Perlen*, with Roelant Crappé on board, and *Jupiter* arrived from Denmark. Jón Ólafsson says of Roelant Crappé that: 'He had made seven voyages to India as a merchant, and has reached his current dignified position. He was unmarried, of poor Dutch family and took to the sea as a young boy. He had first worked as a cabin boy, washing floors and decks, and received his primary education from the sailors'.

Calicut then paid a visit to Roelant Crappé. During the negotiations, Crappé showed him all the armament and cannons; whenever they stopped by a cannon, it was fired, and immediately there was a reply from the ship anchored outside, as was the custom. Calicut was very impressed, and whenever the cannon fired, he shouted 'Abbai'.[91] It was a hot Wednesday, and one of the elephants, whose hind leg was tied to a tree, ran amok and uprooted the tree to which it was tied. The elephant-keeper, who sat smoking with his friends, was able to calm down the elephant. It was believed that elephants understood human speech and, in fact, only lacked the ability to speak. Jón Ólafsson says that once Peter Lollik and he rode on an elephant, which was anything but comfortable.

Calicut was a light-skinned handsome man with a huge belly. He wore a lot of golden jewellery, a gold-embroidered sash around his waist and another full of gold jewellery around his head. A servant carried his magnificent gilded ivory staff. After the peace negotiations, he left the place. Soon after, Crappé followed, with letters and presents for the King of Tanjore: two new copper cannons, decorated with seven human figures, a bed made from cypress wood and a painting of the King of Denmark. The pagan king gave his portrait, together with a bed made from ivory decorated with expensive blankets, which were valued at 100,000 rdl or a barrel of gold. The president, who had refused to provide the lead in the first place, was given a stern warning, as he had endangered the life and property of people and of the king. He could have lost his life; however, he was pardoned and sent on a dangerous trip to the Moluccas.

In June 1624, an English ship arrived at Carical (Karaikal). The officers from the ship asked Naike Ragnato (Raghunatha Nayak) for permission to set up a trading post. The Nayak immediately sent for Roelant Crappé. Crappé left with 12 soldiers, and Jón Ólafsson should have been one of them. However, due to dysentery, he could not travel. Before the general (Roelant Crappé) left, there was a party and everyone had wine. During the night, three of the guards (Peter Arendal, Salomon and Lennart) were found to be asleep, but on the fourth post, where Indian soldiers were keeping watch, they were all alert. The three men were immediately imprisoned, awaiting the return of the general.

The Nayak asked the general (Crappé) what reply he should give to the English, and the general politely said that they should be refused permission to establish trading. The next day, the Nayak told the English that it was courageous of them to seek consent, but their faithlessness was known in all the countries they had occupied, and asked them to leave immediately: 'Pao! Pao!'.[92] The general was in the audience at that time, and he left after a sumptuous meal. The Nayak presented him with two Desmer cats (probably civet cats) – one whose testicles had a scented smell when it died and the other whose excrement had a scented smell as long as it was alive. The latter was worth 60 times the former. When the general returned, the imprisoned guards were assembled for judgment (which was usually the death penalty); however, as the number of people had declined dramatically due to illness, it was decided to put two blank slips and one with the word 'Death' in a hat. Lennart got this slip. He was taken to the pole outside the fort where the sentence was to be carried out. He had to choose five of his best friends to carry out the job. He was blindfolded. They were to shoot all at once, with two of them aiming at his heart and three at his head. When he was taken out, Jón Ólafsson had the gate watch; they bade a tearful and loving farewell to each other. Lennart regretted that he did not get Ólafsson's help to save him, to which Ólafsson replied that he had a gut feeling that Lennart would not be executed that day. After he was tied to the post and his friends were ready to shoot him, the general suddenly signalled a pardon. In the evening, the officers from the English ship visited the fort. They were treated to a good meal. The Danes and the English parted in friendship, as the English would find another place on the coast to set up a trading post.

A year had passed, and now it was time for Jón Ólafsson to travel back to Denmark. The ship *Perlen* was loaded with pepper, cotton clothes, gold, silk and gold-embroidered clothing, jewels to a value of 60,000 rdl in small bags. A natural dye, indigo (extracted from a wonderful herb), and clothing woven with a mixture of cotton and silk were included. Jón Ólafsson, being a gunner, was asked to take care of the cannons, which was against his own wishes (since he knew that *Perlen* had ancient and rusty cannons). As it was strongly forbidden to take any Indian servants, Ólafsson had to say farewell to his servant, who was very depressed.

On 7 September, around 2 in the afternoon, cannons were fired from the fort, and as usual, there was return salute from the ship. After firing 18 cannons, Ólafsson loaded the next, but did not notice that there were still embers in the pores on the inside of the cannon. (These holes arose during the casting process.) The gunpowder caught fire and the piston in the cannon exploded with great force. Three fingers on Jón Ólafsson's right hand were broken, three on the left were badly damaged, and his arms and shoulders were badly burnt. The force of the explosion threw him into the sea. He was saved by a boat that came from the land. The crew did not expect him to survive, but after midnight, he started to breathe normally. Next day, everyone from the fort paid him a tearful visit and praised him for his bravery. The barber (who was also the surgeon, because he had sharp knives) had to remove the damaged fingers with his tongs and removed close to 300 splinters. The general (Crappé) then invited Ólafsson back on shore to stay until he returned to normal health. However, Ólafsson refused, as he longed to go back to Iceland. He lay in the ship for 14 weeks. During eight of these, he was on his back with stretched arms and cushioned by 30 pillows. Seventeen days after the accident, on 24 September 1624, the ship sailed for Europe.

There were 140 people aboard the ship. Several of them died on the way. After enduring a severe storm and several hardships, the ship sighted the island of Scilly on 22 May 1625, and soon after that, Ireland. Since the ship sailed from India, 35 persons had died. During their stay in Ireland, many people from far and wide came to visit them. 53 of the men rented a ship from Ireland, and sailed to Denmark during the autumn of 1625; Ólafsson was promised that his private property would be delivered to him when the *Perlen* returned to Copenhagen.

Jón Ólafsson now petitioned the king and the Danish East India Company to be compensated for the damages he had suffered so that he could live a normal life. However, the king was at war (which he lost) with Germany. Since the situation in the kingdom was bad, Ólafsson could not get any compensation. Besides, his property was lost. However, he had made up his mind to return to Iceland, and the following summer, he returned to Skutilsfjörð. Later, he moved back to his home area of Álftafjörð, where he married Ingibjørg Ólafsdatter. One day, a few years later, Ingibjørg sailed to visit some friends across the fjord, a sudden freak squall threw the boat out of control and she drowned. A few years later, Ólafsson married Thorbjörg Einarrsdatter. The predictions of the young Frederik had come true. Ólafsson now petitioned the new king (Frederik III) to provide him with a livelihood and a place to live. Finally, he was given permission to live on the farm of Eyrardal at Álftafjorð, which belonged to the king, and to use any produce that may arise from the farm for his livelihood. During their old age, Ólafsson and his wife, Einarrsdatter, taught young children reading and writing.

At the age of 67, he wrote down his memoirs. The last part of the memoirs was written by his son, Ólaf Jónsson, after his best recollections. Jón Ólafsson died in his sleep at the age of 87 in the year 1679, two years after his wife's death. Today, at the farm in Súdavik where he spent most of his later life, there is an Arctic Fox Research Centre. A few hundred metres away is the Café Jón Indiafari, where the owner, Heikur, proudly displays a poster summarising the life of Jón Ólafsson.

3

Inebriety, Intrigue and Slavery

We are still at the site of Fort Dansborg, which served as the residence for all the governors until 1784 [Fihl 2017]. This site will be the backdrop for many of the eventful incidents during the period when Willem Leyel was governor. Due to internal wars in Europe, contact between Tranquebar and Denmark was infrequent. After Roelant Crappé left, another Dutch merchant, Behrent (Bernd) Pessart, was director of the East India Company from 1637-1643. It is said of him that he was 'intelligent, but most unreliable' [Kay Larsen 1918]. His accounts were not well-kept, he made high-handed deals only to lose them and the Colony fell into significant

Fig. 3.1: An early map of Tranquebar shows that the market place, where several atrocities by parsons mentioned in the text were committed, was located in front of the entrance to the fort (Hallesche Berichte, Teil 3, Cont. 29).

debt. Two ships *Solen* (The Sun) with Claus Rytter in charge and *Christianshavn* with Leyel, appointed in place of Pessart, left Denmark in 1639. The ships sailed together till they reached the latitude of Madeira, where a massive storm and severe leaks forced Leyel to seek shelter on the island of Tenerife. The governor of Tenerife, however, was not favourably inclined to yield any assistance. While *Solen* reached Tranquebar in 1640 after an uneventful voyage and returned to Copenhagen, *Christianshavn* underwent a brutal treatment at the hands of the Spanish in the Canary Islands for three years and reached Tranquebar only in 1643. Both Pessart and Leyel had the Dansborg fort as their residence. After the arrival of Leyel, there was no contact between Tranquebar and Denmark for 29 years due to a prolonged war with Sweden.

Willem Leyel[93] served the Dutch East India Company for several years before coming to Tranquebar. He had a good knowledge of the commercial possibilities in trading with the Coromandel Coast. He was proficient in Persian, Portuguese, Spanish, Dutch and German. When he finally arrived at Tranquebar, Leyel was met by an unwilling and averse Pessart. Pessart suggested that they sail together to Masulipatnam to fetch goods for the return voyage. At Masulipatnam[94], Leyel was made aware of the precarious situation of the Danish trade. They did not dare go ashore for fear of the creditors demanding their money. In the ensuing confusion, Pessart managed to get away from Leyel and sail towards Tranquebar. When Leyel finally reached Tranquebar, he could not even enter the town, as the Pessart-friendly garrison refused to let him in. Leyel now laid siege on the fort with the help of a few soldiers, forcing the inhabitants to come out. With the orders of the Danish king in his hand, he was able to convince them that he was the rightful governor. Pessart had fled the colony a few days earlier, and he was eventually killed by the natives on a beach in the Philippines. Leyel found the fort in ruins and the accounts in disarray.

Leyel practically had to rebuild the fort from scratch. He managed to assemble a small army, collect a few ships and carry on trade with Golconda, Macassar, Bantam and Ceylon, but also involve himself in piracy, which was common at the time. As no ships from Denmark arrived for almost thirty years, Leyel thrived on piracy and slavery. Eight slaves were exported in August 1647, and just a month later, 165 slaves were exported [Bredsdorff 1999, p. 152]. Leyel and his local partner, Anina Marca, equipped *Skt. Michael*, which had 114 slaves destined for Quetta.

In the long run, the lack of any support from Copenhagen plagued Leyel. Rebellion broke out among his officers. In 1648, Paul Hansen Korsør became the Governor of Tranquebar, after leading the mutiny against Willem Leyel. In Europe, Christian IV got involved in the Thirty Years' War (1618-1648) in 1625. In 1643, a war was fought between Denmark and Sweden. Christian IV had to capitulate in 1645. He died in 1648 and his son Frederik III came to the throne. From 1639 to 1668, the Danes in Tranquebar had to manage their affairs on their own. Willem Leyel managed to return to Copenhagen on a Dutch ship – he died a poor man in 1654.[95] He was given provisions such as rye, barley, butter and meat from the king's stores. Paul Hansen Korsør died in 1655. Eskild Andersen Kongsbakke, a constable, became the next governor. Unknown to those in Tranquebar, efforts were underway to sell Tranquebar to the Dutch, the English or the French. The first Danish East India Company closed its affairs in 1650. When the ship *Færø* finally arrived from Denmark in 1669, Eskild Andersen Kongsbakke was the sole Dane left. Not much is known about Kongsbakke. When he took over from Poul Hansen Korsør, there were no artillery, money or stores left. He himself could neither read nor write. However, he had kept the colony going, establishing trade with Bantam, Java and Macassar. He had also held the fort well fortified, with a defence wall around the entire town. He remained its governor until his death in 1674. *Færø* returned to Denmark in 1670, and the formation of a new East India Company had begun.

A remarkable trial took place during the period of Willem Leyel, involving two chaplains – Niels Andersen Udbyneder and Christen Pedersen Storm. Niels Andersen Udbyneder was employed as a ship chaplain aboard the *St. Anna* on 7 November 1634. When he became a chaplain at Dansborg during the time of Bernt Pessart, he learnt Portuguese and preached in that language for the many people who had moved into Tranquebar. Christen Pedersen Storm came from Stavanger in Norway. Initially, both chaplains were well respected. However, the tropical heat, loneliness, monotonous life and sheer boredom induced them into drinking bouts. The local arrack was consumed in large quantities. Christen Pedersen Storm seems to be the one who initiated these sessions. Not long after, the locals started complaining about them. The chaplains drew the soldiers at the Dansborg into their fold. It is said that they were seen at times running through the streets with only a loincloth and at times completely naked – Niels Andersen with a sabre in his hands [Bredsdorff].

It was customary to hold open-air markets on Sundays in Tranquebar, where farmers came to sell their produce, such as ghee, coconuts, rice, spices, betel nuts and jewellery. Niels Andersen once ran through the market[96] with his sabre in his hand, wreaking havoc. After the people fled, a poor horse belonging to a Muslim was standing in his way, and Niels Andersen attacked it with all his zest until it died. Then he ran amok with his sword and broke several of the clay pots containing ghee.[97] After he returned to the fort, the locals slowly came back to collect whatever was left and to complain to the authorities. The dead horse was dragged to the entrance of the fort and compensation was demanded. The authorities were unrepentant; in fact, the chaplain had the horse skinned and kept the skin as a souvenir. Niels Andersen also mishandled two women to death – and lived with a runaway woman. After intense pressure from Leyel, he married her in 1644, but proceeded to mistreat her so severely that she became a total wreck. In his turn, Christen Pedersen Storm married a Portuguese slave and abused her.

After several complaints, Leyel decided to remove Niels Andersen from the fort and lodge him aboard the ship *Christianshavn*. At about the same time, Christen Pedersen Storm was caught in the act of instigating a mutiny aboard the *Fortuna*. He was imprisoned and brought aboard *Christianshavn*, where a court was set to hear the case in January 1645. The interrogation protocol can still be found in the Archives in Copenhagen. After several witnesses testified against him, he confessed to instigating mutiny. He was condemned to be sewn into a sack with stones and thrown into the sea. His three slaves were to be released to freedom. The judgment was signed by Willem Leyel, Jørgen Hansen, Poul Nielsen, Rasmus Pedersen and Amund Olufsen. The order was executed on the same day. The protocol continues: 'On January 30, the judgment against Christian Pedersen Storm was carried out approximately 40 kms north of Dansborg and 10 kms from the shore'.[98]

Niels Andersen was imprisoned onboard the ship until the autumn. His case came before the court on 1 October 1645. The complaints of several Portuguese who had settled down in Tranquebar were read out. The first witness was Anna Salazar. She complained that Niels Andersen had forced himself into her house; all the people fled except Anna, who was an old lady, together with a maid named Francisca, whom Niels Andersen beat so hard with a stick that she fell to the ground. He returned to his senses after Anna told him that the girl might be dead and he then left the place. The girl was in bed for seven months. Later, Niels Andersen met Francisca again in another house and this time he attacked her so severely that the girl died. Furthermore, Anna said that Niels Andersen had attacked her with a log because she had refused to sell him the wood at half price. She had to run away and dared not return until he was imprisoned. Another witness said that May Giomar, a young Portuguese woman, was attacked by Niels Andersen on her way home from a Catholic mass during Christmas. Her right arm and right thigh were broken. People who witnessed this attack dared not intervene; she was eventually found by her 18-year old son, Manuel, and taken home. She lost her speech and died a year later. Yet another Portuguese girl, Philippa Texera, was likewise said to have been attacked in the street by Niels Andersen with a stick. She received a large wound on her breast. She was close to death and aborted her three or four-months old foetus.

A well-respected Portuguese in Tranquebar, Antonio Pacheo, said that Niels Andersen attacked his servant in the street without any reason. The servant was bedridden for three months and then left the town for fear of the chaplain. He also complained that Niels Andersen had attacked his maid so severely that she was bedridden for two months. Another Portuguese, Juan Borges, said Niels Andersen was so fascinated with his parrot that he and two soldiers had broken into his house and stolen the parrot. A Japanese soldier, Thomas Dono (?), complained that Niels Andersen had stabbed him in the chest with a knife. Even Muslims in the town did not go free. Finally, an Indian girl, Waidy, who used to sell firewood in the town, was attacked with a big stone when she was on her way home. Her face was completely disfigured and she was confined to her bed for six months. She had to sell her only son, who was very young, to pay for the doctor. She exhibited a large scar on her face. Even the Danish soldiers at Dansborg testified against Niels Andersen. Jacob Amager had had his right arm broken by the chaplain and Jens Madsen's rib had been crushed. Finally, Governor Leyel himself maintained that it was an act of lese-majesty against the king when Niels Andersen had prevented him from entering the fort. Once all the witnesses had testified, Niels Andersen was asked whether these statements were true, but he denied the accusations. However, under the threat of torture, he confessed to his acts.

Niels Andersen was found guilty of causing the death of May Giomar and Fransisca, of causing the abortion of Philipa Texera's foetus, of spending most of his time in a state of drunkenness and violence, of living an un-Christian and ungodly life. The sentence passed by the court was the same as that for Christen Pedersen – that Niels Andersen be sunk into the sea in a sack of stones, and that his house and other possessions of value be confiscated and given to his wife, Monica. However, by this time, the opinion of the public was that the chaplain should be shown mercy, as he had been a good and just man in the beginning, and that it was only his association with Christen Pedersen that had driven Niels Andersen into debauchery. Shortly after the judgment was passed, the court received petitions from Christians – both European and Indian – that he be pardoned. The sentence was then commuted to exile in the unexplored jungles of Ceylon. Niels Andersen was forbidden ever again to enter the Danish territory. This judgment was passed on 8 October. He was left on the shores of Ceylon, at a deserted place with only a little food. However, Niels Andersen managed to find a way to the town of Cotiari, a small island about 30 kms south-east of Trincomalee and he lived there for several years. Apparently, he never did change his ways [Bredsdorff].

*

A social problem that persists to this day in several countries, which was also common in and around Tranquebar at that time, is the existence of slavery. Private companies in Denmark exported more than 100,000 slaves from the west coast of Africa to the Danish West Indies (now US Virgin Islands) during the 17th and 18th centuries. Their slave trade began earlier on in India, but this never reached the same heights and numbers [Christensen]. The Danish king, the Danish East India Company and private people were involved in the slave trade in India. From the ship lists of the Danish East India Company during the period 1616-1729 and the year 1732, the number of slaves traded was more than 10,000. The slaves were exported from Coromandel to Atchin and Malacca. During 1695-1696, the ships *Charlotte Amalie* and *Elephanten* transported about 2,500 slaves to Atchin from Tranquebar.[99] Calnein, who was the governor during 1687, earned 12,000 rdl from just one shipment [Olsen]. During the period 14 March 1688 to 4 January 1690, slaves were sold to a value of more than 46,000 rigsdaler. Mourids Christensen, during his sojourn in Tranquebar in 1671, describes how slaves were bought and sold.[100] During periods of famine and high rice prices, many sold themselves or their children into slavery. People who could not repay their loans were also sold as slaves. When the Nayak in Tanjore sold his subjects, the sale went through Tranquebar, and the colony earned a commission for facilitating such transactions. When the 'Malabaris' needed food, they sold their children and wives and, finally, themselves for 1-2 rdl just to get some rice. As slaves, they had to perform heavy manual work throughout their lives and most went almost naked. A person who had too many slaves simply sold some of them abroad. If the slave was handsome or talented, he could work somewhere in town, but had to return to his master's house at the end of the day and deliver all the money he had earned. If it were a pretty girl, she could sell herself, but if she had any children, they remained slaves. She could be given a house, but she had to cook her master's food as well as wash and sew his clothes. He could take her wherever he went, sell her or free her. The prices for slaves were as follows:

A young man	20 rdl
A teenager	13-14 rdl
A small person	10-11 rdl
An old person	10-12 rdl
A pretty girl	14-16 rdl
A small woman	11-12 rdl
An old woman	8-9 rdl

Just to have an idea, 1 rdl from the 1620's would amount to 60 US dollars today. The directors of the Company urged people to treat the locals more humanely, not for humanitarian reasons, but out of fear that people would run away and that commerce would suffer as a consequence [Struwe, p. 208-211]. As late as 1732, there was a considerable slave trade, even though the instructions from Copenhagen did not allow it. Struwe writes how several people sold children between the ages of 2 and 7. The Danish slave trade in East India was carried out by private individuals as well as by the Danish East India Company. The economy of Tranquebar depended

Fig. 3.2: A Selling (or Salangu) of the type used to transport slaves and goods. As there was/is no proper harbour, all goods and persons were transported from the ships anchored off the coast to the town in boats such as these. The boards of the Selling are sewn together with ropes made from coconut fibres. Catamarans (the term comes from the Tamil word kattumaram, meaning logs bound together) are still used for fishing on the southeast coast of India (Tranquebar Maritime Museum, photo: P. S. Ramanujam 2019).

significantly on it.[101] Krieger[102] notes that, in 1646-47, more than 2,000 slaves were sold. There was even a slave house in Tranquebar, which in 1744 was badly in need of repair.[103]

Many slaves were trained in Lutheran churches and schools and these came to be called 'Lutheran slaves'. Many were imported by the Danes, Portuguese and Indians to be sold in Nagapatnam or Madras or were sent to the Cape of Good Hope. Frederik Holmsted, a director in the Danish Westindia-Guinea Company, had the job of acquiring a 'black' slave girl as a present to the queen of Denmark. Twice, the children who were sent died on the way. The third time, a little girl was sent together with a boy whom Governor Panck in Tranquebar sent as a present to the crown prince.[104] Later, when the food situation improved and rice was available in plenty, the slave trade dropped. The slave-traders now resorted to stealing children from their parents and wives from their husbands. Five or six such slave-traders were caught by Tanjorians and lynched. The missionaries tell of how people could become surreptitiously enslaved after having been fed good food and clothed nicely. Another trick was to throw a 'magic powder' on the potential victim. The powder made the victim confused and made him follow the swindler who gave him food and clothing and then sold him.[105]

Slave trading was finally forbidden in 1753; however, people continued to keep slaves for their own 'personal' use. According to the census, fully 4% of the population were house slaves [Architectura 1987]. The earliest converts to Christianity in Tranquebar, through the efforts of the German missionaries Ziegenbalg and Plütschau, were slaves [Ramanujam 2016]. The Jerusalem Church register from 1707 is filled with the names of slaves. We do not know whether these people were house servants or bonded labourers.[106] Did the missionaries buy bonded labourers for their own use? We have no idea how these people were treated in the Danish colony. The Tranquebar census from 1834 shows that most citizens of the town, Indians and Danes alike, possessed at least one slave [Ramanujam 2016]. According to Asger Svane-Knudsen, National Archives in Copenhagen, there is a lot of documentation from the late 17th and early 18th centuries; unfortunately, this is in a poor state and is being restored, and is not yet accessible to the public.[107]

The Dutch also actively promoted slave trade on the Coromandel coast. In a letter written on 26 july 1622 to the president and council in Batavia (Jakarta), Thomas Mills and John Milford write from Pulicat:

> 'Concerning your required provision of 14 to 15 slaves from the age of 16 to 20 years fit for labour and to be sent along in the ship, which at present wee can by no meanes performe, parte in regard of this short warning, besides the tymes much altered in that qualitye, the Dutch having bought all that came to hand since our abiding, and now by a late advice brought by our ship are heer ordered to buy as many as possible can be procured, to the number of four or five thousand of men,

women and children, and, rather than faile, to leave ther other affaires and follow that designe; for which cause they have layd the countery all over, standing uppon no price; for whereas uppon our first seating one might have bought a slave of the age afore prescribed for four or five pag[odas], now you cannot gett the lyke under 12 or 14, and not to be procured as in those tymes… for most of thos slaves brought them to sell are stollen uppon the highways and brough[t] forcibly from their parents and frinds', it is complained.[108]

Governor-General Coen, Dutch East India Company, seems to have stressed the desirability of obtaining as many slaves as possible from the coast of Coromandel, China and Madagascar for the peopling of the Dutch settlements in the Moluccas. The number of slaves exported from the Coromandel Coast by the Dutch between the years 1500 and 1850 is estimated to be approximately 19,000.[109] They were exported primarily to Batavia (Jakarta) and Ceylon (Sri Lanka). The French were no less active in the slave trade. The minimum number of slaves traded by the French within the Indian Ocean Basin between 1500 and 1850 is estimated to be around 350,000 people.[110]

Allen, citing Larson,[111] writes: '…slave trading in the Indian Ocean world was of far greater antiquity than in the Atlantic world and that the total number of slaves exported from sub-Saharan Africa across the Indian Ocean and Sahara probably exceeded that shipped across the Atlantic'.

Slave trade is not new in India. Evidence of slave trade long before Tranquebar came into existence is present in stone inscriptions, palm-leaf manuscripts and government documents. Old palm-leaf manuscripts reveal the existence of slavery in the 15th century.[112] For instance, a man named Kaadi and his younger brother Tavasi from the village of Mathur in Madurai sold their seven children in August 1448. Thirty palm-leaf manuscripts containing servitude agreements between 1448 and 1910 were recently discovered. In 'The First Firangis', Harris [Harris] reports how the Indian slave trade already existed in the 16th century. Even today, India seems to have the highest absolute number of people living in modern slavery (exceeding 18 million) according to the Global Slavery Index, 2016.[113] As late as December 2018, a couple sold their 12-year old son into bonded labour for the sum of 10,000 rupees after they lost all their possession in the aftermath of a cyclone.[114] Hjejle discusses how different types of bondages existed in the villages, communal and private. These seem to be related to the miràsi[115] rights of cultivating the land.[116] Kaarsholm has recently discussed bonded labour and trading in slaves from India in the 17th and 18th centuries.[117]

On 28 September 1802, Wengidasala Chetty complained to Colonel Ewald in the Danish administration that a 'Paraiyan' slave, Soveyen, who had been bought by his father's brother 40 years earlier, had absconded to Pondichery. Wengidasala Chetty went there in person and brought him back, after which Soveyen toiled for him for 15 years in the fields before he died.[118] Following that, Soveyen's wife and son worked for Wengidasala Chetty, until the son decided to seek a job with a European. The son even had the audacity to refuse to work for Wengidasala Chetty and, worse still, was able to borrow 10 pagodas from his aunt (who apparently was also a slave). Wengidasala Chetty pointed out that lending money to another slave without the permission of the master was not a custom in the farming community.[119] Once a slave, always a slave!

Slaves were treated as personal possessions, like dogs or pieces of furniture. Bacchus was a slave bought at an auction by a midwife named Sophie Magdalena Sørensen, at St. Croix in the Danish West Indies (now US Virgin Islands), and he was leased out to labour on a ship. In Spain, Bacchus managed to escape to Tranquebar, where he was 'owned' by the governor Abbesteé. The governor took pains to baptise him, naming him Jean Baptiste. He took him back to Denmark. Bacchus – Jean Baptiste – joined, with the permission of his master, the Royal Regiment as a piper. One day while he was playing, the midwife from St. Croix saw him and demanded that he be returned to her or that she be paid appropriate compensation. The supreme court of Denmark decided that, indeed, Ms Sørensen was the rightful owner of Bacchus. The Royal Regiment, however, would not pay the compensation and nobody knows what actually happened to poor Bacchus.[120]

4

Murders, Property Disputes and Caste Conflicts

Moving out of the fort, we now walk across the parade ground. Keep your eye on the ground, you may find bits and pieces of China from the Danish period, clay pipes and, if you are lucky, you may even find a Danish coin. Today, the white building across from the parade ground houses the Bungalow on the Beach, which is a hotel run by the Neemrana group. We do not know when the original building is from. The British construct-

Fig. 4.1: The Collector's Bungalow from the British era, after renovation. This building is now a hotel run by the Neemrana group 'Bungalow on the Beach'. This was the site of the Black Court in the late 18th century (photo: P. S. Ramanujam 2008).

ed a collector's bungalow for their use. Villiam Nielsen[121] writes that the house belonged to a French cotton merchant by the name of Diclome, who sold the house to a Dane, Petersen. Subsequently, it was sold to a Nadar family.[122] In the middle of the 18th century, this was the site of the Black Court.[123] In a map drawn by Governor Peter Anker in 1798, the position of the Black Court is clearly marked.[124] Earlier, during 1779-1781, the Black Court was situated at Muturady,[125] and we know precisely where this was. The census from 1790 [Ramanujam] positions this close to the town entrance, where the Gate House is today.

The first 100 years of the Danish presence on Indian soil was a struggle for existence. The first Danish East India Company was established in 1616, but it was dissolved in 1650 due to a financial crisis. In 1670, a new company was established, which had to close again in 1729. In 1732, the trade monopoly in East India was handed over to the Asiatic Company, which resulted in connections with other countries in the East, especially China, the main import from there being tea. This deeper involvement in the East necessitated clear rules and regulations regarding the whites and the Indians. According to the original treaty between Raghunatha Nayak and Christian IV, signed in 1620, Danish citizens within the Indian Territory were subject to Danish law and the Indians were subject to Indian law. Clause #10 of the treaty says: 'His Majesty of Denmark shall have jurisdiction in these territories over his subjects who are guilty of a crime, as occasion requires, just as we ourselves have over our subjects'.[126] However, in the middle of the 18th century, the Danish territory expanded because the Maratha kings of Tanjore were unable to pay back their loans to the Danes and subsequently pawned several villages to them. It thus fell on the Danes to maintain order and justice in the local Indian society. Here, the clash of cultures was evident – the Europeans, unaccustomed to the unwritten laws that existed between castes, did not want to get involved in domestic problems [Brimnes 1991].

The Danish judicial system within the Tranquebar territory consisted of several law courts. There was a military as well as a civil court [Nielsen]. There was also a consistory court to decide on matters related to the clergy. The fate of soldiers who came under court-martial was decided in Copenhagen and here Danish law applied. In civil cases, the highest instance was the Secret Council (sekreteråd), which took ultimate decisions. Three persons, with the governor as the chief, were responsible for main-

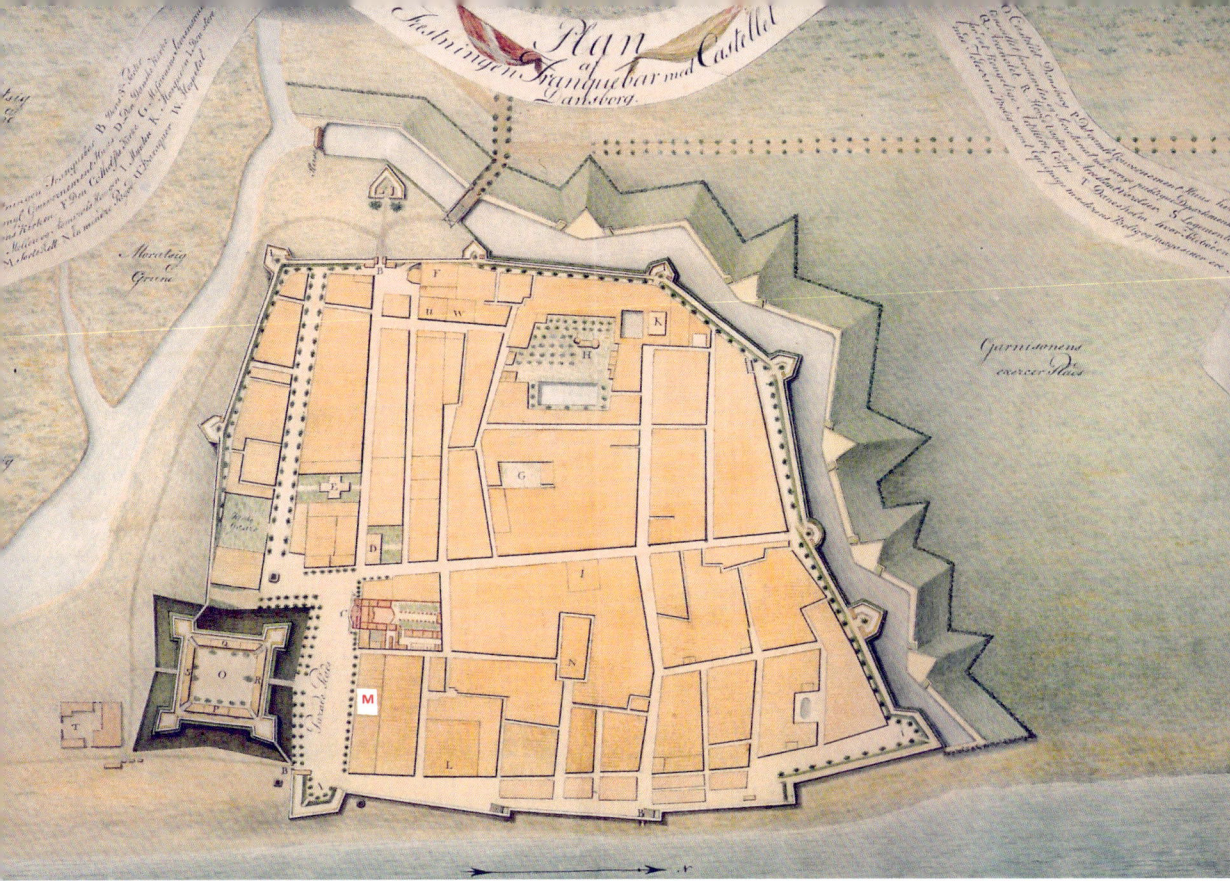

Fig. 4.2: Map of Tranquebar from around 1800, sketched by governor Peter Anker. 'M' marks the place where the Black Court was situated, corresponding approximately to where the Bungalow on the Beach is now (https://www.khm.uio.no/tema/utstillingsarkiv/peteranker).

taining law and order. The lower court consisted of a city court (municipal court), which dealt with criminal cases involving both the Danish and Indian populations and a Black Court to decide on civil matters relating to the Indians. The Black Court decided in 'harmless' cases pertaining to inheritance, debt and probations. Justice was to be administered according to 'the habits and usage of the Indians, as well as right and reason'.[127] All appeals from the lower courts went on to the Secret Council.

Even though, formally speaking, the Indians ought to have been judged under Danish law, it was evident as early as 1735 that this was not the case. In a matter referred to by Olsen [Olsen 1992] and cited by Nielsen [Nielsen 2009], a Tamil, Irlappa, was accused by one Christian Rasmussen Meyer of stealing 46 rdl. Meyer demanded that the money be paid back and that Irlappa be punished in accordance with Danish law regarding disloyal servants. After hearing Meyer's side of the case, Irlappa presented

Fig. 4.3: Rules regarding the administration of justice in Tranquebar promulgated on 8 January 1781, including those for the Black Court. (RA, Kommercekollegiet, Journalsager (1789) (Løbenr. 995) #84). (Photo: P. S. Ramanujam).

his and pleaded not guilty. To demonstrate his innocence, he offered to dip his hand in boiling butter (as was the custom in the area at that time). If the fingers were not burnt, then he was innocent. Meyer accepted this Indian custom. On 12 October 1735, Meyer presented testimony from two Danish doctors, Stolle and Jansen. They were of the view that the fingers were indeed damaged. Irlappa presented his evidence from two Tamil doctors, Muttu and Sidambaram. Sidambaram declared that, in a similar case from Singer Koil, nails and flesh had fallen off as the bandage was removed from the hand of the accused on the third day; however, in the case of Irlappa, this did not happen and thus the fingers had not suffered any injury. As no conclusions could be reached on this basis, it was up to the town bailiff to decide, and his sentence fell in Irlappa's favour. Another unusual case involving swearing on a cow is described by Mohanavelu [Mohanavelu]. Arumugam's father had lent Rengappen a sum of 300 rupees. After his death, Rengappan denied that he borrowed that sum. A European judge asked Rengappan to swear on his cows that he had not borrowed any money, at which Rengappan broke down and admitted his guilt. A case of holy cows!

The first Black Court existed already in 1730. The first two cases are from 1736 and 1738 and the next two from 1755 [Nielsen]. One could appeal to the Asiatic Company's court and, following that, to the Supreme Court in Copenhagen. The Black court usually consisted of a providiteur (local police commissioner), an interpreter, a secretary and six assessors, two of whom were Malabars (Hindus), two Moors (Muslims) and two Christians. A European observer was stationed at the court to ensure correct procedure without having the power to judge. A proclamation from 1781 clarified that judgments should be passed, taking into account the customs and traditions of the Indians.[128] The first article of the proclamation asserts: 'Any European or Indian, inhabitant or stranger, of whichever nation, religion, position he belongs to, should be free and unhindered to seek justice following the instructions according to our Danish Law'.

According to the proclamation (of 1781), the Black Court at Tranquebar 'shall consist of a providiteur[129] as magistrate, an interpreter, a secretary and six assessors, namely: 2 Muslims, 2 Malabars and 2 Mission Christians, and in addition, an observer *sine Voto*, who keeps an eye over the court proceedings and reports to the government or Ministry of Justice, and the same observer, who may be a European, writes a report. The court shall meet twice a week, on Tuesdays and Saturdays, on the Black Court's premises in Tranquebar from 9 in the morning until noon and, after invoking God and the King, the court shall decide all the cases between Indians'.

Swearing an oath in the Black Court was a procedure all of its own. Article 8 of the proclamation reads: 'When someone, either as a witness or due to other causes, must submit their oath, then it shall happen in the presence of the concerned parties, and the principles of the religions shall be carefully followed in such a way that Lutherans, Reformists and Roman Catholics take their oath under the law, Moravian Brothers take the oath according to their principles and Indians in the way their religion pre-

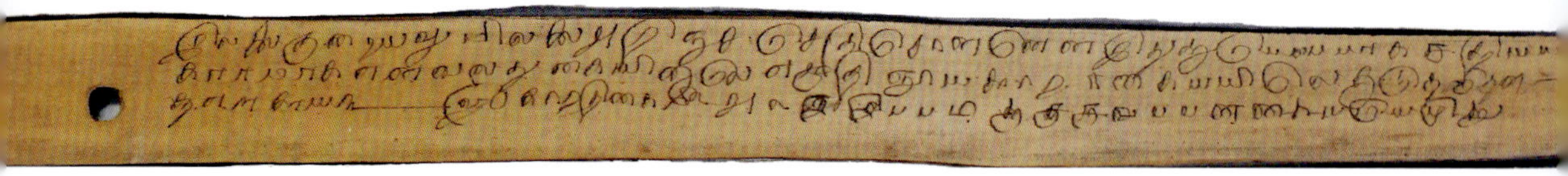

Fig. 4.4: Olai in which Guruvappan swears to tell the truth. Olai is a dried palm leaf, on which inscriptions can be made with a stylus (photo: P. S. Ramanujam).

scribes, according to the ways of their castes'. In 1759, the Danes came to doubt the procedure that was used by the 'Malabarians'. The prosecutor, Falk, sent a request to the Black Court, and Muttea Pulle, Louis de Cruz, Seidu Marcair, Peri-Tambu Markair, Siva Sidambaram Toqvedor, Masselamani, Shawri-Muttu and Dewaprien, all of the Black Court, replied.[130] They had consulted Brahmins – priests and 'doctores theologie Mallabaris' – who were the most erudite with regards to the laws and statutes of the Malabars. According to the Brahmins, distinguished people wrote their testimony on an 'ollis' (same as olai, a palm-leaf), took it in their right hand, told the court their statement, which was written on the palm-leaf and which was correct and true to God and they then handed it over to the court. Remarkably, one such palm-leaf still exists at the National Archives in Copenhagen. On 8 Karthigai 1763 (corresponding to 20 November), one Guruvappan, after writing his testimony, stated that: '…as evidence of swearing, I have written (this) with my right hand and handed (this) over to the court'.[131]

If persons of a lower caste were to take the oath, then they must first proceed to the Ayyanar temple (also known as 'pagode de Brahe'),[132] carry out their ceremonies, ablute themselves in the temple tank, wear the garlands whose flowers had been consecrated, position themselves in front of the main entrance to the temple and, finally, place the fingers of their right hand on the sacrificial stone located just outside the main entrance and profess that their testimony was the pure truth.[133] This practice of swearing at the Ayyanar temple seems to have continued at least until 1841:[134] 'Please force my opponent (the accused) to swear in the usual way at the Ayyanar temple'.

Several proceedings from the Black Court are kept in the National Archives.[135] Most of the cases from the Black Court pertain to loans, debts, inheritance and the like. The first proceedings available cover the period 1736-1779. The early documents are more like complaints than proceedings. A later, quite interesting, case from 10 December 1767[136] serves to illustrate the nature of the cases in general. One Tendajudam (Thandayutham) submitted a document postulating that his paternal uncle, Sidambaram, had adopted him as his own son and that his uncle had given his father an olai (document) promising that Tendajudam might marry Sidambaram's eldest daughter and, provided Tendajudam carried out all the ceremonies when Sidambaam died, he could inherit Sidambaram's property. After the funeral of his uncle Sidambaram, Tendajudam carried out all the ceremonies, as he had promised – however, Sidambaram's widow refused to give him her daughter in marriage. She said that her husband had never talked about adopting Tendajudam as his own son and that the olai was false. But she asserted that Tendajudam had carried out all the ceremonies after her husband's death. The Black Court, with Tendatchi Pullei as the providiteur, Daniel, Seydumareican, Periatambimareican, Siva Sidambaram and Dewaprien, asked Tendajudam at what location he was adopted and who else had been present at the ceremony. Tendajudam answered that he had been adopted at Tivucotte, and only his father and Sidambaram were present along with a few of their relations, but Sidambaram's wife was not present. The court then declared that, according to Malabaric tradition, when a man adopts another man's son as his own, both the man and his wife must be present together with the rest of the family, so there were now doubts about whether the adoption had taken place at all. The Solomonic decision passed by the court was that Sidambaram's widow must swear by oath that her husband never talked to her about the adoption, in which case the olai that Tendajudam had produced would be invalidated, and she was not bound to give her daughter in marriage. On the other hand, if she did not take the oath, then she would have to accept the olai. Besides, she would have to transfer her husband's property to Tendajudam, because he had performed all the ceremonies as required. Tendajudam, on his part, must support her as his own mother if the inheritance came into his possession. However, if Tendajudam and Sidambram's wife were not able to live in unity and peace, the entire property, including any debts, was to be divided into two equal parts, with one half going to Tendajudam and the other half to Sidambaram's widow. The case was settled on 24 June 1768 at Muttradi.

Let us look at two more representative examples, one from 1779 and the other from 1805. On 20 July 1779,[137] the providiteurs Tandatzi Pulle and Daniel Pulle passed judgment in a case between the two visiadors (police officers), Rama Sandra Nayken from Tillaly and his colleague, Rama Nayken from Ourumangalam.[138] Rama Sandra Nayken accused Rama Nayken of selling or giving a construction plot in Poreiar to one Arasur Nayken, a visiador from Tanjore. According to Rama Sandra Nayken, the plot belonged jointly to himself and Rama Nayken. Arasur Nayken sold the ground to Sukker Pullei and this was, in Rama Sandra Nayken's opinion, unfair. Arasur Nayken appeared personally before the court and testified that he had inherited the plot as well as a stone house in Tranquebar from his father 50 years earlier. Two neighbours, Kadamba Pullei and Cuthia Pullei, appeared as witnesses in favour of Arasur Naiken. Kadamba Pullei testified that, when he came to the place about 60 years earlier, there was only a small house belonging to Arasur Nayken's father, in which the witness himself lived with Arasur Nayken's parents, and that about 20 years earlier he had rented the fruit trees on the ground from Arasur Nayken. He produced a contract to that effect. The other witness, Cuthia Pulley, substantiated this claim. Now, Rama Sandra Nayken was asked whether he had any evidence to the contrary, which he did not. The court then decided that, in the absence of any indication to the contrary, there was no hindrance on the part of Arasur Nayken from selling the plot.

The proceedings[139] of the other case, from 1805, are in Tamil. The court was convened on 10 Ani 1805 (21 June 1805) with the assessors Viraraghava Iyengar, Gulam Muhammad and Josef and the interpreter Devasahayam Pullei in place. This was a case between a woman named Sinnacchi and a man named Savarimuthu. Savarimuthu's parents had left his inheritance consisting of land and house in Sathangudi in the care of Sinnacchi. Apparently, Sinnacchi felt that it was her property. The court, in this case, decided that Sinnacchi must give back the land to Savarimuthu; but since she had had it in her possession for such a long time, Savarimuthu must treat Sinnacchi properly, as he would his own mother and sister, for as long as she lived. Savarimuthu was responsible for paying all debts incurred, but he also had the rights to any gains obtained. After Sinnacchi's death, the property would become Savarimuthu's. Both the parties agreed to this suggestion and signed the agreement.[140]

During the late 1790s, efforts were made to reform the Black Court.[141] One of the problems with the Black Court was that the dubashes (interpreters) had almost unlimited power and the public was unhappy with them. Bendix Prahl, who was a town judge, wondered whether it was possible to choose representatives from the different castes for a specified period. After the expiry of their term, new persons from the same castes could be elected for the posts. He speculated whether the Black Court, in general, could be organised in such a way that it would attain confidence among the locals. He felt that arrests and punishments without proper sentence from the court should be abolished, and he was particularly critical of Daniel Pulley, who was a dubash, for acting like a judge. He advocated that the Europeans employed in the Black court be well-versed in the local language and customs. He was also of the view that the powers of the visiador, who was mainly a servant of the King of Tanjore, should be severely restricted. Prahl leveled stinging criticism against Governor Peter Anker for punishing Matturaja Pulley and Thambu Chetty without a proper investigation and trial[142] (see the chapter on 'Pluripotency, Power and Painting'). Prahl protested vehemently when Ramalinga Chetty, a morador (landowner) from Tillali, was punished under orders from one Arumuga Pulle, who was a servant of Governor Peter Anker, without trial or sentence. Perhaps due to his opposition to Anker, Prahl was removed from his post in 1798 and spent the rest of his life in Christiania (now Oslo) in Norway. It is not clear whether these suggested improvements were ever put in place. With the British takeover of Tranquebar, the Black Court was effectively abolished.

In addition to the Black Court, which was a civilian court, there was also a criminal court in Tranquebar. Cases involving more than 100 rdl and criminal cases were adjudged in this court. Article 16 of the proclamation of 1781 says that: '... all cases relating to life, honour, freedom and occupation shall be summoned to the Supreme Court'. Thus, cases resulting in death sentences were always referred to the Supreme Court in Copenhagen for confirmation of the sentence or otherwise.

Jamalgan and Pattagan, two brothers from the town of Siale,[143] attended a wedding celebrated by Ayder Chan in Tranquebar[144] on 3 June 1756. Like most Indian weddings, a pandel[145] was erected across the street. At about 11 pm, after dinner, Jamalgan and Pattagan went out to get some fresh air. Jamalgan stood on one side of the pandel facing north and did not see the three 'blanks' (whites) and a white woman approach him from the south. They were Captain Hesselberg and his wife[146] together with lieutenants Bruuse and Keslow. Two 'black' servants, Reiappa[147] and Muttea, accompanied them. Pattagan was standing on the other side of the street. When they reached the house, Captain Hesselberg bumped Jamalgan aside and told him to move away. Jamalgan felt as if he had been rammed by a goat. Jamalgan insulted the captain by calling him a 'porear' (parayar). 'Are you calling me a 'parayar'?' asked Hesselberg and responded by beating Jamalgan with a cane, and Jamalgan in turn responded in kind by hitting the captain in the head with his fan. As the wedding crowd started to gather around, Keslow, who was a step or two ahead, turned around and came to the rescue of the captain. He began to beat Pattagan, the brother of Jamalgan, with a stick. Pattagan became so confused in the ensuing commotion that he happened to stab Keslow with his knife. Mortally wounded, Keslow was taken to the military barracks, where he died four days later. A post-mortem showed that Keslow was stuck in the breast on his left side between the fourth and fifth ribs, with a wound as broad as three fingers and a punctured lung. Pattagan and his brother were promptly arrested and jailed in Fort Dansborg.

A detailed examination and cross-examination now took place in the city court.[148] Did Pattagan thrust his dagger at Keslow? Pattagan did not know, but he did hold the dagger in his hand. Was the dagger covered with a sheath? It was, but in the commotion, it must have fallen to the ground. Did Pattagan wilfully take the sheath off in order to stab or kill someone with it? No, said Pattagan. Was he aware that the sheath had come off when he stabbed at Keslow? Pattagan said that he was not. It was not intended as revenge for the beating he had received, but had happened inadvertently. Reiappa and Muttea proved to be the most reliable witnesses. Friis, the counsel for the defence, asked whether there was enough space for the captain to pass without shoving Jamalgan aside. Yes, there was enough space, as Jamalgan had already moved. Was the pandel well lit? Yes, there were lamps all around. On which side did Jamalgan stand? On the side where Andal Chetti lived and close to the house with the 'pial'.[149] What clothes were Hesselberg and Keslow wearing? White waistcoats and caps. Did the witness see the culprit draw the knife and stab? Yes. The prosecutor for the Danish East India Company, Ziegenbalg, summed up the case by saying that, according to paragraph 866 article 1 of the law, Pattagan was to lose his head by executioner's axe and his property be divided between the Asiatic Company and the nearest heirs of Keslow. Friis, appearing for the defence, pointed out that the accused came from a town 30 kilometres away, a place not under Danish jurisdiction and not

Fig. 4.5: A portrait of the Nawab of Arcot, Muhammad Ali Khan Wallajah (1717-1795), who pleaded for the life of Pattagan. He was the Nawab of the Mughal province of Arcot in South India. His aristocratic life made him dependent on the British East India Company. He had several contacts to Danish persons of authority, such as Ole Bie and Johann Gerhard Koenig, a German-Danish missionary in his service (picture credit: India Office Library and Records).

covered by Danish law – although the crime had been committed in Danish territory. Friis did not expect his clients to go free, but he appealed for clemency and leniency.

The sentence was passed in the city court on 4 October, according to which the accused was to have his right hand chopped off and thereafter his head with an axe.[150] Because the case against Pattagan was criminal in nature, it was not decided in the Black Court. The sentence was appealed to the Asiatic Company's court in Copenhagen. On 15 October 1759, the same judgment was passed in Copenhagen, even though it was found that the court in Tranquebar had committed several errors, such as not interrogating Keslow, who had, after all, lived for four days after the attack. Questions lingered: Who was Pattagan? Where was he born? What were the ages of the witnesses? Verdict: According to the sixth book of the law, Chapter 6, Article 1: life for life – Pattagan's head was to be be cut off with a sword and his property be shared between the company and Keslow's heir.

In the meantime, the Nawab of Arcot in 1760 wrote from Porto Novo to Governor Herman Jacob Forck pleading for the release of Pattagan.[151] In Denmark, there was an appeal against the Company Court's judgment to the Supreme Court. The Supreme Court passed its judgment on 28 November 1761. All the judges except one concurred with the earlier judgments. This judge found that the accused must be freed because it was a case of self-defence; however, this judge later changed his mind and claimed that, even though it was self-defence, in the strict interpretations of the law this amounted to murder.[152] The case was placed before King Frederik V of Denmark for a possible pardon. King Frederik V took a real interest in the case. He wanted the directors of the Asiatic Company to provide him with information about whether beating with a stick amounted to a shameful act in Tranquebar society. The Asiatic Company produced testimonials from Governor Bonsach and others. The Chancery then sent the question to the Faculty of Law at the University of Copenhagen. The question was whether Pattagan was guilty of the crime he was accused of, as Keslow had, in fact, attacked him with a stick.

The case was referred to the highest instance within the Faculty of Law at the University of Copenhagen. Peder Kofod Ancher,[153] foremost lawyer, professor and Dean of the Faculty of Law, discussed this case extensively in his book 'Answers to a few questions posed to the Faculty of Law' in 1779 and gave his reasons why Pattagan should not lose his life.[154] Question number 18 that he sought to answer was whether a murder, committed by a Moor for the humiliation suffered due to blows inflicted on him with a stick, deserved to be punished with death? He decided that Pattagan could not be judged in accordance with Danish law, even if he might have been capable of committing the crime; it was also felt that Pattagan acted under the sway of emotion. The professors concluded that a murder committed in anger was not morally criticisable to the same extent as premeditated murder. 'The intent of a human being is invisible to the eyes of others, without being apparent in external actions. One must judge the will and intent of the perpetrator from the act and the circumstances under which it was committed',[155] wrote Kofod Ancher. The attestations of several employees of the Company who had lived for a long time in Tranquebar indicated that the Moors (Muslims) were a proud people for whom a blow with a stick inflicted by a 'white' person amounted to the worst humiliation. Even more so during a wedding or another important religious function, in which case it must be avenged. If Jamalgan and Pattagan did not avenge their humiliation at the hands of a white, they would be disparaged by their own. Furthermore, Pattagan was ignorant of Danish law and unfamiliar with Christian beliefs. However, a murder was still a murder and the perpetrator should be punished. It could be in the form of a life in chains or some other punishment '*poena capitali proxima*'. Kofod Ancher wrote further: 'The security of our nation among the Moors demands that the act of committing a murder result in stringent punishment'. The whites had already lost a lot of their respect among the Malabars and the Moors. The sentence was thus commuted to imprisonment for life. The king finally passed the sentence on 5 March 1762.[156] We do not know for how long Pattagan was held in the prison of Dansborg. On 30 June 1756, less than a month after his skirmish with Pattagan, Hesselberg himself died in the Perumal Naik war.

On 8 August 1765, a body was found in the empty house of Lieutenant Windtfeldt. It was that of Peder Andersen Houerup, second mate on the *Callicut*, just returned from Bengal[157] [Larsen 1918]. Houerup (or Hourop) was engaged to marry Agatha Schlerk. Within a few hours, two young people belonging to a lower social class – Lucas Winter, a 26-year-old Portuguese topas, and Ismael, a 22-year-old slave belonging to Windfeldt – were apprehended.[158] Ismael confessed that he, along with Winter, had brought Houerup into the kitchen of Windfeldt's house and hit him with a metre-long iron crowbar on the right side of the throat. As Houerup fell, he was struck on the head and breast by Lucas Winter and was killed. He was buried in a shallow grave in the garden, his shoes, waistcoat buttons and the golden galoon from his hat were taken by Winter. Houerup's clothes were removed and given to a black man. Ismael himself took two golden rings from Houerup. Gruesome details emerged during the trial. Ismael was having an affair with Agatha. Agatha became pregnant once and, after taking an extract from bamboo leaves, she aborted. Two to three months later, she became pregnant again – at least, that is what she told

Ismael. Perhaps she lied both times. About three days before the murder, she encouraged Ismael to kill Houerup as she was not happy with him and would rather have Ismael. Both Winter and Ismael were arrested as was Agatha Schlerk. The proceedings in the town court of Tranquebar are very detailed.[159] The meticulous examination and cross-examination would put a modern court proceeding to shame. Several persons, including Windtfeldt, his servants and slaves, Agatha Schlerks's slave, Kitoria, Christina, the enslaved mother of Ismael, Schwari Muttu, Houerup's boy-slave, and Lucas Winter's brother were produced as witnesses. Agatha Schlerk, who did not know her age, had been confirmed at Zion Church five or six years earlier (so she would have been 19 or 20 years old at the time or murder). Her deceased mother was so poor that she could take care only of herself. After the death of her mother, Agatha joined the household of Windtfeldt, baking and selling 'panniaram'[160] for a living. Before Agatha's mother died, she had asked the Windtfeldts to look after her daughter. Agatha Schlerk's reputation in the town was far from good. Houerup had apparently told his mates that he had heard that his fiancée was a well-known whore in the town, and if he had known it, he would never have become engaged to her. Agatha was present along with the entire Windtfeldt household when the body was dug up – but she exhibited no emotion. Agatha claimed that she did not instigate Ismael to commit the crime. At the end of the proceedings, the prosecution submitted that the male delinquents be taken to the place of the murder for nine consecutive weeks and whipped and caned 100 times; at the end of this period, they be taken in procession from the prison along the streets clad only in loincloths, first to the house where the murder was committed and then along the streets of the town to the place of execution, they should be pinched with hot tongs, have all their bones broken and, without the merciful deathblow, be put on stakes. For instigating the murder, Agatha Schlerk should be forced to watch the execution of the other two, then flogged and sent to work in a spinning house for the rest of her life. The defence pleaded for a mild and moderate sentence. When the judgment was delivered on 23 December 1765, it was, predictably, harsh. The two men were to be paraded in their loincloths, pinched thrice with hot tongs, have their right hands chopped off with an axe and, finally, have their heads severed from the body with an axe, and heads and hands were to be exhibited on stakes. Agatha Schlerk was sentenced to be flogged and subsequently sent to a spinning house for the rest of her life.[161]

As the case involved a murder, it was sent to Copenhagen.[162] The ship *Cron-printzen af Danmark* returned from Copenhagen to Tranquebar during the summer of 1768 with a concurring judgment from 27 November 1767. The two men were executed on 23 July just outside the walls of Tranquebar – with one detail different from the judgment. The execution was carried out with an axe instead of a sword, since no one in Tranquebar was able to wield a sword. The executioner had to come all the way from Nagapatnam.[163] Agatha herself, while in detention, had an illicit relationship with a married man, Lieutenant Michael Sundt, and she had a baby, Johanne Therecia, born in September 1767.[164] Agatha died on 25 January 1769 and the baby died three weeks later, on 14 February.

Andala, a Malabar, murdered a 12-year old boy named Conery, son of Wiraraga Setti. Andala, who was a servant of Wiraraga Setti, was caught stealing arrack bottles. Andala developed such hatred for Wiraraga Chetty that he killed his son and stole all the boy's jewellery before burying him in the house of Rev. Kohlhoff.[165] He confessed to the crime and even showed the place where Conery's body was buried under the neighbour's fence. The prosecutor in this case was Ole Bie, who would later become governor of Serampore. The judgment, as passed by the Municipal Court in Tranquebar and the Asiatic Company's court in Copenhagen, was death. First, Andala was to be paraded from the prison in his regular clothes without a mask, with a noose around his neck and his hands tied behind his back to the place of the murder, where the executioner would pinch him with red-hot tongs, a process to be repeated at all public places, and then then he would have his right hand chopped off with an axe and, finally, his head as well. Afterwards, the body, head and hands would be placed on the stake to serve as a warning. Wiraraga Setti would be given half of Andala's property with the other half going to the Company.[166] The sentences thus passed sound barbaric by modern standards, but were normal in those days.[167]

In another instance, during early 1766, Kammela (probably Kamala), a Malabar woman from Karaikal who had lost her husband eight years earlier, conceived a baby in secret. Two months after coming to Tranquebar, she gave birth to the baby while standing above a hole by the side of the house where she was staying. As the baby fell into the hole, which was about a metre deep, the umbilical cord broke. Immediately, she covered the baby with sand. She did not know whether the baby was alive when it was born. When this was discovered, a sentence was passed that she was to lose her head to an axe and the head displayed on the stake. I do not know whether this sentence was carried out, because J. W. Rafn, defense for Kammela intended to appeal to the supreme court against the sentence. The reason for this severe punishment may be that she was a local (compared to Agatha, who was white) or because she took a direct part in the murder.[168]

Cases pertaining to castes, such as ceremonial rights and inheritance, were to be settled by the castes themselves. The members of the Black Court were apparently not satisfied with their social rank in society; they wanted a recognisable symbol of their dignified status. In an additional proclamation from 1789, they were granted status symbols, such as a stick with a silver head and an umbrella on a pole. In addition, judgments were to be written in Tamil and read aloud in the court before being translated into Danish. Several proceedings of the Black Court can be found in the National Archives, written in Tamil.[169] During the British occupation of Tranquebar in 1808, the Black Court was suspended and, due to increasing operation costs, it was abandoned during 1822-23. The separate courts of Indians and Europeans were from then on united with Danish law forming the basis of the judgments [Brimnes].

By now, the locals had learnt the trick of complaining directly to the governor. There are several intriguing requests, recorded in Tamil, from the period 1837-1845, such as the request to be allowed to sell single bottles of cognac or 'French brandy' instead of the stipulated sale of a dozen bottles at a time by Lakshmana Setti,[170] a pathetic request from Varadayyangar, who was a member of the commission to look into caste unrest and who had taught Christoph Samuel John Tamil, Sanskrit and Telugu, for a pension to support his large family,[171] a request from one Bagyam to marry Annam, the wife of Arulanandam who had left her to live with another woman in Chennai,[172] a request for a loan from Devapirasadam, an employee of the Bethlehem Church in Poreiar, from the poor relief fund to be deducted monthly from his salary,[173] and so on.

Continuing our walk from the Bungalow on the Beach along King Street, we come to a small temple devoted to the elephant god, Ganesha, or Pillaiyar as he is also known. Despite being of diminutive size, this is one of the oldest temples in Tranquebar, predating the Danish occupation, and it was known as 'Poiyatha Pillaiyar Koil', and this name persists to this day. This street, which is currently known as Post Office Street, was referred to in the Danish days as Troquedor Street (Moneychangers' street). The moneychangers worshipped this Poiyatha Pillaiyar as their god. Fuglsang, whom we shall encounter later, writes that the temple was known earlier as Kunandi Pulliar Kovil. This may not be correct, as there is a different Kunandi Pulliar Kovil in Trellund's map of 1733. The Post Office Street was also known as Tendatzie Pullei Street. At the corner of King Street and Post Office Street is, of course, the post office. The history of the Danish Postal Services in the East Indies is treated in an article by Dörnbach in The Post Horn.[174]

5

Pluripotency, Power and Painting

The majestic, newly rebuilt, structure next door to Poiyatha Pillaiyar Kovil was the governor's residence. Until 1784, most of the governors stayed at Dansborg. That year, David Brown, a Dane of Scottish origin, bought a small house from Edward Stevenson and built a magnificent residence to suit a governor. Later, Peter Anker expanded and reconstructed the house.

Peter Anker served as the Danish Governor of Tranquebar between 1788 and 1806. He was a most unusual person in many respects. Peter Anker

Fig. 5.1: The new Governor's residence already looking old. Until 1784, all the governors and their families resided in the fort. David Brown, a Dane with Scottish origin, bought this site, and in 1784, the Danish government bought the building from Brown. Peter Anker, who was the governor from 1788, strongly modified this structure. After the exit of the Danes, the building was used as a salt office. In 2009, funds were provided for by the National Museum of Denmark for a restoration of the building (photo: P. S. Ramanujam, 2019).

Fig. 5.2: Portrait of Governor Peter Anker (photo: Wikimedia).

was born in Frederikshald, south-east of the Norwegian capital, Oslo, on 31 July 1744. Peter Anker's father, Erik Anker, was a businessman and his mother came from a prestigious family. Peter Anker and his brother, Carsten Anker, were sent abroad in 1760 as part of their education. Peter Anker studied architecture in Paris and mineralogy in Freiberg. His later stay in England had important consequences for his life. He learnt English and became acquainted with English society, thinking and politics. In 1773, he became consul in Hull. After three years, he moved to London and was appointed General Consul in 1784. Peter Anker came to admire the English and maintained this enchantment throughout his life. He had a refined taste, acquiring many costly things, such as books and furniture. He also accumulated a lot of debt because of his expensive tastes. He felt that an appointment in India might clear him of his debts and from London he submitted his application to the king of Denmark for the post of governor on 1 May 1786.[175] He arrived in Tranquebar in 1788.

Fig. 5.3: Samples of textiles sent from Tranquebar during the year 1783. South Indian textiles were traded by the Danes in West Africa (photo: P. S. Ramanujam).

When Anker arrived, the area under Danish administration was about 50 square kilometres. From north to south, the colony extended about 15 kms and westwards some 7 or 8 kms. The main export from the Tranquebar territory was textiles.[176] According to a census from 1790, there were 3,821 inhabitants in the town, and it was thus comparable to a large provincial town in Denmark [Brimnes]. Out of these, 3,482 were Indians, and there were 57 houses in which lived 157 Danes; in addition, there were 100 soldiers. Twenty other Europeans and 62 Indo-Portuguese also lived in the town. In the 14 other villages belonging to the Danish colony, there lived 20,000 people. Here, Tillaiyali[177] with 3,000 inhabitants and Poreiar[178] with 5,000 were the other major towns.

The Colony was administered by five persons – the governor was the Chief of Administration and commander of the army; one person oversaw finances and one was in charge of justice. Besides, there was a representative from the military and a secretary. In 1777, there were six other European and 34 Indian civil servants. In 1788, the number of European

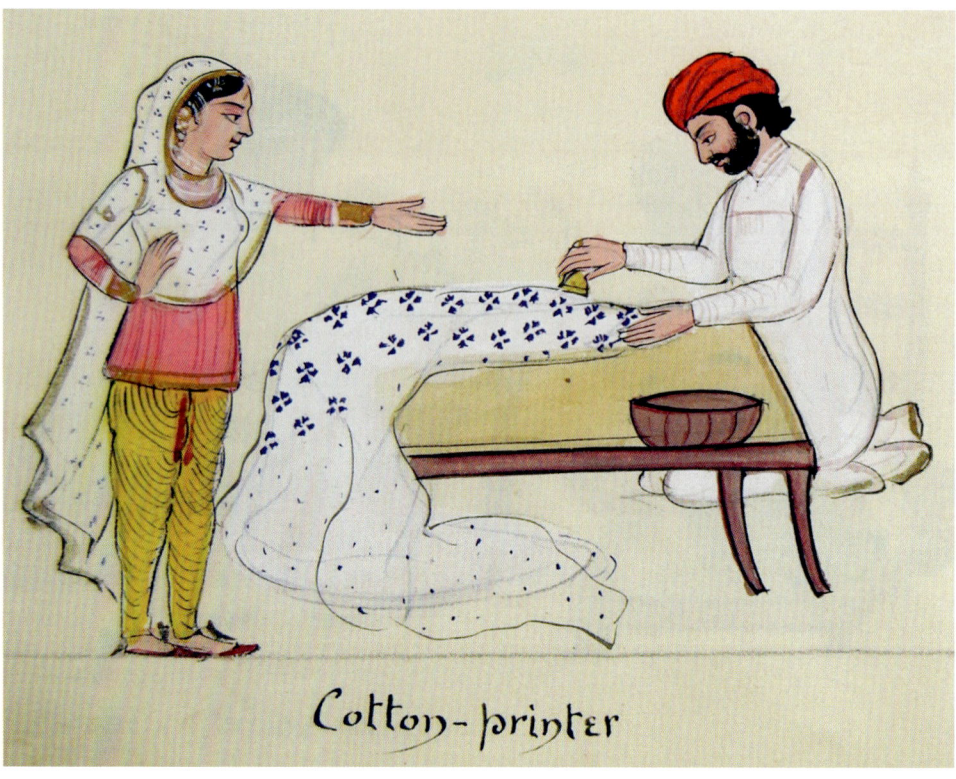

Fig. 5.4: Cotton printer block printing a length of fabric. Chintzes, which were woodblock printed textiles, were immensely popular in South India. The prints consisted of floral patterns in different colours on a light background. During the early 19th century, the sale of cotton textiles decreased in India at the cost of import from the British Isle (picture credit: Royal Asiatic Society of Great Britain and Ireland).

civil servants had grown to 25. It was a challenge for the 250 Europeans to administer 25,000 citizens.

The privy-counsellor was the chief financial officer. He collected the customs duties on rice and other agricultural products as well as land and sea customs. Customs duties on perishable goods were collected at the entrance to the town. In order to collect the duties, Indian contractors were often employed. An overmaniagar[179] (village headman or superintendant) was put in charge of agricultural production. He was responsible for the cultivation of crops, watering etc. Moradors (Mirasdars) leased the land from the state.

Justice was administered by the Chief Justice. As mentioned earlier, the

Danes did not want to get involved in local affairs, such as caste matters. A visiador (police officer) occupied a special position and was nominated by the Raja of Tanjore. However, he received his salary from the Danes. One of his duties was to patrol the borders of the colony. He was responsible for maintaining law and order within the colony and had to arrest and question suspects. He was directly under the command of the governor. Another essential position was that of the providiteur, a kind of overseer and provider for the army. In order to facilitate communications, three interpreters were employed – a Tamil, a Persian and a Marathi. The governor and the council were answerable to the chancery in Copenhagen.

A list of the salaries of the government employees from August 1791 is found in the National Archives.[180] According to this, Peter Anker earned 3,000 rdl, Chief Justice Colbjørnsen 1,000 rdl, Finance Counsellor Lichtenstein 800 rdl, Hermanson 600 rdl, Boalth 400 rdl, the contribution to the missionaries amounted to 462 rdl, Tamil interpreter Christian Daniel 110 rdl, interpreter Piragasam 60 rdl, Persian interpreter Gulam Mohamad 84 rdl, a Marathi interpreter 60 rdl, a Tanjore vakil stationed in Tranquebar 48 rdl, a government vakil stationed in Tanjore 60 rdl, providiteur Tandatzia Pulle 110 rdl, the governor's interpreter 33 rdl, the northern visiador 172 rdl, the southern visiador 66 rdl, canakapla[181] (accountant) about 25 rdl, maniagarren[182] (superintendant) 77 rdl. On the military side, Mühldorff was paid 767 rdl, a head constable 110 rdl, a corporal 65 rdl, a member of the music corps 36 rdl, an Indian premier lieutenant 128 rdl, a sergeant 65 rdl, a sepoy about 40 rdl and, in the hospital, the chief surgeon 150 rdl and a Tamil barber (who acted as a surgeon) 55 rdl.

Prior to Anker's arrival, the first royal governor, Peter Hermann Abbestée, was in office from 1779. Under Abbestée, a close relationship developed between the Danish officers and prominent Indians in the colony. During his period, the dubashes[183] (interpreters), and essentially those in the employment of the Danish councillors were important land lessees. Being a dubash had many advantages. In 1787, the dubash for the privy councillor had leases amounting to more than 22,500 rdl. These earnings were usually shared with the councillors.

Until the mid 1750s, the colony of Tranquebar was able to show a profit, mainly income due from customs duties. Despite the usual minor skirmishes between Danes and Indians, trading had been smooth. However, the situation changed dramatically after 1750 [Gregersen; Struwe].

Peter Hermann Abbestée was governor of Tranquebar 1761–75 and again 1779–88. Abbestée's family belonged to the Reformed Church and left the Netherlands for Denmark in the 17th century due to religious disturbances. Peter Hermann Abbestée, born in 1728, became an assistant at the East India Company in 1752. He was sent to the King of Travancore in order to establish a trading centre at Colachel, in Kerala; he returned to Tranquebar in 1760 and became the interim governor in 1761. He resigned from this post in 1775 and travelled to Denmark. He was elected General Governor of the Danish Establishment and returned to India in 1777 and stayed there until 1783. He wanted to resign from his post, but was asked to continue in Tranquebar due to the difficult war-like situation between England and France. He finally retired in 1789 and died in Denmark in 1794. He was married to Francoise Lange in Tranquebar in 1768 and had two daughters with her. The older of the two daughters, Maria Barbara Abbestée was confirmed in the French Reformed Church in Copenhagen in 1789 and later married Count Conrad Daniel Blücher. The younger daughter, Franziska Genoveve Abbestée was confirmed in the French Reformed Church in 1791 and married to Frederik Carl Ferdinand von Qualen. Both of them moved to the city of Altona. A portrait of Franziska Abbestée, painted by the Danish painter Jens Juel, adorned the Danish 500 kroner bank note between 1977 and 1997.

Fig. 5.5: Franziska Abbestée on a Danish banknote. Franziska was the second daughter of Peter Hermann Abbestée. A series of paintings made by the Danish artist, Jens Juel, made its way onto Danish banknotes between 1974 and 1995 (https://notescollector.eu/pages/en/notes.php?noteId=220).

It is possible that Peter Hermann Abbestée was married before he moved to Tranquebar. The Confirmation Registers for the Reformed Church show that one Johan Ludvig Abbestée was confirmed in 1770 and a Peter Abbestée in 1771. Their age suggest they could be sons of Peter Hermann. It is possible that they travelled to Tranquebar with their father in 1777, but both died before their father returned to Denmark (see 'Familien Abbestée' by C. F. Sommer). Their deaths are not recorded in the Tranquebar registers.

Fig. 5.6: The original portrait by Jens Juel of Franziska Genoveve Abbestée at the Schloss museum, Ahrensburg, Germany (photo: P. S. Ramanujam).

Just after his daughter Franziska was born, Peter Hermann had an affair with a 'Catholic slave' and became the father of Pauline Abbestée in 1772. Pauline later married Christian Tulin Boalth and became the mother of the Boalth sisters (Fanny, Abigail Catharina and Paulina). We shall meet them later in Chapter 10: Philology comes to Town. Three sons also resulted from this marriage.

There were two main caste groups in South India – right hand and left hand castes. Conflicts between the right hand and left hand castes were incessant. After all, they had been going on ever since the Chola period.[184] Tranquebar was dominated by the Vellala caste,[185] which was involved in agriculture. Because the Vellalars considered themselves more important, they were said to belong to the right hand caste. Mackenzie Manuscripts mention that the right hand castes could use white umbrellas and ride white horses. Vellalar, Agambadaiyar, Idaiyar, Kavaraikomutti, Kaikolar, Cedar and Ceniyar (oil-monger) were said to constitute this group.[186] The casteless Parians and Kavarai Chettys or Vadugas, as well as the Janappas also belonged to this caste. The distinction between who belonged to the right and left hand has never been clear. Panchalar[187] was a common name for skilled artisans working in five different branches involving manual skills – goldsmith, carpenter, blacksmith, coppersmith and stonemason [Brimnes 1999, Hastings]. The name comes from 'panch' meaning five and 'al', to melt, because Panchalas were said to melt the five metals: gold, silver, copper, brass and zinc. In the old Madras Presidency, they were also known as Kammalans, whereas the artisans belonged to the left hand caste. Saluppan[188] (known as Chelpa in Danish documents) was a small caste of Telugu weavers from Visakhapatnam, originally engaged in producing gunny bags and coarse clothes. In the old days, a headman called Senapathi governed this caste. The name 'Saluppan' is probably derived from Janappan,[189] originating in Janapa – 'hemp' (sanal[190] is a Tamil word for jute). The left hand caste could use white umbrellas, but never white horses.

Conflicts between the caste groups could start for trivial reasons. As Dubois notes,[191]

> 'Perhaps the sole cause of the contest was the right to wear slippers or to ride through the streets in a palanquin or on horseback during marriage festivals. Sometimes it is the privilege of being escorted on certain occasions by armed retainers; other times that of having a trumpet sounded in front of a procession, or of being accompanied by native musicians at public ceremonies. Perhaps, it is simply the particular kind of musical instrument suitable for such occasions that is in dispute; or perhaps it may be the right to carry flags of certain colours or certain devices during these ceremonies'.

Subramanian, who has translated Modi documents into Tamil, notes: '… matters connected with caste disputes, especially between Valankai (right hand) and Idankai (left hand) groups, which often, even for petty matters like the wearing of slippers, were at loggerheads, included religion, religious ceremonies, *sati*, the sale of women as compensation for debts incurred, *devadasis*, prices of various essential commodities like rice, expenses incurred in the palace for various festivals and ceremonies, *harem* and its role, educational institutions and their upkeep, lands and various types of problems connected with them'.[192]

In 1787, the Danish administration had to intervene in the internal conflict in Tranquebar. On 27 August 1787, Abbestée reported that all castes, except the Chelpa caste, had left the Danish territory and had gathered right outside the borders on the Tanjore king's soil. Their complaint was against Suppremania Setti. Suppremania Setti of the lower Chelpa caste became a dubash, an assessor in the Black Court and a royal employee. Usually, an assembly called 'Maha Naadu Thesattar',[193] consisting of all the right hand castes, settled these disputes internally. This time, however, it was too severe a case. Later, even the left hand caste, represented by artisans such as carpenters, smiths and masons, also joined the exodus, as they had been promised certain ceremonial rights by the right hand castes if they joined the mass departure. The government bowed to the pressure and imprisoned Suppremania Setti for six weeks, promising to appoint a commission to investigate the matter. After a couple of months, most of them returned, apart from the left hand caste because the right hand caste had not fulfilled its promise. Abbestée now promised to set up a commission to investigate the affairs.

It was at this juncture that Peter Anker entered this unfamiliar world on 17 May 1788. He tried more resolutely to punish the offenders, but little did it help. Suppremania Setti was again in prison for a couple of weeks and was released on bail paid by Major Braun. Anker found that many of the government officials collaborated with the 'culprits'. He encountered vigorous opposition when he tried to stop this collaboration, which he believed was harmful to the interests of the government. He challenged the colony's European and Indian elite in Tranquebar, in particular, the financial collaboration between the governing bodies and their dubashes. Thomas Christian Walter, who was the privy councillor, and his dubash, Suppremannia Chetty, were the chief 'plunderers'. According to Anker, bribery of the councillors resulted in lower duties being paid, and dubashes as intermediaries got their share of the booty. One of the officers who enjoyed these special privileges was Major Braun. He was an engineer and chief of the military corps. He was also responsible for the upkeep of the Dansborg Fort and the defensive walls around the town. In 1786, 75,000 rdl were allotted to repairing and improving the defence. However, the construction was of poor quality, as the bricks that had been used were substandard. Braun was responsible for the contract. Peter Anker also complained that Braun did not supervise the work, with the result that even people who were not employed were being paid. Braun had probably also employed the workers to construct his own 'palace'. Again, in the army, people used privately by Braun were paid for by the military and he received a commission whenever a sepoy was employed. Braun was subsequently dismissed from service.

The commission set up to enquire into the charges against Suppremania Setti was still functioning when Peter Anker took over in 1788. Another complaint against Suppremania was that he was responsible for an assault on another well-known merchant Sela Sela Setti (Seshachala Chetti).[194] This happened during August and September of 1787. The right hand caste accused Suppremania Setti and others from Chelpa caste of neglecting their duties during temple festivals, such as bearing torches, greasing the procession cars etc.[195] In short, Suppremania Setti, belonging to the low Chelpa caste, had acquired a high status in the society simply because he was a dubash for the fiscal, Thomas Christian Walter.

In June 1788, there were more inter-caste problems.[196] Anker ordered the arrest of several of Suppremania Setti's accusers. They were released again on 7 July after paying a fine of 100 rdl. In November 1788, history repeated itself. A large group of people left for Karaikal, thereby threatening the valuable rice harvest. In their absence, customs and duties would diminish, decreasing the Danish government's income. Frantz Theodor Lichtenstein was sent to determine the cause of the exodus. This time, conditions stipulated for a return were the release from fines and the arrest of Suppremania Setti. While the former was accepted, the latter was denied. When it became clear that the emigrants would not come back, Suppremania Setti was arrested – and now those who had left came back. During the spring of 1789, Suppremania left the territory of Tranquebar and went to Tanjore. From there, he did his best to harass the administration of the colony. Parallel to this, the disputes between the left hand and right hand castes continued regarding ceremonial rights. Finally, the left hand and right hand castes were allotted their own streets in which they could have ceremonies and ceremonial processions.

Peter Anker characterises Suppremania Setti, as 'a genius for intrigues'. 'He is a black from a mediocre caste who is blessed with the utmost talent for intrigues. He knows how to unite his instinctive Malabarian talents for roguish acts with the tricks of a European attorney; he is an absolute master in the art of covering up so well his worst actions that it is impossible to prove (them) by legal means'.[197]

The relation between Peter Anker and the missionaries was not great either. He accused them of creating a breed of 'rice-Christians', people of the lowest caste who were willing to convert to Christianity for the sake of getting a morsel of rice.[198] The Malabars, who belonged to a caste, did not convert, but 'pariars, who do not have a caste or worship' were considered dishonest. 'I myself had them in my service. But thievery and inebriety are as much inculcated in them as in their unconverted brothers'.[199]

Time and again, Suppremania Setti aggravated the situation by allowing himself to be carried around in a palanquin, a rite that was reserved for the higher castes. This resulted in people leaving Tranquebar and settling outside in Karaikal. Suppremania Setti's son was the dubash for Major Braun, and dubash Daniel Pulley's son-in-law was a good friend of Suppremania Setti.[200] Suppremania Setti served as a dubash for three successive privy counsellors –Lichtenstein, Repstorff and Walter, ending up a rich and influential man. Anker felt that the reason for the conflicts must be found in Suppremania Setti and his Danish employers' financial exploitation of the people. After the death of Walter in 1788, Lichtenstein became privy counsellor, which only made matters worse. In 1789, a new commission was established with a view to investigating the complaints against Suppremania Setti. As a result, he was fined 4,000 rdl in 1794. He had, in fact, previously offered to pay more than double this amount to become free. Anker had given the job of enforcing law and order in the colony to his interpreter Piragasam Pulley.

Whenever Maha Nadu Thesattar wanted to send a complaint to the Danish government, the chiefs of all the castes assembled at Ohrugamangalam.[201] When they had settled on the final wording, it was the business of one of the chiefs to keep it until it was written down and sent off. After a period of lull, in 1794, the chiefs of some of the castes reported to Peter Anker that Suppremania Setti was inciting the locals to leave the Tranquebar area, helped by two of his acquaintances Tambu Chetty and Matturaja Pulle. Tambu Chetty had told people in Poreiar that Daniel Pulley together with Colbjørnsen and Lichtenstein had been planning an exodus for the people from the colony. The locals asked Anker to investigate the matter and arrest the two troublemakers. After a short enquiry, Anker sentenced the two troublemakers to be whipped in public. A consequence of this was the voyage of one Chinnayya to Denmark, as will be discussed in the next chapter. Complaints against Piragasam Pulley for misuse of his position gathered strength in 1795. Anker was reluctant to pursue action against Piragasam for reasons we do not know (perhaps because he had borrowed a large amount of money from Piragasam or because Piragasam Pulley was loyal to Anker). He defended Piragasam Pulley as much as he could. In a letter dated 31 August 1798, addressed to the chancery in Copenhagen, he bitterly complained about the 'negligent and shamefully partisan' atmosphere in the Black Court after Daniel Pulley had been appointed as the assessor instead of Piragasam Pulley.[202]

As a result of Chinnayya's complaints to the Danish king about Peter Anker, a commission was set up to enquire into Anker's punishment of Tambu Chetty and Matturaja Pulley, as well as the behaviour of Piragasam Pulley. The commission consisted of Privy Counsellor Lichtenstein, accountant Schmidt, Captain Otto Stricker and missionaries C. S. John and Rottler. The commission completed its work in 1798, concluding that Chinnayya Naik did not have any foundations for his complaints and that Piragasam Pulley should be dismissed from his employment as a dubash as well as an assessor at the Black Court. Anker himself was reprimanded for his treatment of Tambu Chetty and Matturaja Pulle. It is surprising that John, who sat on the commission and who wrote a 'biography' of Daniel Pulley, did not comment on these incidents.

The situation continued to worsen with more flights from the colony in 1798. The conflicts escalated with Anker and Mühldorff on one side, Lichtenstein and Colbjørnsen on the other. At the same time, England and France were at war in Europe. The neutrality of Denmark was an excellent opportunity to earn a fortune in the East Indian colony. Lichtenstein made good use of this situation. He established commercial contacts through his relations to the French possession of Isle de France (Mauritius). Lichtenstein went under the name of 'le Marchand des Passports notre Ami le 5 p.c.', because he collected 5% of all the customs charges on sea passes. Lichtenstein was also accused by the British government of supporting the French directly. (Lichtenstein's mother was French,[203] and he had a very strong French leaning.) Based on information passed on by Anker to the English government in Madras, a strong complaint was lodged by Lord Mornington.[204] Lord Mornington wrote to Peter Anker that:[205] 'a member of your government is distinctly stated by the French agent of Tippoo Sultan to have aided and abetted the system of correspondence and intrigue carried on by that agent, for the accomplishment of the declared objects of his mission: That person is the Second Governor of Tranquebar whose name I understand to be M. Lichtenstein'. He went on: '...your Excellency should take effectual and speedy measures for securing the person of M. Lichtenstein, the second governor of Tranquebar; and you should by the first opportunity send him to Europe…A denial of this just requisition would amount to a positive violation of neutrality, on the part of the whole Government of Tranquebar, and place them in the same predicament in which M. Lichtenstein now stands; that of a declared enemy of the British Nation'.[206]

Anker replied obediently:[207] 'I have the honour to enclose a Translation of a Declaration made by M. Lichtenstein and sworn to in the presence of the Consul, which solemnly contradicts the insertions against him. M. Lichtenstein has inform'd Governor of his intention of embarking for Europe in the course of next month, and, that he will there be ready to meet the enquiry into his conduct his Danish Majesty shall think proper to direct'. Franz v. Lichtenstein sailed from Tranquebar on 10 May 1799, to Isle de France and from thence to Copenhagen. The Commission set up to inquire into his affairs could not conclude before Lichtenstein's death in 1802.

There was another problem that would not go away. The reason for this, however, was quite different. The problem with Perumal Naik started already in 1742. He was accused by the Danes of murdering 90 persons.[208] Hans Georg Krog was Governor of Tranquebar between 1754 and 1759. Just before the arrival of Krog, the Danish government in Tranquebar had appointed a local naik (visiador) for the northern border districts, without requesting permission from Tanjore. The duty of the visiador was to maintain order at the border. The north naik, Ramalinga, was dead, and the Danes appointed his nephew, Rama Naik, in his place. Krog was told in no uncertain terms that only the King of Tanjore had the power to appoint the local naik. In a conciliatory gesture, Krog sent the king a pet dog, a fine flint stone and a pair of pistols as presents. The king, Pratapa

Fig. 5.7: Temple at Thillaiyali, where Danes were massacred by Perumal Naik's troops. This town was one of the largest towns in the Danish territory in South India. The name of the town alludes to the myth that Vishnu, one of the Hindu trinity of gods, worshipped Shiva, another of the trinity, in the form of the mythical beast, yali (photo: P. S. Ramanujam).

Simhan, appointed Perumal Naik. Perumal Naik had a reputation for brutality and was an archenemy of the Nayak of the southern districts. The problems continued in 1756.[209]

In 1756, Perumal Naik began to gather ammunition and soldiers with help from Tanjore. The 'talliars' (soldiers) belonging to the Asiatic Company who were functioning as border patrol entered Perumal Naik's house surreptitiously and removed the ammunition. It was, however, returned to him through the mediation of the English consul. On 17 June 1756, Perumal Naik stole cattle – buffaloes and 48 cows[210] – belonging to the natives in the Danish territory.[211] Lieutenant Passow, who was sent on reconnaissance, found the cows but had to retreat as cannons protected the animals. The Danish border force was too small to offer any opposition and called for more troops. Captain Strøbel, who was in charge of the border force, was ordered to occupy Anandamangalam, which was under the protection of Perumal. There were clashes at the temple at Anandamangalam; however, a three-month truce was established due to mediation from the subedar of Mayavaram [Struwe].

Perumal Naik acquired more support and was ready to attack. The Danish force at Tillaiyali also received extra troops. On 30 June, as Perumal Naik's troops neared Tillaiyali,[212] they were fired upon by the Danish troops led by Captain Hesselberg together with Attrup and 24 soldiers. At Tillaiyali, the fighting initially took place close to the inn (chattiram) and then the temple where the Danish troops had moved in. However, the result was a massacre of the Danish troops. Captain Peter N. Hesselberg, his brother-in-law H. J. Attrup, who was the standard-bearer, two noncommissioned officers, 24 European soldiers and approximately 20 Indians died. Only one Danish soldier, who had hidden inside the temple, was unhurt. The Mission lost property worth a few hundred rigsdaler, including furniture, windows and doors, tables and chairs from the Church of Bethlehem in Poreiar. Approximately 600 thatched houses and huts were burnt.

In July, the English offered to mediate. The King of Tanjore, Manosiappa, sent a letter to the English:

> 'The sea had washed down the Eastern part of the walls of the fort of Tranquebar, for which reason the Danes intended to take possession of my ground to the distance of two miles to the westward of the said fort, with a design to build a fort on it, and so the [sic] began troubles. The village of Anentamangalam belonging to me lies to the westward of the said fort, which was possessed by them as well as a pagoda, and they broke the images to pieces & burnt or broke the Wahanams /:

or seats belonging to the images :/ and a chariot. They likewise erected batteries on all sides of the pagoda and brought ten or twelve guns from their fort and mounted on the batteries and placed a guard of 100 or 150 Europeans, and topasses, together with seepoys in all 3 or 400 men threat(e)ned my people and drove them away. When this news was brought to me, I sent to demand their reasons for so doing? but the(y) pretended a false story and returned an answer to me that Ramah Naik and Perumal Naik Poligars were indebted to them and they refused to pay it, for which reason they seized the said village.'

George Pigot[213] concurred in this version of the story:

'..the original cause of your taking up arms was some injuries offered you by one Perumal Naik, a Polygar and subject of the king of Tanjour, to obtain justice from whom, you marched a body of troops upon the territories of the said king possessed your selves of the village of Anandamangalam which belongs to him, this act of hostility is on the other hand, made the subject of complaint from the king of Tanjour; to give you our opinion freely on this subject, so far as it is yet stated to us, we must say, it does not appear, that you ever made any application to the court of Tanjour for redress of the injury done you by Perumal Naikker, had you made such application without effect, the law of nations /: which as the case now stands seems rather to speak against you :/ would then have justified you seeking redress by the means of arms....we shall be able to prevail with the king of Tanjour to cause ample reparation to be made you for all the damages you may have unjustly sustained by his subjects and on the other hand to shew a good example of justice, we persuade ourselves you will as readily agree to withdraw your troops within your own bounds and restore to him those territories to which he has a just right'.[214]

After the English intervention, the skirmish quietened down. Krog lost the battle and decided to quit his job. Perumal Naik paid for the damages done by him.

Thirty years later, this Perumal Naik was on the loose again and had been embarrassing the Danish Territories.[215] Anker tried to stop him by complaining to the King of Tanjore, but to no avail. As the King of Tanjore was at this point supported by the British, Anker complained to Mornington[216] that he had been 'for upwards of two years much annoyed by one of the Rajah of Tanjore's polygars'.

> 'The Polygar I allude to, is a Person by the name of Perumal Naik, who's Polygar District under the Rajah of Tanjore extends within the Limits of the Danish Jurisdiction. This Perumal Naik collected an armed Force in the Rajah's Territory for the express Purpose of committing Hostilities in this Settlement. He passed the Boundaries in the night and with his armed Banditti to the Number of 200 broke into the Kings Gardens, attacked the Guard on duty, and killed two of the Kings Sepoys and wounded three in the very Centre of the Danish Jurisdiction; but a gallant Defence of a native Officer with 30 Sepoys compell'd the Assailants to make a precipitate Retreat back to the Rajah's Territory with a Number of killed and wounded. A few days after another Attack was made, by the same Perumal Naik, on a Patrol under Command of a European Officer, and followed by my Second in Command, Colonel Mühldorff, who's Intention was to inspect the military Stations. In passing a small Wood the Patrol received violent Fire of Musquettery, the Sepoys were fortunately dispersed and thereby escaped the Bullets; but it appeared, that Col. Mühldorff was particularly aimed at, as he had a Sepoy killed close to his Horse. The Villains, when pursued, took Shelter in the Rajah's Territory. I was silent for some Time on the Subject of these outragious Proceedings in hopes, that Perumal Naik would be sensible of the Consequences which might attend his criminal Conduct; But it appeared, the Protection he enjoyed under the Rajah of Tanjore was a sufficient Security to enable him to continue to rob and plunder within the Limits of the Danish Jurisdiction, and even to address me some insolent Proposals. It was then I found myself under the absolute necessity of addressing the Rajah of Tanjore. I wrote

his Excellency a letter on the 1st of June, of which I have the honor to inclose a Copy...The Rajah of Tanjore being placed on the Musnud by the English Company as a subordinate Prince and under the Direction of a Servant of the Company, I am flattered with the Hopes your Lordship will do his Danish Majesty the Justice to order the Government of Tanjore to observe a Conduct towards his Majesty the King of Denmark in every respect conformable to that friendly Alliance, which subsists between his Danish Majesty and his Majesty the King of Great Britain. And, that your Lordship will please to order the Government of Tanjore to enforce the Demand I address'd his Excellency the Rajah in my Letter of the 1st of June respecting that audacious Criminal Perumal Naik'.

However, the British Government did not want to get involved. Here is Mornington's reply:[217]

'His Excellency the Rajah of Tanjour is bound by Treaty to hold no intercourse with Foreign States without the sanction of the Company's Government; and although these forms may have been dispensed with on occasions of little importance, yet the Rajah could not consistently with his engagements enter into any arrangement with your Excellency, for the suppression of animosities on the Frontier of the Danish Territories.

I find upon enquiry, that the Polygar Perumal Naik holds a right of Cauvil[218] as well in the Districts subject to the Danish authority, as in those under the Jurisdiction of the Rajah of Tanjore or of the British Government, and that availing himself of this divided authority he had committed depredations upon each of the Districts under circumstances suited to the different occasions.

It is stated in your Excellency's Letter, that the present act of violence of which you complain was committed within the limits of the Danish Territories; and, as it appears to have happened at no great distance from a Military Post, I should have been sincerely glad, if your Troops had been able to inflict immediate punishment'.

England was growing in power, and the Danish foreign trade policies were not to their liking. In 1801, England ordered all the Danish colonies to be occupied. Tranquebar was occupied by the English on 12 May 1801. Anker decided to hand over the colony to them in order to avoid any bloodshed and because the state of fortification left much to be desired. After a peace agreement was reached with England during October 1801, the colony was given back to the Danes on 17 August 1802.

Sick and tired of all the political intrigues, Anker wanted to leave the colony. He wanted to quit already in 1799 but was persuaded by his brother to continue a little longer. His resignation was granted in 1805; he left Tranquebar in 1806 and settled down at his inherited farm, Øraker in what is now Oslo, Norway, in 1808. In 1811, he complained to the chancery about the 'rank tax' he had to pay, thus reducing his effective pension.[219] He did not travel again or get involved in politics, except for a brief stint to help his brother Carsten Anker to obtain British support for Norwegian independence. Peter Anker died on 17 April 1832, at the age of 88.

Peter Anker was highly esteemed in the colony for his fairness and his behaviour towards the local people. An invitation in Tamil and addressed to Peter Anker has been preserved, inviting him to attend the annual chariot festival of the god at Thiruvidaimarudhur and requesting 472 persons to pull the chariot. In 1799, not far from Dansborg, workers found 14 exquisite bronzes belonging to the Chola period carefully buried in the soil. Inger Wulff, citing Peter Anker, writes:

> The Brahmin priests, who were called in to evaluate the situation, decided that the holiness in the statues had disappeared because the soil in which they were buried had been trodden upon by people as well as impure animals, although with the proper invocation, they could be restored to their original glory. However, this process was quite expensive, as new temples worthy of the bronzes must first be built before the idols could be consecrated. No Tamil king in the southern part of Hindustan had the necessary means to perform such an expensive affair.
>
> Therefore, they decided to hand over the statues to me, and they were brought to my country house in a solemn fashion by

Fig. 5.8: Mrs. Mallard's memorial at Peter Anker's summer residence in Thillaiyali – now completely razed to the ground (photo: P. S. Ramanujam 2009).

the Brahmins and the people. As a testimonial to my gratefulness, a quantity of rice was offered in the temples nearby, and betel and rice were distributed among the Brahmins, which was accepted as a friendly gesture'.

Undoubtedly, the bronzes were buried in the soil to escape the hands of the Muslim invaders. Peter Anker kept them on his farm until his death; after he died, they were sold to Christian VIII of Denmark and were then donated to the National Museum of Denmark. To this day, a few of them are exhibited in the ethnographic collections at the National Museum of Denmark in Copenhagen.

As mentioned earlier, Peter Anker had an exquisite taste for all things good. He was also an acclaimed painter. He painted or drew several hundred pictures. After his death, these were donated to the Peter Anker Collection in Oslo.[220] He was always in debt. In fact, one of his reasons for

Fig. 5.9: Portrait of Mrs. F. A. Mallard (or Mollart). Mrs. Mallard was born Lady Mary Seymour; she was a widow and a catholic, which was perhaps the reason Peter Anker did not marry her (unknown painter, National Museum of Art, Architecture and Design, Oslo, Norway).

coming to India was the hope that he would attain sufficient wealth to pay off all debts. He even borrowed money from his interpreter, Piragasam Pullei, and perhaps this was a reason for Anker to defend Piragasam despite all opposition. He went to the extent of asking his brother in Copenhagen, Carsten Anker, to find him a rich widow.

However, he did have a lady friend from England, Mrs. Mallard, a widow, who lived with him at the governor's residence. Anker met her in London and she came to Tranquebar in 1791. Barely a year after her arrival, she died in Tranquebar and was buried in the Church of Zion cemetery. After her death, Peter Anker erected a memorial for her at his summer residence.

Suppremania Setti was still going strong in 1808. In a letter, formulated in both English and Tamil, he complains of the injustice done to him as far back as in 1788: 'The above-mentioned decree from the Royal College in Copenhagen arrived at last but with a refusal of renouncing, as petitioned, the rents stipulated by the government, adlegging the probability of my being the Author of the Inhabitants leaving Tranquebar and consequently unworthy of the indulgence petitioned'.²²¹

Conflicts between the right hand and left hand castes were not resolved with the exit of Peter Anker. Vengitasala Setti, belonging to the left hand caste, celebrated a marriage in Kattucheri in 1818; but the right hand caste, led by Thambu Setti and Thirumalai Naik, caused interruptions during this function. The left hand castes complained²²² to the Danish government. In December 1821, a committee consisting of three prominent Indians granted the left hand caste several ceremonial rights.²²³ Tirumudi Setti and his brother Appu Setti were given the right to travel by palanquin, which was vehemently opposed by the right hand caste. In January 1822, the right hand caste plundered and burnt several houses belonging to the left hand caste. Violent protests continued on both sides. As late as in 1822, several newspapers, such as the Bengali Hurkaru, reported how harmful it was to grant privileges to a specific caste. Here is a report from the India Gazette from 1822:

> 'By Letters from Madras, Pondichery and other parts, intelligence has been received of disturbances of very serious nature having taken place at the Danish Settlement of Tranquebar. According to our information, it originated in some imprudent and impolitic measures adopted by some servants under the Danish Government at that Settlement, who had granted to *Tirumuddy Chetty*, an opulent Native of low caste, all the priveleges which belong exclusively to the higher caste, and should therefore, according to the established custom of the country and fixed opinion or prejudice of the Natives, be exercised only by those who are of what is commonly called the *right hand* caste.
>
> We are sorry to learn that this popular tumult even went so far that several godowns filled with valuable goods were set on fire by the Natives, and property destroyed to a considerable amount. In consequence of these violent proceedings, the Government was at last compelled to lessen their dignity so far as to disgrace the low caste man that had been so unwisely elevated by recalling the privileges granted to him. But not

satisfied with this point being conceded to them, the Natives boldly and peremptorily demanded the dismissal of Mr. Kofoed and Mr. Lorentz, two Officers employed under the Danish Government at that place, who are complained against as having given rise to the disturbance, by granting the unusual privileges already alluded to, to Tirumuddy Chetty. Altho' the letters do not explicitly state, it is to be inferred that the object of the Natives in committing these outrages was merely to intimidate the Government into a revocation of those honours granted to Tirumuddy, which were so inconsistent with their ideas of the proper gradations of and due subordination among men of inferior origin.

We are happy to be able to add that according to the latest accounts, tranquility had been again restored, chiefly owing to the prudent and efficacious measures adopted by Mr. Ratlig, Judge and Magistrate at that place; and the complete confidence the Native population have in him give reason to hope that the peace of the Settlement will not be again disturbed. It is added that the European inhabitants suffered considerable inconvenience during these disturbances from their Native Servants having completely deserted them for several days'.[224]

*

Peter Anker left Tranquebar in 1807, and Peter Hermansen became the new governor for the period of 1806-1808. The French had concluded a peace treaty with Russia in 1807, which led England to make a lightning strike against Denmark, in order that the Danish navy should not fall into the hands of the French. After three days of intense bombardment of Copenhagen, the Danes surrendered their vessels to the English. Commercial Danish vessels were captured everywhere by the English. In February 1807, Tranquebar was again occupied, under the same conditions as during 1801-1802, minimising the losses suffered by the town. Peace was again concluded between Denmark and England in 1814, and the colony was returned to the Danes on 20 September 1815. It was becoming apparent that the future commercial prospects of Tranquebar were not looking good. The English levied a hefty customs duty on all goods. Indian goods,

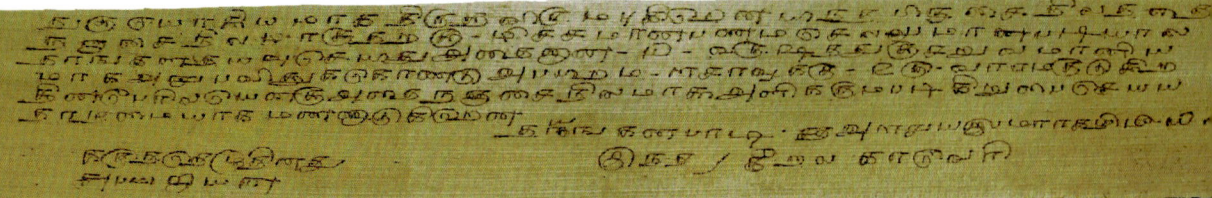

Fig. 5.10: A request by Kaveri to Governor Rehling to convert an existing 'punjai' (an area of dry land) to 'nanjai' (wet land) for a period of 10 years and enjoy its benefits. Wet lands are used for rice cultivation (photo: P. S. Ramanujam).

such as linen, were no longer popular abroad; instead, products such as rice, raw cotton, camphor, indigo, sago, ginger and sugar were the primary export goods [Rasch]. The more affluent class within the local community now began to dress in the English style, and it was getting difficult for the local weavers to make ends meet. Tranquebar was becoming British, and the official language was slowly changing to English. In fact, retired English people and widows of English officers who could not afford the voyage back to England began to settle down in Tranquebar. On the good side, the corruption that had plagued the place during the years prior to 1815 slowly disappeared, and the colony enjoyed more peace and order. Honest and well-educated civil servants started their employment in Tranquebar. On the other hand, the earnings of the Danes began to fall dramatically. Already during the 1780s, the economic situation was not very bright.

Talks were afoot for a sale of the colony to the English. Governor Peter Hermansen died in 1822 and was succeeded by Jens Kofoed who was the governor until May 1823, followed by Schönheyder during 1823-1825 and Brinck-Seidelin between 1825 and 1829. Fjellerup and Brinck-Seidelin both tried to establish textile industries in and around Tranquebar, but neither of them succeeded. Brinck-Seidelin was a difficult man who harassed everyone.[225] Lauritz Christensen, an enterprising man, was the next governor and he tried to paint a very optimistic picture of the future of Tranquebar, attempting bravely to once more colonise the Nicobar Islands – but he came back to the mainland in a barrel of spirit having died on the way.[226] Konrad Emil Mourier followed Lauritz Christensen. Christian Tiemroth, the next governor, was unbearable, often sending his complaints in verse. He sent Johannes Rehling, who was the governor, an

Fig. 5.11: A European officer (photo: P. S. Ramanujam).

Fig. 5.12: An Indian soldier painted in 1822. Despite the tropical heat, the uniforms were made of the same material as in Denmark. (Painter unknown) (RA, Kommercekollegiet, Ostindiske fags sekretariat, Journalsager 1822 (Løbenr. 3268)) (photo: P. S. Ramanujam).

irritating complaint in 17 pages that forced Rehling to take an extended sick leave.[227] The end of the Danish period was drawing near.

The last Danish Governor of Tranquebar was Peder Hansen. Peder Hansen was born 27 November 1798 in the city of Aalborg in Denmark [Madsen]. After finishing his schooling with excellent grades in 1817, he studied law at the University of Copenhagen. He graduated, again with excellent grades, in 1825. As one of the young and talented graduates, he was appointed head clerk to the Government of Tranquebar in 1826. He arrived at Tranquebar on 12 February 1827. Starting at the bottom, he ad-

Fig. 5.13: An intimate portrait of Peder Hansen, the last governor of Tranquebar and the entire Danish establishment. Peder Hansen negotiated with the English regarding the sale of the Danish colony in 1845 (Royal Library, Copenhagen).

vanced through the hierarchy to become the last Governor of Tranquebar between 1842 and 1845. Many of his letters and documents are preserved in the National Archives in Copenhagen, giving an insight into life in Tranquebar.

Reforms were necessary after 1815 in order to reduce expenses. Several posts within the government were removed. The job of surveyor, procurement officers and other administrative positions were abolished. The trading post at Porto Novo was sold in 1829. The relationship with the Halle mission from Germany, which was sending missionaries to Tranquebar, was scrutinised carefully. Gradually the English Mission took over the Danish Mission. Already in 1803, it had been decided that the missionary aim should not be to convert Indians, as they were impossible to convert. The caste system was too strong. Instead, the mission concentrated on general education and health care. The Black Court was dismantled and, initially, the cases were adjudicated in the town court. Six locals from different religions supported the Danish judge. There were far fewer court cases in 1830 compared to earlier. Whipping and beating were still the most common punishment. Peder Hansen started out as an assistant to Justice Rehling. Peder Hansen wrote to his friends in 1827 that the locals complained to him every morning between 6 and 9 about each other. Usually, both parties were sentenced to be whipped. His usual working hours were from 6 in the morning until 6 in the evening, with a short break for lunch. After deciding in the local disputes, finishing this task at 9 in the morning, he functioned as a judge at the court until about 2 in the afternoon when he went home for lunch. Again, at 4 in the afternoon, he judged local disputes. In the evening, probably after a game of whist, he went to bed around 10 at night. 'At ten, I go to bed after a comfortable day's life. Then all the mosquitoes, grasshoppers, bats, rats and mice start fighting for supremacy. Last night, I was disturbed by a bat for four hours. Usually, I wander every night for a few hours on the floor. The next morning the same life begins again and this goes on forever... I still have 112 months to go in a place that should have been paradise, but nobody knows where it is'. His first years in Tranquebar were not very pleasant for him. He says: 'Today it is exactly fifteen months ago that I left Denmark, and I have wished at least 15 million times since that I was back home'. Initially, he found the nature around Tranquebar interesting, with coconuts and other palm trees, but 'after one gets used to this, this is gloomier than a spruce forest'.

Peder Hansen did not have any contacts with the locals. He lamented that: 'The majority of Malabarians are cultivated people with beautiful and regular traits, and many of them are proficient in several European languages', but 'they were also great liars whose greatest pleasure was to carry out lawsuits against each other'; 'They are the most 'backward' people one can think of, and they have the opposite habits compared to Europe. Their ladies show their respect by showing their backs and turning the heads away. To belch and to fart are a fashion at their parties, to show that they have had enough to eat. When you wave your hands, they leave, and when you gesticulate with your hands, they come. At night, they are merry, making a lot of noise with bassoons and trumpets so that you go mad. ... Brahmins are the worst. It probably lies in their priesthood. You should see such a Brahmin, almost naked, but with a solemn look and gesture, make himself curved like an eel, and bend with his head touching the earth, all the time lies and compliments pour out from his mouth. I have beaten many a rogue down the stairs, but he bowed low and said it is the pleasure of your Lordship' [Madsen].[228]

Peder Hansen married Harriet Maria Smyth, who was half-Scottish and half-Danish, at the Church of Zion in 1829, and their first child was baptised there the following year. Harriet was only 15 years old at the time of her wedding. After giving birth to several children, she died on her 14th wedding anniversary, 29 years old; Hansen was later appointed chief of Serampore in Bengal. After Rehling's death, Hansen became Governor of Tranquebar in 1841, and within a few days he began negotiations to sell the colony. During the first negotiations, Hansen did not name a price, but proposed that this should be calculated on the basis of the annual income of the colony together with the value of the public buildings, such as the fort. Setting the annual income to 50,000 company rupees, at 5% interest over 20 years gave a value of 11 lakhs (1.1 million rupees), plus the buildings. The English would only offer 10 lakhs. Finally, the English accepted a price of 12½ lakhs[229] Company rupees (1,125,000 rigsdaler), including the public buildings. The final contract was signed in Calcutta on 22 February 1845, by Hardinge for the English and Elberling for the Danish. Otto Rehling, son of Governor Johannes Rehling, wrote to his family in Denmark on 10 November 1845: 'Finally Tranquebar has become English. On the 5th of this month, Lewin, the judge from Kumbakonam and Sir Henry Montgomery Gertie, Collector of Tanjore came down here and at 2 p.m. on 7 July, the English flag was hoisted without any ceremony at Dansborg castle. I did not want to see the English flag go up, so I stayed at home'.[230]

After the sale of Tranquebar, Hansen spent a few years trying to establish commercial trade with China. He was appointed Governor of the Danish West-indies (present Virgin Islands) in 1848, a post he served for three years before returning to Denmark. Between 1854 and 1861, he served in the Danish parliament. After 1861, at the age of 62, he continued to occupy public posts for another 20 years. He died in Denmark in 1880, at the age of 82.

6

A Stowaway from Tranquebar

His name was Chinnayya Naik. He was born in Tranquebar[231] – but where, we do not know. As his story is intimately connected with that of Peter Anker, he appears here. Chinnayya Naik was a young man of about 25 years. (Danish documents at the National Archives in Copenhagen name him as Sennia Naik; most of the later documents call him Sennapa Naik, but he signed all his documents in Tamil as Chinnaayyanaa…).[232] Chinnayya left Tranquebar on 4 February 1795, as a stowaway on the ship *Juliane Marie* belonging to the Asiatic Company. The ship's log for 5

Fig. 6.1: The ship 'Juliane Marie' on which Chinnayya Naik sailed from Tranquebar to Copenhagen (M/S Museet for Søfart, Helsingør, Denmark).

February says: 'Found that a black sailor by the name of Senepa had crept aboard the ship and hidden between the pumps for protection'.²³³ When questioned by the captain, he declared that he wanted to become a Christian and be employed as a sailor. Captain Lemming ordered that now that he was on the ship, and because there was a shortage of sailors, he be given the job at a salary of 5 rdl. per month [Waaben].²³⁴ Later, he confessed to the captain that his real intention with the trip was to complain about the then Governor of Tranquebar, Peter Anker. The ship reached Copenhagen on 27 July 1795. Chinnayya immediately went into action. He was granted an audience with Crown Prince Frederik (later King Frederik VI) within a few days of his arrival. On 29 July, he sent his complaint formally in writing – in Danish.²³⁵

After this, several meetings between the Board of Economics and Commerce and Chinnayya took place. During November of the same year, the Board of Trade was able to piece together Chinnayya's complaints: That Governor Peter Anker, with the help of his dubash Piragasam Pillai, was amassing wealth from his economic dealings. When the heads of the castes were preparing a complaint to the king, Anker intervened and jailed two of the locals – Maturaja Pillai and Tambu Chetti. According to Chinnayya, these documents were in his chest, which was removed by Piragasam Pillai, and Chinnayya himself had to hide. Peter Anker tried by threat and force to convince the two locals that his authority was just; when they refused to accept this, it was decided to 'punish the black dogs' physically and in public. According to Chinnayya, the caste leaders decided to send him to Copenhagen to make a complaint about Peter Anker and to ask that he be suspended from the post of governor.

Two documents were produced by Chinnayya – one was signed by nine individuals as representatives of the castes and the other was a letter from Chinnayya's father. These documents had been sent with the *Prinsesse Lovisa Augusta,* which had left Tranquebar in March and reached Copenhagen in August. Chinnayya wanted a commission of enquiry with P. H. Lindam as the head. At this juncture, Carsten Anker, the brother of Peter Anker, who was employed as a director by the Asiatic Company, went into action to protect his brother. He was sure that Chinnayya did not have the proper credentials. Through the public notary, he formulated eight questions regarding Chinnayya and his background, such as whether the official knew that Chinnayya's father was an ordinary person who sold milk and that he was neither of a noble nor a spiritual family? Whether he knew that Chinnayya himself and his family had been accused as well as punished in India?

Next, Carsten Anker contacted seven of the largest commercial companies in Copenhagen, 'not as his friend, but as friends of the truth', and asked whether they knew of the conditions in Tranquebar as these had been described by Chinnayya. Could they, based on their contacts in India, testify to these conditions in the colony? He received a reply from all of them during a day – of course, none of them had heard anything negative about the governor. Carsten Anker presented his documents before the Board of Trade. There was more bad news for Chinnayya – news was received in Copenhagen that Chinnayya did not have the social status he claimed to have and that he carried out only meagre services for ship's officers. It was also said that his brother had been punished and that he himself was a person of questionable character. One of the officers, Blume, had had to dismiss Chinnayya from his job because some gold thread had gone missing from Blume's possession. The king now resolved to set up a committee to investigate the accusations from either side.

On 3 February 1796, the king decided that the Danish East India Company should pay Chinnayya 1 rdl per day for sustenance from 25 November 1795 onwards. Chinnayya was then paid until 16 September 1796, an amount totalling 302 rdl. This was a large sum of money for an ordinary man – however, Chinnayya was no ordinary man. He had very expensive habits. On 24 May 1796, he applied for a loan of 4,000 rdl. He claimed that Peter Anker prevented the sending of any money to him. He received 2 times 300 rdl from the Board of Trade (in addition to receiving 1 rdl per day until May 1798). But this was not enough – Chinnayya started to borrow money. The first documented debt amounted to 38 rdl owed to one Schwabe, for which the above-mentioned Lindham was the guarantor (Schwabe later took Lindham to court). Soon, Chinnayya became acquainted with Carl Wilhem Carlsen, who paid off all his loans and in addition lent him a large sum. In December 1796, Chinnayya owed Carlsen more than 6,000 rdl. On 6 September 1797, Chinnayya was sentenced by the court to pay Carlsen the 6,000 rdl. There are indications that Chinnayya borrowed 10,000 rdl from a man called von Strambow, but no documents prove this. Chinnayya managed to borrow large sums of money on the pretext that he was descended from a noble and rich family in India and, with a little bit of patience, all the debts would be repaid in due course.

An expensive habit grew on Chinnayya – he began to use paid transport (hackney). He travelled to several places in and around Copenhagen using carriages. Probably he believed that if he used such a means for transport, he would be considered an important person and it would then be easier to borrow money. One of the carriage drivers (A. C. Friis) said that he believed Chinnayya to be an important envoy. Later, Friis sued Chinnayya for not having paid him – Chinnayya retorted that no one accused him of misuse of the carriage. Chinnayya spent an extensive amount of time visiting officers from ships as well as sailors who returned from Tranquebar to get hold of the local news, hoping that he would get some support, but to no avail. Meanwhile, his list of expenses grew. The cost of board and lodging during 1796 was 30 rdl, which was paid by Carlsen. Once a month, Chinnayya had a haircut costing 1 rdl. The greatest expenses were spent on clothing (as he had to dress befitting an envoy). In 1798, Chinnayya estimated that he had an expenditure of 5-600 rdl for clothing. At the same time, there was an unpaid invoice of 57 rdl to a tailor named Hildeman.

1797 was a bad year for Chinnayya. He had no funds, and now illness started to plague him. On 15 April 1797, he was admitted to the hospital in Frederiksberg for two weeks. The Board of Trade paid his bill of 12 rdl and 1 mark, out of which 4 rdl and 4 marks went to having a servant on call for 14 nights and 2 days. He subsequently spent six weeks in the countryside at Suserup mill close to the town of Sorø. On 15 August 1797, Chinnayya was imprisoned at the notorious Blåtårn ('Blue Tower'– this does not exist anymore). While in prison he became sick, but one of the wardens took care of him, and the Board of Trade granted him an additional amount of 16 shillings per day. Documents show that Chinnayya was provided with coffee, tea, beer, wine, sandwiches as well as dinner. He was admitted to Frederik's Hospital in Frederiksberg again between 26 September and 25 November. The bill of 112 rdl was once again covered by the Board of Trade. Chinnayya then went back to the Blue Tower. He contacted a noted criminal, Johan Christian Heuss, who had been sentenced to life for the fabrication of false banknotes. Later, Heuss appealed to the Commerce Department to refund him 24 rdl, which Chinnayya owed him for letters written in French on his behalf. (While in the Blue Tower together, Heuss made a seal for Chinnayya, containing the words

'Trangoebarske Nation af Sinnia Naisher', complete with the emblem of a crown, a lion and a sword). He sat in the Blue Tower until June 1798. On 14 February 1798, Chinnayya complained that he had not received his clothes from the miller, Lassen; on 25 September, he complained that miller Lassen had stolen his clothes and requested money to pay for warmer clothes as the winter was fast approaching and he was almost naked.[236] 'Please let me know how much I owe His Majesty, and I shall pay as soon as I come to Tranquebar', he said in another letter of 15 October 1798.[237] Letter after letter followed, requesting the government's and His Majesty's support in paying off all the debts that Chinnayya had incurred.

In January 1798, the Commerce Department issued a 60-page long report.[238] The committee found that both Tambu Setti and Maturaja Pillai did receive punishment on the direct orders of Peter Anker. Tambu Setti was detained for a total period of 7½ months, and Maturaja Pillai for 5 months. Tambu Setti received two times 25 lashes at two different places in the town, while Maturaja Pillai received 25 lashes. His punishment was stopped through an agreement between Piragasam Pillai and Mühldorff. The Department also found that the complaints from Chinnayya were unjustified and that it was doubtful whether he had really been sent as a representative for the different castes. Three of the persons he had given as references denied that they ever gave a power of attorney to Chinnayya, while four refused to testify and one had died in the meantime. The royal decree of February 1798, based on this report, criticised the governor only in very vague terms; Piragasam Pillai was removed from his office, even though accusations against him were unproved. Despite this decree, Chinnayya continued his tirade against Peter Anker and Mühldorff. In his opinion, these two men were enemies of his Nation[239] and should be removed from office.

Chinnayya now started to claim that before he left Tranquebar in 1795, he had been contacted by the King of Ceylon who wanted to buy warships from Copenhagen and that he had received a bag of diamonds for this purpose. However, these had been taken from him by Peter Anker. (One of the witnesses, Møller, did indeed testify that prior to leaving Tranquebar Chinnayya had told him about an anonymous enquiry from the King of Ceylon and that Møller himself was asked by the king to buy warships, a request which he had refused.)

In August 1798, the King of Denmark set up a commission consisting of three people (Ove Sehested, Christian Lawaetz and Andreas Wendelboe) together with Rasmus Lange to investigate the matter. Even during this period, Chinnayya was still treated very favourably by the government. His debt of 39 rdl to a tailor for a frock, waistcoat, dress coats, trousers etc., was paid. The shoemaker Petersen received money for boots and shoes. A large suitcase with double locks, six pairs of cotton socks, two black silk scarves and cloth for 12 shirts and payment for stitching were all provided for. However, in March 1799, all these luxuries came to an end. Nobody believed in Chinnayya anymore and the daily allowance was stopped. During April 1799, emergency appeals were made to the king, the prince and the Commerce Department. On May 30, Chinnayya withdrew all the accusations – 'My own hatred and that of my Nation against Piragasam Pillai and his suppression of the castes had provoked me into making accusations against Peter Anker and other gentlemen in the government as taking part in the injustice created by Piragasam Pillai.[240] Now that the department has limited the power of this man, my mission is fulfilled. My accusations against Anker for taking diamonds from me were unjustified. I hope that the departments will forgive me and recommend me to the king for support' [Waaben, my translation from Danish].

Carsten Anker, the brother of Peter Anker, had for a long time been dissatisfied with the Board of Trade's handling of the Chinnayya case. On behalf of his brother, he now summoned the 'Hof og Stadsretten' (District Court) on 6 July 1799. By this time, Chinnayya was back behind bars for his debt to the coach-driver, Friis. Anker's advocate, Klingenberg, started the proceedings, saying: 'A few years ago, the accused Malabarian or East-Indian, who calls himself Sinnia Naicker, but whose real name is Senopa, was inspired to go on an adventure' [Waaben]. The process took some time, as the documents from Tranquebar had to be translated. On 20 January 1800, Chinnayya was sentenced for injuries;[241] the High Court confirmed this judgment. In both cases, Chinnayya received a free trial, subject to the condition that, if he won, he would have to pay 3 rdl to the non-commissioned officers who served in the court. As expected, the judgment went against Chinnayya – he was declared 'undesirable' (meaning he must leave the country); in addition, he had to pay several fines: 60 rdl plus the cost of the expenses incurred by his counterpart (80 rdl) (this was later renounced by Carsten Anker) plus 24 rdl for unnecessary proceedings plus 9 rdl to pay the translator. Anker was not happy with the

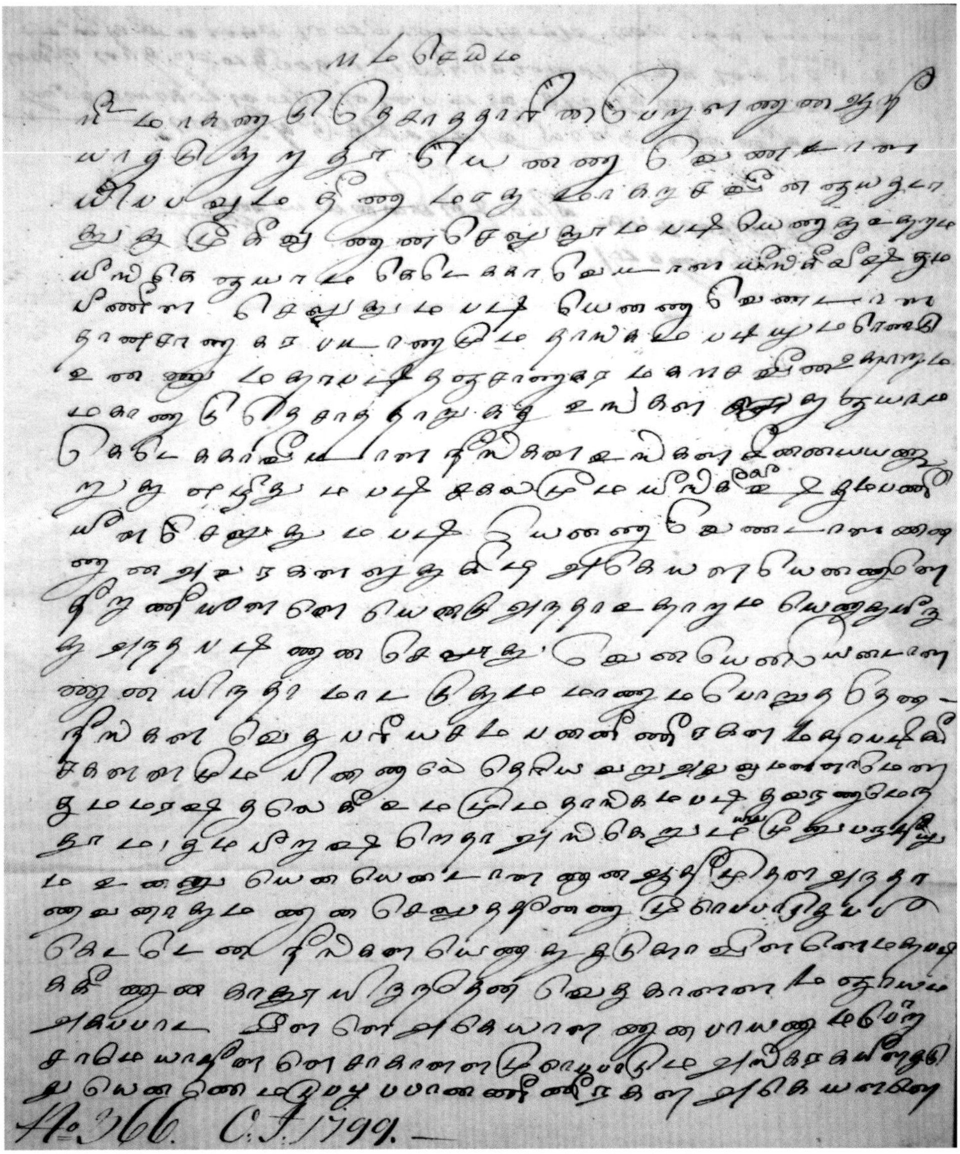

Fig. 6.2: Chinnayya's only letter in Tamil written on 22 August 1799 – the letter begins with 'Ramaseyam'. It is hard to figure out what Chinnayya is trying to say in this letter. It is clear that Chinnayya was not an educated person (Kommercekollegiet, Ostindiskefagssekretariat, "Sager vedr. den til København ankomne inder, Sennappa Naik, samt dennes klager over Guvernør Anker 1795-1802"). (Photo: P. S. Ramanujam).

verdict. He thought that it was too mild; had judgment been passed in India, the accused would lose his nose and eyes. Carsten Anker knew that the king did not favour substantial punishment. He wrote of the Crown Prince Frederik (in a coded message) that he would never become an important person; he was ignorant, obstinate, suspicious, and conceited and despite some good qualities, would never prove to be an able king. Carsten Anker was very friendly with the future king of Denmark, Christian Frederik (later Christian VIII-1786-1848) to whom he confided his feelings. The young prince wrote in his diary later: 'Only the righteous and just nature of Carsten Anker and the Crown Prince saved Peter Anker from being transported to Europe in chains, on account of a runaway mulat slave pretending to be a prince'.

Amid all these investigations, on 30 January 1799, it was announced that a marriage had taken place between the 'Indian Sennaja Naicker and Madam Birgitte Ytting'. Birgitte Tønnesen, née Yding, was divorced from her husband in 1792 and had applied for permission to remarry in August 1798. Chinnayya also requested the Board to pay half his salary as a pension to his wife after his death. He moreover mentioned that his greatest wish was to return to Tranquebar and his country of birth. A couple of months later, Chinnayya sought permission to marry Birgitte Tønnesen. The Chancery had granted permission to Birgitte Tønnesen but did not reply to Chinnayya. In fact, it was clearly stated in the Chancery's resolution that Chinnayya's application should be passed over in silence. However, when they applied together for permission to get married, the Chancery replied that it would stand by the consent that it had given to Birgitte Yding. The couple probably married a few days after receiving that answer. Obviously, it was not possible to marry someone who was neither baptised nor confirmed – so the Chancery requested the bishop to check whether Pastor Cruse, who conducted the marriage ceremony, had checked the 'qualifications' of Chinnayya. It turned out that the pastor had performed the service without any evidence that Chinnayya had ever been baptised, nor did he seek the king's approval. Cruse, who was mentally disturbed, was later fined 50 rdl (about one-fifth of his annual salary).

Cruse maintained that there had been an announcement in 1797 in the Adresseavisen, the first Danish newspaper based on advertisements, regarding Chinnayya's baptism. This notification of 30 December 1797 runs as follows: 'The Indian Sinnia Naicker has accepted the Christian faith and took the name Carl Christian Friderich at his baptism in the month of May'. Chinnayya wrote to the Board of Trade on 1 June 1797: 'After long and careful reflection, I have decided to convert to the Christian religion. I am being taught the Christian religion and will soon receive my baptism. Unfortunately, I am unable to pay the costs connected to this; therefore, I request an advance of 300 rdl which I shall repay as soon as Captain Schultz, who is expected this month, returns'. This request was not granted, and Chinnayya did not later mention anything about his baptism, nor did he take the name of Carl Christian Friedrich. In June 1798, he wrote: 'As I have made such a long journey from the country of my birth, changed my religion and lived among Europeans, during which time I have embraced the Christian religion, I cannot live with my parents or my nation. I have experienced much pain on behalf of my nation. Therefore, I request the Esteemed Board to appoint (me) as a Vakil in Tranquebar with free Quarters and 1,000 pagodas annually'. However, as the only letter in Tamil written by Chinnayya in the Archives shows, he still maintained his Hindu faith as late as 1799. This letter in Tamil written in the year 1799 begins with 'Ramaseyam'[242] (Victory to Rama), which means he still adhered to the Hindu faith – however, he claimed several times in 1798 that he had converted to Christianity.

In 1799, Chinnayya wrote to the king once again requesting that he be allowed to stay in Denmark: 'I beg your Royal Highness to show me kindness and grant me so much money annually that I and my wife can live on it, as I do not wish to travel to East India anymore, but would like to spend the rest of my time in Denmark and live in such a way that I can pay back the amount I have borrowed, as I have a little too much pain and am mostly ill, and in addition as my wife will give birth later this month...'.

In January 1799, Birgitte and Chinnayya were married in Frederiksberg, Denmark.[243] On 3 May 1799, they had a daughter; she was born in a public maternity hospital in Copenhagen and was baptised on 11 May 1799, receiving the name Caroline Siringomalia.[244] Her baptism is recorded in the Archives and the documents are available on the internet. Apparently, her name later was shortened to Caroline Sirini Amalia.[245] In the census of 1801, Birgitte Sinnaicka lived with her mother, Anne Marie Jacobsen, and brother, Jens Ytting, at Selskabet Harmoniens Huse in Copenhagen.[246] There is no sign of what happened to her daughter, Caroline. Either she was dead or had been adopted by another family.

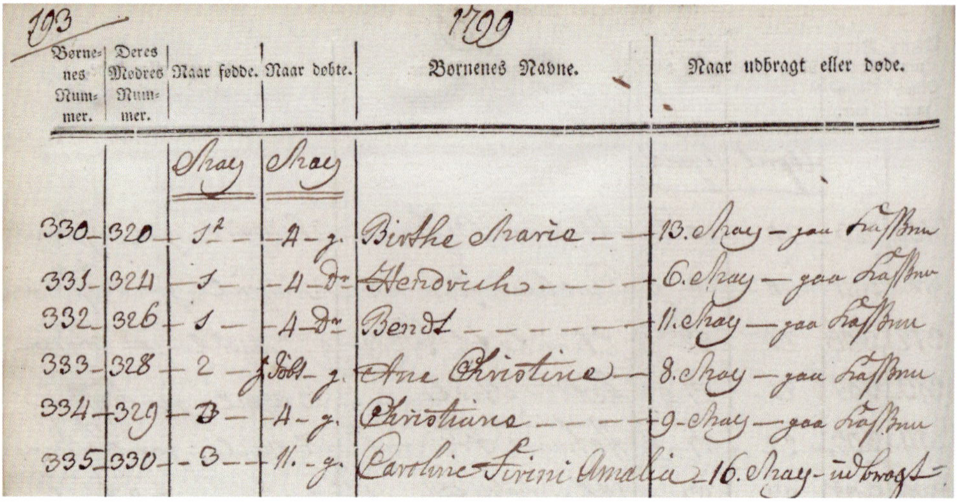

Fig. 6.3: The birth registry of Chinnayya's daughter – Caroline Sirini Amalia (https://www.sa.dk/ao-soegesider/da/billedviser?bsid=2#2,630).

Steps were now taken to deport the family to India. Birgitte Yding and Chinnayya made a list of items that they would need for the trip. Chinnayya had received some funding for his travel. The requested items included handkerchiefs, a hat, stockings, chamber pot, beer glasses, tobacco, sewing thread and needles, knives and forks etc.

The king granted 110 rdl to be spent on purchases for the journey. The Asiatic Company was willing to pay 20 rdl per person for travel and board. The Board of Trade asked them to be ready to travel on 29 June 1799. However, they were unable to leave, because the coach driver, Friis, wanted Chinnayya arrested for not paying his debt to him. Chinnayya served a few more months in the Blue Tower and was released in March 1800. On 12 July 1800, Chinnayya requested that both he and his wife be allowed to leave. However, Carsten Anker now appealed to the Supreme Court. Chinnayya was again imprisoned until 1801. In November 1801, he applied for some monetary support for his mother-in-law, who complained that she was too poor to take care of herself, but this was refused, as Chinnayya had already been paid several large amounts.

At this point, a war between England and Denmark seemed imminent – and on 21 March 1801, Chinnayya offered to fight for Denmark. This offer was refused. In September 1801, negotiations were made with the merchant and ship-owner Duntzfeldt regarding Chinnayya's jour-

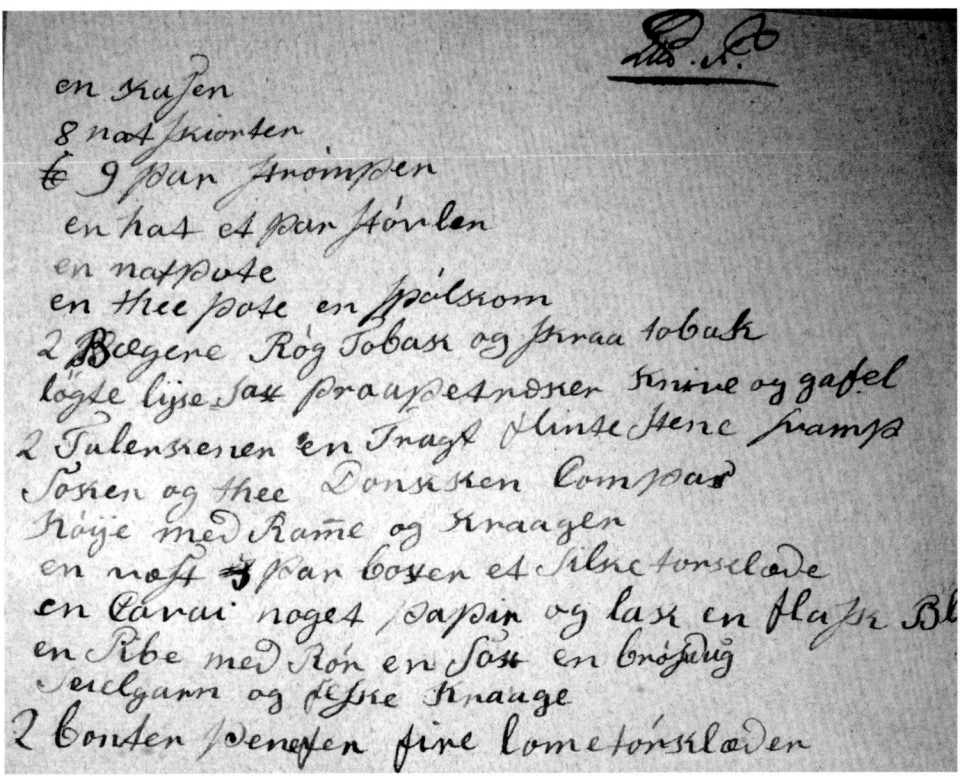

Fig. 6.4: A partial list of articles that Chinnayya and his wife wanted to take with them to India. The list included among other things socks, shirts, boots, a chamber pot, tea bags, tobacco, a compass, handkerchiefs, a hat, a silk scarf, sewing needles, buttons and plates (RA: Kommercekollegiet – Ostindiske Sekretariat, Journalsager 1792 (Løbenr. 1007) #116). (Photo: P. S. Ramanujam).

ney. (Duntzfeldt was born in East India and had returned to Denmark in 1791). Duntzfeldt demanded 30 rdl per person per month, paid in advance. The Department of Commerce was only willing to pay 25 rdl per month for Chinnayya. At this point, it became clear that only Chinnayya would be allowed to leave Denmark. On 18 November 1801, Chinnayya's mother-in-law wrote bitterly to the Lords of the Board of Commerce about how she had had to take care of Seneje's (Chinnayya's) wife (her daughter) for two and a half years, and how he kept on making empty promises to pay her when he left, but all she got from him was verbal abuse.[247] It was assumed that he would be sent either to Cape Town or Batavia (present Jakarta) and from there on to Bengal. After Chinnayya's departure, Bergitte Sinnia Naiken appealed to the Board of Commerce for support.²⁴⁸ Judging by the census of 1801, she appeared to be living alone. On 25 January 1802, Bergitte (Birgitte) appealed for some support from the Board of Commerce²⁴⁹ – again without any mention of her daughter.

There is one last message regarding Chinnayya from Simon's Bay (now Simon's Town) in South Africa,²⁵⁰ dating from March 1804 and written by a Henry Roselt:

> 'Upon your request to be informed with the history of the Indian Person Sannia Naiker, I have the pleasure of giving you the following narrative; he came here in the Danish ship *Marianne*. Captn. Lars Holm who informed me on the 21st of May 1802, being ready to leave this place, that the said Naiker had deserted the ship, and after having informed Admiral Sir Roger Curtis of this business, and after a long conversation on the subject, as Sir Roger seemed to be very much inclined to assist the said naiker, who spoke to the Admiral before, I was desired to go on Board the *Marianne* and to take what goods belonged to Naiker from the Captain which I did, and for which goods viz: 1 locked chest contents unknown, 1 trunk containing some old cloth, 1 cott with Bedding and 92 sp: Dollars, I have given a receit to the Captn, on the 30th following Naicker came to me and said that he was engaged on Board the *Henry Dundas*, and therefore desired me to let him have his goods and Money, all which except the money I ordered him to be given, and told him that he was to desire the Captn to come to me for it, but finding a few Days afterwards from the several Complaints lodged against him, that he was making Debts, runn'd about and said that I ow'd him a great deal of Money, I had him apprehended on the 6th of June and kept him as a civil Prisoner to the 11th when he was released, and by the Admiral's order sent on Board the *Henry Dundas*, very much against the inclination of the Captain and about the middle of August he went on board of the Dutch Man of War *Juno*, Commodore Melisse who upon the request of the Admiral and me took him on Board, but left that ship soon after and came again in goal (gaol?) after having spent all his Money, and by the Admiral's order was sent to Cape town –

what is become of him after I do not know, except that the Admiral told me he would care of him – in consideration of his being sent out by the Economical Board of Danmark we have taken care of him and have had a great deal more trouble than he deserved –'

The total cost of the whole affair was 3,926 rdl – a daily allowance of 1 rdl since the middle of May 1798 amounting to 902 rdl, treatment during his sickness for 295 rdl, board and lodging for 1,065 rdl, cash for his travel amounting to 300 rdl and payment to the Commission in Tranquebar.

*

We continue to saunter along King Street. We now come to the corner of King Street and Queen Street. Here, we turn north along Queen Street. The dilapidated building to the right used to be the house of the Danish commander and was later used as a hospital. The structure has been renovated recently by the Tranquebar Association and part of it is now a maritime museum.

The building on the left side (northern side) at the corner is the Church of Zion, the façade of which is European in style, but with a pointed dome, which is typical of Indian temple construction, thus unifying two different cultures. There is a churchyard behind it, which can be seen from Queen Street. The church was built in 1701[251] as a replacement for the earlier church inside the fort and is the oldest Protestant church in India. However, the initial construction was shoddy. In 1782, the church was partly demolished and rebuilt. The material that was removed from it was auctioned off and bought for 196 rdl.[252] Until 1839, the church had a flat roof. Muttien, a local master builder, was given a contract for restructuring the church in 1839. The church was shortened from 125 feet in length to 80 feet. A new vault supported by an internal wall was constructed, the doors shortened and a new sacristy on the eastern side was built.[253] The work lasted 196 days, and Muttien received 1,850 rupees for the construction.

An exciting archive material is the 'List of marriages registered in the Danish church register of Zion Church, Tranquebar 1767-1845'. This was composed by Knud Heiberg and published by the Government Press, Madras in 1935. In the introduction, Heiberg brings out some interesting statistics:

> 'The registers contain Danish, Portuguese, French, Dutch, German and a great number of English and Scottish names. Marriages between the English and the Danes have been frequent both in time of war and of peace. Several Anglo-Indian families in South India descend from these Brito-Danish marriage… Re-marriages were very common in Tranquebar. We find, for example, that Ellen Christine Panck during the short period of less than six years married three times. On 11 December 1770, she married the Pastor of the Zion Church, the Reverend Peder Mandrup Tuxen. He died on 17 May 1772, and on 7 September 1772 she married his successor the Reverend Caspar Const. Möller; after his death on May 27, 1778 she married her third husband, accountant Ivar Lyche, on November 13, 1778… The great majority of marriages were solemnised in private residences, very few in the church itself. Under the British occupation of Tranquebar 1808-1815, it looks as if wedding celebrations in the church itself became more common, and on April 24, 1809, the English chaplain solemnised in Zion Church the marriage of A. H. Kelso, Esq., the English Commissioner, to Miss Maria Rosalia Colbjörnsen, not yet 16 years old, the daughter of Jacob Edward Colbjörnsen, Chief Justice and Member of the Council in the Danish service'.

The church also provided a relief fund for the poor. It is moreover a curious fact that the church contributed a sum of 180 Porto Novo pagodas and 967 Rdl. in relief for those affected by the fire of Copenhagen in 1795[254] – equivalent to approximately 145,000 US dollars in today's currency.

Walking just a bit further down, we come to Borgen Street. The Zion Church and the house next door to it in Borgen Street provided the living and working quarters of perhaps the most charismatic figure during the entire Danish rule in India – that of Henning Munch Engelhart, priest, astronomer, scientist, historian, linguist, philosopher and reformer. According to the census of 1790, Engelhart lived at #82, Prints Joergens Street (later renamed Borgen Street).

7

A Forgotten Astronomer – A Forgotten Blessed Soul

One of the most significant astronomical events that occurred in the 1760s was the transit of the planet Venus across the Sun's disc. Edmund Halley had proposed earlier[255] that by measuring accurately the time when the diminutive disc of Venus touched the Sun and the time when it emerged

Fig. 7.1: Zion Church, Tranquebar as it appears today. Constructed in 1701, this served the white population in and around Tranquebar. The façade of the church is European in style as observed from King Street; however, seen from a distance, elements of South Indian temple structure, such as the structure of the vault, become visible. The church was rebuilt in 1782. In 1839, the church was shortened to 80 feet (24 metres). (Photo: P. S. Ramanujam 2019).

from the Sun's disc, one could estimate the solar parallax, which would enable astronomers to estimate the distance between the earth and the Sun. This, in turn, could be used to determine the size of the known solar system. The transits of Venus were predicted to occur in 1761 and 1769. Great preparations were made to observe these phenomena from different parts of the globe.[256]

> The story of **Le Gentil** (1725-1792), a student of Cassini in France who was sent to study the transit of Venus across the disc of the Sun in 1761, is captivating. It can be read in Daniel Hudon's 'A (not so) brief history of the transit of Venus'. Le Gentil, whose full name was Guillaume Joseph Hyacinthe Jean-Baptiste Le Gentil de la Galaisière, set out from Paris on 26 March 1760 to Pondichery to observe the transit of Venus. He was to change ships at Isle de France (Mauritius). When he arrived in Mauritius in July 1760, he found that no ships sailed to Pondichery because of the war between France and Britain. Six months later, he was still waiting. Just as he was about to give up, a French ship arrived on 26 February 1761, assuring him that he would safely reach Pondichery. When they arrived at Mahe in July 1761, he was informed that Pondichery was in the hands of the English and that the captain had decided to return to Mauritius. On 6 June 1761, he viewed the transit of Venus from on board the ship, unable to make any exact observations due to the rolling of the ship. The transit of Venus is a rare event – but strangely enough, it occurs in pairs with an interval of eight years. Instead of travelling back to France, Le Gentil was determined to stay in Pondichery and make observations during the next transit, which was to to occur in 1769. He decided to make use of his time by carrying out as many observations as he could with regards to geography, natural history, physics, astronomy, navigation, winds and tides.
>
> In the meantime, he found that the best place to observe the next transit would be Manila in the Philippines. He arrived in Manila in August 1766 and found that the Spanish Consul was ill-disposed towards him and France. He was then informed by

one of his colleagues from Paris that Pondichery might after all be a better place to observe the transit than Manila; by this time Pondichery had changed hands and had once more become French. Le Gentil arrived there in March 1768. During the next several months, he spent his time studying the astronomy of the Brahmins and the local customs. The day before the transit – 4 June 1769 – the skies were clear. However, at 2 a.m. the skies became overcast. A freak storm covered the sky with clouds, and the Sun was completely obscured during the transit. Afterwards, the skies cleared up and there was brilliant sunshine for the rest of the day. To make matters worse, Manila had been cloudless on the day of the transit. Le Gentil now just wanted to return home. However, he became ill and could not leave Pondichery until March 1770, only to reach Mauritius, where he found himself too ill to continue. He set out again in November, but had to return to Mauritius due to storms and a damaged ship. He left once more on 31 March 1771 and was yet again halted by storms at the Cape of Good Hope. Finally, he reached France on 8 October 1771, a full eleven years after he left in the first place, only to find that his estate had been taken over by his relatives, who had given him up for dead.

Catholic Jesuit priests[257] observed the transit of 1761 from Tranquebar, possibly from the Catholic Church in King Street. Their accurate observations, which were presumably made with the aid of a telescope, were published in Novi Commentarii[258] and were reported in 'The Gentleman's Magazine and Historical Chronicle'[259] as well as 'The Gentleman's and London Magazine'.[260] A little known fact is that, just 50 metres down King Street, the Lutheran missionaries were making their own observations. This is recorded in their report to Halle. The entry for 6 June reads:[261] 'Today, Venus transited the Sun's disc. The entrance occurred at approximately 6 h 51 minutes (in the morning). The exit at 1 h 49 minutes (in the afternoon). This conjunction of Venus with the Sun occurs very seldom, not seen since 1639'.[262] There is a remarkable difference between the observations of the Jesuits and the Missionaries – the Jesuits mention that the ingress started at 7 hours 29 minutes 39 seconds while the Missionaries claim that this had happened 38 minutes earlier. According to a prevailing simulation, the transit began at 7 hours 32 minutes (first contact) and ended at 14 hrs 07 minutes (fourth contact).[263]

The missionaries were prepared for an observation in 1769 as well. Alas! The infamous clouds that disappointed Le Gentil stretched from Pondichery to Tranquebar. The missionaries report: 'As we endeavoured to observe the passage of Venus across the Sun, it was a total impossibility because the entire horizon in the east was covered with clouds, and we could not see the Sun until 7; after 7, one could see where the sun stood, but it was so hidden in the haze so as not to be seen clearly, and it did not shine brightly the whole day'.[264]

A reference to observations of the transit from Tranquebar for the years 1761 and 1769 can, however, be found in 'An Account of the Observations on the Transit of Venus over the Sun, on the 3d of June, 1769, by the Committee appointed to observe it at Philadelphia; drawn up, and presented to the American Philosophical Society, held at Philadelphia, for promoting useful Knowledge' [Ewing].[265]

1769 was a great year for astronomy in Tranquebar. The missionaries carried out their work with zeal. They observed a comet in August 1769. The entry for 29 August reads: 'As I came out of my tent at about 4 in the morning and looked at the sky, I observed a comet in the constellation of Taurus with a very long tail' reports a missionary[266] from Cuddalore. By 7 September, the comet had moved into the constellation of Orion and was very bright. It was also observed by the missionaries in Tranquebar. On the 4 September, it was close to Orion's shield, with Venus and Saturn providing an enchanting spectacle. 'On the 10th, just before 2 (in the morning), it was in Minoceros, in a direct line with Sirius northwards. Its tail extended from Orion to Taurus'.[267] They continued to watch the comet until October. In January 1771, there was another bonanza – a new comet appeared. 'From 9 till 13 January, we have observed a comet. It has also been visible in Madras' write Kohlhoff, Zeglin, Maderup, Klein, König and Leidemann from Tranquebar.[268]

All these magnificent developments required a new strategy. The 18th century saw a rapid development of science and technology across the European countries and their colonies. Buoyed by the scientific success of the Venus expeditions, Thomas Bugge, a well-known Danish astronomer, was interested in astronomical observations made in the Danish establishments.²⁶⁹ Christoph Samuel John, a Missionary from Germany interested in natural sciences, was proposed as the first astronomer in Tranquebar. In a letter to the Danish Chancery, Luxdorph requested 100 rdl towards the appointment of Christoph Samuel John.

Yet, John never did become the astronomer, since he expressed the desire to visit his relatives back in Germany at this time. In his stead, a young astronomer named Henning Munch Engelhart, who was to be the second chaplain at the Zion Church, was intent on establishing an observatory at Tranquebar. Henning Munch Engelhart was born on 17 January 1757 at Rendalen in Norway, the son of Bastian Engelhardt and Marine Munch [Norsk Biografisk Leksikon]. He graduated in 1773 from the Latin school of Christiania (Oslo) and took a degree in theology at the University of Copenhagen in 1782. Besides, he studied mathematics, astronomy and geography. He worked as a ship's chaplain during 1783-1785 in the South China seas, completing a Malayan-Danish dictionary and encyclopaedia. In 1786, he was appointed the second chaplain at Zion Church in Tranquebar. Soon after his arrival in Tranquebar, he established 'The Tranquebarian Society for Information on India', the prime purpose of which was to focus on scientific methods and information for the betterment of Denmark and the local society in India and to improve European knowledge about India.²⁷⁰ Governor Abbestée became protector of the society, Fugl became president, Lindam cashier and Engelhart himself secretary. The intentions of the society were divided into 21 points: Questions such as how does India's location, climate and occupants influence the physical and moral constitution of the Europeans, the influence of slaves on the European colonies in India, how convenient Tranquebar would be for trade, what would be the best use of the natural products from Tranquebar, on the national character of the Malabars, castes and their rights, and so on. The society had a set of by-laws and regulations. The first and only issue of the proceedings of the society contained articles on suggestions for the establishment of a botanical garden (written by C. S. John), on the translation of Athichudi[271] and Konraivendan,[272] and Mudurei[273] of Avvaiyar,[274] a Tamil poet (C. S. John), a description of various snakes (C. S. John), Rottler's description of the palm tree and Engelhart's description of his astronomical observatory.

During 1789-1790, Engelhart also took upon himself the task of registering the Danish archives in India. He had access to all the documents that the Asiatic Company had not sent to Copenhagen. Based on these documents, he wrote a 'History of the Danish East Indian Establishments' for the period 1610-1770[275], but he was able to complete only the period up until 1687. This work contains all the treaties made between the Danes and the Indian kings in various parts of the country and was dedicated to the Tranquebar Society.[276]

In 1788, he wrote his 'Thoughts about the dissemination of knowledge among Indians'.[277] He encouraged educated Europeans to teach the Indians about their rights, and he suggested that teaching a slave that he is not a slave is more beneficial than to show pity on the slave. When the Europeans came to India, they found people who were 'black' and therefore not Christians, and they used this as an excuse for their shameless violations of humaneness and international law. Perhaps as a direct retort to Svend Bredstrup, another chaplain at the Zion Church, Engelhart says that one blames the Indians for want of a religion (understood as Christianity), for being irresponsible, for exhibiting scant regard for marriage, for their unwillingness to work and for their unbridled passion for lust. But these are not specific to India, he says. Wherever there are people and societies, one is bound to find them. He suggested five ways of alleviating the situation: 1) to educate the Indians about their rights and duties, 2) to teach them their own history, 3) to teach them their own holistic religion, 4) to teach them astronomy and natural sciences, and 5) to teach them European history. He concluded that this ought to be done as a repayment for the willingness with which the Indian nations opened their harbours and lands to the Europeans, provided them with property and allowed them to become such dreadful abusers of their benefactors. However, his advice was not followed.

His most important job was to be an astronomer. Thomas Bugge had assembled a network of colleagues dotted about the many Danish colonies: Rasmus Lievog in Iceland, Andreas Ginge in Greenland, Abraham Pihl in Norway and Engelhart in Tranquebar. The clergy was often taught natural sciences as part of their curriculum. With the help of his professor of astronomy, Thomas Bugge, Engelhart brought several meteorological, geographic and astronomical instruments to Tranquebar and established an astronomical observatory in the tower of the Zion Church. At his disposal were a transit instrument, an astronomical circle, a Dollond telescope and an astronomical clock. The transit instrument, which was an invention by

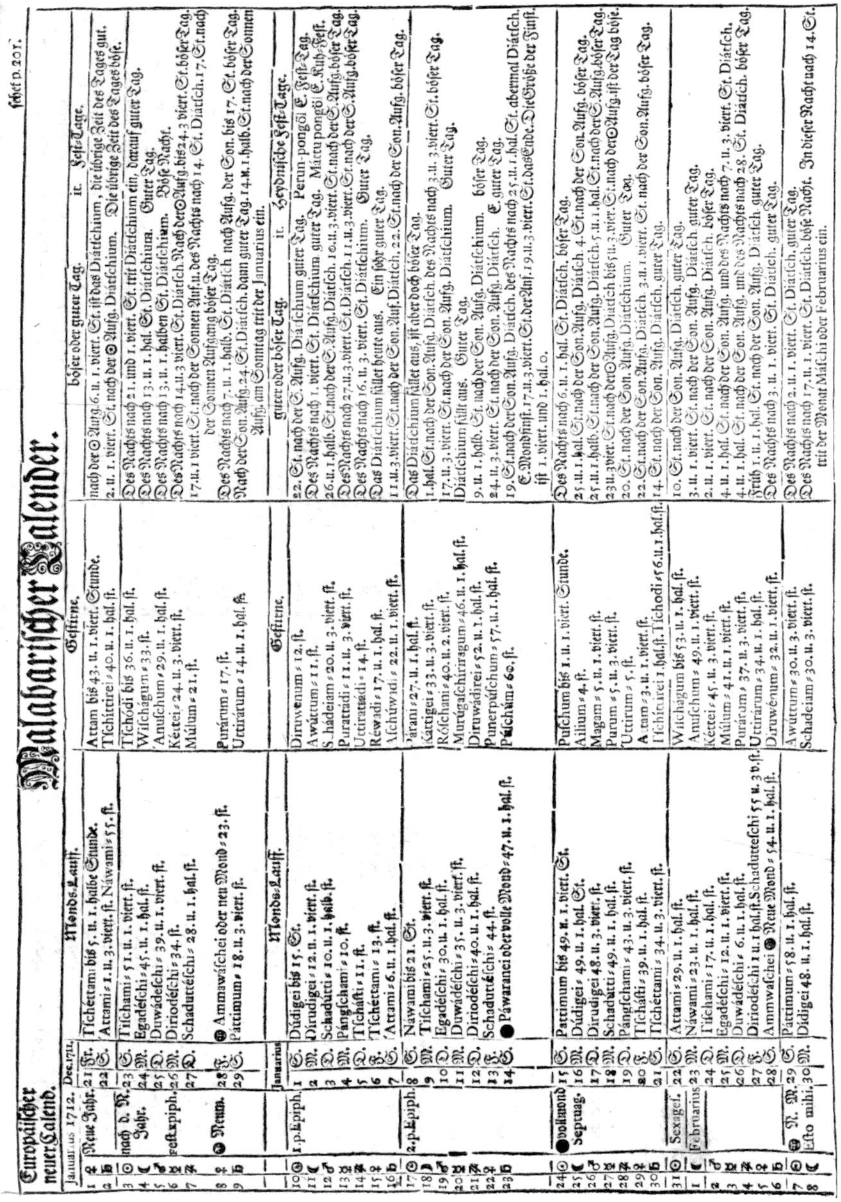

Fig. 7.2: A page from a Tamil Almanac ('Malabarischer Calender') for January and February 1712 translated by the German missionary Gründler. The first column features the Gregorian dates used in Germany and the fourth column features the Julian dates used in Tamil Nadu. The sixth column shows the moon's phases (Tschettami or Sapthami), the seventh column shows the star of the day (Attam or Hastham) and the last column indicates whether it will be a good day or a bad day for conducting auspicious rites (Ostindische Berichte (Hallesche Berichte), Teil 1, Cont.5 (1712) p. 200-201).

another Danish astronomer, Ole Christian Rømer, is mounted on a strictly east-west axis and is free to rotate in the north-south direction, along the meridian. This instrument is used to observe transits of heavenly objects across the meridian. Also, Engelhart most certainly carried a copy of The Nautical Almanac and the Astronomical Ephemeris for the year 1789 (and received an example for 1790 through the post) as well as different logarithmic tables.

He described the construction of the first European observatory in India in the Proceedings of the Tranquebar Society:

> 'With the help of His Royal Highness, it has been possible to acquire in October 1786 a set of astronomical instruments for use in India. The instruments, which were purchased with the help of Mr. Councillor Bugge, were brought by me to Trankebar. Upon my arrival in Trankebar in July, the Royal Government decided to construct an observatory. The best place for this was found to be the tower of the Zion Church. The spire on the church could be removed, permitting the establishment of an observatory above. The work of demolishing the spire was begun immediately, but because of riots in the colony, the workers could not complete the work before the end of August 1788.
>
> The observatory in Tranquebar is the tallest building in the town and has an unobstructed view to all sides. A short distance to the east is the sea. To the south, one can observe the district of Tranquebar, the English and French establishments at Nagor, Nagapatnam and Karaikal. To the west, the avenues of Tranquebar and the villages acquired later. To the north, one sees the border to the royal possession at Tanjore. There are no hills anywhere.
>
> The height of the tower from the ground to the floor of the observatory is 40 feet, and the thickness of the walls is 3 feet. One climbs up to the balcony of the Zion Church and, from the flight of stairs with 22 steps, one is led to the observatory, which has a gallery on one side. The tower is in the form

of a rectangle, 13 ½ feet in length and 12 feet in breadth. The inside length of the observatory is 11 ½ feet and it is 10 feet broad. The walls are thicker at the corners. The height of the observatory is 6 ½ feet towards the east and west and it is 3¼ feet higher on the other two sides. This difference in height provides a vertical meridional opening. The observatory is provided with windows on all sides, which are large compared to the size of the observatory. Half the roof, towards the east and west, is solid and has a slight inclination. The other half consists of two hatches, which because of their inclination provide space for two small beams; this leads to a horizontal meridional opening, which can be closed with the hatches. The floor of the observatory consists of a strong brick arch on whose northern side the pillars for the transit-instruments are placed. These are 6 feet high up to the axes and have a width of 17 feet at the low point and 10 feet at the higher level. The sidepieces for the movable bearings are screwed to the cross iron, which are cemented into the pillars. There are meridional marks in both the north and south to verify the transit-instruments. There is a round elevation made of brick, approximately in the middle of the observatory, about 4 feet in diameter and 16 inches high, on which the instrument with its stand is placed in such a way that it can be positioned according to the transit-instrument's meridional marks, and on which one can stand or sit during observations. It is possible to make measurements or observe with the telescope across the entire sky when the hatches are opened.

The astronomical clock is immovably attached to iron built into the wall and placed in such a way that it can easily be read during observations.

The Tranquebar observatory is provided with the following instruments:
1) An astronomical circle with a diameter of 2 feet. This instrument, which can also measure angles on a horizontal plane, is made explicitly for geographical travels in India,

Fig. 7.3: An impressive transit instrument at the Kroppedal Museum in Denmark used to measure the transits of stars across the meridian, as well as their altitudes. It is likely that Engelhart had a similar instrument at the Zion Church observatory in Tranquebar (photo: P. S. Ramanujam).

according to the Royal General Land Economic and Commerce Departments' Requirement of 12 May 1787. It is hoped that a larger instrument of similar construction will be donated to the observatory for permanent use.
2) A transit-instrument with a 3 foot astronomical telescope.
3) An astronomical clock.[278]
4) A 2 foot achromatic telescope with 2 objectives.'

Unfortunately, this printed report, of which there exists only one copy, stops here. The rest of the pages containing the observations could not be found. However, substantially the same information can be found in two handwritten reports in the National Archives in Copenhagen. The first, covering the period 1788-1789, deals mainly with the construction of the observatory in the Zion Church and a determination of the latitude of Tranquebar. The second report provides a table of Engelhart's observations.

Here are his observations from 1790:[279]

'Report regarding the astronomical observatory in Tranquebar for the year 1789.
Regarding the condition of the observatory and of the instruments, I refer to the report sent via the ship *Danmark*, which sailed from here in January 1789.
The telescopes are becoming more useless with time. The sharpness of the air[280] causes noticeable deterioration, and it is not in my power to stop or correct this. The other instruments have not escaped these detrimental effects and much worse, as the observatory cannot endure rain.
After the departure of the ship *Danmark* from here last January, I have been afflicted by a nervous weakness, which required me to keep away from the observatory. In June and July, the sky was covered with thin, white clouds and was, most of the time, unsuitable for observations. The rainy season began in August and continued, unusually, until the end of the year, except for late December. Thus, there have been natural obstructions in the way of my duties as an astronomer in Tranquebar. However, I have made use of every lucky opportunity that was available. No immersion or emersion of the satellites of Jupiter has been neglected, and the reason for a large number of these not having been observed or recorded is partly because most of these immersions have occurred during the rainy season, partly because the measurements made during opposition[281] periods could not be verified, and partly because of the generally impure air, as well as the mediocre or bad quality of my telescope.
According to the observations sent by me last year, the latitude of Tranquebar has been determined at 11° 1' 20" N (11 degrees 1 minute 20 seconds north). A more accurate deter-

> **Beobachtungen zu Tranquebar in Oftindien angeftellt von Herrn Engelhart.**
>
> Herr Engelhart ift mit einem 3füſsigen Mittags Fernrohr, einem aftronomiſchen Kreis von 2 Fuſs im Diam.; einem 8füſsigen achromatiſchen Fernrohr und zweyen Uhren verſehen. Den Anfang feiner aftronomiſchen Arbeit hat er mit Beftimmung der Breite ſeiner Sternwarte gemacht, die er aus 113 mit dem erwehnten Kreis angeftellten Mittagshöhen von Sternen und der Sonne, im Mittel 11° 1′ 20″ Nordlich gefunden. Er hat dabey den Kreis durch ein wechfelfeitiges Umwenden gegen Often und Weften verificirt.
>
> 1788

Fig. 7.4: Engelhart's measurements as communicated by Thomas Bugge (Astronomisches Jahrbuch für das Jahr 1793).

> *Beobachtungen und Nachrichten.*   101
>
> 1788 den 8. Oct. Auſtritt des III. Trab. ♃. 14U. 16′ 16″
>   25. - Eintritt - II.   -   12   54   2½
>   29. - Eintritt - I.   -   13   49   10   zweifelh.
>   1. Nov. Eintritt - II. -   15   28   46
>   5. - Eintritt - I.   -   15   42   42

Fig. 7.5: Engelhart's measurements showing both the latitude measurements and eclipses of Jupiter's moons (photo: P. S. Ramanujam).

mination can hardly be made with the current astronomical circle.

This time, I hope to determine the longitude of the observatory with sufficient accuracy. I have compared my measurements with those calculated from the Nautical Almanac, as corresponding observations are lacking'.

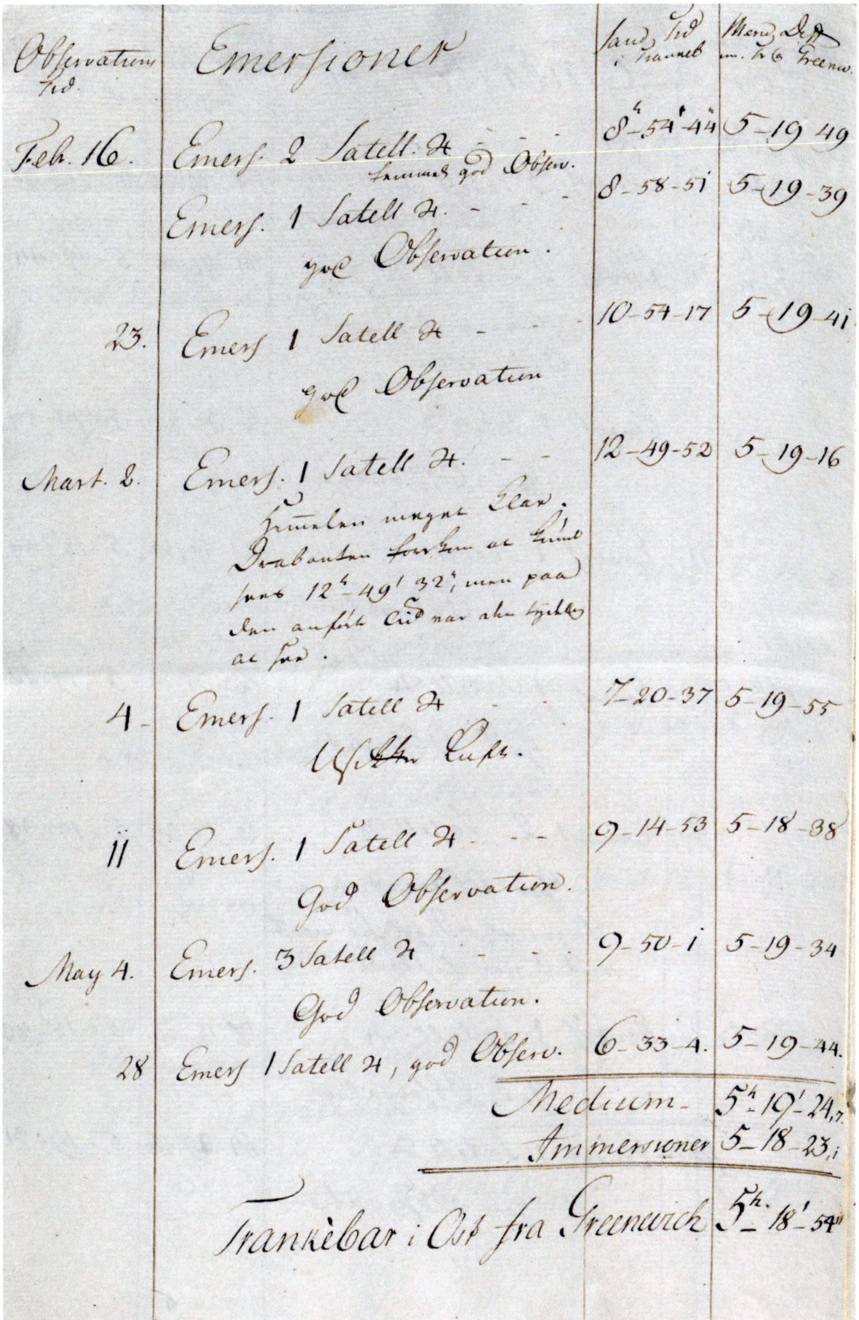

Observations Tid.	Emersioner	Sand Tid i Tranneb	Mean Tid to G Greenw.
Feb. 16.	Emers. 2 Satell. ♃ — — — Immers god Obsev.	8ʰ-52'-44"	5-19-49
	Emers. 1 Satell ♃ — — — god Observation.	8-58-51	5-19-39
23.	Emers 1 Satell ♃ — — — god Observation	10-54-17	5-19-41
Mart. 2.	Emers. 1 Satell ♃ — — Trabanten meget klar; Trabanten forsvan at være fans 12ʰ 49' 32"; men paa den anseet Tid nar den spilles at Sud.	12-49-52	5-19-16
4.	Emers. 1 Satell ♃ Uften Luft.	7-20-37	5-19-55
11	Emers. 1 Satell ♃ — — — God Observation.	9-14-53	5-18-38
May 4.	Emers. 3 Satell ♃ — — God Observation.	9-50-1	5-19-34
28	Emers 1 Satell ♃, god Obsev.	6-33-4.	5-19-44.
	Medium		5ʰ-19'-24"₇
	Immersioner		5-18-23,₁
	Tranlebar i Ost fra Greenwich		5ʰ-18'-54"

Fig. 7.6: Engelhart's observations showing the mean time difference between Tranquebar and Greenwich (RA, Kommercekollegiet, Ostindiske Sekretariat, Journalsager (1790) Løbenr. 1001).

The transit instrument at the observatory served two essential purposes. By measuring the altitudes of the stars (the height of the stars above the horizon) crossing the meridian, and knowing the declination of the stars (which is available from standard tables), it is possible to calculate the latitude of the place. Night after night, Engelhart toiled to measure over 100 altitudes of the stars from which he was able to arrive at a figure of 11 degrees 1 minute and 20 seconds. We shall shortly come to the other important reason to measure the transit of the stars.

From the point of view of navigation, an important measurement to perform in the 18th century was the determination of the longitude of a place. The importance of determining the longitude correctly while sailing (to India) has been illustrated by Gøbel.[282] While trading for pepper in 1744, the navigator of *Prinsesse Louise* thought that he was at 99 degrees east, while he was actually at 74 degrees east in the Maldive islands, resulting in the loss of the ship. This is an error of almost 2,500 kilometres in distance. Before the advent of the advanced chronometers made by Harrison [Sobel], Galileo himself suggested using the eclipses of Jupiter's moons as a clock. These could be predicted with high accuracy, and the Nautical Almanac and Astronomical Ephemeris carried these for the longitude of Greenwich for each year ahead of time. It was possible to find the time difference between Greenwich and a given place with a copy of these tables in hand and observing the actual time of eclipses at that place. Through observation of the moons of Jupiter, Engelhart determined the time difference (longitude) between Tranquebar and Greenwich. By taking the difference between the third column of Engelhart's observations and the corresponding calculated values from the Nautical Almanac, one arrives at the time difference between Greenwich and Tranquebar, which is shown in the fourth column of Engelhart's table. He arrived at a mean time difference of 5 hours 18 minutes 54 seconds. The actual value is 5 hours 19 minutes 25 seconds. Engelhart determined the latitude of Tranquebar to be 11 degrees 1 minute 20 seconds whereas the correct value is 11 degrees 1 minute 34 seconds. Thomas Bugge reported the measurements of the latitude of Tranquebar, as well as the occultations of the satellites of Jupiter, in Engelhart's name in the Berliner Astronomisches Jahrbuch, 1793.

John Goldingham, an astronomer in Madras,[283] published two articles in the Philosophical Transactions of the Royal Society. A part of his table on the longitude of the Madras Observatory is shown in Fig. 7.8.:

III.		MAY 1789.			[51]
Days of the Month.	Semidiameter of the Sun.	Time of D° passing the Meridian.	Hourly Motion of the Sun.	Logarithm of the Sun's Distance.	Place of the Moon's Node.
	M. S.	M. S.	M. S.		S. D. M.
1	15. 54,5	1. 5,9	2. 25,3	0.003787	7. 29. 35
7	15. 53,1	1. 6,4	2. 24,9	0.004380	7. 29. 16
13	15. 51,9	1. 6,9	2. 24,6	0.004947	7. 28. 57
19	15. 50,8	1. 7,4	2. 24,2	0.005479	7. 28. 38
25	15. 49,8	1. 7,9	2. 23,9	0.005941	7. 28. 18

Eclipses of the SATELLITES of JUPITER.

I. Satellite. Emersions.		II. Satellite. Emersions.		III. Satellite.	
Days	H. M. S.	Days	H. M. S.	Days	H. M. S.
*1	12. 2. 34	1	19. 29. 28	4	0. 57. 51 I
3	6. 31. 29	*5	8. 48. 28	4	4. 30. 27 E
5	1. 0. 23	8	22. 7. 15	11	4. 57. 55 I
6	19. 29. 16	*12	11. 25. 53	11	8. 30. 44 E
8	13. 58. 5	16	0. 44. 21	*18	8. 57. 28 I
10	8. 26. 54	19	14. 2. 40	18	12. 30. 27 E
12	2. 55. 41	23	3. 20. 48	25	12. 56. 25 I
13	21. 24. 25	26	16. 38. 45	25	16. 29. 33 E
15	15. 53. 9	30	5. 56. 34		
*17	10. 21. 50			IV. Satellite.	
19	4. 50. 29			11	20. 8. 18 I
20	23. 19. 7			12	0. 41. 21 E
22	17. 47. 42			28	14. 9. 14 I
24	12. 16. 16			28	18. 44. 36 E
26	6. 44. 49				
28	1. 13. 20				
29	19. 41. 49				
31	14. 10. 18				

Fig. 7.7: A copy of the page from the Nautical Almanac for May 1789 showing eclipse times for Greenwich. The Nautical Almanac published immersion and emersion times for four of Jupiter's satellites several years in advance.

> *Longitude of the Madras Observatory by the Eclipses of the Satellites of Jupiter, from 1787 to 1801, corrected for the difference of the Tables from the Observations taken at Greenwich at or about the time of each Eclipse.*
>
> | 1789. | | | | | |
> |---|---|---|---|---|---|
> | Jan. 29 | Tranquebar. | 2 E | 14 21 10 | 9 1 26 | 5 19 44 |
> | 31 | —— | 1 E | 10 40 54 | 5 22 5 | 5 18 49 |
> | Feb. 14 | —— | 1 E | 14 29 56 | 9 10 25 | 5 19 31 |
> | 23 | —— | 1 E | 10 54 17 | 5 34 36 | 5 19 41 |
> | May 28 | —— | 1 E | 6 33 4 | 1 13 20 | 5 19 44 |
> | 1790. | | | | | |
> | Jan. 23 | —— | 2 I | 10 10 12 | 4 51 46 | 5 18 26 |
> | 25 | —— | 1 I | 15 5 52 | 9 47 23 | 5 18 29 |
> | 30 | —— | 2 I | 12 43 29 | 7 25 39 | 5 17 50 |

Fig. 7.8: Table published by Goldingham on the longitude of the Madras Observatory. In the third column, 'E' stands for Emersion and 'I' for immersion of the satellites.

> The Coringa, Masulipatam, and Tranquebar observations were taken by the late Mr. TOPPING: the Calcutta observations also by the late Mr. TOPPING: the Bombay observations by myself.

Fig. 7.9: Places of measurement for the longitudes.

Goldingham noted that the observations for Tranquebar had been made by the late Mr. Topping. However, these observations are identical to those made by Engelhart, as shown in his report above. Goldingham credited the wrong man! Engelhart's observations also include measurements on several stars using 'instruments on the west'. He notes that the observations were made with an 8-foot Dollond telescope, which was one of the finest instruments for that period.

After two years in an observatory without a proper roof, the optical instruments were failing due to the salt in the air, being so close to the sea. Engelhart was on to a new adventure. The Danish colony of Tranquebar was getting squeezed between the two super-powers of England and France. Its policy of neutrality, on the one hand, was responsible for its well-being, but on the other hand, this was also its headache. Already in 1754, Denmark was looking to colonise the Nicobar Islands.[284] The Nicobar archipelago consists of 24 islands. Being tropical, the islands had

Fig. 7.10: A sketch of the residences built on the Nicobars, from Engelhart's archives. The drawings were made by Wickede in Tranquebar after Engelhart's sketches. Friedrich Bernhard August von Wickede (1774-1822) was a Danish army officer (RA, Kommercekollegiet, Ostindiske Sekretariat, Journalsager (1792) (Løbenr. 1007).

the potential to provide the essential timber for the construction of ships and thus looked promising in terms of export. The first Danish colony was established on New Year's Day, 1756, but was vacated again already in 1757. During January 1791, Engelhart sailed to the Nicobars to make a survey of the islands (also called Friedriks Islands) with a view to their colonisation. He was to create a map of the islands, examine the forests, the soil, stones and minerals, water, climate, plants and animals. While sailing to the islands and on arrival in Nancowri, he made several astronomical and meteorological observations that can be found in the extracts from his journal, covering the period up until 16 March 1791. Part of his work concerned determining the latitude and longitude of the islands. The principle of determining the longitude was the same – to establish the difference in time between a known location such as Tranquebar and the current position of the ship. To this end, Engelhart had an astronomical clock made by John Arnold of Madras on the ship. He spent almost a week calibrating the clock before leaving Tranquebar.

Calibrating the clock involved extensive observations of heavenly objects such as stars in transit. Due to the revolution of the earth around the sun, a given star crosses the meridian precisely 3 minutes and 56 seconds earlier each day (sidereal time). For example, for a period of five days, this would amount to 19 minutes and 40 seconds, which can be compared to the stationary clock. This would reveal whether the stationary clock is gaining or losing time and it can thus be adjusted. The heavenly clock is very accurate. This is the other reason to use the transit instrument for the observation of the transits across the meridian. Unfortunately, Engelhart did not have enough time for his calibration and was therefore not able to make quite the right measurements.

Engelhart calculated the local time at the location of the ship using an ingenious method, which was known in the literature. If the hour-angle of the sun could be determined at a given time, then one could estimate the time until noon (or from noon) and thus determine the local time. The hour-angle was calculated from spherical astronomy, knowing the latitude, the declination and the sun's altitude, which was measured.[285] Engelhart applied several corrections to his measurements, such as the semi-diameter of the sun, dip of the horizon, refraction through the atmosphere and parallax.

Engelhart's measurements give the mean latitude as 8 degrees 3 minutes 12 seconds for Nancowri. On 13 March 1791, using an astronomical circle to determine the solar altitude, he also determined that Nancowri was 11 degrees 25 minutes 15 seconds east of Tranquebar, which will give its longitude to be about 91 degrees 11 minutes East. The actual value is 93 degrees 32 minutes East. A comparison with recent measurements shows that Englhart was about 250 kilometres off the mark. His results are to the west of what they should be. I believe that the problem was due to the calibration of the clock, which showed Tranquebar time. Engelhart simply ran out of time before his departure. Making an error of 1 minute in calculating the time difference would result in an error of about 30 kilometres in longitude. If Engelhart's clock from Madras had been gaining time by about 7 or 8 minutes over 40 days (or about 10-12 seconds per day), this would result in the observed inaccuracy.

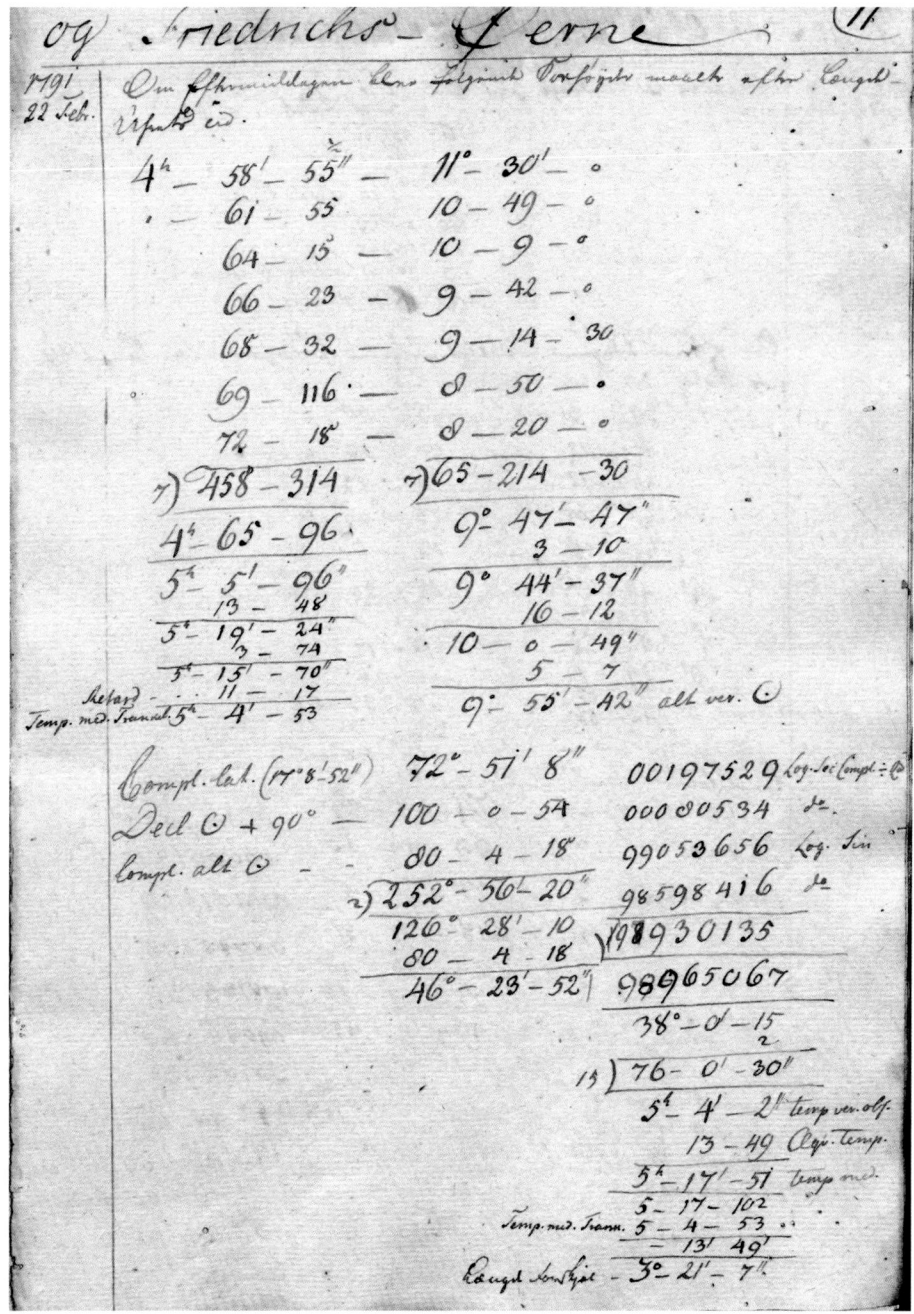

Fig. 7.11: A page from Engelhart's Nicobar journal, with his measurements for the calculation of the longitude of the ship's position. His remarks 'Log-sec compl.' and 'Log sin' reveal his method of calculation using the half-angle method (photo: P. S. Ramanujam).

One of the most elegant applications of a branch of mathematics, known as '**Spherical Trigonometry**' was carried out by Henning Munch Engelhart to determine the longitude of a given place at sea. The art of measuring the longitude of an unknown location boils down to a measurement of the time difference between the unknown location and a location whose longitude (and the time) is known. Engelhart knew the longitude of Tranquebar from previous measurements, and he had a clock on board the ship that showed the time in Tranquebar. To measure the local time in the midst of an ocean, where no landmark is visible, Engelhart determined the hour-angle of the sun. Engelhart uses a well-known formula ('half-angle method') for a spherical triangle (ex. 'A treatise on spherical trigonometry with applications to spherical geometry - Part I', W. J. Mclelland og T. Preston, Macmillan & co., (1897). For an astronomical or polar triangle, (PZX in the figure), 't' is the hour-angle of the sun, $x = 90 - h$, (compl. alt in Engelhart's notation) is the complementary altitude, $y = 90 - d$, (90+dekl in Engelhart's notation, as d is negative (southerly declination in northern latitudes)) is the complementary declination, $z = 90 - b$, is the complementary latitude (compl. lat in Engelhart's notation). The sun crosses the meridian at 1200 hours. The sun's hour-angle indicates how far the sun is from the meridian, i. e., the local time.

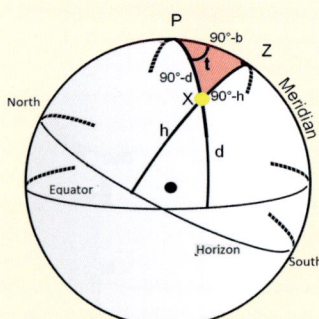

Fig. 7.12: Astronomical triangle (figure: P. S. Ramanujam).

$$\operatorname{Cos} \frac{t}{2} = \sqrt{(\sin(s) \sin(s - x) \sec(b) \sec(d))} \text{, where } s = \frac{x+y+z}{2}$$

Taking logarithms, this boils down to simple addition and subtraction.

The latitude of the place can be determined from $b = 90 - h \pm d$.

The next piece of information about Engelhart comes from a letter signed by Anker, Colbiörnsen, Lichtenstein and Hermansen, dated 29 August 1791, announcing his death:[286]

> Towards the end of May, we received the sad and unfortunate news about the death of chaplain Engelhart and Squire Lachmann in Nikkobar, both died on the expedition ketch Jutengport on 12 April; Lachmann in the morning and Engelhart in the afternoon on account of the fatal Nikkobar fever, due to a misuse of the medicine. According to the report of the ship's captain, Engelhart had an abundant zeal when he arrived in the Nicobars on 11 March and did not exercise the necessary precautions in the unhealthy climate, which resulted in his getting the Nicobar fever. As the condition of the chaplain worsened, a cruise in the sea breeze was undertaken on 1 April. A few days before, Lachmann had an attack of the fever, and on 12 April, he took 1½ times the dose of the emetic and, as it did not have an immediate effect, he took a large amount of boiled water, which brought him to the grave in a few minutes. Both these promising young men whose premature loss will be mourned by compatriots were buried solemnly on the island of Taraka. It is unfortunate that, judging by all circumstances, both are themselves responsible for their own hasty deaths, and not the notorious climate of the Nicobars, as one could incorrectly surmise'.[287]

Bendix Prahl, who was a good friend of Engelhart, paid a glowing tribute to him after his death: 'I do not refer to my friend Engelhart as a blessed soul just because he is dead, but because he carried his blessedness in his good heart as he walked among us, and he was a true philosopher whose aim and purpose was to enlighten his brothers' [Prahl]. Laurids Christensen, who became the Governor of Tranquebar later and died in the Nicobars, noted down in Englhart's log-book that there were six Tamilian servants with him and Lachman on the ship when they were in the Nicobars. One of them, David, survived the trip and at the age of 60 he met Christensen in 1831. David was 17 or 20 at the time he sailed with Engelhart.

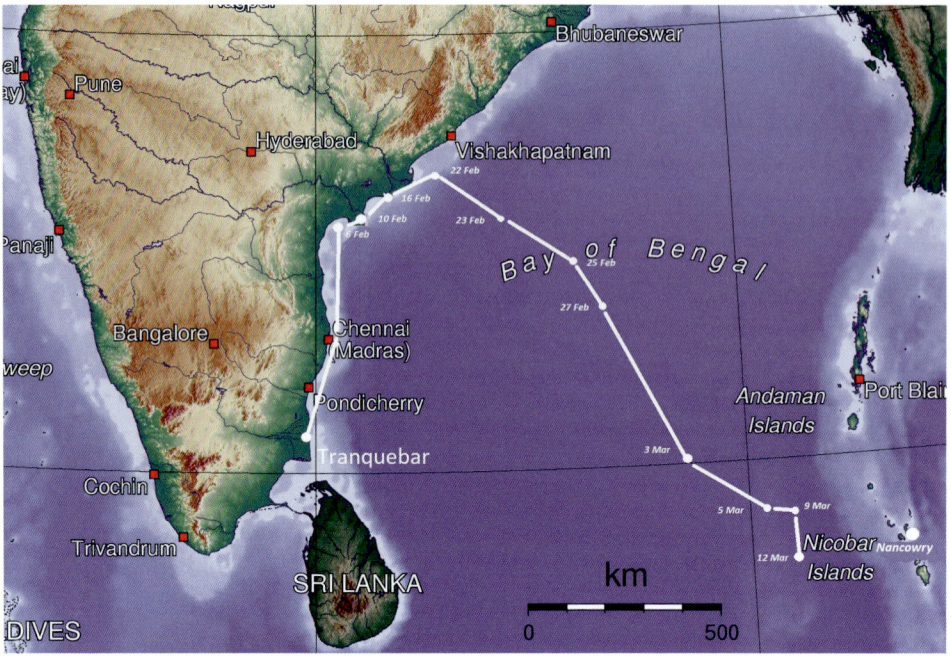

Fig. 7.13: Engelhart's voyage across the Bay of Bengal. The points have been calculated in Microsoft Excel. Engelhart's calculated position for Nancowri was approximately 250 kilometres to the west of the actual position (figure: P. S. Ramanujam).

It is very likely that Niels Studsgaard Fuglsang was appointed as the astronomer in Tranquebar after Engelhart. His application, dated 9 October 1792, to the government for the post together with a recommendation from Thomas Bugge can be found in the National Archives.[288] After the death of Engelhart, the Tranquebar Society collapsed. Not many written records survive.

Gensichen, a German Protestant missiologist, mentions that: 'Among the old houses which are left in King Street mention should be made of the so-called 'Mr. John's House' with its now rather ruinous tower. It was built towards the end of the 18th century by the German missionary John who had a boarding school for European children there' [Gensichen]. It is reported that C. S. John constructed an observation tower in this house, next to Mühldorf's house on King Street, and continued astronomy [Architectura 1987]. I have not seen any observations by John in the National Archives. Photographs show that the tower existed as late as the

20th century. The fate of the astronomical instruments is unfortunately not known.

*

Now that we are here, let us take a quick look at the Zion Churchyard. Not many gravestones are left today. But important people such as Gowan Harrop, Thomas Christian Walter, Johannes Rehling and family, and Harriet Maria Smyth were buried here.

Let us continue our walk along Queen Street. The next corner is interesting. The street on the left is called Perumal Koil Street (there is a temple devoted to Vishnu, also called Perumal, at the western end of the street) and the street to the right is Masilamani Street, after the old temple devoted to Siva. It is very unusual in the South Indian context to have temples dedicated to Siva and Vishnu in the same street.

Fig. 7.14: Harriet Maria Smyth and her son, Harry Benoni O'Grady Hansen, lie buried under this jumble in the Zion Churchyard. Harriet Maria Smyth was the wife of governor, Peder Hansen. She married him at the age of 15 and died on her 14th wedding anniversary, after giving birth to seven children. Harry Benoni O'Grady Hansen, her last child, died less than a year after her (photo: P. S. Ramanujam).

8

Death, Despotism and Destruction

Further along Queen Street, we come to Admiral Street. We will come back here at the end of this chapter – but a little bit further along Queen Street lived, according to the census of 1790, the missionary Christoph Samuel John and Daniel Pulley, a dubash of Tamilian descent.

Daniel Pulley was an enigmatic interpreter (dubash) for the Danes during the latter half of the 18th century. What Ananda Ranga Pillai was to

Fig. 8.1: This plot, which today is empty, could have been the place where Daniel Pulley lived. This plot on Queen Street is close to the intersection of Goldsmith Street and Mosque Street (photo: P. S. Ramanujam).

the French and Pachaiyappa Mudali was to the English, Daniel Pulley was to the Danes. He played an important role in the political and religious life of Tranquebar during this period. An unusual and remarkable fact is that several sources of documents concerning Daniel Pulley exist in at least three different countries. More than 120 letters in Tamil written by Daniel Pulley during 1782-1785 are preserved at the National Archives in Copenhagen[289] and possibly several more in Germany. The letters of Daniel Pulley from the National Archives in Copenhagen can be seen at www.tharangampadi.dk. The archive registry by Rise-Hansen simply states that the documents relate to the pawning of certain villages. However, this collection is in fact much more interesting, containing several accounts of Daniel Pulley's stay at Heider Ali's camp as a 'voluntary' hostage. Later, from 1788, Daniel Pulley seems to have been involved in local caste conflicts. At the National Archives in Oslo, Norway, in Governor Peter Anker's Private archives, one can find documents relating to the part played by Daniel Pulley during a conflict between the dubashes [Hodne]. Lastly, he seems to have told the story of his life to Christoph Samuel John, who wrote it down and sent it to Germany. The 36-page handwritten manuscript is still available at the Archiv Frankesche Stiftungen, Halle, and a slightly modified printed version is available as a Google book.

Daniel Pulley was born around 1740. His grandfather, Johann d'Almeida, had converted from Catholicism to Protestantism and was a catechist at Tranquebar between 1707 and 1744 [Liebau 2013]. We know little about Daniel's parents, except that they were Protestants. Daniel's father died early, and his grandfather on his mother's side brought him up. Johann d'Almeida died in 1746. As a young man, Daniel learnt German and used every opportunity to learn more of it. From 1755, he taught Tamil to the missionaries David Poltzenhagen (1726-1756), Petrus Dame (1731-1766) and Ole Maderup (1711-1776). Besides German, Daniel Pulley also learnt Danish. He undertook the post of the second interpreter (dubash) at the recommendation of H. J. Forck. Daniel's brother, Peter Rajappan was employed by the Danish-Halle Mission and later by the Moravian Brothers' (Herrnhuter) Mission. Peter Rajappan died in 1782. Daniel Pulley advanced to the post of first interpreter under the governorship of Peter Hermann Abbestée, a post that he held until the end of his life. As a dubash, he had an influential position in the political life of the Danish colony, as well as a high standing with the Raja of Tanjore, Tulsaji.

Fig. 8.2: Tippu Sultan in procession – a mural from Tipu Sultan's summer palace at Seringapatna. Tippu Sultan (1750-1799) was the eldest son of Heider Ali (photo: P. S. Ramanujam).

As he was also proficient in Hindustani, he was sent several times to negotiate with Heider Ali and his son, Tippu Sultan.

Heider Ali and Tippu Sultan provided a brief obstacle to British rule in India. Heider Ali was born around 1720, as the son of a naik at Budikote in Karnataka. His date of birth is unknown but is said to be between 1717 and 1722. He assisted his brother in the Mysore army and familiarised himself with the military tactics of the French. In 1749, at the siege of Devanhalli, his skills were noticed and he became a commander. During the next 12 years, his power grew and he became the de facto ruler of Mysore. During the war with the Marathas, the British promised him help. However, in 1772 the Marathas defeated him, because the British did not come to his aid. Furious, he was determined to throw the British out of India with the help of the French.

In 1780, Heider Ali came down from Bangalore with more than 80,000 troops and with the support of French officers, determined to exterminate the British in South India.[290] This started the Second Anglo-Mysore War. The troops were divided into three – one division under the command of Tippu Sultan went on a rampage to the north, another commanded by Heider himself. This first Battle of Pollilur[291] has been well described in the literature.[292] The third, under the command of Karim Saheb, another son of Heider Ali, was sent to plunder Porto Novo in July 1780. The Danish and the Dutch residents (representatives) at Porto Novo were captured as hostages.

During the Second Anglo-Mysore War (1779-1784), Daniel Pulley was taken 'hostage'[293] several times, and at the same time, he served as a negotiating partner and official representative of the Danish Government. When Lala Saheb, one of Heider Ali's generals, invaded Porto Novo, Chidambaram and Siali [Sirkazhi], Daniel Pulley was sent to negotiate with him. Daniel Pulley was successful in stopping the plunder of the Tranquebar area.[294] In 1780, Daniel Pulley accompanied the Secretary of the Asiatic Company to negotiate with Heider Ali. The secretary was to hand over 140,000 rupees demanded by Heider Ali as the Danes had sold weapons to the Nawab of Arcot. On 18 February 1781, Daniel Pulley was sent again to negotiate with a division of Heider Ali's army, which was camping close to Tranquebar with his troops. He was taken hostage once again and taken to Karaikal. In April 1782, he was once again a hostage of Heider Ali near Poraiyar.

At the Battle of Pollilur, Heider Ali defeated Hector Munro's 3,800 strong troops. Heider Ali was close to invading Tranquebar in 1781. In order to avoid a siege, the Danish rulers paid a rather large ransom to Heider Ali. He carried out a regime of terror around Tanjore. Water supply was of paramount importance to the rice bowl of the south. Heider Ali destroyed several sluices and canals near Tiruchirappalli, which supplied water to the rice fields around Tanjore and Tranquebar, resulting in a famine in 1781. The duties paid by farmers to the government depended heavily on the rice harvest. In 1781-82, this was around 2,600 tonnes per year and it fell to 380 tonnes in 1782.

General Eyre Coote, who had been sent down from Bengal to reinforce the British troops, defeated Heider at Porto Novo in 1781. However, he came back strongly with the help of French, under the command of

Admiral Suffrein. During the Second Anglo-Mysore War, Tippu Sultan defeated Colonel Braithwaite's troops at Annagudi near Tanjore, not far from Tranquebar on 18 February 1782. Tippu Sultan captured the entire detachment and seized their guns.

Denmark tried to remain 'neutral' in this war between the English and the French – by trying to help both sides a little. The English accused the Danes of helping the French, while the French accused them of supporting the English. In between, the Dutch from Nagapatnam and the Malacca Straits harassed the Danes. A very bleak report from 1782[295] sent by Abbestée clearly expresses the distress and dismay experienced by the Danes. Abbestée wrote that the English had driven out Heider Ali several times from Tanjore. Four sea battles between the English and the French were fought within sight of Tranquebar. The famine caused by the war was so bad that dead bodies lay everywhere. Commercial production came to a standstill. Import of food supplies from Bengal was forbidden by the English. Tippu Sultan, son of Heider Ali, demanded that his arrival in Tanjore be welcomed by a European from Denmark. Lieutenant Mühldorff undertook this journey, bringing presents. Tippu Sultan insisted that a European be sent as an emissary to the court of Heider Ali in order to assist the French and refuse any help to the English. A town clerk named Siersted, who came from the town of Ringsted in Denmark, was sent as the envoy on 8 April. Secretary Fugl and copywriters Westerholdt and Liebe were assigned to accompany him on the way. No sooner did the trio get outside the city limits of Tranquebar, than they were surrounded by 300 soldiers from Tippu's army, who had plundered the town of Poreiar. Westerholdt and Liebe ran back to the safety of Tranquebar, leaving Siersted to make the journey to Heider's camp alone. News later arrived that both Siersted and Daniel Pulley had been taken as captives. Heider Ali wanted many foreign merchants, who had taken refuge in Tranquebar, including Mucramia, a wealthy Muslim family, delivered to him. The family left Tranquebar secretly.

Siersted was harassed every day for not delivering the Mucramia family and a ransom of 500,000 pagodas was demanded for him. Due to this harassment and due to an unhealthy climate, Siersted died in captivity. Heider Ali wanted another European replacement for Siersted. He also wanted the Danish government to deliver arms and necessities to the French. The French were badly in need of timber to repair their battle-

Fig. 8.3: The seal of Daniel Pulley – apart from featuring the figure of a lion and flag, Daniel's name is also included in Tamil, English and Hindustani (photo: P. S. Ramanujam).

ships. However, the timber that the Danes possessed was too valuable, because they needed it themselves, and so the Danes had to refuse to sell it to the French. Heider Ali was livid and asked Monsieur Suffrein whether they should not occupy Tranquebar. Suffrein, who had a short temper, was finally pacified by Guignace, Lonay and Count Bussy and other French military personalities. As a replacement for Siersted, the copywriter Olivarius was sent as a resident. The entire affair was embittered by the false accusations of one Irulappa, who took sides with Heider Ali and Tippu Sultan for his own good.

Daniel Pulley's letters, now held at the National Archives in Copenhagen, give a personal portrayal of these wars, providing a vivid description of the troop movements and the sufferings of the ordinary people. In his biography, which he narrated to Christoph Samuel John, he paints the horrors caused by the wars. Most of the letters carry only the month and date, but no year, except those written from Heider's camp. The contents of the archive are not in chronological order, making it difficult to date the letters. However, most of them seem to have been written between 1782 and 1785.

Below are my translations from Tamil of some of the letters written by Daniel Pulley in 1782 from the camps of Heider Ali. They describe in first person the gruesomeness of wars and their consequences. Explanations of names, places, persons and events are given below each letter, wherev-

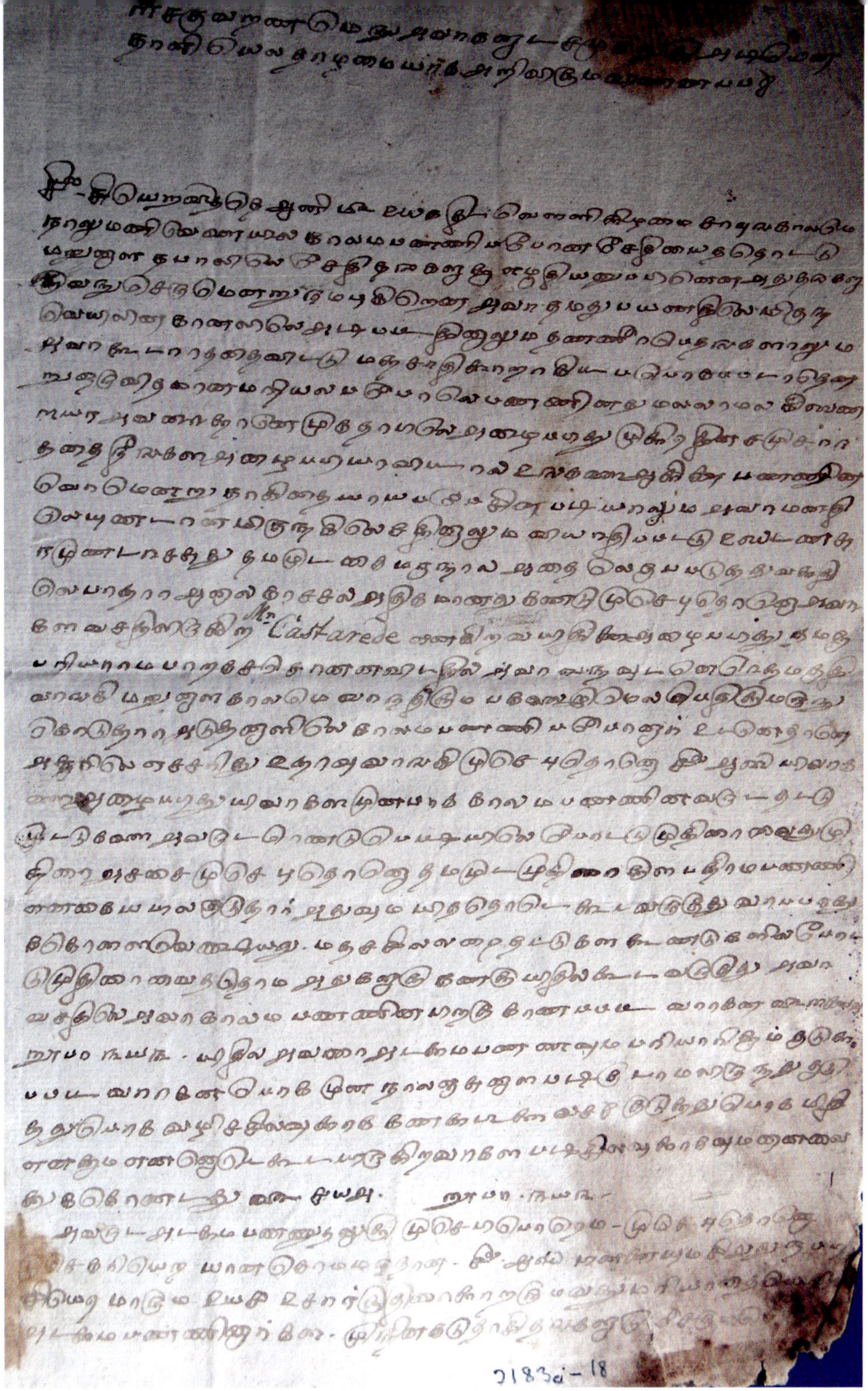

Fig. 8.4: *Letter from Daniel Pulley on the death of Siersted. Bertel Siersted was a secretary for the Danish government in Tranquebar and was sent as a resident to the court of Heider Ali (photo: P. S. Ramanujam).*

er possible. Daniel Pulley wrote the personal names in Tamil as they are pronounced in their native languages (French or Danish). All letters below have been translated from Tamil by me.

Letter from Daniel dated 2 July 1782 (22 Ani)[296]

To the Royal Government

I hope that you have received the news that I sent through the post, on the death of Mr. Siersted[297] on Friday evening at 4 on 21 Ani.[298] Because of exhausting travels in the intense sun and due to water-borne diseases, he was not allowed to meet others. Furthermore, Krishna Rayan[299] threatened him if he did not perform his normal duties. This mental stress caused a high fever. He tried to cure it with his own medicine. As the fever increased, Mr. Castarede,[300] a doctor with Mons. Boudenot,[301] tried to treat him through bloodletting and giving him medicine against diarrhoea. However, he died the day after. Immediately, his personal belongings were sealed in a box in front of Mons. Boudenot and Mr. Hasz[302] and Mons. Boudenot handed over the documents to me. They are included with this letter. Please collect them. We have sealed the other sundries, and the accounts are enclosed. He had about Rs. 33 (in his possession) at the time when he died. After paying for his funeral and other expenses, I have kept the remainder.

At his funeral, Mons. Piveron,[303] Mons. Boudenot, Mons. Kariyer,[304] myself, Commander Mr. Hasz, a few officers and 24 horse riders honoured him with their presence. After the funeral, I told Mon. Piveron through Mons. Boudenot that I was the interpreter for the Royal Government (of Denmark). They (Heider's troops) brought me here as a friend and treated me like an enemy. Just a few years ago, our Governor of Tranquebar was responsible for procuring the release of Surappa Mudali, the father of the interpreter for Mons. Duchemin,[305] who was kidnapped by Muhammad Ali.[306] It would be fair if you can discuss with the Nawab. I am sure that the Tranquebar government has written to Mons. Duchemin. I am sure that the Nawab will release me if you put in a word to Mons. Boudenot. It took us two days to send the personal belongings of Mr. Siersted. But his servant was not released. Krishna Rayan wanted permission (to release the servant). I do not have enough money to support the two of us as well as the people around us. Please send us funds for our expenditure. When I went to the Nawab[307] to get permission to send the personal belongings, he said that another white man must be sent (as envoy) as soon as possible. I told him that there were not enough white people. The person who died came just last year. He was sent here because he came from abroad only the previous year. Therefore, it is not possible to get another white man. He said that they would send another man if I wrote. Krishna Rayan remarked that a person destined to die would die anywhere. My modest intellect tells me that you should write a letter saying that we do not have any white person and that you will send Nagayyan, with the help of Vakil Venkatesu Ayyan. Please remember to include my case.

Mr. Siersted had completed the account for the month of Chittirai [April/May] and, in his worry, he had also wanted to make a copy. However, because of his illness and worry, this was not possible. Accounts will be submitted for the period 8 Chittirai until 24 Ani[308]… Mr. Siersted had given some money to Nawab's personnel, and he had recorded this in the accounts.

Otherwise, the man sent to Chennai for negotiating peace has not come back yet. I am sure that Nagayyan had informed you that three medicine boxes and three cannons were captured by Tippu Sultan from the troops who were on their way to Chennapattnam[309] after taking a rest at Vellore and that this event was celebrated with a small arms salute. The day after, people at Vellore sent 2,000 Carnatic servants and 500 sepoys. They did not know about the ambush the day before and were captured as well. This event was also celebrated with salutes. I should be writing this to you in Danish, however, because of the disturbances, I am writing in Tamil. Please excuse me for this. Please send your instructions to me in Danish.

                    Your faithful servant
                            Daniel

Dhobikedi Sambarkedi[310] 1782
Ani 22.

Daniel addresses Siersted as 'si' (for Signor); the French are referred to as 'musé' (for Monsieur).

Letter from Daniel dated 5 July 1782 (25 Ani)[311]

To the Royal Government

Received your letter dated Ani 14, addressed to Mr. Siersted and Hazrat Nawab[312] together with the 2 bundles of sugarcanes and 2,000 almonds. I had to open the letter in a hurry in order to get the information from the letter to Siersted. As mentioned, I gave the sugarcanes and the almonds to Krishna Rayan with your regards along with the request from the governor for me to meet the Nawab. Appu Muhammad was very helpful. We had promised him 500 rupees if he was helpful. The reason for this is that Krishna Rayan has never listened to us and has always been angry. I was allowed to meet the Nawab. I met the Nawab on the 24th and gave him your letter. After going through the letter, he asked me the reason for the death of Mr. Siersted. I told him that, as a white man, he was used to moving around to keep good health. As Mr. Siersted was ordered not to move out of his tent and not meet his French and Dutch friends, he was stressed and acquired a fever and died because of it. Then Krishna Rayan, who was nearby intervened and said: 'That white man had recently arrived from abroad and was already ill'. The Nawab said: 'Mons. Piveron who has been here after arriving from abroad a long time ago is not dead. When I saw Mr. Siersted the last time, he looked in good cheer'. I replied: 'What I told you earlier is the cause of his death'. The Nawab said: 'I never prevented Mr. Siersted's meeting his friends or moving around. I shall write to the Governor of Tranquebar; you must also write, mentioning that they should not send a new man, but an experienced person'. I said: 'If they send an experienced person, he should be allowed to move around and contact his friends. However, there are no white persons at Tranquebar. There are not enough employees'. The Nawab said: 'There must be an experienced person at each Royal Court. According to the agreement with the governor, there should be a white man here as an envoy'. I replied: 'I shall write according to your orders. Mr. Siersted has informed them of the way he has been treated here; your cavalry came to Tranquebar and gave me a friendly invitation to come here, which was allowed by the governor, and now I have been here for three months. The governor is also very sad about the looting in Tranquebar and is probably suspicious about your intentions'. The Nawab said: 'We shall not ask for money when an experienced envoy comes here. As with the presence of the French and Dutch envoys here, his presence will be an indication of the friendship, and We will be happy. According to this letter from the governor, we have helped the French and Dutch ships at Tranquebar not because of you. It says: 'The envoy there and Daniel are at your mercy' and does not mention anything about sending you back. I also mentioned that the English ship captured 3 Frenchmen. He asked me about the number of people in Tranquebar, and I told him that I did not think that there were new foreigners.

When I complained to Appu Muhammad about a new white resident, he said that such a person would be necessary for maintaining good relations between the Governor and the Nawab. Krishna Rayan does not want to discuss this issue. I have sent Nagayyan back. I need to pay for the palanquin bearer. Please pay their salaries to their homes. The news from Mons. Suffrein[313] and conveyed by Mons. Piveron on the 16th to the Nawab was celebrated with a 21-gun salute. Mons. Suffrein has sent a letter to the Nawab inviting him to Pondichery to discuss further proceedings with Mons. Duchemin. The Nawab is in two minds as to whether to wait for the news about peace from Chennapatnam or to go to Pondichery. I have given Kittharan Pillai and the palanquin bearer 4#. Since I have sent the sealed box containing Mr. Siersted's medicines, I request to you send them to me. Otherwise, I remain your faithful servant

Daniel

Dhobikedi Sambarkedi
Ani 25.

There is an interesting reply from Piragasam Pullei to this letter. While most of the message is in Tamil, there is one strange, interspersing line: 'ragasiyma irukkira sedigalei Tamulil eludamel Paseiil suruchamay eludijanuppiwica sonnargal'. This is Tamil written in the Latin alphabet, to make it impossible for people who could not read that alphabet to understand this message. The message says: 'They say that secret messages should not be written in Tamil but expressed precisely in the 'foreign tongue'.[314] The foreign tongue referred to is probably Danish. The later part of the message talks about 12-25 English ships, which have arrived from the south to 'our' port, which is the secret information. Heider Ali was not happy that the Danes supported the English indirectly.

Letter from Daniel on 1 August 1782 (20 Adi)[315]

To the Royal Government

Humbly written by Daniel. Your letter of Aani 26 (26 July) written to Mr. Siersted arrived here on the evening of Aadi 8 (20 July). I showed Krishna Rayan the contradicting orders in the letter, which was eagerly awaited by him and about which he had asked me so much. The vakil demanded to see the letter to the Nawab and asked for a great deal of money to be paid.

I told him to send a vakil to Tranquebar so that the governor could confirm that things did not happen as claimed. Krishna Rayan intervened to say that his vakil might not know all that was going on at Tranquebar. I told him that: 'If the vakil does not know what is happening at Tranquebar, how can you accuse us based on his letter? Our Governor has been helping the Nawab all the time; he has helped the French ships as requested. Our Governor has written to me that the Nawab will not request us to do unjust things. So please inform the Nawab'. Next day, he told me that it would help a lot if the Governor sent a white, experienced envoy. As I know that he (Krishna Rayan) will not be satisfied with small amounts, I have not agreed to pay him anything. I have told him that I will obey his orders. He said that: 'The horse that was ordered by Appu Muhammad for 500 rupees when Mr. Siersted was alive, has come to Tranquebar. Find out about the cost of the horse and its pedigree'. He is asking about it – I await your orders.

A few days ago, the Nawab sent a letter to Chennapatnam, supposedly written by General Braithwaite who is under arrest here. He mentioned in it that nations are being destroyed by the war and that it will be good to have peace. The Colonel replied that he would send his message if the Nawab sent a wise man (to Madras or Chennapatnam for negotiations). Through this man, they replied from Chennappattinam that the Nawab had destroyed enough and that it would be good if he returned to his own place. However, the Nawab sent a message to Chennapattinam that he refused to leave unless he got the town of Tiruchinappalli and 100,000 varahans.[316] He is still awaiting an answer. An experienced white man is expected here. In the meantime, the Nawab, after taking some rest in Vellore, caught a few people belonging to Bommaraja and cut their noses off. About 600 people had their noses cut. The English troops are at Kanchipuram. A two-day march separates the troops. People are afraid here that the English will fight well. It is believed that Maratti cavalry may help the English. It looks as if God will unleash a fury in a few days. The Nawab has unwillingly paid 1 lakh to the French, in addition to the 2 lakhs before. Mons. Piveron has gone to get the French troops. We do not know when they will come. Mons. Piveron mentioned to me that Brigadier Abbestée helped quite a bit twice during the Siege of Pondichery. He wanted me to inform you that if they (the Danes) wanted to act in a friendly manner, they should not support the English. I replied: 'Only Brigadier Abbestée knows how to conduct himself. There are a few Frenchmen in Tranquebar, and they spread misinformation about us. I beseech you in the name of the Government of Tranquebar – Please do not believe them'. He said that there are people like that. I also talked to Mons. Lally.[317] He expected that there would be a peace agreement between the Nawab and the English soon.

Your merciful, humble servant
Daniel
Sambarkedi
Aadi 20

The Nawab has kept 2 hircar (spies) with me in addition to the Brahmin.

Letter from Daniel dated 1 August 1782 (26 Adi)[318]

Daniel writing with great humility to the Royal Government at Tranquebar

I hope that you received the letter sent through the ayyangar[319] Brahmin. I have sent three letters following that. Since these were sent by post and as I have not received any reply, I do not know whether you have received them. The most important news in them is that the Nawab called me aside and told me that: 'According to information from Mons. Suffrein, Mons. Piveron complains that the Governor Tranquebar is supplying arms to the English, whereas when the French ask, he denies this. If he wants to remain in Tranquebar, he must refuse the English, but support the French. If they cannot pay, then we will pay. We have asked Tranquebar for information about ships, but the Governor of Tranquebar is not responding. Please make sure that the news is conveyed by post – this will help our friendship'. The information he told me to write to you about sending a white, experienced envoy was also in those letters. Now the Nawab is 5 naazhi[320] west of Cuddalore on the evening of the 25th. He often asks whether there is any reply to his letters. When I gave him the message informing that the envoy could not be sent, he asked whether there were English ships at the port. I replied: 'Not in our port, but at Nagapattinam'. He did not say anything. Appu Muhammad says that not sending a white man (as an envoy) will be a cause for enmity. He keeps on asking about the horses and money. Mons. Suffrein and 10-12 officers met the Nawab on the 24th. Mons. Suffrein gave a horse, two diamond rings, two pieces of golden clothing to everyone. They all had their food in the house or the tent of the Nawab on the 27th. The Nawab and Mons. Suffrein talked together for a long time. The outcome is not known. Mons. Suffrein donated a watch made of gold, worth 40,000 rupees, to the Nawab. They will continue their discussions today. In the meantime, rumours say that the Nawab may go south in order to purchase Nagappatinam and give it to the Dutch. He suspects that Tranquebar is helping the English as well as their ships. The Nawab demanded that I ask: 'Has there been a ship at Tranquebar? Has Mons. Bussy sailed past with 35 ships? Why has this news not been passed on to me?' I said: 'If this were true, then they would have written. Perhaps they could not send the post because of the disturbances along the route'. 'Why should they not send by 'salangu'[321] mail?' he then asked. It is said that the French captured an English ship with Colonel Ahren[322] along with 8 officers. Mons. Duchemin is still very weak and is not allowed out. Because of the water situation, Tippu Sahib is still at Kattumannar.[323] If the water level goes down, he may go to Tanjore. Because of the current situation, it is urgent to send a white envoy as well as inform us about the situation as often as possible. Since the Nawab is still at Cuddalore and if you are willing to send a white envoy, it may be better to send him to the French at Cuddalore, and inform them that the news they are spreading about us is false. Further, please ask them to treat the envoy with respect, and please send me back to Tranquebar. It may be worthwhile for the governor to send a message to the Nawab. Since I am not sure whether you received my previous letters, I hope that my repetition is not a problem

Otherwise, I remain your humble servant awaiting your orders
Daniel

Pattambakkam[324]
Aadi 26, 1782.

Letter from Daniel dated 19 August, 1782 (7 Aavani)[325]

To the Royal Government

My humble request. Received the letters sent by you to the Nawab and to me on Aadi 31 (12 August), on Aavani 5 (17 August). I informed the Nawab about all the things described in my letter. He said that the reason for your reply to his previous letter might be that the letter was sent through Mons. Suffrein. After hearing the rest of the news, he was happy that Mons. Abbestée has conducted himself with wisdom and care in all matters and that, because the Danes are Christians, they have been honest. He said that it is not a sin to sell goods to both the English and the French; however, for our sake, when the English ask for something, they should say that they do not have it; they can sell the stuff to the French for good money. It will please Us. I told him that this was the reason why the Governor has told the French to buy whatever they wished. I said to him that Mons. de Lannoy[326] was accompanied all the way to Cuddalore on a Danish ship, just to please him. He asked me what kind of ship it was, and I replied that it was the same ship that brought his people. He remarked that, as written earlier, it is best to help the French. He said that the envoy who was expected must be an experienced and wise man. I replied that our Governor would only send a wise man.

I told Appu Muhammad and Krishna Rayar that you have written that they should treat the new envoy with respect. They promised to do so. In order to understand their behaviour as well as for them to speak advantageously about us, it is necessary to give a lot (of cash) to Munshi-Krishna Rayan-La-la-Samayya.[327] Therefore, it occurs to my modest brain that you should send enough cash through the new envoy.

You may know about my conversations with Mons. De Lannoy and his letter to the Brigadier from my previous letter. He is at Cuddalore now. Mons. Duchemin is very ill and may not survive. I have spoken to Mons. Piveron. He said that the Brigadier would send you a letter. When I told Mr. Hasz the contents of your letter, he said that the Governor has been kind to the foreigners. Talking about English ships, he said that they are now in Chennappattinam…

Awaiting your orders and your mercy

Your humble servant
Daniel

Pattambakkam
Aavani 7, 1782.

On Aadi 29 [10 August], I sent a letter to Mons. Brigadier de Lannoy and Mons. Guignace[328] through our hircar Saminathayyan. He was caught at Siyazhi for taking letters to the French. His clothing and turban were taken from him, and he was arrested. He escaped and told me the news. I had written that Mons. de Lannoy gave a letter to the Nawab from the King of France on the night of the 24th. This received a 21-gun salute. He was presented with two diamond rings, two horses, two pearls # (undecipherable) and a turban. Next day, he gave me the letter you sent through Piragasam Pillai and handed over a letter to the Brigadier to facilitate our errands with the Nawab. I told him all that was necessary.

There was another letter written to Piragasam along with that letter. It contained a mistake as it was written in a hurry to the government on the 20th. It claimed that our king had informed the Nawab along with other kings that America, belonging to the English, is now ours. Please correct this mistake. 24 horsemen who came with the Nawab went on a killing spree. 9 people were tied to the right leg of an elephant and dragged through the streets. Another 12 people were hanged. You may receive all these letters if they are allowed through Tranquebar. It would be nice if you can write to Mons. de Lannoy and Mons. Guignace about their letters being intercepted.

Daniel

Letter from Daniel dated 8 September 1782 (27 Aavani)[329]

To the Royal Government of Tranquebar

My humble message. As I wrote on Aavani 16 (28 August), we left Pattambakkam on the night of the 20th (1 September) and arrived west of Pondichery to Vazhudavur[330] on the 21st (2 September). When Colonel Coote left for Chennappattinam after resting at Vellore, an Englishman came here. He said that there were 800 white men, 1,600 sepoys and 200 horsemen. Heider[331] said that he is only talking about the company people. He said that kallars (spies) there had informed him that there were 4,000 white people, 15,000 sepoys, and 4,000 horsemen. About 100 sepoys left on the 22nd (3 September) for Thayilapuram and arrived on the 23rd (4 September). They will leave on the 28th (9 September) to support the English. 8,000 people accompany 2 ships. Heider has stored 1,000 ox-loads of rice at Vellore. Therefore, there should be enough food at Vellore for 6 months. This news was conveyed to the Nawab by 3 Englishmen. There is no rice for the troops; they loot and eat… There the few things sent by the Colonel from Chennappattinam along with Colonel Braithwaite[332] arrived – silk, dhoti, trousers – one thin Cheppe (Chappals – Indian footwear?), delicate silk tablecloths, several alcoholic spirits, several cases of tea – all because these will be good for the Nawab. He tried the chappals(?) on his legs, and said that they were very soft, removed them and sent everything back to Mr. Braithwaite along with 10 orange fruits in a golden bowl. The important news in that letter to the Colonel: You can be sure that I will see you in three months. Heider was very surprised at these words. How can this be possible? People close to him were telling him things that he wanted to hear. On the 25th (6 September), the troops camped at Thellam close to Vandhavasi.[333] 200 white men and 200 sepoys, together with 100 soldiers who left Cuddalore on the 25th, joined them. One commander, one Captain and 2 officials accompanied them. The Nawab did not want so many. He hated the fact that he had to pay so much for all these. The birthday of Louis, King of France was celebrated. There was a 20-gun salute. There was a big tiger in the place where we stayed. They shot it and showed it to Heider. After arriving at Satthamangalam on the 24th (5 September), due to heavy rains, we came here on the 27th (8 September). The Nawab intends to go to Virinchipuram close to his place. It involves three journeys. It is said that he may go to Chennappattinam from there. It seems that 4-5 district chiefs (Palaykkarar) are supplying grass and hay to the English, which is forbidden. Therefore, he wants to fight them. Some say that as there is much water in Kollidam,[334] the Nawab would like to go back to his place from whence he can attack Tanjore since there is not much strength (many troops) in that place. Some others say that he is awaiting Mons. Bussy.[335] If he does not arrive, he may conclude a peace treaty with the English before returning to his place. Only God knows which will prove true. I have had a fever for the past three days. You should know that Mr. Olivarius[336] has arrived[†]. Otherwise, living by your kind mercy and obeying your orders

Your humble servant
Daniel

Written on Aavani 27 at Satthamangalam

+ Mr. Hasz told me what he heard through his French connection: At Chennapatnam, Admiral Hughes[337] wanted to take 400 soldiers and 1,000 sepoys on his ship; this was rejected by Colonel Coote.[338] Then Admiral Hughes asked the Council. The Council gave him permission to take the soldiers and the sepoys aboard the ship. We heard that Colonel Coote then grew angry and said that he would not interfere in the affairs of the troops anymore.

Letter from Daniel dated 12 September 1782 (31 Aavani)

To the Royal Government in short

My message to you. Mr. Olivarius arrived at the camp at Chettupet, on 28 Aavani (9 September), in the evening. The camp moved to Kamakkur on the 29 (10 September). The troops scheduled to leave for the west of Vellore the next day, hearing the news that the English camp had left Chennappattinam and are near Chengleput, have moved to Arcot believing that the English troops are heading for Cuddalore. If the English troops leave for Cuddalore, the Nawab has been thinking of following them. We are at Kamakkur[339] on the 30-31(11-12 September). We leave on the 1st (13 September). Last night, he talked to Mons. Guignace. He gave him a horse. He did not speak to me. Tonight, we will talk to him. The news here is that the troops split into two at Chennappatinam; one part leaving as if heading north towards Chengleput, then went west and after a day's journey 450 horses out of 2,000 were attacked and wounded severely. The Nawab sent 2,000 Carnatic soldiers to help at Cuddalore … The Nawab is taking everything in his stride as he expects Mons. Bussy's help in a few days. Sometimes he scolds the French. He says that they are beggars. That is the news here. If God helps me, I will come back soon. Living by your kind mercy,

Your humble servant

Daniel

Kamakkur
1782 Aavani 31 (12 September).

The events described in the above letters are corroborated through the letters that Daniel Pulley sent to the missionaries. Some of these letters have been translated into German and have been published in '*Neuere Geschichte der Evangelischen Missions- Anstalten zu Bekehrung der Heiden in Ostindien*' from the year 1784. A translation of the letters is given below, as they supplement the information in the above letters (my translation from German).

Letter dated 23 May 1782

Everywhere I have been, I have seen places burnt down and people who have died due to hunger and thirst lying in fields and valleys, torn apart by wild animals and birds. Wherever we have stopped, beggars, small children, orphans and widows pitifully ask: Please give us some kanji (rice brew). When we reach our camps, we see several dead bodies lying about… On the night of 22 May, the French general had an audience with Hazrat Nawab. The Nawab presented him with an elephant, a horse, a breast ornament, a diamond ring and a shawl. Tomorrow, the camp moves to Pondichery.

Letter dated 1 June 1782

…I have translated the twelfth chapter of the Tenth book (in the Bible) into Tamil.

The Brahmin, who is my watchman, took the writings from me as he thought that it might be a letter to Tranquebar, and after reading it he asked: 'Is your law so agreeable?' He read it aloud for his chief, who said: 'I must have a copy'. As I have written it under so much duress, there are probably several mistakes. I am anxious to read it once again if it were in better Tamil with proper meaning. Therefore, I request you to show me the favour to copy what I am sending and correct the mistakes, and once more write it down and bind it as a book and send it to me. Whoever copies it twice will be paid by my son-in-law. As I would like my wife to read this also, I would appreciate if it can be copied a third time with larger letters.

Incidentally, Hazrat Nabab (Heider) is marching south to Wabudaur,[340] which lies about 10 Naazhi (two German miles) west of Pondichery after capturing Perumuckel[341] and from there to Kodukur.[342] During this period, the English have moved towards Wandawasi with 20 divisions. As soon as Heider heard this, he sent some troops to counteract this and went there himself. We were in Peier. So far, we have not met them. It looks as if we will march from the south to the north and camp where we have camped before. It seems as if we will be moving further north. We do not know the will of God.

Letter dated 2 July 1782

On the 14th of this month, I and Mr. Sürstädt[343] were called and threatened: Where is the Moor family (whom Heider had ordered to be delivered)? (Daniel is referring to the Mucramia family). If they do not arrive here, you must pay 5 lakhs (half a million) pagodas. If there is no reply in eight days, you will be chastised. That is what Kischtnarayan, the Privy Council of the Nabab (said). He is an infuriating person. Mr. Sürstädt was very upset by these threats. He said: 'You can take my life – but you cannot kill my soul'. He had an increasing fever during this period. He took the medicine that he had, but the illness had the upper hand. The French doctor saw him. The doctor did bloodletting and gave him medication for vomiting and purging. The fever increased, and he went to his Lord during the evening of the 21st. The patience, courage and friendliness that he displayed until his death puts me to shame. He could accept the mistakes of others with equanimity. At the beginning of the journey, when the kulis (bearers) and other people were disorderly, I told him: 'You must get angry and scold, as otherwise, these people will not obey'. He, however, answered: 'It has never been my habit. How can I scold them? I do not understand this'. Once when I in my unhappiness mentioned how we suffer because of Tranquebar, he said: 'Our sin is also responsible for this'. At another time, when I said: 'My regrets and worries are evident', he replied: 'The Lord is now testing our faith. When we are faithful, the end will be good. He will not leave us completely'. Incidentally, he has mentioned several times that: 'I will die here. I do not believe that I will come back to Tranquebar'. Two days before he died, when he had much pain and thirst, I told him: 'I have read the Epistle to the Philippians, where Paul says with great confidence – Christ is my Life and Death is my Reward. Everything will be swept away if Jesus Christ wants', and he said: 'I know what I believe'. When he was dying, I asked him: 'Are you firm in your belief that Jesus Christ will take care of you?' He looked at me and said: 'God grant me that belief'. Those were his last words. He died around half past 4. All the local French of repute came and buried him with respect. The place where he is buried is barely twenty steps from my tent. I look at it often and think that the Lord has placed him there so that you (I) can think of your (my) own death. After that, I have sent all the servants and palanquin-bearers away, and I am alone. However, the Lord is with me.

The letter from Tranquebar arrived on the 24th when I was feeling depressed. There was also a letter to the Nabab with it. As I had to give him the letter, I was allowed a second audience. He conversed in a friendly way. I told him that: 'The deceased Mr. Sürstädt was not treated like an envoy. He died of worry since he had been accused'. The Nabab replied: 'I had not ordered this. This will not happen again. Ask another white man to come'. (He has himself received a letter from the governor). When I said: 'Should I not go back?', he replied: 'It is not said in this letter from Tranquebar that you should come back. It depends on whether the Tranquebar government could send another envoy. If this does not happen, there will be thousands of difficulties, and it may take a long time before I can come back…

Due to peace negotiations, an envoy has been to Madras and has returned. He has been sent back there again. However, peace looks very doubtful, since the Nabab does not discuss the treaty with anyone because the government in Madras has not accepted his suggestions; time will show. It looks as if the Nabab will go to Pondichery for discussions with the French. No one knows how that will go.

Letter dated 29 July 1782

Due to the lack of time, a brief report: I received your letter at Vannanturuvam[344] where we camped. I read the letter on the way, on the 21st. I was moved to tears by the kind words. The Nabab has begun peace negotiations with the English. Then the French reported that they are expecting 35 ships and Mons. Bussy will arrive soon. They invited him to come to Cuddalore to discuss things of importance. After that, the camp broke up and we went to Padtampackam, about 5 nazhigai (about a German mile) west of Cudelur. The English stationed at Kanchipuram have retreated. We do not know the reason for this. We came here on the 25th. As soon as we came, all the cannons in Cudelur (Cuddalore) and on all the ships were fired because of the arrival of the Nabab. On the 26th, Mons. Suffrein and a few other French officers had an audience with the Nabab. Mons. de Souffrein received two diamond rings, a pair of slippers, jewellery with precious stones to be placed on the head, two pairs of garments woven with gold. The others also received garments and other presents. On the 27th, the Nabab gave them food, when they told him that they had captured an English ship with Colonel Harper and eight other officers. On the 28th, Mons. Souffrein came with some other Frenchmen and held talks with the Nabab. What was discussed has not been divulged. The Nabab has been informed that Tranquebar has provided the English with ship masts and other war provisions. It is believed that the Nabab wants to obliterate Tranquebar. He does not believe in the lies that are spoken in Tranquebar. God will govern his heart that he may keep the sympathy he has for Tranquebar. It will be good if the government sends an envoy soon. If not, danger lurks. May the Lord and Jesus show mercy on Tranquebar and all of us.

Letter dated 27 August 1782

The way to Cudelur was challenging – may be the Lord did not want me to go back, but probably wants to send me to Tranquebar? When the Nabab arrived in Cudelur, a European came to me and said that I could go home. That was of great comfort to me.

On the 21st of August, the camp moved to Warhudaur[345] west of Pondichery.

During this period, General Coote had gone to Velur with his camp and then back to Madras. He had 1,000 ox-loads of rice, which came from Heider country and which was to be sent to the camp, but it was captured. One part of it was sent to Velur, the other to Madras. Therefore, he now has provisions in Velur for six months. We heard this from three English deserters, who came to us. A sergeant, who came from General Coote's camp, said that 28 ships with 8,000 soldiers were apparently on their way from Europe, and two of these ships should have arrived at Madras. The Nabab has made this renegade (the sergeant) chief of the sepoys. He had told him that the English camp has 800 whites, 10,000 sepoys and 200 horsemen. The Nabab replied that this estimate is too high. He seems to have news that is more accurate. Through his spies and kallars,[346] who have been in Madras, he thinks that there are 4,000 Europeans, 15,000 sepoys, 400 Palayakkarars and 600 cavalrymen.

In the camp, there has been a significant increase in prices. Rice cannot be bought for money. Several oxen and horses have died due to the lack of grass and other fodder. Because of this, Heider would like to get closer to his own country. On the 22nd, we came to Teilaburam[347] and on the 23rd to Weiraburam,[348] where the blessed Sürstädt and I received our first audience with the Nabab.

On the 24th, we came to Tellaru[349] close to Wandawasi. 200 French, 200 sepoys and a few 'kaffers', a German captain and two other officers came to the nabab from the French camp at Manjalkuppam to stay with the nabab. The French general had promised to send more, but the nabab said that he should not send more than 500 men, as it will be too expensive.

On the 25th, the French celebrated the birthday of their king. They shot a large tiger in the forest close by.

On the 26th, we came to Sattamangalam.[350] Here, there is a large hill on which two beautiful temples have been built. In the middle of the mountain, there is a huge palm tree. People used to live around this; now all the houses are destroyed. In the forest, bushes and on the hill, one sees the beauty of the Lord's work. It rained quite heavily this night, so we could not continue our travel. On the morning of the 28th, we had to break the journey. The Nabab is getting closer to his own country, from the Wirurschi side. However, it is still three days of travel. Due to the strenuous march, several have died. Five Palayakkarars north of Madras seem to be supplying grass, straw, rice and provisions to the English camp. The Nabab is talking about going there and fighting them.

Letter dated 4 September 1782

On the 1st the English, 20,000 strong, came to Chengleput and have captured several riders and horses belonging to Heider. It looks as if they are going to Cudelur. After hearing this, Heider wants to go to Cudelur in the morning. He has already sent 3,000 infantry soldiers to help the French.

Samuel (*) has come. I would like to give him all possible instructions to make his stay useful. On the evening of 3 September, we had an audience with Heider. He would like to prove that he can hold a friendly conversation with me and gave me leave to depart. I must wait for his answer to the government. At last, the Lord in all his mercy will bring me back to Tranquebar.

The English have advanced to Karumkurichipalayam.[351] Heider would like to stay, fearing an attack on Cudelur by the English. It is raining quite a lot and horses die frequently. Heider has sent 30,000 'podi'[352] (ox-loads) of rice to Cudelur. There is nothing here, and Heider is mortified. Heider is moving forwards and backwards, hoping Mons. Bussy will arrive in a few days. He always says: 'We shall see'. If the English move south, he will follow them for sure. It is up to the hand of the Lord how things will go. A few ships and 1,000 soldiers should be coming from Madras. It is rumoured that the French fleet has left for Trincomalee in order to battle the English fleet there.

I received permission to return to Tranquebar yesterday, with the Lord's mercy. I hope as you had written in your last letter that the Lord would bless my return to Tranquebar as He did when I left. Please pray to the Lord that He will do so.

The Lord had decided in all his wisdom to take my elder brother in my absence. I am comforted by the will of God. He (my brother)[353] had been ill for a long time. My absence has given him the opportunity to contemplate the state of his soul and decide its fate (?). As my younger brother is far away, I do not have any comfort in my own illness. Now I will turn to God and seek solace in Jesus....

(*) Samuel probably is the new envoy in place of Daniel.

Johann Jacob Klein

A few remarks about Heider Ali, which I collected from Daniel Pulley (Klein's remarks):

He is a man approximately 65 years old, does not use spectacles, not that it is necessary for him, as he can neither read nor write. He signs his name, as he is used to it. It is doubtful whether he is a Muhammadan. That he is a heathen is demonstrated by the following: Every Saturday, he distributes alms to 30 Brahmins, one rupee each, one portion of oil (for a head wash, Nallennai[354]), one portion of rice and a brass vessel with water. It is rumoured that he has a small golden idol which he worships every Sunday. He does not cut his beard, but twice a week has his hair plucked. He eats together with male members of his family. He chews a lot of betel-arak, not filling his mouth as other big lords, kings or nababs do, but like other Tamils takes it from a golden plate and keeps it in his clothing, chewing when he wants to. He drinks everything, including tea, but not coffee. He takes a bath every day and washes his head once a week. He has about 20 to 30 wives, who follow him, hidden from view. He has several salaried doctors as well as a French doctor, who can correspond with the English in Madras. During the five months Daniel Pulley has been in his camp, not once was Heider indisposed. He is very eager to know the latest news, whether favourable or not. He gets all the provisions for the camp from his land, wheat, rice and wonderful fruits, grapes and so on for his table. He is very ambitious. He is a very dependable ally of the French..? He waits mainly for General Bussy and the fleet that should come with him.

Daniel Pulley holds him in high esteem. He (Daniel) was given the tent used by Colonel Baillie,[355] who was defeated in 1780 and whose name was there still. Because of its blue colour, it had an advantage in the strong sunshine. The white ants were a pestilence in the camp because they ruined all the carpets that were put on the ground. Heider has about 1,000 farmers with him, who receive very little money from him, as they live on their own farmlands. He pays them 2 rupees for each head of a white person they bring, and they probably lose their own heads afterwards. Heider entertained the French admiral and other naval officers at Cudelur. He wondered why they ate so little until he was told that he had not given them enough wine.

In particular, all the English officers, who were either prisoners of war captured in the battles or from the forts, were released to their country. Only Colonel Braithwaite, captured by his [Heider's] son Tippu Sahib in February of this year at Colaram and kept at his place, was allowed to correspond with Madras and allowed to spend his time as he wished. Once, he received from Madras a batch of garments, elegant stockings, a pretty hat and tea. Heider wanted to look at them all. He took his turban off his head, put on the hat and remarked that this was a fine piece. He put on one of the stockings. He also opened the tea (buzette?), smelt it, asked for some of his own and compared the two. Afterwards, he passed on everything to the colonel.

He has tremendous respect for General Coote. He tries to avoid him. Once they met. General Coote had camped in a forest. Heider divided his army into three, one commanded by himself, another by his son and the third by Lally. Heider has the habit of advancing and firing even in the heat of midday. General Coote let him use all the fire until 3 in the afternoon. After 3 O'clock, when it became a bit cooler, General Coote started a deadly round of firing so that Heider's people were fleeing by 5 O'clock. Heider himself was in danger of being killed or captured.

During the Second Anglo-Mysore War in 1784, Christian Frederik Schwartz (used interchangeably with Schwarz) reported the abduction of 12,000 children by Tippu Sultan. The invaders plundered the country and took away all the cattle and grain, raising terror in the minds of the people. It looked as if the English were losing the war when suddenly Heider Ali died in 1782 of cancer in the neck. His eldest son, Tippu Sultan, was defeated during the Third and Fourth Anglo-Mysore Wars and finally died defending Srirangapattana in Karnataka in 1799.

Between 1782 and 1785, Daniel Pulley had several times to act as a mediator between the Danish government and Amarasimha, Raja of Tanjore in the matter of the pawning of several villages. In 1780, the territory around Thirukalacheri was leased to the Danes for a period of 90 years. Daniel Pulley negotiated during October 1784 with the Raja of Tanjore, and a month later, the negotiations were concluded successfully [Strandberg]. The result of the negotiations was the pawning of 14 villages to the Danes. During 1786, new negotiations took place, resulting in the Danes obtaining an area around Thiruvidakalli to an estimated value of 35,000 pagodas. Daniel Pulley was also instrumental in negotiations during the caste crisis in August 1787.

Many of the letters from Daniel Pulley in the Archives are addressed to Piragasam Pullei, who was the personal interpreter to Governor Abbestée. These letters seem to point to a close relationship between Daniel Pulley and Piragasam Pullei until 1785. The following invocations at the beginning of the letters can be cited as examples of the close relationship: 'To my beloved Pillai Piragasam Pillai, may God show you mercy and wisdom',[356] 'Wishing my dear Piragasa Pillai that he would love only Jesus, considering life on earth as waste',[357] 'To my dear Piragasa Pillai, who is much loved by me'.[358] Here is what Piragasam Pillai says: 'Let all good things happen to Daniel Pulley'. In 1788, this relationship seemed to sour, as the new governor, Peter Anker, was appointed in place of Hermann Abbestée. According to Hodne [Hodne], Daniel Pulley was passed over with regards the post of chief interpreter, which went to Piragasam Pullei, as Daniel Pulley seems to have supported Suppremania Setti, a chief suspect for instigating caste conflicts. Daniel Pulley also appears to have accused Piragasam Pullei and his father, Salomon Pullei, of misusing their offices in the Black Court.[359] Peter Anker was later forced to appoint Daniel Pulley as an assessor in the Black Court instead of Piragasam Pullei. Perhaps, there might be another reason for the conflict between Daniel Pulley and Piragasam Pullei, which is hinted at in one of Daniel's letters to Salomon Pullei (my translation from Tamil):[360]

To my dear wise brother Salomon Pillai, who is much loved by our Saviour Jesus Christ, Daniel surviving due to the good wishes of God for your sake is writing with prayers.

    I hope that you receive this letter while you are in good cheers and health. As you know, I have enough problems here due to my involvement with the palace (in Tanjore). In this case, you know how difficult it is for me to be involved in matters concerning others. I have heard that Gurupada Upadesiar is looking for a suitable girl for his son, Thoppila Pillai. Last year when you talked to me, you agreed that my brother's daughter would be a suitable match, as you are like her father. I think you said that his father would come when the month of Thai starts and finish the marriage. I have also written a letter to Gurupada Upadesiar to say that I concur with the decision made by Salomon Pillai and that he could come here and perform the marriage with no difficulties. I am now surprised that they are looking for a girl. At least I expected you to write to me. I would like to know whether this is true. The Lord has, in his scheme of things, already decided the match between a boy and a girl. So, I should not force matters. People by now would know that this girl was rejected. The girl's mother and others would think that I am responsible for the cancellation of the marriage. Even now, I am not opposed to the marriage. I would like to consult you before giving my opinion. I thought Gurupatha Pillai belonged to the same caste. Probably the Lord wanted it differently if they are now changing their mind. As you are like her father, I hope that you will do your best. I am putting this pressure on you for the sake of the fatherless girl in the name of the Lord

Aani 10   Daniel

Was Salomon Pullei related to Thoppila Pillai and Gurupada Upadesiar mentioned in this letter? Could this have been the start of a family feud?
    Towards the end of his life, Daniel Pulley seems to have told the story of his life to Christoph Samuel John, whose manuscript can be found in

Halle. In this manuscript, entitled[361] '*Short Biography of Daniel Pulley – First interpreter for the Royal Government, Assessor in Black or Tamil Court and Head of the Christian Mission's Congregation in Trankebar. Born 1740 Died 1802*', C. S. John says: 'Subsequently, he led a distraught life in Tranquebar. Despite his prestige (in society) and the advantages accrued to him, the hubris of the second interpreter, especially his ingratitude, hurt him no end, particularly because of all the help and benefits he had showered on that interpreter'. This must be a reference to his relationship with Piragasam Pullei.

The narrative continues:

'His wife was no source of comfort either, thanks to her sharp tongue, which she freely let loose on him. She died of oral cancer and had the grace to regret her bad behaviour prior to her death. Likewise, he did not experience any joy from his 2 sons. The eldest had no talents and was lazy, but he believed that he could have been trained to work at the mission, which, however, did not happen. However, for the sake of his father, he was nominated to become his successor. The second was more gifted and learned German and English taught at the English National School founded by Mr. Schwarz, but he abandoned it and joined the English service, developed a fondness for alcohol and died suddenly in Madras in his prime. One of his daughters was feeble of mind. The other 3 became good Christian-minded wives. Two of the sons-in-law had serious illnesses; one of them encouraged his wife to cause constant annoyance to her father'.

Daniel Pulley also served as an assessor in the Black Court in addition to his job as a dubash. He had six children – two sons and four daughters. The missionary Joseph Daniel Jänicke in Tanjore educated both of his sons. Daniel himself was married twice. During his later years, Daniel Pulley seems to have turned more and more to religion for support. He appears to have translated several works of Christian literature into Tamil, as well as publishing his own compositions and composing a Christian prayer book 'Bhakti Manjari' [Liebau]. A few books written by him can be found at the library of the British Museum. Dennis Hudson, in 'Protestant Origins in India: Tamil Evangelical Christians 1706-1835', mentions several books written by Daniel Pulley. Daniel Pulley stopped working for the government after the takeover of the colony by the British in 1801.

Christoph Samuel John records that Daniel Pulley died in 1802 in Tranquebar. In the end, he was too weak even to talk. However, he always welcomed the missionaries when they came to visit him. Daniel Pulley had a house in Queen Street no. 109[362] where he lived with one 'slave'. After his death, items auctioned off from his house fetched 39.6 Porto Novo pagodas.[363] Krieger further notes that there were 5 mirrors and 9 paintings, diverse pieces of furniture and books in the house, indicating Daniel Pulley's rank in society. In addition, he seemed to have had a house in Tanjore according to the Danish archives, as well as one in Poreiar.

His son, Johan (John) Daniel Pulley appears to have inherited his father's job at the Black Court. We can follow the family of Daniel Pulley for another forty years. Apparently, Christian Daniel Pulley's granddaughter, Gnanammal, was not treating her husband, Salomon, well. Here is an amusing petition from Salomon to Governor Rehling:[364]

> My humble petition to the respected Governor, Colonel and Knight of Dansborg, Johan Rehling at Tharanganpadi
>
> I, the undersigned humble man, would like to request your permission to present to you the torture committed by my wife Gnanammal and my son, Johan Daniel. From the day I married Gnanammal, the daughter of the interpreter Johan Daniel, I have been treated with frequent disrespect by her, and she has been a disobedient wife. All the people in this town who know me know this for a fact. You are aware these facts very well yourself and have ordered her to leave this town and go to her husband's place in Tanjore. However, under the pretence of obeying your command, she nevertheless did not follow me to Tanjore. I have tolerated her strange and rough behaviour so far. Despite my efforts through letters and through my son, Johan Daniel, to improve her behaviour, her heart has hardened. Despite this, I have found a suitable girl from my own family circle as a wife for him. She has refused

this offer and has found another girl of her own choice. Until this day, it is unusual, either in this society or in other countries, to carry out a marriage and other vital functions without the presence of the father. You can easily see the mad deeds and acts against the accepted customs of the temple (church) and the society carried out by the above-mentioned Gnanammal. Even though I would like to live with her in peace, she continues to be hostile.

Therefore, my humble request to you, Sir, who know the customs and traditions of the Tamil society, is to take pity on me and force her to live with me in peace during my old and weakened age; otherwise, please ask her to pay me the Rs. 500 that I spent on my marriage and towards the jewellery I gave her; and ensure that my son, Johan Daniel, carry out the daily rites after my death and distributes food and clothing. I am confident that you will heed my kind request.

Yours humbly
Salomon

Tharangampadi
10 Ayppasi 1840.

Interestingly, the year after, in 1841, Gnanammal and her sister, Mariyammal complained to Governor Tiemroth about the waterlogging of their rice fields[365] at Mottukannamoolai[366] due to the malicious destruction of the water banks. We do not know what result came of this complaint or whether she ever reconciled with her husband.

On a recent visit to Poreiar, I went looking for the grave of Daniel Pulley. Much to my surprise, I found a recent grave of a Daniel Pulley (born: 1893, died 1981). With an unusual name like this, it is tempting to assume that this grave belongs to a family member of the old Daniel Pulley.

If we continue along Queen Street, we reach Goldsmith Street towards the east and Mosque Street towards the west. Most of the Muslim population lived in the north-western part of the town, close to the mosque. The origin of the Muslim community dates to the 14th century. There is a walled compound containing two mosques, the tomb of a saint and housing for mosque employees and a Muslim cemetery.[367] Two pirs,[368] Sheikh Ismail Sadaat Valiyullah and Seiyadina Saiyad Sahib Sadat Valiyullah, whose tomb is in the old mosque, are celebrated in three chariot festivals, where the chariots symbolising the two pirs are drawn through the streets of Tranquebar in May or June[369] [Schönbeck 2012].

9

Pietism, Printing and Peccadillos

We make a U-turn on Queen Street and trace our steps back until we come to Admiral Street. Engelhart, in his history of the East Indian Establishments, says that the street was named after Admiral Ove Gedde. A few metres down the road (towards the west), we see on the right side, a vast and impressive complex that houses the abode of Bartholomæus Ziegenbalg and the old prayer hall.

Visitors to Tranquebar today may be taken by mild surprise when they see two old churches on the main street, which is King Street, right across

Fig. 9.1: Ziegenbalg's house and Prayer Hall on Admiral Street. Ziegenbalg's house is a museum today and the rest of this complex functions as a school. It has been here since 1741 (photo: P. S. Ramanujam).

from each other. Even before the arrival of the missionaries, the Zion Church in Tranquebar was built for employees of the Danish East India Company. At the same time, the locals remained 'heathens'. Pietist movements arose in Europe during the late 17th century. Frederik IV of Denmark had for a long time considered sending evangelical missions to East India to convert the heathens to Christianity. He encountered Professor August Hermann Francke of Halle in Germany through his pastor, Franz Julius Lütkens. As no suitable persons could be found in Denmark, the king requested Francke to look for appropriate people in Germany. Francke found two young and energetic missionaries who volunteered to shoulder this task.

Bartholomæus Ziegenbalg was born on 24th June 1683 to Catharina and Bartholamæus Sr. in Pulsnitz in Germany. He lost both his parents at a young age. Of his father, it is said that, one time when he was gravely ill, a fire broke out in the town and threatened the house where he lay. He was put into a coffin, which he had in readiness, and was transported to the open-air market place where he died[370] [Singh]. We do not know whether this is true. The young Ziegenbalg stayed with his sister, attended the Gymnasium (high school or pre-university) in Görlitz and was very interested in theology. Soon, he encountered Francke, who advised him to continue his studies in Berlin. After finishing his studies in Berlin, he found that the University of Halle provided him with the best opportunities for his theological studies. He was persuaded by Francke to take up the profession of a preacher of the Gospels in pagan countries. It was about this time that the request from Lütkens (and Frederik IV) came for him to serve in a foreign country. He was to be accompanied by his school and university friend, Heinrich Plütschau. They left Berlin in October 1705 for Copenhagen. They had no idea where they were being sent to, but they both took up learning Portuguese. Just before they were due to leave Copenhagen, they were told that their destination was Tranquebar. They sailed off on the 29 November on board the ship *Sophia Hedewig*. In April 1706, they reached the Cape of Good Hope and arrived in Tranquebar on the 9 July 1706. When they arrived, they received no support from the Danish merchants and officials for their undertaking. In fact, no one took care of them when they disembarked from the ship. For several hours, they were left standing at the bazaar in Tranquebar in the hot sun. Finally, in the evening, Attrup, who was secretary to the government, took pity on them and lodged them

Fig. 9.2: Ziegenbalg's baptismal font, which is now in the Ziegenbalg Museum, Tranquebar. Made of tin, this was probably donated to the German Church in 1663. Engraved are the words: 'Lasset die kindlein zu mir kommen und wehret ihnen nicht, denn solcher ist das Reich Gottes' ('Let the little children come to me, and forbid them not, for of such is the kingdom of heaven'), Math 19:14. (Photo: P. S. Ramanujam).

with his father-in-law. However, this reception did not discourage them at all; they were totally determined to be missionaries in the unknown land.

Ziegenbalg says the following about the people among whom he had come to live: 'The inhabitants consist partly of white Europeans, partly of half-white Portuguese, partly of yellow Moors, but principally of black-brown Malabarians.[371] I do not exactly know the number of these various inhabitants, but I must say that Tranquebar is a well-peopled town, swarming with old and young, especially as its trade attracts men of all nationalities both on sea and land' [Fenger]. He comments that the Tamils write 'their books and letters with an iron stylus on palm-leaves' and are experts in many trades and handicrafts as well as almost all sciences.

Ziegenbalg says that the Malabarians understood that there was only one Supreme Being. When one of the natives, who was well versed in the Hindu religion, was asked why they worshipped many gods when they knew so well that there was but one, he replied: 'A schoolmaster would prove himself very perverted, if he began teaching his scholars to read by giving them a difficult poem; he must begin with the A, B, C. So, it is with the knowledge of God; one must begin with the little gods and rise step by step, till one reaches the highest Being...' [Fenger].

The two missionaries started by learning the common languages – Portuguese and Tamil, the former because of the presence of a substantial number of Portuguese descended from European fathers and Indian mothers. According to Fenger: 'Their colour varied according to their degree of distance from European blood. Those natives who had adopted the European dress and Portuguese language, because many generations back they may have descended from a European, were called black Portuguese'. It was not easy for the missionaries to learn Tamil because there was no printed and written assistance. After several months, they found an old Malabarian schoolmaster, who was willing to teach them Tamil. The missionaries sat with the children on the floor and traced out their letters in sand, just as the children did. Although they learnt the letters and words, they did not understand their meaning, as the schoolmaster could not translate them into Portuguese (which they were now accustomed to). Later, they found Aleppa, a 46-year-old who was proficient in several Indian languages, as well as in Portuguese, Danish, German and Dutch. Over the course of two years, starting in October 1706, they learnt the language from him. They read and translated Tamil manuscripts every day. Ziegenbalg notes that during the three years they were in India he scarcely read a book in German or Latin. By 1707, he was already proficient enough to write books in Tamil. The Tamil books he collected can still be seen at Halle in Germany. He divided these books into four classes – the first consisting of 14 books written by himself, the next of 21 books written by Roman Catholic missionaries, the third of 119 books written by Hindus and the last class consisted of 14 books written by Muslims. Since it would have taken a long time to copy the books, he bought them, mostly from Brahmins who were willing to sell them for a trifle. With the help of the teacher, Aleppa, a native poet and a Malabar writer, Ziegenbalg now produced a dictionary containing 20,000 words and he completed it in two years. The dictionary consists of one column in Tamil characters, one column in Roman to aid pronunciation, and a third with the meaning of the word in German. The dictionary consists of historical, theological, philosophical, medical and philological terms. After four years, this had grown to 40,000 words. He also made a poetic dictionary consisting of 17,000 words. The purpose of this dictionary was to help him understand the 'worship of the heathen from their own books', and to oppose their belief. He concluded that the difference between the daily language and the poetic language was like the difference between German and Latin.

The missionaries began to catechise the people in January 1707. As Ziegenbalg was the one more fluent in Tamil, he concentrated on this while Plütschau focused on Portuguese. They translated several hymns and prayers into both languages, using European melodies. The first baptism took place in May 1707. The missionaries now started contemplating the construction of their own church. The first stone for the Jerusalem Church was laid in June and was consecrated on 4 August 1707.[372] Before the end of the year, both a Danish-Portuguese and a Tamil school were erected.

This very idea of teaching the idol-worshippers to read and write was not welcomed by the Danish officers since the commandant appointed by the Company, like many of the Danish soldiers, could not read or write [Olsen], and many could not even sign their names (most managed to write just their initials). Even one of the early governors, Eskild Andersen Kongsbakke, copied his name after someone wrote it for him. There was one other catch: The mission was a private project of the king's (Frederik IV), and the East India Company had not been notified that missionaries were being sent to Tranquebar. The commandant obeyed the company laws –not the king's.[373] The persecution of the missionaries increased steadily.

Uneasy with the prospect of the missionaries gaining the upper hand, Commandant Hassius imprisoned Ziegenbalg in the fort for four months from November 1708 onwards. Ziegenbalg found it necessary to appeal to the king for protection, not only for himself but also for his congregation, which had grown to about 100 members. Just before going into prison, Ziegenbalg had started to translate the New Testament into Tamil. However, he was now denied even pen, ink and paper to continue his work in prison. Despite this, he did not nurture any hatred toward the commandant, but invited him and his wife to come and visit him in prison. Soon after this, he was released.

Obstacles continued to be put in the path of the mission's work, and Ziegenbalg himself decided to travel to Europe in 1714. The commandant, Hassius, and the council became very uneasy at the prospect of Ziegenbalg complaining to the king about the persecution and offered him a peace treaty. Ziegenbalg also wanted to inform Francke of the situation in India and of his own position. He left on 30 October 1714 aboard the ship *Frederick IV* and landed at Bergen in Norway on 1 June 1715. In order to keep his knowledge of Tamil fresh in memory, Ziegenbalg had Peter Maleiappen to accompany him. They met with the king. Ziegenbalg returned to Germany and spent most of his time in Halle, marrying Maria Dorothea Salzmann, who was one of his former pupils. During this stay, the Danish king made him Provost to the Tranquebar Mission. Ziegenbalg returned to Madras in August 1716.

We now travel 300 years forward in time. During his stay in Germany, Rev. Dr. Christian Samraj, Ambassador for Overseas Affairs of the TELC-India was given, around Christmas of 2014, a guest-book from 1713.

The book was presented by Mrs. Schott of the Emmrich family. During their visit to Germany in 1715, Ziegenbalg and Maleiappen stayed with this family as guests and took time to write in the guest book. For the first time, one can see Ziegenbalg's and Maleiappan's Tamil writing. Christian Samraj donated the book in January 2019 to the Ziegenbalg Museum in Tranquebar, which runs under the guidance of Jasmin Eppert.

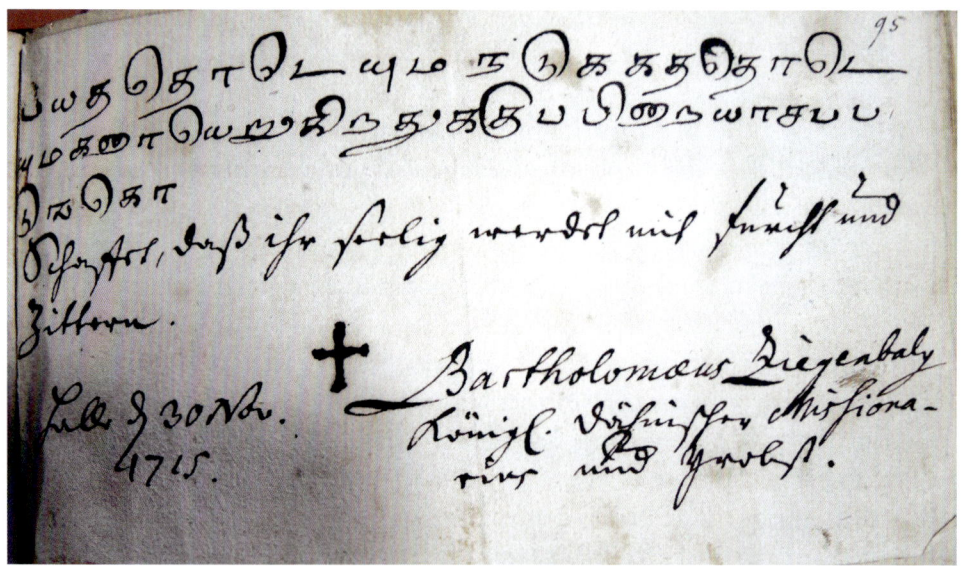

Fig. 9.3: Ziegenbalg and Maleiappen's observations in the guest book (Ziegenbalg writes: 'பயத்தொடெயும் நடுக்கதொடெயும் கரையெறுகிறதுக்குப் பிறையாசைப் படுங்கொ – Schaffet, dass ihr seelig werdet mit Furcht und Zittern: Bartholomæus Ziegenbalg, Königl. Dänischer Missionarius und Probst, Halle d. 30 Nov. 1715'. (Philip 2:12)) ('Continue to work out your salvation with fear and trembling'). (Photo: P. S. Ramanujam).

During 1709 a ship carrying much-needed funding, as well yet another missionary, Johann Ernst Gründler, arrived in Tranquebar. The day after his arrival, Gründler watched a Malabar meal for the first time: 'The children sat on the ground with their feet crossed under them. Each one had an earthen bowl before him, filled with rice boiled in water, and on it lay a small baked fish... Instead of a knife, they made skilful use of their two first fingers... They lie on a mat on the ground and require neither coverlet nor pillow. The same piece of linen with which boys and men cover the lower parts of the body by day serves them as a cover by night' [Fenger].

Commenting on the culture of the locals, Ziegenbalg observes: 'Most Christians in Europe suppose the Malabarians to be a very barbarous people, but this arises from the Europeans who have been amongst them not understanding their language, so that they have not been able to read their books, but have drawn their conclusions from outward appearances. I must acknowledge that, when I first came amongst them, I could not imagine that their language had proper rules, or that their life had the laws of civil order, and I took up all sorts of false ideas about their actions, as

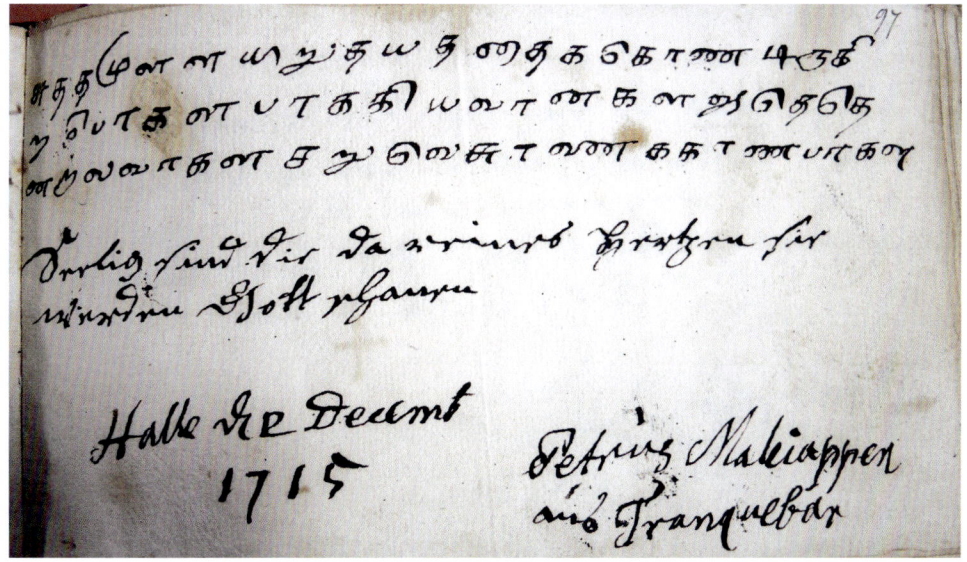

Fig. 9.4: Maleiappen writes: 'சுத்தமுள்ளயிறுதயத்தைக் கொண்டிருக்கிற பேர்கள் பாக்கியவான்கள் அதெதென்றால் சறுவெசுரனைக் காண்பார்கள் *– Seelig sind die da reines hertzen sie werden Gott schauen: Petrus Maleiappen aus Tranquebar, Halle d. 2 Decemb. 1715'. (Math. 5:8) (Blessed are the pure in heart: for they shall see God). (Photo: P. S. Ramanujam).*

if they had neither a civil nor a moral law – but as soon as I had gained a little acquaintance with their language and could talk to them about various subjects, I began to have a much better opinion of them and, when at last I was able to read their own books, I found that the Malabarians discussed the same philosophical subjects as the Savants of Europe and that they had a regular written law wherein all theological subjects were treated of and demonstrated. This surprised me extremely, and I was delighted to be thoroughly instructed in their heathenism from their own writings' [Fenger].

Ziegenbalg was interested from the beginning in imparting education to the local children. In 1711, the Society for Promoting Christian Knowledge had offered to provide and maintain one or more charity schools in Madras through the agency of the Danish missionaries. The Madras Government supported these initiatives. It was resolved to establish a charity school for Protestant children, giving them food and free education. 'While they are entertained in the school, the boys shall be taught to read, write, cast accounts, or what they may be further capable of, and the girls shall be instructed in reading and the necessary parts of house-wifery'.[374]

Ziegenbalg continued his translation of the New Testament and completed the project on 21 March 1711. By this time, the work of the missionaries had aroused great sympathy in Denmark, Germany and England. The English were the first to send a printing press to the mission. The Society for Promoting Christian Knowledge (SPCK) became an important actor. The Society dispatched a printing press with Roman letters and a trained printer, Jónas Fincke, to Tranquebar during the spring of 1711. But the ship veered off course to Brazil, where it was captured and plundered and Fincke was arrested. The ship, together with Fincke, was released afterwards, but he then contracted a violent fever and died at the Cape of Good Hope. The printing press, however, reached India safely during August 1712. Fortunately, one of the soldiers in Tranquebar had some knowledge of printing. The missionaries soon started printing books in Portuguese.

The German friends of the Mission promptly supplied them with a printing press in Tamil, mostly with funds collected in Halle. The Germans, with no knowledge of Tamil, managed to fabricate Tamil fonts, and the first part of the New Testament was printed by them. Johann Berlin, Johann Gottlieb Adler and his 14-year-old brother were sent to

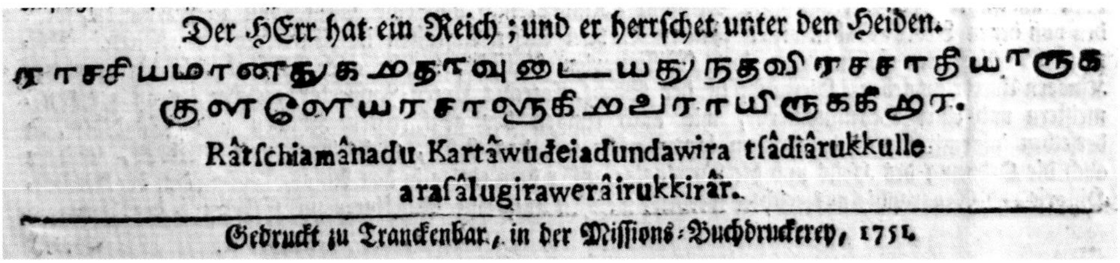
Der HErr hat ein Reich; und er herrschet unter den Heiden.

Râtschiamânadu Kartâwudeiadundawira tsâdiârukkulle arasâlugirawerâirukkirâr.

Gedruckt zu Tranckenbar, in der Missions-Buchdruckerey, 1751.

Fig. 9.5: At the end of each report from the Mission, the New Testament is cited in German and Tamil. This one is from 1751. (RA, Missionskollegiet og Direktionen for Vajsenhuset 1738-1808). (Photo: P. S. Ramanujam).

Tranquebar to help with the printing. Adler served for many years as the letter-founder and mechanic, as the fonts sent from Europe were too large. Since getting paper from Europe proved expensive, a paper mill was set up at Poreiar. The king of Denmark provided much needed monetary support. Frederik IV, saddened by the missionaries' reports of their ill-treatment, also sent orders to the Commandant and Council of Tranquebar not to use force or severity towards the missionaries, but to help them in every way. The first part of the New Testament, including the Gospels and the Acts of the Apostles, was printed using the early types, while the remaining books were printed with smaller letters during 1715. Ziegenbalg now started translating the Old Testament. He did not live to complete this; instead, it was finished by his compatriot, Benjamin Schulze.

Ziegenbalg corresponded regularly with the natives; in three months, he had received 55 letters, which he put together and dedicated to Crown Prince Christian (later Christian VI), and he soon added another 44 letters to his collection. Plütschau returned to Germany in 1711 and became a pastor in Beyenflieth in Holstein.

As early as 1710, the missionaries corresponded copiously with the Francke Foundations. This correspondence was later published under the name of 'Der Königlich dänischen Missionarien aus Ost-Indien eingesandter ausführlichen Berichten erster Theil, Halle 1710'. After the death of Francke in 1725 followed another publication, 'Halle Reports'[375] (Hallesche Berichte), covering the period up until 1772.[376] Seventeen volumes of the Halle Reports, each containing more than 1,000 pages holding a wealth of information, were published. The material sent from Tranquebar to Halle was censored and edited, and many footnotes were included. From 1770 onwards, a new series was started under the name of 'Neuere

Geschichte der Evangelischen Missionsanstalten zu Bekehrung der Heiden in Ostindien' ('Recent History of the Evangelical Mission Institutions for the Conversion of the Heathens in the East Indies'). The publications continued under the name of 'Missionsnachrichten der ostindischen Missionsanstalt zu Halle' ('News from the East Indian Mission to Halle') until 1880. These reports contain letters, sermons, diaries, travelogues, reports on missionary work and general reports pertaining to India. The country's topography, the nature of the landscape and the soil, irrigation, nature of the vegetation, types of buildings, food, clothes and currency were described [Forchhammer]. The cultivation of different types of rice was of interest.[377] There is a description of the kingdoms and/or principalities of Thanjavur, Madurai, Gingee and their relations with each other.

Ziegenbalg immersed himself in understanding the local conditions. Because he knew the local language, Tamil, he was able to converse freely with the locals. His 'Genealogy of the Malabar Gods' attests to his scholarship. Ziegenbalg translated Needhi Venba, Konrai Vendan and Ulaga Needhi,[378] examples of moral literature in Taminadu. He realized that the European literature on India had not been well founded, mainly because of a lack of knowledge of the local languages. However, Francke was not interested in the local news. He wanted the missionaries to preach and convert the heathens [Lehmann] and Ziegenbalg's Indological work was not well appreciated.

The 'New Jerusalem' church built in 1707 was already too small. On the 9th February 1717, the foundation stone for a new church was laid, and 11th October 1718 the 'New Jerusalem' church was consecrated. The old church was given to the catechists and was also used for funerals. This building has since disappeared into the sea. As a political and diplomatic tour de force, the façade of the new building was ornamented with the monogram of Frederik IV. This church, with the monogram and the year of consecration, is still in use in King Street in Tranquebar.

The Royal Library in Copenhagen boasts several palm leaf manuscripts in Tamil ascribable to Ziegenbalg. Ziegenbalg also collected Tamil literature and sent the manuscripts to Halle in Germany.[379] He had a library of Tamil manuscripts, called 'Bibliotheca Malabarica'.[380] Ziegenbalg's health started to fail during the last months of 1718; on 10th February 1719, he gave up the superintendence of the Mission, the accounts and documents to Gründler. He died in his armchair on 23 February 1719. Gründler continued for a year, but suffered severe bouts of diarrhoea and died on 19 March 1720. They are buried on either side of the altar in the New Jerusalem Church.

Ziegenbalg and his wife, Maria Dorothea Salzmann, had three sons. The eldest, Ernst Gottlieb Ziegenbalg, born in 1716, became a professor of mathematics at the University of Copenhagen, and he died in Copenhagen in 1758; the second son, Johan Christian Lebrecht Ziegenbalg, was born in 1718 and died in 1719 in Tranquebar; he was buried at the New Jerusalem Church; the third son, Bartholomæus Lebrecht Ziegenbalg, was born in 1719,[381] became an employee of the Danish East India Company and served for many years both in Tranquebar and Serampore. After the death of Ziegenbalg, Maria Dorothea Salzmann married Oluf Lygaard and moved to Denmark, and after the death of Lygaard she moved to Flensburg in Germany.[382]

The work of the missionaries continued, all of them being selected by Francke's Foundation in Halle. After the elder Francke had died, his son took his place. Benjamin Schulze, who succeeded Ziegenbalg, was the first missionary to settle down in Madras [Muthiah]. Johann P. Fabricius, who in turn succeeded Schulze, started printing in Vepery, Madras, with a printing press looted from the French in Pondichery by the English. Muthiah reports that, in 1766, Fabricius expanded the press with another printing press, possibly acquired from Tranquebar, with fonts cast in Halle. This wing of the Vepery Press later developed into the SPCK Press and then into the CLS Press of today. Gründler also visited Madras and was permitted to establish two charity schools – one in the 'White Town' and the other in 'Black Town'. However, neither of these schools was successful. The Vepery Anglo-Vernacular School was started by Schulze and is known today as the Fabricius School (Muthiah). After the printing press was established in Tranquebar, the missionaries printed annual reports and sent them to Halle and Copenhagen.

Johann Gerhard König (1728–1785) was a botanist and physician born in 1728 in Ungerhof in Polish Livland. He was a private pupil of Carl von Linné (1707-1778) in 1757 and lived in Denmark from 1759 to 1767. From 1773 to 1785, he worked as a naturalist for the Nawab of Arcot in India. He was in Tranquebar with the Danish medical mission from 1773 to 1785. In 1773, he received a Doctor's degree in absentia from the University of Copenhagen. As naturalist to the Nawab of Arcot, he

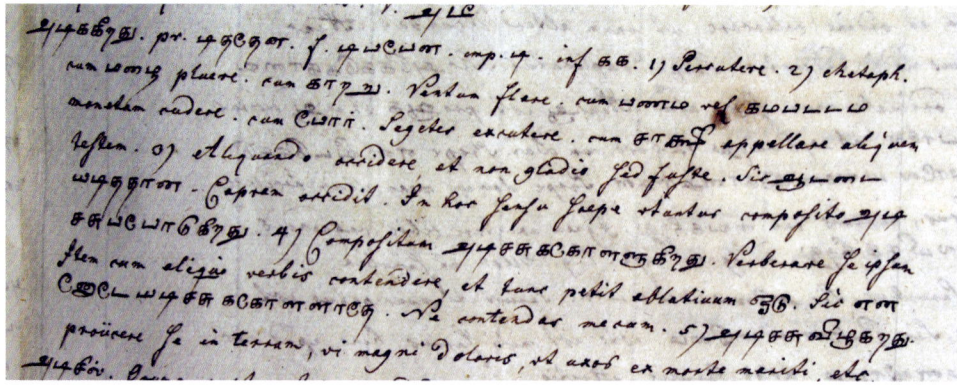

Fig. 9.6: A part of the Tamil-Latin Lexicon (RA, Det kgl. Ostindiske Guvernement, Kolonien Trankebar, 1776-1778), (Løbenr. 1450c). (Photo: P. S. Ramanujam).

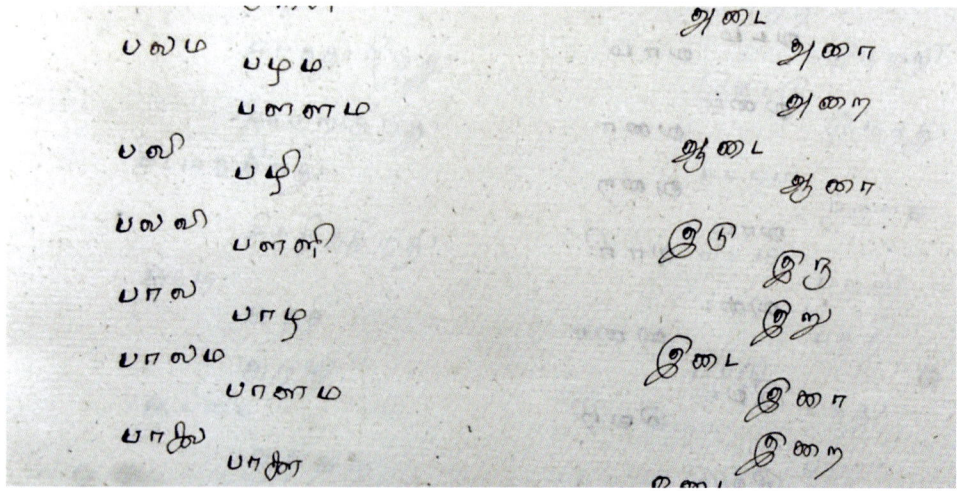

Fig. 9.7: The picture shows words, which have a similar pronunciation, but very different meaning.

embarked on a voyage to the mountains north of Madras and to Ceylon, and he later published a description of this in a Danish scientific journal. He started his 'medical voyage' to 'discover' different disease-curing plants and herbs with the help of Indian doctors, covering the areas from 'the mountains north to Madras and to Ceylon', and published his findings in a Danish scientific journal. In 1778, König was transferred to a post with the British East India Company where he remained until his death, undertaking several scientific journeys and working with notable scientists, such as William Roxburgh. He died in Jagannathapuram near Kakinada in 1785. König compiled a Tamil-Latin encyclopaedia, containing several thousand words.

He described many plants used in Indian medicine. An indispensable ingredient in the South Indian kitchen, curry-leaves[383] (*Murraya koenigii*) is named after him [wikipedia.org]. He bequeathed his collections and manuscripts to Sir Joseph Banks, and these are now at the British Museum (Natural History), where they have remained unpublished. Lehmann writes that his missionary work was a failure: 'Dr. Koenig travelled out in 1768. On the way, he lost his wife and married the widow of a Danish preacher. He was a botanical expert but knew less about the practice of medicine, least of all surgery. The missionaries complained: 'the circumstances of our doctor are depressing and trying'; for the doctor withdrew himself more and more from the Germans, never appeared in any church, did not even send greetings for the New Year and towards the last, he wrote poisonous letters' [Lehmann].

Christoph Samuel John (1747-1813) was a missionary who succeeded König in 1771. John arrived in Tranquebar in June 1771 and died there in 1813. As instructed by König, he set to work collecting and preserving samples, which he packed and forwarded to William Roxburgh. He advocated the use of Indian derivatives and extracts of *Bassia Butyracea* (*Polyandria Monogynia*), *Bassia Longifolia*[384] etc., which were of economic interest. He took an interest in Indian fish. Employing Indian professional painters, he collected many samples in jars and illustrations in books, and sent them to Professor Marcus Eliezer Bloch in Berlin. Based on the data and information received from India, he published 12 volumes on the natural history of fish. He also helped Professor Johann Reinhold Forster in Halle, who was interested in snakes, snakebites and the antidotes prescribed by the Brahmins. In the Proceedings of the Trankebar Society (unpublished), he proposed the establishment of a botanical garden in Tranquebar, and he also gave several descriptions of Indian snakes.

John received an honorary doctorate in 1795 for his studies in Natural History. He was renowned for his collection of shells and the botanical garden he had laid out in the mission; however, he failed to persuade the Danish governor to let him create a similar garden in the town. He was instrumental in setting up an integrated school for European and Tamil children in 1779, and advocated similar schools wherever the Danish

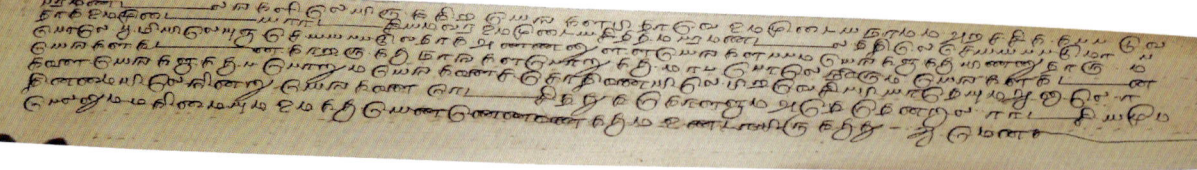

Fig. 9.8: The Lord's prayer in Tamil and Telugu on palm leaves, probably collected by Benjamin Schulze (Royal Library, Copenhagen). (Photo: P. S. Ramanujam).

Halle Mission worked. John mentions that Engelhart taught mathematical sciences in his school, while Johan Peter Rottler taught botany and religion and that there was an artist and a piano teacher in his school.[385] John published a book on Indian civilisation in London in 1813, which examined the traditional Indian school system. He also translated Athichudi, Muthurai and Konraivendan of Avvaiyar into Danish. He is buried in the New Jerusalem Church.

Johan Peter Rottler was another important missionary. He was born in Strasbourg in 1749. He was enrolled at the age of 17 at Strasbourg University and studied there for 9 years. He arrived in Tranquebar on 5 August 1776. Within a year, he was able to hold his first sermon in Tamil. In 1779, he married a Dutch lady who was the widow of a ship's captain. His interest in botany had been so vigorous that he made 'botanical excursion' around the 'Tranquebar countryside and as far away as Ceylon' to collect Indian medicinal books, formulations, drugs and medicines. He published descriptions of new species in European journals and verified the names of plants collected by two other members of the mission – Johann Klein and Benjamin Heyne. He served in Tranquebar until 1803 and then moved to Madras, working for the Madras Mission. He worked as a chaplain and secretary to the female asylum (Women's Hospital). During a short period when he was cut off from missionary work, he wrote 'A Dictionary of the Tamil and English Languages', containing the names of many South Indian plants. He became a missionary in 1812 and oversaw a small congregation at Black Town, Madras. He took over the Vepery Mission again in 1817 and remained there for the next 18 years. He died on 24 January 1836 and was buried in the Vepery Mission churchyard [Stansfield]. Thus, he worked for 60 years in Tamil Nadu. He collected more than 2,000 plants and sent them to Europe. All three of these missionaries – John, Klein and Rottler – received doctorates for their fieldwork [Krishnarao]. Rottler bequeathed his books, manuscripts and herbarium to the Vepery Mission [Stansfield]. Subsequently, the books were sent to the Madras Medical College, and the herbarium to King's College, London, from whence, in 1872, they were transferred to the Royal Botanic Gardens in Kew. According to Rottler's manuscript catalogue, there were 5,000 items in the collection.

Johann Gottfried Klein also made positive contributions to rationalism in Tranquebar. He was born in Tranquebar in 1766. His father, Jacob Klein, was a Royal Danish Missionary and his mother, Anna Dorothea Obuch, was the daughter of another Royal Danish Missionary in Tranquebar. Johann Klein was sent to Germany at the age of 11 for his studies and, after studying medicine in Copenhagen in Denmark, returned to Tranquebar in 1791. He started assisting at the maternity hospital at King Street in Tranquebar. There are supposed to be about 700 of Klein's plants at the Willednow Herbarium in Berlin. Klein had collected the specimens between 1792 and 1817, travelling to Gingee in 1792, to Tanjore in 1793 and to Ceylon in 1796. He also collected many plants from Tirunelveli and in the mountains around Courtallam [Stansfield].

After Ziegenbalg, Christian Frederick Schwartz was probably the most remarkable person in the history of the Tranquebar Mission. Schwartz was born on 26 October 1726, in Sonnenburg, Germany. He came to Halle in 1746, where he met Benjamin Schulze, who had just returned from Tranquebar. Schwartz learnt Tamil from Schulze. He arrived at Tranquebar in July 1750 and delivered his first sermon in Tamil before the end of the year. For the first ten years, he led a quiet life in Tranquebar. In 1762, Schwartz first went to Tanjore and then to Trichinopoly. At the time, the town was under the control of a Nawab to whom the King of Tanjore paid tributes. Most importantly, there was an English garrison, and Schwartz was determined to help them. He was asked to conduct public worship for the English on Sundays, and at the same time he did not neglect the Portuguese and the Tamil congregations. Later, with support from the Nawab, a church was built within the fort in May 1766. Schwartz was content with very little for himself. An Englishman, William Chambers, who visited him, says:

> 'Certainly his dress was worn and of a very old-fashioned make, but in his whole appearance there was something exactly the reverse of what one could call dismal or repelling. Picture to yourself a well-grown man somewhat above middle height, holding himself naturally yet erect, of rather dark yet healthy completion, with black curly hair and a powerful manly glance expressing unaffected modesty, uprightness and benevolence, and then you have an idea of the impression which the first sight of Schwartz makes on a stranger. A platefull of rice, boiled after the fashion of the country with a few vegetables (curry) formed the daily meal to which he sat down with a cheerful countenance; and a piece of native cloth, dyed black, formed the materials of his dress for a year' [Fenger].

In 1769, Heider Ali dominated politics in South India. After the English had concluded peace with him, Schwartz went to Tanjore. On 30 April 1769, the King of Tanjore, Tulasi Raja, sent word to meet him. 'Then I was led through many dark passages to the King, who sat in a four-cornered space on a bed, which was made fast at the top so that he could rock himself. His servants were ranged at his feet on both sides. Opposite to him, at a distance of 10 or 12 feet, a chair was placed for me. The Persian interpreter said that the King had heard me very well spoken of and that he had sent for me on that account… I begged his permission to speak in Tamil' [Fenger]. A lengthy discussion of Christian doctrines took place. The king was delighted. After this, the king decided that Schwarz should remain by his side, and 'be his Padre'. The relations between the king, the Nawab and the English had soured, and there was a war. Tanjore was besieged during 1771. The king requested peace after the walls of the fort had been breached and, in exchange for peace, the king had to give up one his most important forts as well as considerable amounts of money. In 1772, Schwartz went again to Tanjore; the king wanted him to be his advocate with the English. In 1773, war broke out again between the Nawab and the English on one side, and Tulasi Raja on the other. The king was now taken prisoner. The Nawab held him as a prisoner for two and a half years and was determined to execute him. However, this was contrary to the policy of the English, and the king was eventually released. Schwarz tried very hard to convert the king to Christian beliefs, but to no avail. Nonetheless, it is said that Tulasi Raja remarked to General Munro that 'he was sure that Christianity was a thousand times better than idolatry' [Fenger]. From 1778, Schwarz took up permanent residence in Tanjore. During 1778, he visited Tirunelveli and baptised Clarinda, a Marathi Brahmin married to an English officer. Clarinda erected a small church in Palayamkottai, which was consecrated by Schwarz in 1785.

When his end was near, Tulasi Raja, who had adopted a nine-year-old child, sent for Schwarz and said: 'this is not my son but yours; you must be his guardian and protector' [Fenger]. The king's brother, Amarda Singh,[386] agreed in this. Tulasi Raja died in January 1787. Amarda Singh, who ascended the throne, was in favour of the Mission. However, Schwarz felt that the life of the child was in danger and sent him to the care of the British in Madras. This child was Serfoji II, who ascended the throne in 1798. Serfoji called Schwarz his

Fig. 9.9: Painted glass portrait of Christian Frederik Schwartz in St. Peter's Church, Tanjore. Schwarz is buried in this church with an epitaph coined by Raja Serfoji. Petronella Kohlhoff (born Thors) and her son, John Caspar Kohlhoff are buried next to Schwarz (photo: P. S. Ramanujam).

father and benefactor. By 1798, Schwarz's health was failing, and he died on 13 February 1798. Serfoji visited him several times and came to look at him before the coffin was closed; he remained present for the funeral. According to 'The Remains of the Rev. C. F. Schwartz': 'On the day following, between four and five in the afternoon, we committed his body to the grave we had made for him in the garden. In the village where Schwartz dwells, the Soetra Christians reside on one side, and the Pariar Christians on the other. The whole village is built around a spacious garden, within which are the dwellings of the Missionaries, the church and the English schools'. A granite stone with an inscription composed by Serfoji covers the grave in front of the altar in St. Peter's Church in Tanjore. This garden was given to Schwartz by Tulasi Raja. Schwartz, who lived to the age of 72 years, had spent 47 years in India.

There is also a magnificent painted glass window with a portrait of Schwartz on the sidewall of the altar in St. Peter's Church in Tanjore.

After the death of Schwartz, Serfoji was instrumental in erecting a monument in the Schwartz Church very close to the Brhadisvara Temple within the Sivaganga Little Fort in Tanjore, close to the Sivaganga Gardens. Initially, the church was a mud-walled Protestant church erected by Major Stevens. It was then called Christ Church. Serfoji II rebuilt the church with brick and plaster and named it after Rev. C.F. Schwartz. A marble sculpture in bas-relief showing the deathbed of Schwartz decorates the west wall of the church. Those surrounding the bed include Gerické, three students from the Schwartz School and two native attendants. Serfoji is shown grasping the hand and receiving the blessings of the dying Schwartz. The panel was sculpted by Flaxman.

Within the complex of St. Peter's Church, Tanjore, there are two magnificent buildings – a house in which Schwarz was supposed to have lived and a large church. Unfortunately, both buildings are now dilapidated. They have been used as schools; today, the church is used as a storeroom.

There is an interesting aside to the story of Schwarz. He was a confirmed bachelor. When he returned from a trip to Ceylon in 1760, he received a message that a wife from Copenhagen was awaiting him. There was another missionary, named John Balthasar Kohlhoff, living in Tranquebar. John Balthasar Kohlhoff was born on 15 November 1711, at Neuwarp in Pomerania and arrived in Tranquebar on 19 August 1737. His first marriage to Ms. Vosges produced two children. After he was widowed, he found it challenging to take care of his children. As there were no suitable ladies in Tranquebar, he thought of importing a pious lady from Denmark. Madam Zeglin (wife of Zeglin, who worked as a missionary in Tranquebar), who was helping Kohlhoff take care of the children, drew his attention to her relatives in Kolding and Sønderborg in the south of Jylland, Denmark. It was decided that two of her relations should come to Tranquebar, one to be the wife of Kohlhoff and the other to stay with the Zeglins. The ship's chaplain, Böhme, returning from Tranquebar, was put in charge of

Fig. 9.10: Schwartz's house (presumed) in dilapidated condition (photo: P. S. Ramanujam).

the project. Zeglin's relations refused the offer, and Kohlhoff was willing to forget the whole affair. However, Böhme managed to find and send two girls, Petronella Thorsen (called Pernille Thors) as a wife for Kohlhoff, and Anne Sophie Pap, as a wife for Schwarz under the care of a mission assistant, Bliesner, and his wife. When Kohlhoff heard that Böhme was selecting a wife for him, he immediately responded by forbidding this; however, the letter probably arrived after the girls had left. The Bliesners were clearly not very happy with the conduct of Anne Sophie Pap. When the ship arrived in Tranquebar, they made a point of contacting the missionaries, saying that she was not worthy of entering the house of a missionary. However, Anne Sophie Pap denied all the allegations and said that Bliesner's wife had taken a dislike to her from the beginning. Schwarz had never expressed any desire to get married and, on his return from Ceylon, clearly indicated that he had not given Böhme a commission to choose any woman as a companion for him. In the end, Kohlhoff decided to marry Pernille Thors in September 1760. In the case of Anne Sophie Pap, Governor Forch inquired among the company's servants, whether any one of them was willing to take her in marriage. An old lieutenant, Haldager, was willing and the marriage was solemnised at the fort. However, Anne Sophie did not live long – she died during childbirth that year.

Kohlhoff died on 17 December 1790. He is buried in the New Jerusalem churchyard. Pernille Thors is buried at St. Peter's Church in Mission Street, Tanjore, under the name of Petronia Kohlhoff. On the gravestone, she is said to have been born in Copenhagen. Today, the Kohlhoff family is large and spread throughout the world with branches continuing in India. John Balthasar Kohlhoff had four children by Pernille Thors. The eldest son from this marriage, John Caspar Kohlhoff, was adopted and brought up by C. F. Schwarz. John Caspar Kohlhoff is also buried at St. Peter's Church, Tanjore. Their third son, Daniel Frederick Kohlhoff, served as Chief Secretary to Serfoji Raja.

Continuing the commentary on the mission, the next prominent missionary who deserves to be mentioned is Johann Philipp Fabricius. His talent lay in languages. He came to Cuddalore at the age of 29 on 28 August 1740. He settled down in Madras in 1742. He seems to have mastered literary Tamil and the colloquial language to a high degree of perfection, and he is famous for his work on a Tamil-English dictionary. The first Malabar-English Dictionary was printed in 1779. It contained 9,000 words. Rottler expanded it to 37,000 words, and Winslow included 67,000 words in his revision. These are available, on the internet at http://dsal.uchicago.edu/dictionaries/fabricius and at http://dsal.uchicago.edu/dictionaries/winslow. An interesting footnote here is that 'On the 18th of February 1753, they (Margaret Maskelyne and Robert Clive) were married in St. Mary's Church by the Reverend Mr. Fabricius, a Danish Missionary, who was officiating after the sad death of the Company's Chaplain' [Reid].

After the last Halle missionary, A. F. Caemmerer, the Leipziger Mission took over the mission's work in Tranquebar. After the sale of the colony to the British, the Anglican Society for the Propagation of the Gospel took control. After the Leipziger Mission, an independent Tamil Evangelical Lutheran Church (TELC) was formed and is still in charge today.

Generally, the work of the missionaries was viewed positively. However, the mission was not without blemish. Ziegenbalg himself took pride in smashing figures of local gods from temples.[387] Fenger also mentions: 'Ziegenbalg had put an end to the Missionary-Conference in a very arbitrary way and had taken complete possession of the money, which came from Halle, keeping it in a separate chest, which might be called a hellish, instead of Hallish chest, for it became a regular apple of discord' [Fenger]. Some of the missionaries took to drinking and fighting. The missionary

Martin Bosse had to be sent home for his drunkenness. Even the respected Benjamin Schultze was an illegal wine merchant and personally engaged in distilling alcohol.[388] The relation between the missionaries and the civil servants of the government was not cordial. The missionaries tried to be judges in cases involving adultery, fighting, drunkenness, theft, fights and insubordination of the ethnic Christians. However, the government refused to oblige them. There were several complaints from the citizens, such as people who had been beaten and/or suspended by the legs.[389] Christoph Samuel John and A. F. Caemmerer were accused of forcibly evicting people, destroying testaments and appropriating their properties[390] for the Bethlehem Church in nearby Poreiar. Tiagapen of Tranquebar complained that he was beaten and that a testament belonging to him was destroyed by John and Caemmerer. Peter Anker tried to suppress the increasing power of the missionaries. Later, government counsellor Lindgreen and bailiff Rehling accused the mission of forcing the inhabitants to draw testaments in its favour. Rehling remarked that it was impossible to believe such things could happen in the beginning of 19th century. Another example of alcohol misuse was the case of Lambert Christian Früchtenicht. His colleagues found it impossible to work with him. He was eventually imprisoned and forced to leave for Denmark. Such behaviour obviously did not endear the mission to the local population.

Another chaplain, Svend Bredstrup, wrote an article for the Tranquebar Society edited by Engelhart. It was never published, but the manuscript can be seen in the National Archives.[391] In it he characterises the Tamils as irresponsible, cowardly, deceptive and impassive. Any loss, whether substantial or not, did not seem to create an impression on them. They were indifferent whether it was just one pagoda, or 20 rigsdaler or a thousand that was lost. They were so indifferent that they would see someone die of hunger outside their door, rather than pity the person and give them some food. They could sit and talk for hours together, just to keep awake. When someone died in their family, people were paid to come and cry and howl for seven days.

Worse was the behaviour of Christian Christoffer Eibye, a sacristan at the Zion Church who arrived in Tranquebar in 1829. In 1837, Boanaventure David complains that his eldest son 'but now since this one weaks ago Mr. Eibye punished the boy very severely, and disappointed him of not coming any more to school; on account he neglected of coming to church on sunday time'.³⁹² On 9 September 1835, the 40-year-old Eibye married Lucil Götting, who was just over 18 years old. Ever since Eibye got married to Ms. Götting, Sophia Thaae wrote to Governor Mourier in 1836,³⁹³ he tried on all possible occasions to have a chat with her privately, which she refused. After a church service, he asked her whether he could visit her that night, which again she declined. In the evening, she retired to the topmost room of the house, with strict orders to the house servant to refuse entry to Eibye when he showed up. Eibye came to her place at about 10:15 that night after the lights were off, dressed only in his night-gown, and demanded that the servants open the door. The servant refused to let him in. Eibye lost a piece of the gown on this occasion. Eibye stood outside the door and shouted: 'This is Eibye. You know me well. Let me in'. Sophia Thaae, 32 years old, had been a widow for 4 years and lived in the house with three children. She requested the governor to stop Eibye from making advances to her. She writes that she does not want to pursue the issue in a court trial, as it would be shameful for Eibye, being a servant of the church. The Danish government was not happy with Eibye's work as a sacristan³⁹⁴ – but he continued to work as a clerk. Poor Lucil Götting!

The Zion Church
The Zion Church had several pastors from Denmark over the years, including Henning Munch Engelhart. Niels Studsgaaard Fuglsang, who succeeded Engelhart, studied Tamil and gathered many palm leaves in that language, which he eventually sold to the Royal Library in Copenhagen. The oldest palm-leaf collection is an Indian almanac from the year 1734.

The Catholic Church
Long before the Danes came to Tranquebar, a Catholic Church served the members of the large Indo-Portuguese congregation living in and around the town. Although Catholicism was prohibited in Denmark following the Reformation and up until 1849, the Catholic Church in Tranquebar thrived. The Catholic Chapel was served by the Jesuits. In fact, the Jesuits started a printing press in Cochin in 1577, and Tamil printing was established in 1673. (The first Tamil book was printed in Lisbon, Portugal, in 1554 (http://karkanirka.wordpress.com/2010/04/14/first_tamil_book/)). In the early years, this chapel was situated inside the Dansborg Fort [Frendrup]. The first church to be built under Danish rule was a proper Catho-

lic church in 1645. It was Willem Leyel who gave permission for the construction of this church, which was housed in the residence of Christian Pedersen Storm. The church was located just inside the town gate on the northern side. According to the census of 1790 and 1834, Catholics represented between 5 and 8% of the population.

When the Pietist missionaries arrived from Germany, conflicts arose between the missionaries and the Catholics. Ziegenbalg complained several times to the governor regarding the religious behaviour of the Catholics, such as using fireworks and conducting public processions and plays [Frendrup]. However, Ziegenbalg also had great respect for the Catholic mission because it allowed Indians to become missionaries. After the death of Ziegenbalg and the departure of Governor Hassius, the situation improved. The Jesuits were allowed to establish a Catholic cemetery in Poreiar. Several prominent persons married Catholics and moved into Tranquebar. Jean-Jaques Gautier, a governor from Chandernagore in Bengal, who had married a Catholic, could now settle in Tranquebar. Peter Herman Abbestée, who was Governor of Tranquebar, had a Catholic wife; however, their children were baptised Lutheran. Frantz Lichtenstein, who was a key actor in the caste conflicts during the late 18th century, was also married to a Catholic.

A new Catholic church was built outside the city limits of Tranquebar, and the old church remained closed until 1958 when it was handed over to the Theresa School. Until 2004, this served as a chapel. The building has since been pulled down, and a new school has been built in the area where the church and the churchyard stood. The schools now consist of St. John's Primary School for girls, St. Theresa's Girls' High School and St. Theresa's Teachers Training College. Board and lodging for the students are at Rehling's house on King Street.

There was also a small chapel devoted to Francis Xavier, south of Fort Dansborg on the south bank of the Uppanaru River.

The Moravian Brethren
While on the subject of missionaries, one should also mention the Moravian Brethren (Herrnhuters). A group of fourteen men led by Georg Johann Stahlmann arrived in Tranquebar 2 July 1760.[395] They established a typical settlement at the *Brüdergarten* (Garden of the Brethren). Oluf Maderup, a missionary at the Jerusalem Church, seems to have stated: 'I cannot de-

Fig. 9.11: The sad remnants of the Salomon Garden in Sathangudi. This garden was the place where the Moravian Brothers stayed and carried out their mission. They were sent from here to the Nicobar Islands to preach Christianity (photo: P. S. Ramanujam).

scribe how the Moravians have insinuated themselves in so short a time into the good will of Danes, French and even Hindus by their voluntary humility and angel-like conduct... If they were as pure in their doctrine and teaching as their life is outwardly to the eyes of the world, there would not be a sect or race to equal them in the whole of Asia'.[396] They were sent with the express purpose of preaching in the Nicobar Islands, with Tranquebar as their base. The relationship between the missionaries from Halle and the Moravian Brethren was anything but cordial. They bought a garden close to Poraiyar and planted trees, kept cattle, dug a well and planted rice while their artisans found plenty of work in Tranquebar [Lehmann]. All the members of the community, 14 of them, lived in the same house and ate at one table. At the end of 1767, 23 persons were living in the garden. According to Fenger, the Moravians made themselves general favourites in Tranquebar. Finally, they got passage on a ship bound

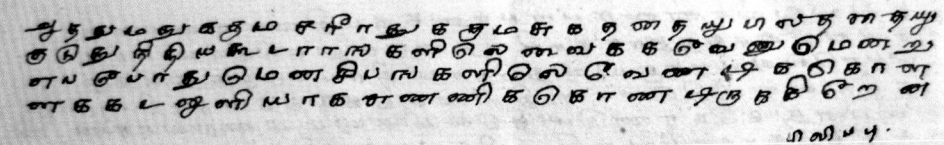

Fig. 9.12: Part of a letter by Philipp to Halle (ஆத்துமத்துக்கும் சரீரத்துக்கும் சுகத்தையும் பிலத்தையும் குடுத்து நித்திய கூடாரங்களிலெ வைக்க வேணுமென்று எப்போதுமென் சிபங்களிலெ வேண்டிக்கொள்ள கடனாளியாக எண்ணிக்கொண்டிருக்கிறேன் / பிலிப்பு). (Photo: P. S. Ramanujam).

for Sumatra, stopping over at the Nicobars. Eventually, the 'Brother-garden' at Sathangudi was abandoned (and sold in 1803), and the remaining Moravians left for Europe in 1801.

The Jesuits
In 1761, after Pondichery was taken by the English, about 8-10 Jesuits fled to Tranquebar [Fenger]. They soon acquired a piece of ground in Poreiar and rented a house, requesting the government to allow them to perform worship. This was refused, as the missionaries in Tranquebar objected. They then rented a house in Tranquebar and started a school. The Mission-College in Tranquebar did everything to stop this, too. However, as we have seen earlier, this did not prevent them from making astronomical observations, such as the transit of Venus across the Sun.

Indian Missionaries
The first Lutheran Indian Christian was in all probability Kanabadi (Ganapathi?) Wathiar.[397] He was the son of Ziegenbalg's Tamil teacher and belonged to the community of washermen. He was also a poet. The missionaries employed him in their school in 1709, when he was 24. He was well-versed in four languages as well as in Carnatic music. Against the wishes of his parents and relatives, he allowed himself to be baptised. He was firm in his new faith, but he returned to Hinduism after pressure from his family. The next person was Modaliapa, whom Ziegenbalg brought with him to Europe on his trip.

The missionaries from Halle had ordained several Indians as co-workers. The first ordination of a Tamil, Aaron, took place on 20 December 1733 [Lehmann] in the Jerusalem Church. Aaron was born in Cuddalore as the

Fig. 9.13: Portrait of Aaron (1698-1745), the first Tamil Missionary. Born into the Vellala caste, he was named Arumugam by his parents. In 1718, he converted to Christianity and was ordained as a minister in 1733 (Ostindische Berichte, Teil 6 (1754)).

son of Sokkanatha Pillai, in 1698 or 1699. The catechist Savarimuthu and the missionary Ziegenbalg influenced him greatly. There are a few letters written by him, which survive in the National Archives. Aaron died on 25 June 1745. The second Indian pastor was Diogo, who was born in a Catholic family in 1709 and died in 1781. There are also a few surviving letters from him in Tamil. The third pastor was Ambrose, who died in 1777. The fourth was Philipp, who was probably born in 1731. His Tamil name was Pulleimuttu. There is an exciting story of how he became a Christian. Apparently, a slave-trader abducted him at the age of ten. His mother was directed to Tranquebar in her search for him. When she saw the church, she was told that that was the House of God. She prayed to God to show her her child. She found him just as he was about to be dragged onto the ship. She went to the church and prayed again, promising that if the child were freed, she and her children would come to the church. She managed to get her child free, but forgot her promise, and instead she made an offering to the Hindu idols. Then, in a dream, she was reminded of her commitment, after which they converted to Christianity. Philipp died on 4 February 1788.

The fifth Indian to be ordained was Rajappen in 1778. However, all was not well with the Indian catechists and pastors. Lehmann writes: 'Catechist Muttiappan swindled others out of money and jewels. Another assistant had to be suspended because he had taken part in the slave traffic. Also, the 'blameless' pastors Diogo and Ambrosius gave cause for complaint. The famous catechist, Rajanaiken, who had brought hundreds to the church, had debts, mostly due to drinking' [Lehmann].

The name of Vedanayagam Sastri must be mentioned in this connection. He was educated by Schwarz and studied under John. He became the first Protestant poet in Tamil, writing more than 120 literary works. His works contained references to anatomy, botany, astronomy, geography and natural history. Later, he became a court poet under Serfoji II.

Before we leave Ziegenbalg's house, look at the facade of the old Prayer Hall; there is an inscription in Tamil: 'சூலை சக 17 ஏடு 41' *(July saka 1741)*; Saka 1741 would correspond to 1819. This inscription is not correct, but is a late addition. The building is from 1739-1741.[398]

*

We continue our stroll along Admiral Street towards the west and at the end of the street we turn left (south). This street, called Prints Christian Street, ends at King Street, where we turn left again (east) along King Street. We stop to admire the stately houses along the street. The magnificent pillared house on the right was built by the engineer Mathias Jürgen Mühldorff. Shaik Alladin's family owns this house now. Mühldorff was born in 1750 and arrived in Tranquebar on 23 July 1788 [Architectura 1987] as part of the engineer corps. Initially, he had a house on New Street (Nygade), which runs parallel to King Street on the south side, and in 1788, he constructed this house. As an engineer, he designed his own home. In 1790, Mühldorff, his wife, two children and two slaves lived here. His salary in 1791 was about one-fourth of that of the governor, Peter Anker.[399] Perhaps this was not enough for Mühldorff and family. 'Due to an unfortunate coincidence of circumstances, which made my husband owe money to the Royal Treasury' wrote his wife, Maria Barbara,

Fig. 9.14: Mühldorff's house, as it appeared in 2010. Mathias Jürgen Mühldorff (1750-1836) came to Tranquebar in 1778. He lived in this house until his death (photo: P. S. Ramanujam).

in 1809 to the king, 'his entire pension had to be paid back to the treasury. I tried my hand at a bit of trading, but this opportunity disappeared when Tranquebar surrendered (to the British). My husband's entire pension of 29 Porto Novo pagodas was quite insufficient even before. Please allow us at least two-thirds of the pension, so that we may live'.[400] The reason for this misery was that Mühldorff, who oversaw the administration of Tranquebar's new districts, owed more than 4,100 Tranquebar Courant to the Treasury. When confronted with the situation, he pledged his entire pension till the sum was paid off, driven by a sense of honour and forgetting that he had a wife and family to support. The Chamber of Commerce recommended to the king that Mühldorff be paid half the pension to support himself and his family against a mortgage of his houses, valued between 10,000 and 12,000 rdl.[401]

As an engineer, he redesigned Nygade, making it broader and thus turning it into one of the most elegant streets in Tranquebar. He was responsible for the construction of sluices and dams across the territory. He was also a stabilising factor in the government, assisting Governor Peter

Fig. 9.15: Ib Andersen's sketch of the garden entrance to Mühldorff's house (M/S Museet for Søfart, Helsingør, Denmark).

Anker in several situations, especially where caste conflicts were involved. The town entrance (Landporten) was designed and constructed by him. A similar portal – but smaller, was designed by him for his garden in 1791. It contained a puzzling inscription on the top: 'D. E. M. E. P.' [Kryger and Gasparski 2003]. He claimed that he was an illegitimate son of King Frederik V and that the letters above described the secret of his life. If one replaces the above letters with the next letters of the alphabet, the resulting 'E. F. N. F. Q.' forms a sentence in Latin: *'Ego Filius Naturalis Friderici Quinti'*, meaning 'I was the natural son of Frederik V'. Only DNA analysis of his descendants would be able to confirm this.[402] Mühldorff and his wife Maria Barbara Sundt had 14 children. It is said that several Anglo-Indian families are derived from them as well as several descendants in Australia.

According to a census of 1835, he was at that time still living in the house, with a daughter and a grandchild. He lived until the ripe old age of 86, having spent 58 years in Tranquebar, and he is buried in the churchyard in Nygade [Kryger and Gasparski]. He had the misfortune to see several of his children die, including one at the age of 12 who accidentally drowned in the river.

The large house across the street, popularly called Rehling's Mansion, was occupied by one of the later governors – Johannes Rehling. He did not build the house, but he bought it in 1823 and his family stayed there until the colony was sold to the English in 1845. Johannes Rehling was appointed colonel in 1834 and became governor in 1837. In 1833, on the occasion of Rehling's travel to Denmark with his family, several of the natives wrote a letter in Tamil expressing great sorrow.[403] He was apparently well-liked by the locals. Johannes Rehling died in 1841. His son, Otto Christian Rehling, was employed in the Danish government until 1845. After the sale of Tranquebar to the British, the family returned to Denmark. This is perhaps the stateliest mansion in town, valued at 2,000 rupees in 1834. In 1762, the building was owned by Hillaire Polycar Bourgine, it was then bought by Michael Sundt in 1772 and in 1784 Johan Carl Wilhelm von Braun bought the house. Today, the building is owned by the St. Theresa foundation.[404] The Rehlings, and the closely related Strickers and Tiemroths, continue to live in Denmark today.[405]

10

Philology comes to Town

In the 18th century, Tranquebar began to evolve as a hub of learning. After the arrival of the missionaries, Tranquebar, strangely enough, became more 'rationalised', with people like Christoph Samuel John beginning to collect local flora and fauna and literature. The Danish surgeon T. L. F. Folly likewise began to record the medical skills of the local Malabar doctors.[406] Scientific material collected by the Arabian expedition (more on this later) was sent to Tranquebar for conservation and repacking.[407]

Fig. 10.1: Rehling's house, where Rasmus Rask stayed. The first mention of the house is from 1762 and in 1818 governor Peter Hermanson bought the house. After the death of Peter Hermanson, Rehling, who later became governor, bought the house in 1824. After the death of Johannes Rehling, his widow continued to live there (photo: P. S. Ramanujam).

Fig. 10.2: Portrait of Rasmus Rask (1787-1832) with his signature. Rasmus Christian Rask, a self-taught philologist, developed a system for classifying the languages of the world, and in his quest for finding the mother of all languages he came to India before returning to Denmark ('Beretning om gravmælet over Prof. R. Rask', K. Gislason et al., 1842).

A remarkable person visited Tranquebar in 1823 during Rehling's period as head of the government (regieringsråd) and he stayed in this house. This was Rasmus Christian Rask, an unusual, self-taught philologist, who was interested in searching for the mother of all languages. He was also interested in the comparison and relationship between all the languages of the world and treated etymology at the same level as natural sciences. His theory on the origin of words in different languages depended on two concepts – the meaning of the word based on encyclopaedic connections and the explanation of the language based on grammatical connections.

Rasmus Rask was born on 22 November 1787 in the tiny village of Brændekilde close to the city of Odense in Denmark. His father, Niels Christian Hansen Rasch, was a tailor and very religious. He was married three times and fathered many children, but not many survived. His first wife, Gertrud Jørgensdatter, died a few days after giving birth to a

Fig. 10.3: Rasmus Rask's house in the town of Brændekilde, Denmark, painted by Hans Andersen Brendekilde about fifty years after the death of Rasmus Rask (Photo: Wikimedia).

daughter. He then married Birthe Rasmusdatter in 1780. Rasmus Rask was their third child. Rasmus' elder sister, Maren, and his elder brother, Hans Christian, both died within a few days of each other in 1796. Rask's father seems to have remarked that the Lord took away what was good and left him the dirt. Rasmus learnt reading and writing and a bit of German from his father. He notes that someone he knew once tried to give him a large amount of arsenic in a sandwich, either to avenge Rasmus Rask or his father.[408] Rask survived and, indeed, forgave the person. Even as a boy, Rasmus displayed a fantastic memory. Soon, he had read all the books his father possessed and became deeply fascinated with Nordic history. It was decided to send Rasmus to the Latin school in the town of Odense. At the age of 13, he passed the entrance test to the school. Sadly for him, his mother died in August 1801, 48 years old, just as he was about to begin his schooling. The school was of the 'old' type – the subjects he had to study were religion, Latin, Greek and Hebrew. Only a few hours were allotted to mathematics, history and geography. Later, he was taught French, German and Danish together with the sciences. Rasmus impressed people with his capacity for clear thinking and analysis, and he was often called the 'little professor'.

A few months after the death of Rasmus' mother, his father married for the third time – this time to Anne Katrine Henriksdatter. Rasmus respected his stepmother and grew fond of her. Anne Katrine and Niels had several children; two of them, Hans Kristian and Maren, were named after the children, who had died earlier. It is said that Rasmus did not require much sleep and worked like a man possessed. His response to the inferiority complex from which he suffered was to work harder. One of his teachers, Mr. Suhr, had a large collection of books, one of which was Schöningen's edition of the Icelander Snorri Sturluson's work on the history of the ancient Norwegian kings. Rask did not even know what language it was in, but his teacher told him that it was Icelandic. The fascination for Icelandic never left him. He started learning the Icelandic language by himself in order to understand the Nordic past. As no dictionaries or encyclopaedias were available, he had to learn the language himself. By comparing available Danish translations with the original Icelandic, he not only learnt the language, but was also able to write the first Icelandic grammar as well as work out rules of inflexion (bøjningslære) and syntax by writing down all the different forms in which a word appeared. Then, on his own, he wrote a dictionary of Icelandic, giving the meaning of a word not only in Danish, but also in Dutch, German, Swedish, English etc. In 1811, at the age of 24, he wrote his first dissertation 'A guide to Icelandic or old Nordic language'. He was to rely on this technique as a means of developing an understanding of the grammar and syntax of many languages. In school, he learnt Greek, Hebrew, Latin, German and French. Then, on his own, he learnt Icelandic, English, Swedish, Old English, Dutch, Frisian, Faroese and Greenlandic.

In 1807, Rasmus Rask left Odense to study theology in Copenhagen. He soon found out that his interest was, however, 'only' in languages. In 1813, he travelled to Iceland to study the language in depth. After returning to Copenhagen, his ideas began to take a concrete form. He soon showed that all the Nordic languages, as well as Anglo-Saxon, Dutch, Friesian and German are derived from a common Gothic language, whereas

Greenlandic had a completely different origin. In his search for the source of the Gothic languages, his attention turned to Sanskrit, and he set out to examine whether this might be the source. With a small scholarship from King Frederik VI of Denmark, he first travelled to Sweden, then to Finland and Russia and learnt all these languages. After arriving in St. Petersburg, he started to learn Sanskrit. In his thesis, he showed that Finnish and Hungarian are related languages, and he was instrumental in the publication of a Finnish-German-Latin dictionary.

While in Russia, the Russian ship *Rurik* arrived from an expedition to the Bering Straits. Onboard were two Aleutians from a group of islands west of Alaska. Rasmus Rask used this opportunity to learn Aleutian, which is an Inuit language, and helped one of them to make a small Aleutian-Russian dictionary. From these conversations, he found that Aleutian was related to Greenlandic. From his studies, he also discovered that only one of the Caucasian languages, namely Ossetian, was Indo-European in origin. This strengthened his notion that he had to travel to India to find the source of the Indo-European languages as well as Greek. Again, while in Russia, he started to learn Persian and Armenian. From St. Petersburg, he came to Tbilisi, Georgia, through Moscow, Sarepta and Astrakhan. On the way, he learnt Ossetian. At Tbilisi, he was taught Turkish and learnt Georgian on his own.

In March 1820, he reached Jerevan and went on from there to Tabriz in Persia. He wrote to one of his friends that, when he did not have anything else to do, he studied Central Asian languages – Tatar, Mongolian and Manchu – and made comparisons between them. Travelling through Persia, Rask reached Shiraz and Persepolis. Here, he stood before the centuries-old monuments and gazed at the still undeciphered cuneiform script – a script Carsten Niebuhr [Niebuhr] had carefully copied almost 60 years earlier.

In 1761, King Frederik V of Denmark had sent out an expedition to elucidate questions regarding statements in the Old Testament as well as carry out investigations pertaining to nature, language, culture and the populations of Arabia.[409] The expedition consisted of the Swedish scientist Peter Forsskål, the Danish philologist Christian Frederik von Haven, the Danish-German cartographer and mathematician Carsten Niebuhr, the medical doctor von Krämer, the artist Bauernfeind and Berggren, their servant. The team landed in Alexandria, proceeded through Suez to Sinai, reaching Mocha in Yemen in 1763. Here, von Haven and, soon after, Peter Forsskål died. The remaining members continued to Bombay. Bauernfeind and Berggren died on the way and, shortly after reaching India, von Krämer also died. That left only Carsten Niebuhr as the sole surviving member. Niebuhr became very sick in India, but slowly he recovered from his illness. During his stay in India, he travelled to the Elephanta caves and made sketches of all the figures there. He also copied the Marathi script meticulously. According to the original plans, he was to have crossed southern India to reach Tranquebar and find a ship to sail him to England and thence to Denmark. However, having recovered his strength, he decided to continue the trip on land through Persia. He travelled to Muscat in Oman and to Bushire, Shiraz and Persepolis in Persia. He was taken by the splendour of the monuments in Persepolis, which had been a magnificent city during the 3rd and 2nd centuries BCE until it was burnt down by Alexander the Great. Niebuhr spent more than three weeks copying all the cuneiform scripts that were found in Persepolis. He returned to Denmark in 1767 via Babylon, Baghdad, Mosul, Aleppo, Cyprus, Jerusalem, Constantinople and then through present-day Poland. Despite the expedition's dramatic fate, the team had been able to collect much material in the form of plants, insects, manuscripts, sketches and maps. Niebuhr's copies of the cuneiform script were to revolutionise Assyriology.

Attempts to decipher the cuneiform fared badly well into the 19th century. Georg Friederich Grotefend (1775-1853) was the first to try to crack the script. Niebuhr had guessed that the text should be read from the left to the right. Grotefend conjectured correctly that the writing was alphabetic, not syllabic; he guessed that the script consisted of 40 letters and deciphered a specific word as 'king', another as 'king of kings' and a third as 'son of king'. From the Achaemenian history, he guessed these names to be Xerxes, Darius and Hystaspes. Rasmus Rask did not decipher the script as he stood and gazed at the writing on the walls. But later, in 1820 when he was in India working on Zendavesta, he realised from the genetive suffix ending the phrase 'king of kings' what the declension 'anam' looked like and he was thus able to recognise the two letters 'n' and 'm'.[410] In Sanskrit, this was the genetive plural from which he concluded that the 'old Persian' language of Avestan was related to Sanskrit.[411]

He reached Teheran in April 1820. By this time, he was getting homesick; he found the journey desolate and cold and the people disinterested in their own languages. However, there was no way back – he had to get around India. In September, he reached Bombay on the ship *Benares* after travelling through Isfahan, Persepolis and Shiraz. His primary interest in coming to India was to acquire and buy old handwritten palm leaf manuscripts. He wrote in his diary that he had collected rare Zend and Pahlavi manuscripts. The languages that he now wanted to study were Avestan and Pahlavi. He also studied Zend, a Zoroastrian language, and wrote down its rules for inflexion and grammar. He concluded that the words were similar to Persian, while the inflexion was more like Sanskrit. His work on Zend and Zendavesta[412], published posthumously, remains one of the tour-de-force pieces of literature.[413]

In November 1820, Rask began his journey towards Calcutta via Pune. At Asirghar, he learnt Marathi from a Brahmin. After travelling through Ujjain, Bhopal, Gwalior, and Benares he came to the Danish trading post at Serampore in May 1821. On 5 May, he notes in his diary: 'I greeted Madam Fjellerup' and on 12 May: 'Had tea with Madam Fjellerup where the doctor displayed fireworks for the youngest daughter's birthday'.[414] By this time, he was both physically and mentally exhausted and very sick. He started having nightmares and sores all over his body. Doctor Christopher Mundt at Serampore tried to convince him that he was imagining things – but to no avail. Rasmus Rask felt that the locals were haunting him. Just as suddenly as he came, he left for Madras aboard the *Glorioso*.

The missionaries Harboue and Rottler looked after him when he was at Vepery, Madras. He stayed in Madras for three months, recovering from his illness. He started studying Spanish, Sanskrit and the South Indian languages. He also completed a book in English on Zend. While in Madras, he moreover worked on Tamil and Tamilnadu. In his manuscript 'Remarks on the Zend language and the Zendavesta',[415] Rask says:

> '...seeing that the grammatical structure of the *Telugu, Tamil, Carnatacá,* and *Malayal'ma* [sic] agrees exactly with the Finnish and Tartar dialects in Northern and Central Asia, I imagine that one great race of men, which may be stiled the Scythians, in the most ancient times, extended from the Frozen Sea to the Indian Ocean, until the chain was broken by a great inundation of people of our own race, which, for want of a more convenient name, I shall venture to call the *Japhetic*,

issuing from Eastern Persia, and taking possession of somewhat more than *Hindústan*. Observing on the map how the above-mentioned Indian aborigines of *Malayalam*, of *Carnata*, of *Sholen*, of *Telingana*, &c. are now situated in the southern extremity and along the eastern coast of the country, it appears most likely that they were driven into that situation by the torrent of a warlike people from the west. Another circumstance tends to corroborate this hypothesis: although the northern dialects in India are all derived from the *Sanskrit*, yet they contain a number of words of uncertain origin; for instance, in *Hindústáni*, rúþi (roti-*bread)*, þopi (thopi-*hat)* &c.; most of these words will be found in the Tamil dialects of the south, and therefore seem to be remnants of the aborigines, who were not altogether exterminated or expelled, although greatly overpowered, just as one might find some Gaelic words in modern French, which properly belong to Welsh or *Erse*.' (italics from the original)

He worded his general impressions of the language and country thus: 'Tamulisk – (Tamla or Tamulah) called High Tamil, is estimated to be the oldest and most indigenous language and is a source for other languages. It is also distinguished by a richer and more self-contained literature. The country likewise contains more remarkable ruins from ancient times than anywhere else that is inhabited by this nation'.

There is at least one notebook at the Royal Library in Copenhagen containing studies in Tamil by Rasmus Rask. In vol. 73 of his manuscript,[416] he comments on the structure and grammar of the language. Here is a short extract (my translation from Danish):[417]

> 'Reading is from left to right in Tamil as in other languages, but here it is exceedingly difficult and complex, impossible for one who does not understand the language, since imperfections in the writing system have made it necessary to attribute to the same letter different sounds depending on the context. Moreover, the words are merged, so that the first letter of the following word is affixed to the end of the preceding one and, finally, fail to distinguish the different possible pronunciations for different expressions.'

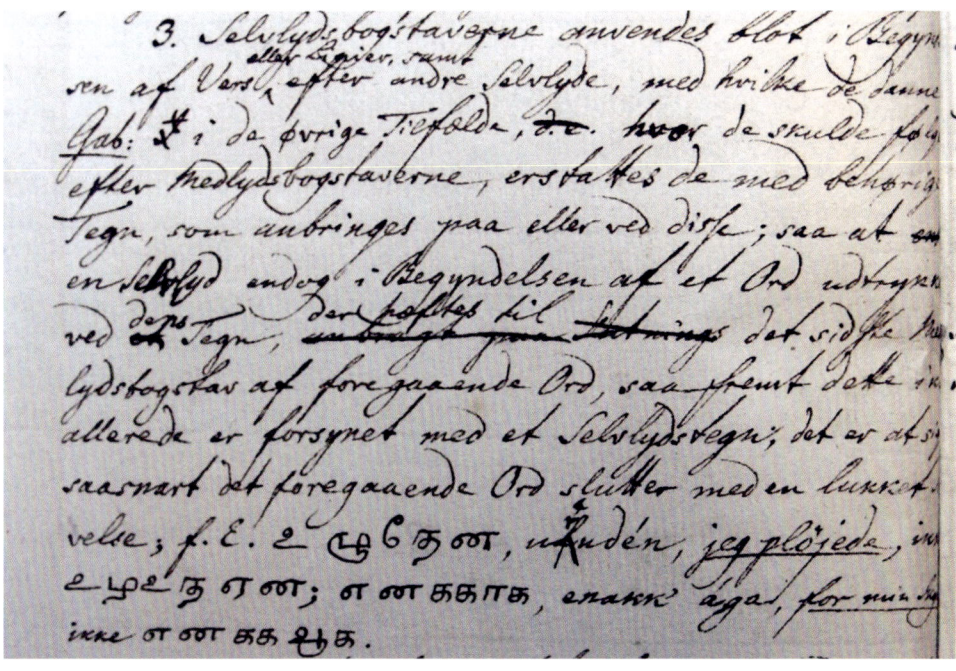

Fig. 10.4: A page from Rasmus Rask's study of Tamil (The Royal Library, Copenhagen, NKS 149 c kvart). (Photo: P. S. Ramanujam).

He points out how the Malabarian languages are strictly without gender, like Finnish. In almost all cases, the Bible was his starting point. Since the Bible had been translated into several languages, he could compare the same text in order to understand the structure of a language. Later in life, he said that just from the Lord's Prayer in each language, he could construct the inflexions for that language.[418] True to this saying, the Lord's Prayer in several different Indian languages can be found in his notebooks, with the morphology of the language given below.

His diary for the month of August 1821 is a testimony to his energy in learning and reading other languages: 'Aug. 1: I begin to study Tamil; Aug. 2: Dutch in Mrs. Rottler's books – Baldwin Janson's Grammar of the Dutch Language, London, 1798; Aug. 8: Watched English and Tamil examinations at the Mission school; Aug. 9: Started on Telugu after which I began to write the first draft on a Sanskrit library of printed literature; Aug. 18: Sent for Mr. Andrew, a Singhalese, in order to begin a self-study; agreed with a Kannada Brahmin, Thirumalachari from Seringapatam, about tuition in Kannada; Aug. 21: Visited by a Telugu-Sanskrit teacher who had a translator with him, and by a Persian-Hindustani teacher, Mir Ghulam Destagir; Aug. 31: Read Tamil again with Haubroe a couple of times a week, Sept. 6: Started working on a Danish Greek vocabulary; Sept. 17. Began to study Sakuntalam; Sept. 23: Visited St. Thomas Mount, saw the cave in the Catholic church on the little mountain, where St. Thomas hid when he was persecuted, Oct. 3: Finished my thesis on the age of the Zend language and the genuineness of Zendavesta'.

On 17 October, he left for Tranquebar over land. On the very first day, his baggage fell into a river. He tried to dry his precious books during the following days. On 25 October, he arrived at the choultry at 'Tenpakkum, 25 English miles from Pondichery'. Rasmus Rask arrived in Tranquebar on 28 October 1821 and stayed there only for a week. On 28 October he wrote: 'In the morning, a man from Mr. Rehling arrived to receive me. I had had my lunch by then. He brought me two letters from Mr. Rehling, and when I arrived at Tranquebar, he took to me to the Councillor of the State, Hermanson, Councillor to the Government, Kofod, Secretary to the Government, Lorenz, sexton Wodschow, Major Luther, who was not at home'.

A couple of days later, he started preparations for his travel to Ceylon. On Nov. 1: 'I dried my books, read a little Sanskrit, packed and prepared for travel. The Councillor for the Government, Kofoed, presented me with a black boy, Lindor, 9 years old. On Sunday, the 4th, I listened to Wodschow's sermon in Danish and organ music, was pretty good. I left the next morning'.

On 5 December 1821, a letter was sent from his mentor, Rasmus Nyerup, asking him to trace the Sanskrit library of Christoph Samuel John in Tranquebar.[419] We do not know whether John had any knowledge of Sanskrit, or whether he collected a Sanskrit library, neither do we know whether Rask was able to trace it.

During the day, he used his time searching for and buying precious palm leaf scripts in Pali and Singhalese. By now, he had little strength left. He managed to complete a project in which all Indian languages were written in the Latin alphabet instead of the complex, local scripts. He also managed to write a Singhalese textbook in Danish. In March 1822, he started his journey back to Calcutta. However, at Galle in Ceylon, the ship was damaged in a storm and started sinking. Several of his Pali and Singhalese manuscripts were lost – and he lost all his money. He contacted

Governor Rehling at Tranquebar to send him funds. He left again on 18 August. On 1 September 1823, he reached Tranquebar and was received by Rehling.

In a report to the Danish government on his travel[420] so far, he thanked it for the sum of 2,000 Madras Rupees,[421] which he had received and which had saved him from the embarrassment caused by the shipwreck. He continues: 'I left my ancestral land in 1816 and travelled through Sweden, Finland and Russia to visit the region of Tavris, to examine what was left of our ancestors in the land of Goths, but found nothing. The closer to the place I got, the more I was convinced that the roving Tatars have wiped out all the traces over hundreds of years. I therefore wrote to Prof. Dr. Theol. P. F. Müller to propose to the government that my present travel could become more fruitful to the literary world, if I were allowed to travel to Persia and India. This is for the purpose of investigating whether the old Persian-Indian languages, religions and peoples are related to Europe. My travel was extended by two years, during which I was lucky to cross the Tatar, Caucasian and Persian deserts to reach the inexhaustibly educational India. Unfortunately, the travel cost more money and time. But I was lucky already in Bombay to collect rare Persian manuscripts, and in Ceylon, a richer and rarer collection of Buddhistic manuscripts in Pali and Singhalese'.

When Rask returned from Ceylon, he again stayed with Rehling.[422] In Tranquebar, he visited Rehling's gardens, both private and public, and Koefoed's garden, 'beautifully furnished with flowers; it is very close to the Government House'. He sailed for Madras on 6 September and arrived on 9 September 1822. On 14 September, he notes in his diary: 'I visited Clarke and listened to an interesting recitation in Sanskrit, Telugu and Tamil in different verse forms. The last one was very pleasing and resembled Danish or perhaps, even more, the Danish warrior songs or folk melodies. I attended the Tamil service preached by Harboue'. On 19 September: 'Visited Mavalipuram. The ruins of the pagodas and the carvings on the rocks were beautiful; however, it was not possible to decipher the inscriptions on a whole wall in one of the pagodas, as they were whitewashed some time ago'.

He left for Calcutta on 3 November. He was still working on his Tamil and French on the evening of the 9th and on the 12th, and the whole of the 15th was spent on the Tamil language. He came to Serampore on the

Fig. 10.5: This used to be Rehling's garden in Erukattancheri, which was much appreciated by Rasmus Rask. There were several gardens around Tranquebar, which were owned by Danish officials used as places of relaxation (photo: P. S. Ramanujam).

4th where he stayed with Governor Bie. While in Calcutta, he met with Ram Mohan Roy: 'He talked about visiting Europe and spoke English very well; understood a bit of Latin and four European languages. He presented me with a few his books'.

Rasmus Rask sailed back to Denmark on 1 December 1822, reaching Copenhagen on 5 May 1823, having spent 6½ years travelling. Back in Copenhagen, he had one objective: To write down the grammars of as many languages as possible, based on the same set of fundamental principles. In 1823, he even worked on constructing one common language for the entire world. Unfortunately for Rasmus Rask, he was so full of new ideas that he never carried them through. After several unsuccessful attempts to gain a professorship, he was finally appointed Professor of Asian Languages in 1832. By now, his health was failing; on 11 October 1832, he wrote to the Board of Directors of the University that he would be unable to carry out his lectures because of his ill health. He died of tuberculosis on 14 November 1832, 45 years old.

Rasmus Rask was said to have understood approximately 55 languages.[423] He could 'speak in Sanskrit with a Hindu and Latvian with a Lett'. There is an extensive collection of letters and manuscripts attributed to Rasmus Rask at the Royal Library in Copenhagen. This includes a draft of Sanskrit grammar and notes relating to Sanskrit texts, collections, drafts and notes for a Danish-Sanskrit dictionary, notes on Gujarati, notes on Kanarese, notes on Mahratti, remarks on Tamil, notes on Tamil literature, collections on Telugu, the Lord's Prayer in more than 30 Indian languages. There are collections for a Pali grammar, notes on Singhalese grammar and collections regarding Caucasian languages, Persian languages, Malay, Magindano, Semitic languages and Syrian. He donated all his precious manuscripts in Persian, Bali and Singalese to the Royal Library in Copenhagen. A catalogue of his collected unpublished works has later been published by his half-brother, Hans Kristian Rask.[424]

Rasmus Rask never married, even though he had entertained the idea of having a wife. On the voyage from India, he fell in love, perhaps for the first time in his life. With him on the ship were three daughters of Christian Tullin (or Thulin) Boalth with whom he had occasions to chat. Christian Tullin Boalth was born in Bergen in Norway in 1767. He had applied for the post of copy-writer in Tranquebar along with his elder brother, Jens Boalth, and they arrived in Tranquebar in 1786. While in Tranquebar, Christian Tullin Boalth married Pauline Abbestée, an illegitimate daughter of Governor Peter Herman Abbestée with an Indian 'slave', and they had six children. Abbestée was 'officially' married to Francoise Lange with whom he had two daughters, Maria Barbara and Franciska Genoveve.[425] Maria Barbara married Count Blücher, and Franciska Genoveve married a nobleman called Frederik Karl Ferdinand von Qualen, and both lived in Altona. Boalth had three daughters in his marriage to Pauline Abbestée, who died at an early age of 29. The three daughters lived with Christian Tullin Boalth until his demise in 1822, in his spatial villa in Cuddalore.[426] The three Boalths left for Altona to be brought up by their step-aunt, Maria Barbara, and her wealthy husband, Count Blücher. They travelled on the same ship as Rasmus Rask.

Rask notes in his diary: 'Miss Boalth left me a copy of V. Kr. Hjort's 'Gudfrygtige Sømænds Sjælero'.[427] …Dance in the evening…Infinite-

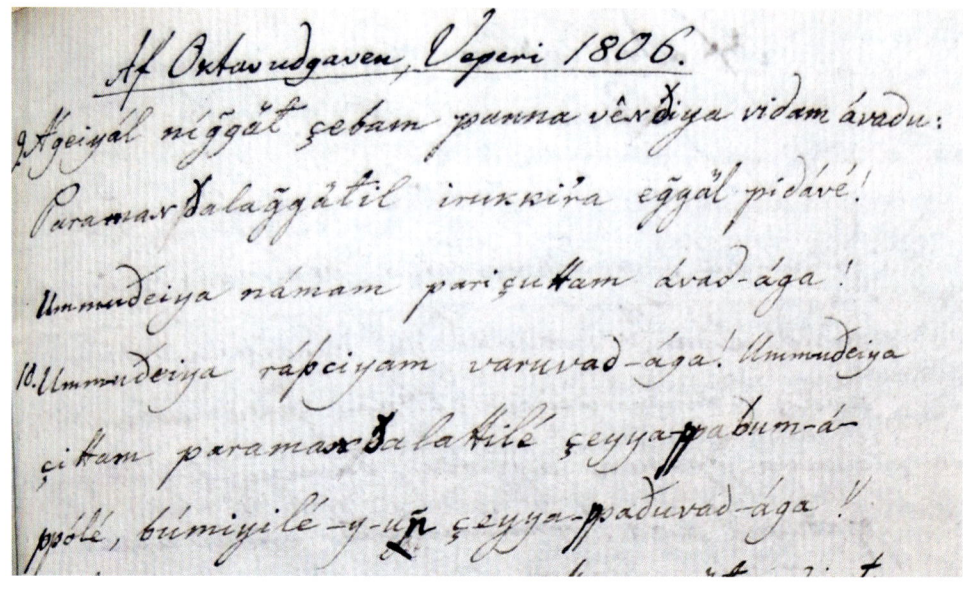

Fig. 10.6: The Lord's Prayer in Tamil, written with the Latin alphabet from Rasmus Rask's collection at the Royal Library, Copenhagen (photo: P. S. Ramanujam).

ly beautiful mornings and evenings'.[428] Rasmus Rask proposed to one of them. He himself did not mention anything about this in his diaries. After his death, his friend Niels Mathias Petersen wrote a biography of him. In one copy of this, which is available at the Royal Library in Copenhagen,[429] a hand-written comment from Rask's half-brother, Hans Kristian Rask, says: '11 May 1824. Rejection from F. B. in Altona, after careful deliberation. Letter sent to her on 18 April 1824. 4 letters on this matter destroyed 22 Aug. 1871, as no one after my death should have this information'[430] (my translation from Danish) [Diderichsen, p. 214].

Marie Bjerrum, who is an authority on Rasmus Rask, says that she found in Kay Larsen's 'Dansk Ostindiske Personalia og Data' a Pauline Boalth, who she thought was the unnamed 'F. B.'. Subsequent authors, such as Markey, have stuck to this explanation; Kirsten Rask in her book says that only Pauline Boalth was a passenger on the ship, and that three Miss Boalths could be three sisters, or two sisters and one unmarried aunt. She also thinks that F. B. could simply stand for 'Frøken Boalth' (Miss Boalth). From the Tranquebar Church Registers [Ramanujam], one can see that the three sisters were: Fanny Boalth (baptised 22 January 1796), Abigael Catharina Boalth (baptised 20 September 1797) and Paulina Boalth (bap-

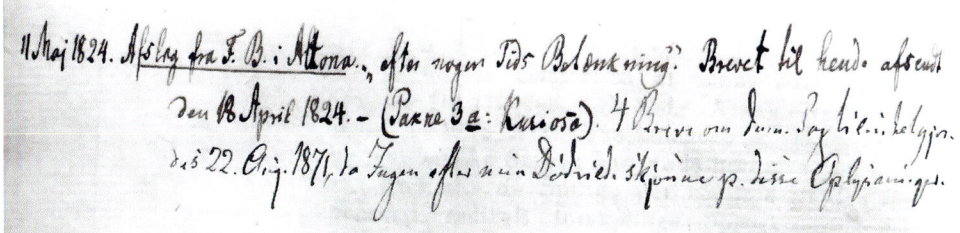

Fig. 10.7: Hans Kristian Rask's comments in Rasmus Rask's biography. ('Bidrag til R. Kr. Rasks levnet (Kbh 1834) – Tilføjelser af H. K. Rask', NKS 389 en oktav, The Royal Library, Copenhagen). (Photo: P. S. Ramanujam).

tised 25 May 1800). I believe that Rask proposed to Fanny Boalth (F. B.). Fanny Boalth married William von Halling. She died in Copenhagen just a year after Rask in 1833. It is very likely that Fanny was named after her other step-aunt, Franciska Genoveve.[431] According to some notes left by Hans Kristian Rask, Rasmus Rask proposed to her a year after returning to Copenhagen, but was rejected. Later, Rask would propose to Louise Nyerup, his mentor's daughter – but that is another story.

Fig. 10.8: Tombstone of Rasmus Rask at the Assistens Kirkegård in Copenhagen, showing the Sanskrit inscription. The stone was raised about 10 years after Rasmus Rask's death (By Pinnerup – Own work, CC BY-SA 4.0, Wikimedia).[432]

Rasmus Rask is buried at the Assistens Cemetery in Copenhagen. His gravestone has inscriptions in Arabic, Runes, Sanskrit and Danish.[433] The Sanskrit text is from the 5th-century Indian philosopher Bhartrhari's Niti-sataka and reads: 'There is no better friend than diligence. He who exhibits this does not perish' (nAstyudyamasamo bandhuH kurvANo nAvasIdati).[434] Rask did not choose this citation for his grave; it was a full ten years after his death that the stone was put in place. However, Rask did live his life in complete accordance with this citation.

*

We continue our walk along King Street. The house next to that of Rehling's is popularly known as van Teylingen's house. Van Teylingen was a Dutch doctor, who stayed on until Tranquebar was sold to the English. The retired westerners, who remained in Tranquebar, received their pensions from van Teylingen. Today, the house has been renovated and remodelled inside and belongs to the Danish textile mogul Troels Holch Povlsen of the Danish company Bestseller. Across the street was the house of Colbjörnsen and, next to it, was the majestic house in which Thomas Christian Walter lived.

11

Pride, Pomp and Circumstance

In the year 1787, Thulaja Raja (Tullasa rajah in the Danish documents) died, and the new king Amarsingh (Amarda Singh in the Danish documents) ascended the throne. Although Thulaja Raja on his deathbed asked his half-brother, Amarsingh, to take care of his adopted child – the future Serfoji II – and requested him to take over the throne, Amarsingh's coronation was delayed, pending orders from the English government in Madras. The English governor from Madras then undertook a journey to Tanjore, where a gathering of 16 Brahmins declared the adoption of Serfoji illegal because the child's parents had not given their consent, because

Fig. 11.1: Location of Walter's house on King Street. The two-storied house behind the pole was the place where the abode of Thomas Christian Walter once stood (photo: P. S. Ramanujam 2008).

Fig. 11.2: Royal Procession with Raja Amar Singh (Reigned 1787-1798) of Thanjavur. Notice the Englishman (Macleod?) sitting next to Amar Singh (photo: Wikimedia).

the child had not spent one year with Amarsingh in order to show respect to him as a father, and because the child was immature. General Campbell then demanded that Amarsingh accept various conditions. Among these, the king should pay Nawab Mohammad Ali Khan 5 million rupees, followed by an annual payment of 100,000 pagodas, and pay the Danish East India Company 700,000 pagodas together with an annual subsidy of 300,000 pagodas. The Company demanded that, in lieu of these payments, the Rajah pay a sum of 700,000 pagodas the first summer, then 300,000 pagodas annually to the Company and 100,000 pagodas to the Nawab until the debts were paid off. Following the advice of the missionary Schwarz, the Rajah refused to pay the amount as his country was totally in ruins after the wars against Nawab Mohammad Ali. However, now there were two more pretenders to the throne – the rightful father of Serfoji and another distant family member. With the real possibility of the throne being usurped from him, Amarsingh decided to accept the harsh conditions, knowing well that if he did not pay the required 680,000 pagodas, Tanjore would fall into the hands of the English. The coronation could now take place.

Tradition required that the Danes send a delegation to the court of the new king with presents and to renegotiate the contracts and treaties signed under the old raja. And what an impressive delegation it was – at the head of the procession was Thomas Christian Walter, the Danish government's number two, followed by Mathias Jürgen Mühldorff, Daniel Pulley and Suppremania Setti as the private dubash of Walter. The presents for the king included an elephant worth 600 Porto Novo pagodas,[435] a gold-plated silver filigree enamel casket, a horse, one pair of steel pistols with inlaid silver, golden dress, a calabash with rose water, two red dresses and brocade.[436] Presents for the chief minister, Sevarayen, included 5 gold dresses, for Sandapa, five gold dresses and one satin piece, as well as various presents for Kullanapa, Papanna and other officials, and several gifts for the subehdars in Papanasam and Mayavaram. The procession included 122 coolies, torch-bearers, palanquin bearers, umbrella bearers, cooks, haricars, dancers, 15 attendants for Mühldorff, 22 for Daniel Pulley and 25 for Walter, medicine for the elephant, 'kollu'[437] for the horse, various pieces of expensive clothing, such as turbans, pano comprido for jackets and liveries for the servants. The cost of the entire delegation, detailed to the last piece of rope to tie the elephant, was a bit more than 2,078 Porto Novo pagodas, the current value of which would be approximately 100,000 USD.

On the morning of 28 April 1787, the delegation left Tranquebar. Imagine what a spectacle it must have made. The procession reached Mayavaram in the evening, where a traditional guard of honour was presented. The subedar was not present, but Walter himself did not complain about this. However, the haricars (spies) reported this to the king of Tanjore, and the subedar was promptly fined 120 gold fanoes. On 29 April, the procession arrived at Kumbakonam, where again a guard of honour was presented – yet again the subedar excused himself. The Danes protested – they would go back to Tranquebar if he did not present himself. He came immediately; this time, the incident cost him 240 gold fanoes. On 30 April, the delegation reached Ayenpettah,[438] where a Brahmin sent by the king invited them to Tanjore. The delegation demanded and received the guard of honour with a 13-cannon salute. The English envoy Macleod, invited the delegation to stay with him, which it declined as this might be

Fig. 11.3: Portrait of Thomas Christian Walter by the Italian painter Angelo Crescimbeni 1734-1781. Oil on canvas, 76.5 x 57.2 cm, 1778 (picture credit: Museo internazionale e biblioteca della musica di Bologna).

Fig. 11.4: Walter's portrait. Carl Philipp Emanuel Bach had this portrait hanging on the wall (photo: Staatsbibliothek zu Berlin – Preußischer Kulturbesitz, Germany).

construed as being impolite to the king. The delegation was then led to the eastern side of the Kavery River that flows through Tanjore area.

On 1 May, the king's father-in-law, Kadera and another member of his family, Venkata Rau Kadera, two Brahmins and a servant came to congratulate them on their visit and led them to Tanjore, which lay on the other side of the river. Again, the delegation was received with a 13-cannon salute, and the king's own guard welcomed it with a fanfare. The king sat on his throne with a canopy made of gold cloth over him. To his left sat the English envoy Macleod and next to him, Colonel Stuart. The Danish delegation sat on the right side of the king. After the presents were given to the king, Walter addressed the gathering and explained, through the dubash Daniel, how a lasting friendship had been forged between the kings of Tanjore and His Majesty, the King of Denmark, for over 150 years. The Danish king wanted to maintain peaceful relations with the king of Tanjore, since the present king was descendent of the famous Pratab Singh, whose valiant deeds were well-known. It was a personal honour for the

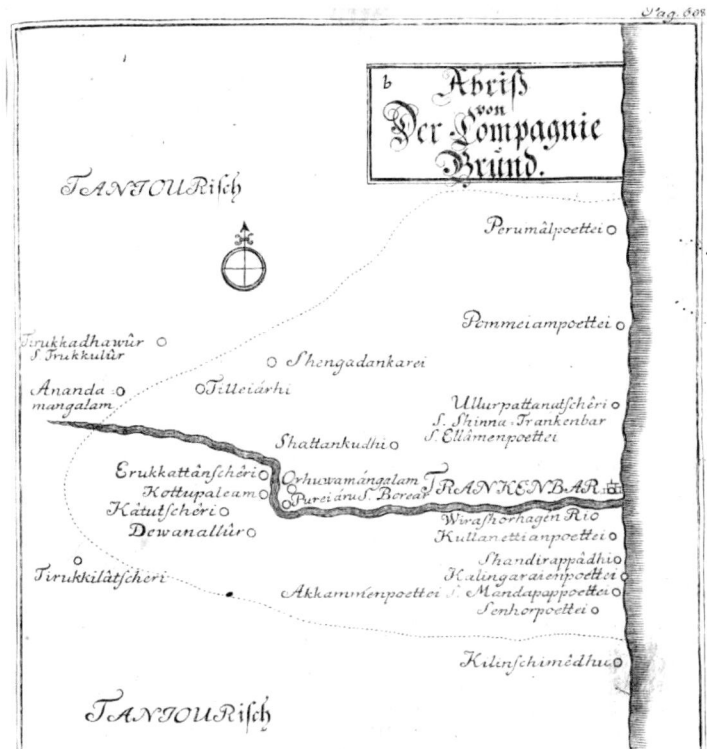

Fig. 11.5: Map of the Tanjore district, showing the environs of Tranquebar (RA, General Toldkammer – og Kommercekollegiet, Generalguvernør P. Hansens Embedsarkiv, Diverse sager (1829-1842), (Løbenr. 3335)).

delegation to deliver a letter from the Danish governor in Tranquebar, Governor-General Major Abbestée, and would the king kindly accept the presents as an indication of the friendship between the countries? The king said in return that he appreciated the gifts, that he knew that Denmark and Tanjore had also been good friends and that the friendship would continue. After this, he allowed the delegation to retire as they were fatigued, with all the traditional ceremonies with flower garlands and gold cloths.

Negotiations began on 2 May. Daniel Pulley was sent to greet Sevarayen, chief minister for the king, bringing the presents that had been bought for this purpose. Four points needed to be negotiated: 1) the king must ratify the bond executed by his half-brother, Thulaja Raja, for the sum of 32,000 pagodas regarding the lease of fourteen villages in Tiruvidakalli's[439] district for a period of 25 years instead of just 8 years. The Danes maintained that this was a wasteland that must first be made cultivable and that they should be allowed to profit from the land for a few years, before handing it over to Tanjore jurisdiction; 2) the remission of the duties (called tribute) amounting to 3,150 pardau annually paid on the Tranquebar territory. As neither the Dutch paid duties for Nagapatnam, nor the English for Nagore, the Danes should also be released from this bond – and they were willing to pay a capital sum in exchange for the annual tribute. 3) Lease of 6 villages in Triclatchery's[440] district for 6,000 pardau for 25 years, instead of the 6,500 pardau being paid annually, and 4) repair of the sluice at Mudalei Madagu in the Triculuur district. These four propositions were translated by Daniel Pulley and presented to Sevarayen. Missionary Schwartz, who was well respected by the king, was present on the Danish side, albeit without directly partaking in the negotiations. Walter instructed Daniel Pulley to promise Sevarayen a handsome income if he would support the Danes in their claims. Finally, after several days of negotiations, on 10 May, the following results were reached: 1) the lease of Tiruvidakalli district extended for 15 years instead of the original 8 years; 2) the lease of the Tricalatschery district for a period of 10 years at 6,500 pardau – it was possible that Daniel could negotiate it for a period of 15 years for 6,000 pardaus; 3) duties on the Tranquebar's territory would be decided in the future, and 4) the sluice construction would be carried out without delay.

Towards the end of the negotiations, Amarsingh requested two favours: 1) a big European horse (Walter explained to him that it had to be transported on a ship that could take 6-7 months, so it might be difficult). In the absence of a horse, the king requested a few small European dogs, and 2) a desire to see the large sailing ships. (Walter replied that if the king visited Tranquebar, he would be received with all the honours and would also have the opportunity to visit the ships). The question of the duties on the Tranquebar territory could be decided then. (This was, in fact, never decided and the Danes continued to pay the duties until they sold the colony).

This was a masterpiece of diplomatic negotiations exhibited by Walter. He knew the fine line between on the one hand treading on the toes of the English, who were quite sure that they would take over the kingdom in less than 18 months, as the king would not be able to pay his debts, and on the other hand pressing Amarsingh too far, since he had the power to harass the Danes by preventing the entry of fuel and provision to the

Danish territory, to cut-off for the water supply or charge higher customs on the cultivated products.

On 11 May 1787, the procession left Tanjore to the sound of a 13-gun salute and headed for Tranquebar and reached the place on 13 May.

In his report to the government, Walter characterises the rule of Amarsingh as confusing, as if the lengthy incarceration had made him weary. The palace was untidy and the decision-making was very slow. He was evidently terrified of the English. Sevarayen was full of duplicity. Innermost, he was against Amarsingh and supported the adopted child, Serfoji II. He was very positive towards the English, but much more so towards his own interests.

Finally, Walter touched on the difficult problem of negotiating in a foreign country, where a skilled translator was an absolute necessity in order to express the thoughts of both parties, as these would otherwise be lost. It was forbidden to talk directly to the ministers, because their houses were

Fig. 11.6: Cover of 'Soliman den anden' – composed by Thomas Christian Walter. The entire partiture is available at the Royal Library in Copenhagen.

not open to foreigners, and they dare not come to the foreigners for fear of arousing suspicion. Likewise, etiquette forbade arranging a meeting in the house of a Malabar, which a European was allowed to enter, without a lot of ceremonies.

Walter's personal life was most unusual. He was baptised 'Thomas Christian Walter' on 12 February in 1749 in Copenhagen as a son of Thomas Saur and Edele Margaret Walter.[441] Following the early death of both his parents, he was brought up by his mother's father, Christian Walter, who was in the chancery and was also a councillor of state. The industrial magnate of that time, Johan Fredrik Classen, was a significant influence on Thomas Christian Walter to whom he was related on his mother's side. In fact, Classen paid for Walter's education and upbringing [Paludan-Müller, Erichsen]. According to Paludan-Müller, Walter was taught by one Colbiörnsen, who had several high-level contacts, and Classen paid for his education in German, French, English, drawing, piano and violin lessons, dance, horse riding as well as his clothes and pocket-money. Classen had a big manor house in Corselitze, Denmark, where he entertained guests with Walter playing the piano. However, Erichsen[442] notes that the talented young Walter did not live up to expectations. All the efforts expended by General Classen ended in his own disappointment. Or did they? It was probably through Walter's efforts that Classen's cannons ended up in Tranquebar. A cannon made by Classen at his factory in Frederiksværk in Denmark can still be seen outside the museum in Chennai, India.

With Classen's assistance, Walter became a government official. Walter was also related on his father's side to Thomas Bugge, the most influential astronomer of his time. He was a highly cultured, decorous person with scientific interests. In 1765, he became the secretary of commerce. However, his talents were in the realm of music. In 1772, he made his debut into the musical world with an Italian aria. His musical talents attracted the attention of the directors of the Royal Theatre, who needed an efficient instructor. He taught one of the greatest singers of the day – Caroline Halle, and they were married in 1774. He was appointed 'directeur de Théâtre' of the Royal Theatre in Copenhagen in 1773, with a salary of 600 rdl, but he quit the post the following year. 1773 saw his debut as a ballad opera composer with the work Silphen. This was followed shortly by 'Tried Fidelity' (Det prøvede Troskab), which was his attempt at emulating the Italian composer G. Sarti. But neither work turned out a success. In 1775, he received a stipend for three years to travel and compose. He made an attempt in Hamburg in 1775 with 'Soliman den anden' (a comedy in three acts for voices and orchestra), in Stockholm in 1776 with 'Adonis' (voices, orchestra with 2 flutes, 2 horns, strings), and in Bologna with 'Arsène' (a comedy in four acts by Charles-Simon Favart). They all ended as failures in the eyes of the public.

What a pity! Carl Philipp Emanuel Bach, son of Johan Sebastian Bach, in Hamburg in 1775 may have met Walter and may have heard him play. Walter's portrait in golden frames hung on Bach's walls. As Richards[443] notes:

> 'When Bach looked at his charming portrait of the young Danish composer and government official, Thomas Christian Walter, hanging on his wall in a golden frame,[444] he could have admired the quality of the drawing and perhaps recalled details of Walter's musical abilities that have not gone down in the historical record. Walter was in Hamburg in 1775 and may have met and played for Bach – the presence of the drawing in the collection suggests that the two were acquainted. More likely, though, the sensitivity and delicacy conveyed by the fragile lines and subtle coloring brought to mind the man's sad story: married, against the wishes of his (foster?)parents, to the singer Caroline Fridericha Halle, they separated and later divorced when she fell in love with the violinist Christian Friedrich Müller and fled with him to Sweden'.[445]

Citing Gerber, Richards continues: '(Walter) is better known outside his own country for the story of his marriage with the famous singer Madame Müller than through his services to music'.

In 1775, he became father to a daughter, Friderica Charlotte Margrethe.[446] Lots of mystery surrounds the life of Caroline Halle and Thomas Christian Walter.[447] After the failure of 'Arsène' and his subsequent divorce, he decided to quit music and received an appointment as a secretary for the Government of Tranquebar. There is some evidence that he had financial problems in Denmark. On 4 November 1777, he sent an application to the The Board of Trade (Kommercekollegiet):

'Secretary of Commerce, Thomas Christ(ian) Walther would like to ap-

Fig. 11.7: A cannon made at Classen's factory in Frederiksværk, Denmark, with the monogram of Christian VII. It is placed outside the Government Museum in Chennai. Johan Frederik Classen (1725-1792) was an industrialist, producing cannons, gunpowder and all kinds of weaponry (photo: P. S. Ramanujam).

ply for the position of Secretary to the Government of Tranquebar, with a small increment to the fixed salary as this would in such an expensive place otherwise be insufficient. He has worked for the Chamber of Commerce for 12 years, as a volunteer and as a secretary, during which period he has used his spare time to study languages and sciences. He completed his studies in 1770 with a commendable grade in public jurisdiction and, finally, he received a royal travel grant allowing him to pursue his passion in music'.[448]

He arrived in Tranquebar as a Counsellor to the Chancery in 1780 and became the Counsellor of Finance and Counsellor of Justice in 1782. The governor in charge of the colony was Peter Herman Abbestée, who was perceived as a weak person.

The situation in and around Tranquebar during this period was very volatile. Internally, the colony was plagued by the disputes between the left hand and right hand castes. Externally, Heider Ali and Tippu Sultan were waging wars around Tranquebar. Walter retained the services of Suppremannia Setti, who belonged to the chellapa caste, as his dubash. Suppremannia Setti was involved in the leasing of agricultural lands and earned a lot through this [Brimnes 1991]. No doubt, some of this was passed on to Walter.

During late 1781 and early 1782, Tanjore and surroundings experienced severe famine. As the town is situated in the Kavery delta, it is usually protected from the ravages of famine. However, this time the famine was caused by the invasion of Heider Ali's troops.[449] The output of crops dwindled to about a sixth of what it normally was. The missionary Schwartz apparently said that:

> 'As the famine was so great and of such long duration, people have been affected by it who seemed beyond its reach. A vigorous and strong man is scarcely to be met with; in outward appearance, men are like wandering skeletons… When it is considered that Haidar Ali has carried off so many thousands of people and that many thousands have died of want, it is not at all surprising to find desolated villages… Such distress I have never before witnessed and may God grant that I never shall again'.[450]

In their letters to Halle, the German missionaries note that the sight of thousands of people whom gnawing hunger had turned into faded skeletons covered with skin was unsettling. Many people died from unnatural foods rather than from hunger. If rice or nellu was carried through the streets, several of these skeletons would follow, seeking every falling grain, picking up from the sand and swallowing it. If something was spilt, violent quarrelling and fighting would ensue. Bones and crab shells were gathered, crushed with stones and eaten. Horns of the cattle, leather from palanquins, slimy creatures, tree leaves, grass and even pure earth got stuffed into the hungry mouths. A dead horse on the street was lacerat-

Fig. 11.8: Portrait of Suppremania Setti, painted by Peter Anker. Suppremania Setti, one of the most powerful Tamilians in Tranquebar, was the dubash of Thomas Christian Walter (photo: Wikimedia).

ed and consumed. There were rumours that a mother ate her own child. Many offered themselves as slaves, or sold their children for a few fano or even offered them for free.[451]

Abbestée, Lichtenstein, Hetting and Walter reported from Tranquebar on 28 January 1782[452] that Heider Ali's troops had taken over almost the entire Tanjore district before Colonel Braithwaite and Colonel Nixon had marched to Nagore to challenge him. General Munro arrived from Madras, and the combined forces were able to capture Nagapatnam. On 13 January, Heider's troops entered Karaikal's territory; however, except for some cattle stealing, no damage was done. The Danish government continued to receive both threats and compliments from Heider Ali – and the troops were never very far away. Heider Ali died later that year, but the terror nonetheless continued from Tippu Sultan.

Thomas Christian Walter Esquire, situated about two miles from the fort. The garden has a number of excellent fruit trees, vines etc.' were sold to Colbiörnsen for 501 rdl. In addition, a storage area in the Trocador Street in Tranquebar belonged to Walter, and this was bought by Sukkermany Chetty (this is the same person as Suppremania Setti we have encountered earlier) for 81 Porto Novo pagodas. The total value of Walter's property was 25,261 rdl; once his debts were payed off, 740 rdl remained. Walter's estate would be worth about 700,000 USD in today's currency, based on consumer price index[458].

The question of not only what Walter possessed and what was sold, but also who bought what and for how much, could form the subject of extensive research. In a closed community, such as Tranquebar, everyone from the governor to ordinary servants working for the government bought something or other. Even Indian citizens had enough cash to buy expensive things: Irulappa Pulle bought a gold container studded with diamonds and pearls valued at 100 rdl for 152 rdl, two large mirrors for 81 rdl, pana comprido for 32 rdl, a turban with golden flowers and a table. Cuppa Chetty bought a gold buckle, sauce spoons; Sinay bought a breast-pin for 71 rdl and 2 pairs of globes for 65 rdl; Thiagappa bought a dozen forks and a table clock; Vedarasa Chetty acquired a cabinet for 41 rdl and Rama Naik a palanquin. Of books, Savary acquired *Dictionary Poetique Portatif (Portable poetic dictionary), Sechia Rupita (La Secchia Rapita?) (The stolen bucket), Experiences de Physique (Experiments in physics), Encyclopedie Portative (2 vols) (Portable encyclopedia), Historie Philosophique et Politique, (Philosophical and political history) Elements de Musique Theorique & Practique, (Elements of music – Theory and practice), History of the Revolutions of Portugal, Dictionaire Philosophique Portatif (Portable philosophical dictionary) and Dictionaire des Rimes par Monsieur Richelet (Monsieur Richelet's dictionary of rhymes)*. All the persons mentioned above were ordinary citizens of Tranquebar.

Thomas Christian Walter was not the only one to live a life of luxury in Tranquebar. Just a few years before Walter, Christian Albrecht von Passow lived a comfortable life in Tranquebar. His life parallels Walter's life very closely. Passow's family came from the area of Passau in southern Germany. He was born in Denmark. Von Passow married Anne Catherina von Lübe, who was a famous singer in Denmark. Under the artistic name of Jomfru Materna, she wrote and produced several ballads. After their marriage, von Passow left for Tranquebar. He, too, borrowed heavily and spent most of the money on luxurious items. Items auctioned off after his disappearance in 1758 reveal the extent of the wealth[459] he enjoyed. His house had four rooms with backyard and cattle shed. One of the living rooms was furnished with two armchairs and two pillows, 8 round and 12 ordinary chairs, a small writing desk with inlaid ivory and silver brackets, a bureau made of redwood with silver brackets, a cabinet and a writing desk. On the wall was a mirror with two sconces, a gun and two pistols. The contents of the cabinet included an elegant Chinese tea container, a coffee grinder, wine decanters and a few jars. In his other sitting room, Passow had an ebony cabinet and on top of it a clock. In addition, cabinets and a gilded mirror decorated the room. In one of the other rooms, Passow had his weapon collection, his library and yet another desk. His weapon collection consisted of 6 guns, a silver rapier, a Malabar sword, 2 brass rapiers and sword blades. His book collection consisted of about a hundred books with 22 volumes of French travelogues, an atlas and other geographic publications, books on mathematics, medical, surgical, philosophical books as well as books on constitutional law; moreover, he owned Bibles, a Portuguese hymn book, Holberg's history of Denmark etc. On the desk was his pen set, ink bottles and mathematical instruments, binoculars (he was also an engineer and cartographer). Another room was used as a wine cellar. Coffee beans, 3 bottles of French brandy and 1,300 empty wine bottles were stored here. Besides, a cabinet containing many wine glasses, porcelain items, coffee and teapots and other things was in this room. His wardrobe was just as remarkable. The lieutenant had 17 different sets of attire, including an exquisite red silk apparel with golden tresses, gold-embroidered hats with black and white feathers, at least 44 shirts and some silk stockings. In all the cabinets, he had a store of velvet, silk, scarfs, Indian and Chinese goods intended for sale in India. He also possessed a white horse worth 600 rdl, a palanquin and a barge moored in the harbour.

A look through the various probates reveals a wealth of details on how the Danes lived and spent their time in Tranquebar.[460] They seem to have spent a lot of time reading. As Krieger [Krieger 2006] notes, these documents also reveal the societal standing of a person. He writes: 'Household inventories generally yield an excellent insight into the contemporary lifestyle, adoption of fashions, and can be taken as an indicator for social identities and cultural transfer'. The interiors of the European houses in Tranquebar generally reflected the taste in 18th-century Europe. Boxes and chests, wardrobes and cupboards, writing desks, dining tables and card tables are amply represented in the Danish houses in Tranquebar. The presence of porcelain, expensive cutlery and wine show the residents' wealth. Krieger cites the case of Mons. Monier who had 132 bottles of red wine as well as 248 bottles of white wine; Wodschow possessed 120 bottles of red wine and 144 bottles of white wine.

*

We now must do a bit of walking before we reach our next destination. We continue our walk along King's Street towards the east and look at some of the properties still standing from the Danish period. The two houses next to van Teylingen's house are The Small Mission House ('Lille Missionshus') or 'Kröckels House' and The Big Mission House ('Store Missionshus'). These houses belonged to the Mission and today they have been merged into one. On 23 July 1709, Anton Gunter Würger, a merchant in the town, sold a house situated between the Zion Church and the Company's warehouse. Ziegenbalg was the buyer – he acquired it for 1,000 rdl. The Mission house served as living quarters for four of the missionaries, but it was also a school, which later became known as the Big Mission House. In 1785, C. S. John made considerable changes to this house, and it is likely that the garden, whose plans were discussed by John, was located here. In 1716, Hassius sold the plot to the north to the missionaries for 100 rdl; this remains an open space whose other side opens onto Borgen Street. To the west of this ground lay Kröckel's[461] house, which he sold for 500 rdl in 1713. This became the Little Mission House ('Lille Missionshus'). The portico on King Street is probably from 1740. The first printing press imported by Ziegenbalg was initially situated here before it was moved to Borgen Street. Today, the Big Mission House functions as the Ziegenbalg Spiritual Centre and belongs to the Tamil Evangelic Lutheran Church (TELC).

Opposite the Little Mission House on the southern side of King Street is the New Jerusalem Church, with the impressive monogram of Frederik

Fig. 11.9: The 'small' and the 'large' Mission houses from the time of Ziegenbalg have today been merged into one building. Missionaries owned these buildings for more than 250 years. Anthon Gunter Würger sold the plots where these houses now stand to Ziegenbalg for 1000 rdl. in 1709. These buildings housed the first four missionaries as well as a school and a printing press, which printed the first books in Tamil (photo: P. S. Ramanujam).

IV. The first New Jerusalem Church, which was built at the eastern end of Goldsmith Street, was consecrated on 14 August 1707 and demolished during 1823-1825.[462] The ground on which the present church stands was bought in 1714-15 by Mrs. Bonsach for 850 rdl. In 1716, Ziegenbalg returned from his European trip with money and work could begin. Teakwood, glass windows and lead were bought from Nagapatnam. Construction started on 7 January 1717 and the foundations were laid on 9 February 1717. A copper plaque marking the occasion can still be seen above the main entrance to the church. Monetary and material presents helped along the construction work. A glazier was hired to come through from Nagapatnam to install the windows. During January 1718, a ship was sent to Jaffna in Ceylon (Sri Lanka) to fetch palm wood for the roof. The six columns on King Street were modelled after a German professor Sturm's sketches. A recent excavation at one of the columns showed that the street level was about half-a-metre lower – sand blown in from the beaches has it filled in. In July 1718, the English governor in Cuddalore presented

600 balusters for railings. The floor of the church was paved with granite from Sadraspatnam (close to Kalpakkam) and the path from the street to the door was paved with red stone from St. Thomas Mount, Madras. The church was consecrated on 11 October 1718. As this was also the birthday of Frederik IV, the cannons at Fort Dansborg saluted the occasion. Substantial repairs were made in 1748, but the shape and form of the church remain unchanged.[463] Ziegenbalg did not live to see the church in use, but he is buried inside of it along with Gründler. Today, it is the property of the Tamil Evangelical Lutheran Church (TELC). Several interesting details about the Zion Church as well as the New Jerusalem Church can be found in Gross et al.[464] The census of 1790 states that there was also an 'Old Jerusalem Church' in Admiral Street.[465]

The Church Register of the Jerusalem Church is found in the National Archives.[466] While the New Jerusalem Church is from 1718, the church register predates it, going back to 1707. It is remarkable that the register started just one year after the arrival of Ziegenbalg in India. Until the year 1800, all registrations are in German, as the missionaries came from Halle in Germany. England occupied Tranquebar from 1801, and this shift is reflected in the language of the register: All the entries between 1800 and 1880, long after the Danes left India, are in English. Unfortunately, the part of the register in German is in poor shape – either the ink is too weak to be legible or the pages have been damaged by water. The question of whether there was any social intercourse between the Danes and the local Indians, such as intermarriages, can be partly answered by consulting the register. Officially, there was no intercultural exchange, but several 'illegitimate' children of mixed parentage are nonetheless found in the registry: Benjamin born to a Malabar (heathen) and A. M. Susanna, Paulo Welusen born to Velayudam and Agatha, several children born to Mutukomaren and Charlotta David, children of Rahmasahmy and Catherina (wife of Billy Folly), children of Adimuhrty and Ellena (Hellena), 'Hendriana, illegitimate daughter of (the couple) Daniel (who is from) low caste and Maria Clemente' and many more.

Let us look to the left at the front of the Zion Church. Substantial remodelling of the Church was made in 1839; the church building, which was originally 120' in length, was shortened to 80'. It is likely that, during the 1839 reconstruction, a dome and spire were added to the tower. We have a letter in Tamil from the mason, Muthian, who was responsible for

Fig. 11.10: New Jerusalem Church, with a few of the graves. The church was consecrated in 1718 on Frederik IV's birthday and maintains its appearance until today. The walls have folded pilasters and cornices and a magnificent balustrade. The ground for the church was bought from Mrs. Bonsack, wife of governor Bonsack, in 1714-1715 (Mrs. Bonsack lived in a small house on this ground). Above the entrance to the church is a copper plaque with an inscription commemorating the laying of the first stone (photo: P. S. Ramanujam).

the reconstruction of the church, requesting 200 rupees for a continuation of the work.[467] The church was sold to the English in 1848, and today it belongs to the Church of South India.

We now reach the intersection of King Street and Queen Street. The parade ground lies in front of us, and we turn to the right along the western side of the parade ground, heading towards the fort. Here, on this corner, stood the house in which the last Dane, Arabella Due, lived. She was born in Tranquebar in 1820 and died in 1889; she was buried at the Old Churchyard (Nygade). In the census of 1835, she is registered as aged

Fig. 11.11: Interior of the New Jerusalem Church with the graves of Ziegenbalg and Gründler on the wall (photo: P. S. Ramanujam).

16. When Ihle, a missionary, visited Tranquebar in 1888, there were three old Danish ladies. Ihle describes his visit to her thus: 'Good old Danish pictures in flat frames, a mirror which has been made useless by humidity and age and a floor scrubbed clean, but so thin and unsteady that one was afraid of going through. The kind old lady came in. Did she remember Danish? Yes, when she read it, but speaking was difficult… One of her friends had left for the mountains and the other was sick. She always sat on the veranda from around 4 in afternoon, watching the parade ground and the majestic residence of the governor'.

In the house next door lived Madam Fjellerup – she who served tea for Rasmus Rask in Serampore – and her daughter, Harriet Anna Fjellerup. Madam Fjellerup – whose actual name was Catherina Elisabeth Braun –

Fig. 11.12: Harriet Anna Elberling and Frederik Emil Elberling. Frederik Emil Elberling was on his way to Serampore when he met Harriet Anna Fjellerup. He signed the documents that transferred the possession of Tranquebar to the British in 1845. Later, he worked a few years at the Danish Colony in the Danish West Indies (now U.S. Virgin Islands) before settling down in the town of Roskilde in Denmark with his wife and children (picture credit: Susanne Lindhard).

was the granddaughter of Gowan Harrop, whom we will meet a few chapters hence. Hans Jakob Fjellerup, Harriet's father, had died in 1835 and on this very day Harriet would meet her future husband, Frederik Emil Elberling.[468]

Frederik Emil Elberling was born in Copenhagen in 1804, completed his degree in law and was on his way to the Danish colony of Serampore to serve as the secretary to the Danish government. He had to stop by in Tranquebar for a few months before continuing his journey. He was an eligible bachelor aged 30; Harriet Anna was barely 14. After the death of Harriet's father, the family was moving to Balasore (Baleshwar in Odisha) close to Calcutta to live with her older sister and her family. Elberling travelled on the same ship and had plenty of time to observe the family. Two years later, he proposed to Harriet Anna, which was accepted and they were married in the Danish church in Serampore. Elberling oversaw the Danish census for Serampore in 1835, he was active in the establishment of a hospital in Serampore and served as its accountant for several years.

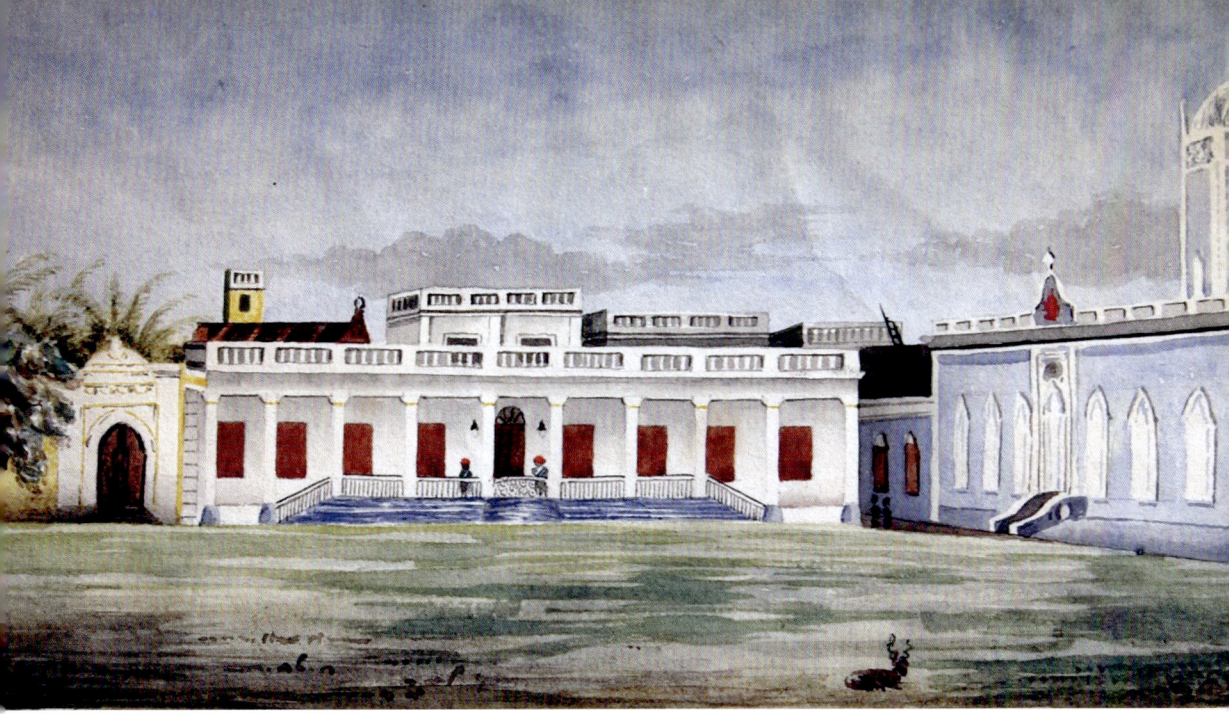

Fig. 11.13: The house in which Arabella Due lived until her death. The house was called 'Jørgensen's house'. The roof of the New Jerusalem Church and the tower from John's house can be seen behind. Zion Church is the blue building to the right (from a water colour by Selby, made in 1839, Danish Maritime Museum, Helsingør, Denmark).

In Serampore, the Hindus, Muslims and British all had different laws; Elberling was the first to gather all these laws into one monograph: 'A treatise on inheritance, gift, will, sale and mortgage: With an introduction on the laws of the Bengal presidency'.[469] At the time when Elberling was in Serampore, Peder Hansen, whom we have read about in an earlier chapter, was the governor. Peder Hansen was already in the process of negotiating the sale of the Danish colony. It was Frederik Emil Elberling, who authored the final documents regarding the sale. Later, moved to the Danish West-Indies (now US Virgin Islands) before returning to Denmark. Harriet Anna Fjellerup and Frederik Emil Elberling were to have 16 children, and their descendants are spread across several continents today. Elberling did not seem to have a high opinion of the Indians that he worked with.[470]

12

The Old Cemetery

When we reach the end of the street, we turn right (west) onto what was previously Nygade (now Athangarai Street). We see the old Danish cemetery on the left hand side – this is where we are heading. More than 600 people were buried here during the period 1767-1845. (During the same period, more than 130 people were buried at the Zion Churchyard.) We can estimate that perhaps another 1,000 people were buried here between 1620 and 1767. Unfortunately, there are only a few gravestones left; some of the prominent ones still standing are that of C. C. Eibye to right of the

Fig. 12.1: The Danish Churchyard in Nygade (Athangarai Street). One can just glimpse the ionic column belonging to the grave of Dr. Rühde in front of the back wall (photo: P. S. Ramanujam).

Fig. 12.2: The grave of Arabella Due, the last Dane to die in Tranquebar. She was born in Tranquebar in 1820 and died in 1889 (photo: P. S. Ramanujam).

entrance, a complex belonging to the Mühldorff family towards the back and that of the last Dane in town, Arabella Due. We shall look at two of the fascinating persons buried here, one from the early Danish period, the other close to the end of the Danish rule.

> 'The lover of truth, the enemy of vice, the prophet of his fatherland, the Danish Apostle of India, Magister Jacob Worm, who knew not how to deceive, but knew well how to punish sin and vice, who taught the erring and unbelieving both by his pen and by his mouth, rests in this place for the truth's sake; for though banished from his native country, he was not burnt out by the heat of the sun, but naturally and happily, after his sea-voyage, short stay in India, and much education

amongst the natives, he was received by Christ into the heavenly kingdom'. [Fenger]

This rather flattering epitaph was written on a monument in a corner of the churchyard we are now visiting, it concerned the Danish parson Jacob Worm and was allegedly composed by himself. However, the circumstances of his arrival in Tranquebar were far from exalting, given the fact that he was exiled from Denmark for 'unlawful' activities.

Political satire, especially against the monarchy, was not well tolerated during the 17th century. Yet, that was what Jacob Worm was good at, and he would suffer the grave consequences of that skill. Born in the village of Kirke-Helsinge in Denmark on 8 December 1642 as the son of the local pastor Peder Jacobsen Worm and his wife Anneke Heichon, Jacob Worm had the misfortune of losing his mother at an early age.[471] His father married the 17 years younger Sille Balkenborg in 1648, and three daughters and one son resulted from that marriage. Jacob Worm received his primary education from his father; later, he became a student at Slagelse Latin School. In 1661, Thomas Kingo, a well-known religious poet, was appointed as the curate in the same church as Peder Jacobsen. The relationship between Kingo and Jacob Worm was not good even from the beginning. There are unconfirmed reports that several of Jacob Worm's siblings were really the children of Thomas Kingo with Sille Balkenborg, and that Jacob Worm knew this, which may have been the cause of their feud.

Jacob Worm entered the University of Copenhagen in 1663. He became proficient in several languages, including Greek, Hebrew and Latin, and wrote 21 dissertations during his studies in theology and philosophy. In 1667, he received a Master's degree to which he responded by writing verses in Hebrew and Greek. Already during this period, he began to compose political satire. Shortly after obtaining his degree, he had the opportunity to preach for Frederik III, who promised him a lectureship at Viborg Cathedral, when one became vacant, with a good chance of becoming a bishop in due course. However, the position at Viborg was not to become vacant for a long time. Eventually, Jacob became rector of the grammar school in Slangerup until 1677. As irony would have it, Thomas Kingo was his chief here – a potentially explosive situation. (Jacob Worm acquired his Master's degree several years before Thomas Kingo did, which did not help the situation).

At this point, the feud escalated into an exchange of satirical of verses. Thomas Kingo apparently had a habit of wearing a calotte, which he never took off even when greeting people of high social standing. Here is an extract of what Jacob Worm wrote: [472]

> Borne by a clergyman, which he newly became
> It sits on his head so firm
> He would not remove it for anyone one without a squirm
> I know a Calotte
> It warms his head, it does him good a lot
> To wear a calotte.[473]

Biting satire against one of the most revered bishops in Denmark – and coming from the target's step-son. In ten stanzas, Worm lampoons Kingo's vanity, his ego and his drinking habits. All the verses end with the word 'Calotte' to make a rhyme with the second-last line. On Kingo's fondness for the bottle and pub crawls, he says:

> He fills his gut with beer and wine
> And lies in [the pub] like a drunken swine.[474]

The poem ends thus:

> And when you have quaffed all your beer
> [Put water in your calotte to make your throat clear]
> If at night you need a (chamber) pot
> Then use your calotte.[475]

Thomas Kingo responded in kind, but using much coarser language. However, Jacob Worm won the first round, and it was clear that his satire had punch. Both Kingo and Worm were looking to move on. One of the most important persons in the country at this time was Peder Schumacher (who later became known as Griffenfeld) who probably knew Kingo through Sille Balkenborg and was perhaps aware of the feud between Kingo and Worm. Worm, at any rate, was not successful in finding a new job and felt that this might be due to Peder Schumacher. Worm took his revenge on Peder Schumacher in the form of several stinging verses. Ironically, Peder

Fig. 12.3: Crucifix from the Greyfriars Church, Viborg, Denmark, where Jacob Worm preached. This is now at the Blackfriars Church, Viborg (photo: P. S. Ramanujam).

Schumacher was himself accused of treason and was later imprisoned on the little island of Munkholm off the coast at Trondheim in Norway, while Thomas Kingo advanced to the post of Bishop of Odense, one of the major Danish towns.

In 1677, Worm found that he could work for Pastor Anders Christensen Achton at the Church of Greyfriars in the town of Viborg. The custom in those days was that whenever the position of pastor became vacant, the new pastor had to marry either the widow or the daughter of his predecessor so that the previous pastor's family could continue to live in the parish. Jacob Worm married the daughter, Abild Achton, of his predecessor. Jacob Worm dreamt of merging the Greyfriars and the Cathedral of Viborg and he prepared to apply for the position of provost. Right from the beginning, he made enemies on all sides. Being very eloquent, he turned to vehemently rebuking the vices and crimes of society, regardless of who committed them. He found fault with several overlords in Copenhagen. What he was not allowed to preach directly, he vented indirectly in scathing satire. His targets included not only the Church, but also the war that was being fought against Sweden by Christian V (1646-1699). His poetic parodies include 'Studiosus Lamentans' and the 'Horologium Regium' and in prose 'Visio Abrahamstrupensis' and 'Idola Jeroboami'. In these, he practically accused the king directly of leading an immoral life and his ministers of committing various crimes. It is said that in 1680, at a dinner given in honour of the king's birthday, Jacob Worm refused to drink to the health of the illegitimate sons of Christian V, calling them 'whore's children'. This did not go unnoticed in Copenhagen.

> 'An officer of justice was sent to Viborg to search Worm's house for such papers as would justify legal prosecution… Jacob Worm gave up his keys, apologising for not going around with the officer as he had to preach the next day, and therefore remained in his chair in the study. The Officer could not find any incriminating evidence. The next day Jacob Worm based his sermon on the 34th and 35th verses of the 31st chapter of the book of Genesis, where it says that Rachel *sat* upon her father's images so that Laban sought them in vain. The Officer, who was in the congregation, immediately left the Church, and went to Worm's house and searched the chair where Worm had been sitting the day before. In a hidden drawer in the chair, he found the satires he was looking for' [Fenger].

Another story says that his mother-in-law had burnt the incriminating papers before the officers returned for the second search. Jacob Worm was promptly imprisoned. While he was in prison, he claimed that his words were taken from the Scripture and that he was accusing humankind in general, not individuals. However, this was all to no avail, and he was sentenced to lose his honour, life and estate. His estate was to be burnt, he was to lose three fingers and, finally, his head by the sword. Jacob Worm now got cold feet and appealed to several persons, pleading with them to save his life. Ironically, the only person who supported Jacob Worm was Thomas Kingo, albeit in the form of a not very flattering poem. Abild Achton, Jacob Worm's wife pleaded untiringly for her husband's life. In the end, he was spared, probably because the authorities were unable to find any conspiracy behind the satirical works. The sentence was commuted to exile in Tranquebar. Jacob Worm pleaded that he should be allowed to spend his time in the prisons of Denmark.

On the king's birthday, he appealed in the following manner:

> He has, to withstand India's sun, no energy
> But is better suited for the Danish clergy.

And further:

> I would be happier with water and bread at your place
> Than with the daily East Indian pudding of rice.[476]

Alas, to no avail. Sometime after arriving in Tranquebar, he was appointed precentor and was granted permission to serve as a chaplain, if the Danish East India Company so desired. The Company did not wish this. There is no record of what he did in Tranquebar. However, one event was recorded. The Danish Governor of Tranquebar at the time was Axel Juel. During his term, the economic situation in Tranquebar was deteriorating. In June 1684, Axel Juel decided to cut all salaries, except his own. This led to widespread protest, and Jacob Worm joined in plotting a coup against Axel Juel. It is not known how deeply involved he was. An informer seems to have revealed the plot to Axel Juel. In 1685, two of those involved were executed at Dansborg, and Jacob Worm himself was imprisoned in the fort. The claims against Axel Juel reached Copenhagen, and the king sent an official (Kalnein) to make an independent enquiry, which resulted in Axel Juel being sent back to Denmark on charges of embezzlement of government funds.

It is rumoured that Jacob Worm translated the Bible into Tamil, but there is no evidence of this. It is also said that he performed a miracle by stopping a temple procession amid his preaching. He is said to have died on the 17 December 1691 and was buried at Nygade Cemetery in Tranquebar. When Ihle visited Tranquebar in 1888, his epitaph was still there to be read [Ihle].

****

Fig. 12.4: Rühde's grave at the Athangarai (Nygade) Churchyard. His epitaph can be seen in the Zion Church. Anthon Wilhelm Friedrich Rühde (1777-1832) was the son of a gardener in Borreby, Denmark. After specializing in medicine, he came to Tranquebar in 1804 and served for 28 years (photo: P. S. Ramanujam).

The most eye-catching grave at the southern end of the graveyard sports an Ionic column at the top and this is the grave of Dr. Rühde. Anthon Friederich Wilhelm Rühde was born in 1773 as the son of a gardener in Sjælland, Denmark.[477] He studied medicine at the University of Copenhagen and became a surgeon in 1802. We do not know what brought him to Tranquebar – only that he applied for the position of regimental surgeon after Dr. Folly. He left Copenhagen in 1804 on a salary of 429 Rdl per annum[478] and arrived in Tranquebar to work as a surgeon. In 1808, Magdalena Elizabeth was born out of wedlock to Dr. Rühde and Chavari

Ammal.[479] On 10 May 1810, he married Agatha Margretha Mühldorff in Zion Church. His second daughter, Sara Minerva, was born on 13 November 1810. After 27 years of service in Tranquebar, Rühde died on 29 August 1832, 53 years old. His wife died 69 years old in Ootacamund, India.[480] From the census of 1834, we can infer that the Rhüdes lived up the street towards the west.

Rühde was, of course, not the first European doctor or surgeon in Tranquebar. Dr. Samuel Benjamin Knoll (also known as Cnoll) had his dispensary and chemistry laboratory in the Halle Mission's school in King Street in 1734 [Jensen 2019]. He not only looked after the missionaries' health but also that of the children in the Mission schools as well as carry out research in local medical knowledge. He sent hundreds of local dried plants to nine herbariums in Europe. One of them still exists at the University of Göttingen, Germany, and it consists of over 500 dried plants from the Coromandel Coast. Knoll was succeeded by Johan Gottfried König. The next person of importance was Dr. Theodor Ludvig Fredrich Folly [Jensen 2005]. Folly was employed as a second surgeon on a ship belonging to Asiatic Company in 1769. He arrived in Tranquebar in 1779 and worked as a second surgeon at the hospital until 1786. After the death of head surgeon Gottlieb Friedrich Böttger, Folly took over this position and became regimental surgeon. Folly wrote 'Notes on the Surgical Skills of the Malabar Doctors', which has been transcribed and translated by Jensen [Jensen 2005]. Dr. Folly is also buried in this churchyard.

Dr. Rühde's legacy lives on in a noteworthy article on Tranquebar's general health, which he wrote in 1831.[481] By and large, Dr. Rühde's narrative follows that of Dr. Folly. Before getting into the different illnesses and diseases that affect the people, Rühde talks about the lay of the land and its climate.

Rühde says that the air was warm most of the time and hot for 7 months of the year and that the climate was tropical between April and September. The temperature in the sun could reach 140 degrees Fahrenheit (60 degrees Celsius) at 4 in the afternoon. He also noticed that the transition from the south-west monsoon to the north-east monsoon was faster than from the north-east to the south-west. Indians were not affected as much by the heat as the Europeans were. The Indians ate and slept well and could sleep anytime. Dyspepsia, dysentery, diarrhoea, boils, general weakness and intermittent sleep affected the Europeans, especially the newcomers as well as women. Some Europeans could not get even two hours sleep during the hot season.

Rühde claims to have relieved these symptoms by using mild laxatives, gentle rubbing of the back and hot baths. In temperatures ranging between 37 and 60 degrees Celsius, people tended to develop Rubella – German measles. After a few years in such weather, the skin became less sensitive and people suffered less. During periods of flooding, malaria became prevalent. Intermediate fevers were cured with quinine – however, this did not seem to work with Indians. In the case of two Europeans, treatment with quinine was not enough; Rühde cured them with strychnine.

Another common illness among Indian children and youths during the rainy season was related to the eyes, which the European doctors on the Coromandel Coast called *Taraxis Indica*. Indian doctors treated this with a paste made from a copper mineral that was rubbed in breast milk on a stone and applied to the eyes. Another method was to use iron filings mixed with lime juice. The organist, Thannen,[482] was unfortunate enough to end up with the tip of a penknife in his eye while he was carving wood. He was treated both with a copper mineral and iron filings, but he nonetheless lost the ability to see with his eye. Rühde's own medicament against this affliction of the eye consisted of a little bit of zinc sulphate dissolved in an ounce of water to which he added a few drops of opium tincture. One drop was to be administered every two hours into the affected eye. If the eye was swollen, then frequent rinsing with a lead acetate solution was recommended. If the eye was so swollen that it could not be opened, then a pea size mixture of crude alum and pure opium mixed with pure unsalted butter was rubbed onto the corner of the eye every two hours. The sexton and the teacher, Wodschow, often prevented the disease from spreading using this treatment on schoolchildren.

During September, there was no wind and the temperature could reach 34 degrees Celsius during the middle of the day. Southeastern winds prevailed, turning to northeast, forecasting the beginning of the northeast monsoon. Insurance companies recommended that ships do not approach the Coromandel Coast from mid-October to mid-December. The rain was not as persistent as in Africa, but there were heavy showers from black clouds for about two hours each day. During the rainy season, water could be found at a depth of 50-90 centimetres. Floors and walls turned musty. Even though temperatures did not drop below approximately 21 degrees

Celsius, warm clothing was comfortable. Indians felt cold during this period. Fever, coughing, rheumatism, diarrhoea and dysentery were common, resulting in death for the weak and infirm. However, Europeans thrived during this period. Their appetite increased and their vitality returned. The temperature changed by about 7-8 degrees Celsius between January and June.

Most of the year, the air was clear and without clouds. The light from the planet Venus was strong enough to cast shadows. Moonlit nights were even clearer than frosty nights in Europe. The behaviour of the atmosphere was strange – the air pressure showed an ebb and flow, just like the tides. Apparently, Lieutenant Obelitz wrote to Rühde in 1824 that the air pressure seemed to be at its highest in the mornings and evenings at around 10, and at its lowest at 4 in the evening and 4 in the morning. Perhaps this could explain the fact that people who were most sensitive were awake at 2 in the morning due to the low pressure.

Rühde also wrote a note on quackery in and around Tranquebar:

> The preparation of any medicine by a person outside of a caste is rejected by others; however, when the need arose, they were willing to seek the help of European doctors. In connection with measures against the spread of cholera, the Tranquebar police stated that there were 66 Malabar doctors in 14 villages in and around Tranquebar, 18 in Poreiar and 11 in Tillali.

Rühde remarks that he never got a coherent explanation of the methods used by the Malabarian doctors:

> The Indians demanded to know from the doctor how many days their illness would last. A servant of mine requested permission to be absent from work so that he could punish a doctor, who had been unable to cure his mother within the promised period. 'Doctors' with several such cases often abscond from the territory with their fees, as they ask to be paid beforehand. They acquire the confidence of their patients through politeness and glib talk. However, many of their medicines are harmful and contain mercury. They have no knowledge of

surgery. The empirical understanding revealed by the doctors inland was much better than those in the coastal area.

Rühde put considerable effort into describing children's diseases and childbirth:

> (I) did not find a single case of scarlet fever among children, and measles was so mild as not to cause any consternation. Diphtheria, or 'putrid sore throat' as it was known, was observed only once during my 24-year stay. Whooping cough is epidemic, but not every year. The local doctors prescribe several practices, such as no milk for children. They charge 4 to 7 Rupees to feel someone's pulse and regulate their diet. Thus, the children, unnecessarily, go without nourishing food for half a year. Dealing with childbirth is in the hands of ignorant women. There is no adequately educated midwife all along this coast, not even in Madras. Civil servants and ladies of better standing have to seek the help of doctors when delivering a child.

Rühde helped to deliver 115 babies during his 24 years of service. He lost three pregnant women before they could deliver their babies and another two due to gangrene in the uterus; he was never asked to deliver a Muslim woman. According to Rühde, the Hindu was always worried about his wife and child and happily accepted help when necessary. However, Rühde experienced one Hindu case where the pregnant wife needed help, but the husband believed that she was unfaithful to him and that the child was illegitimate, and he let both die.

Rühde goes on to describe public healthcare facilities in Tranquebar:

> The hospital is situated in Bazaar Street, also called Pagoda Street, close to the Permaul Temple.[483] The hospital is divided into two sections, one for Indians and one for Europeans. In 1805, there were barracks for 150 men from the European garrison. When the Indian sepoys became sick, they were sent home for convalescence – only if they were seriously ill were

they admitted to the hospital along with the Europeans. In 1815, under Bille's administration, the hospital received several improvements, good beds and linens and good food for the military. After Bille's death in 1816, the garrison became smaller and the barracks thus became available. It was suggested that the barracks be included as part of a civil and military hospital to serve both Europeans and Indians. From February 1818, the hospital admitted all citizens of Tranquebar for treatment, without charging any fees for housing, food, bed, linen or medicine. A sick Indian soldier could bring as many of his family members as necessary for his care. There was an open shed in the courtyard where they could prepare their own food. If the Indian soldier did not want to see a European doctor, for religious or other reasons, he was welcome to be treated by a Tamulian (Tamil) doctor. When a patient lay dying, he could return home to have the prescribed rituals performed in the presence of a Brahmin. Indians had no faith in their own surgeons. During the 11 years that the hospital existed, several surgeries were performed and several people from and around Tranquebar were restored to health.

Rühde then describes the daily consultations:

Because the garrison was large, the hospital was always full of patients, and there was no fixed time for consulting poor patients. I set up my consultation for the poor between 7 and 8:30 in the morning in my own house. In the beginning, medicaments were imported from the Royal Pharmacy in Copenhagen on a requisition from the Danish doctor. Later, there were three local sources: 1) from the local market, 2) from the hospital's laboratory established by the doctor and 3) from the pharmacy in Madras. The first two sources are much cheaper. Vaccines are a totally different story because of the apathy and indifference of the locals. It is not the lack of encouragement from the authorities or the doctor to bring their unvaccinated children to be vaccinated. I promised them petty cash if they showed up for vaccination against cowpox: In the beginning, this brought several people, but after a few days, nobody came. It should be noted that no European or no one in the Mission schools was ever treated for smallpox (because they had been vaccinated). Leprosy is a bigger problem in the colony. It was brought to the Coromandel Coast by Africans kept as slaves by the Dutch in Nagapatnam. It is unknown in the areas further away from the coast. One of the sons of the former chief of the garrison, Colonel Stricker, returned from Europe in 1808. He had the disease when he was staying at the institute of Brahe-Trolleborg in the island of Fyn. He was sent to the Frederik's Hospital and from there on to Tranquebar with a certificate declaring that he was suffering from an unknown and incurable disease. After spending many months here, and after Colonel Stricker had paid a lot of money to a Tamil pretender practising quackery, the young man was sent to Bengal, where the disease spread even more, and he died there in a miserable condition. Medical treatises had nothing to say about this disease. Dr. Klein had a book that mentioned leprosy, and there was a discussion of it in 'G. G. Schillingii de Lepra commentiones. Recensuit J. D. Hahn Lugduni Batavorum 1778'. (Comments on leprosy by G. G. Schilling – Reviewed by J. D. Hahn). This doctor had spent a considerable time in Surinam and encountered the disease in a climate like that of Tranquebar, among the African slaves brought by the Dutch. Schilling does not mention that the disease is incurable, but a cure is almost impossible.[484] English doctors tried to cure it by means of arsenic, the French by fumigations of sulphur and the Malabar doctors by all the hocus-pocus of their quackery.

Diabetes Mellitus and anthrax affect a lot of Indians. The first is incurable, mainly because the locals refuse to give up their vegetable diet. It takes many years before the disease becomes deadly. During the last stages of the illness, people get carbuncles in the face or on the neck, which become lethal. Where carbuncles occur not in conjunction with this disease, patients have been cured with mercury in combination with a linseed carbon poultice. Only one European patient, a child of four, was seen with diabetes. Hepatitis is an illness that is encountered less than would be expected.

Rühde says that he treated two such patients after his arrival in 1804. Inflammation of the intestines (*Caput Coli*) was, on the other hand, widespread.

> The range of patients consisted of the garrison, Europeans and European families and those locals who dressed like Europeans. The garrison consisted of a sepoy corps composed of an artillery corps of 12-14 Europeans, some invalids, and senior citizens and about 30 cannon soldiers together with an infantry corps of about 50 sepoys. The second rank consisted of 15 civil and military personnel. They were all attended to free of charge and provided with medicine for themselves, but their families were not provided for. During the first quarter of 1829, 150 people were registered for treatment; 89 of them were treated at the doctor's house, 20 at the hospital and 41 in their own houses. Six children of soldiers died. Six European and 10 Indian soldiers have been sick in the garrison. Thanks to the generosity of the king, the position of the doctor has increased remarkably. He can now live a decent life.

*

Today, only a few grave monuments are left. Even about 20 years ago, there were several more. Most had a practical use – they were used for drying cow dung.

13

A Musician and His Tragic Fate

As we continue walking along Athangarai Street (Nygade) heading west, somewhere in the middle of the street on the right hand side was a house – now demolished – in which Carl Ludvig Runge lived, perhaps the most tragic figure in our history.[485]

Runge was born the same year as Walter, probably in Berlin (he later claimed an inheritance of 565 rdl from Berlin).[486] A government resolution asserts that Runge "came to Tranquebar as an oboist. He was em-

Fig. 13.1: Ib Andersen's painting of Nygade from 1948. The large house with the colonnade on the left belonged to Palle Krog Hoff Wodschow, brother of Runge's son-in-law, Jens Jacob Wodschow. This house has since been pulled down (M/S Maritime Museum of Denmark).

ployed as a cantor, 'the only person who could sing', at the Zion Church on 1 September 1780".[487] From the Zion parish register, we gather that he was married to Anna Elisabeth Tannen on 12 July 1781.[488] Their eldest daughter, Sophia Magdalena, was born in 1785, and in 1787, Charlotte Amalia was born. Heindrich George was born in 1789. Their last child, Carl Ludvig Runge, was born in 1790 but died the day after. From the census of 1790, we also know that Runge lived with his wife and three children as well as two servants in 'Nye Gade'. Everything looked idyllic. He even bought a few of the items that were auctioned after Thomas Christian Walter – one cup, two large pictures with gilded frames, one painting of Pastor Hans Madsen, one Chinese teapot, a dozen red and white cups, a colander, 32 panes, 1 palanquin, 4 bottles of liquor and 1 dozen silver teaspoons.[489]

Unfortunately, Runge had a darker side to his life: he was very short-tempered. On 25 March 1792, he threatened to shoot the missionary Johan Friderich König in the sacristy of the Zion Church. König promptly complained to the governor, Peter Anker: 'Last Sunday, Sexton Runge told Mr. Caemmerer in the sacristy that he was going to shoot me. He has uttered to several others in town – Jens Due, Beck, Colbiörnsen and Folly – that I will be shot the moment I said 'Amen'. I request the government to take necessary measures to prevent the sexton's evil intention'.[490]

Article 12 of the law (Proclamation of 1781) says that: 'When the clergy is to be examined for offences committed in their offices, then the governor will set up a Consistory Court, which shall consist of all members of the government and two or four pastors and missionaries of the Zion Church, depending on the nature and character of the case, and these people are to investigate and judge. The sentenced person can appeal his sentence to the Supreme Court. Should the governor feel the sentence to be too lenient, he can appeal to the Supreme Court for the sentence to be increased by sending all the documents pertaining to the case, in accordance with the Resolution of 8 October 1777. Should the defendant's offence be of such a kind as to require a suspension, then he remains suspended with the benefit of doubt until our Supreme Court's judgment. All other cases, which do not relate to the offices and relations of the clergy, come under the normal court, like the military cases'.

The governor, Peter Anker, found it necessary to arrest Runge and imprison him in the Dansborg fort. He also convened a consistorial court consisting of Councillor of Justice J. E. Colbiörnsen, Councillor of Finance Frantz Theodor Lichtenstein, missionaries Christoph Samuel John and Johan Peter Rottler and Secretary to the Government Johan Peter Hermansson.[491]

Several witnesses were called to testify. The first one was copywriter Beck – Claus Peter Beck who was 25 years old, of Lutheran religion and not related to either of the parties. He testified that, one morning a few days earlier, as he was walking past Runge's house, Runge called him over and complained to him that Madam Martini owed him some money, which she refused to pay him, because she claimed that Runge also owed her money. When Runge complained about this to König and requested him to collect the money on his behalf, König behaved indifferently. Beck also testified that Runge wanted to sue Madam Martini and, if he should be unsuccessful in getting a favourable verdict, he would shoot König in the forehead when he said 'Amen'. Runge apparently wanted to borrow Beck's pistol and intended to bring it into the church.

The next witness was August Friederich Caemmerer.[492] He presented his statement in German and a Danish translation was made. He testified that, on Sunday 25 March, it was his turn to preach, and Runge had come to him and told him about his quarrels with König regarding a few pagodas that were outstanding between Runge and Madam Martini. Runge requested Caemmerer to help him collect the money owed to him; otherwise, he would shoot König in the pulpit. When Caemmerer admonished Runge for his behaviour, Runge began to cry but insisted that he was going to shoot König.

Jens Due was the next witness – 37 years old, born in Jylland in Denmark and of Lutheran faith; he was not related to either of the parties. He testified that Runge had come to his house and complained about some outstanding amount with Madam Martini and had said that he wanted to shoot König in the pulpit of the church. When asked what he had against König, Runge allegedly said that he had asked König to get his money and König had replied: 'You won't get anything' ('Sie kriegen nichts'). When Due exhorted him against doing anything stupid, Runge had replied that if he were to die, it did not matter whether he died a day earlier or later. When Runge requested him to sell his pistols, Due said that he had already sold them to Captain Steed.

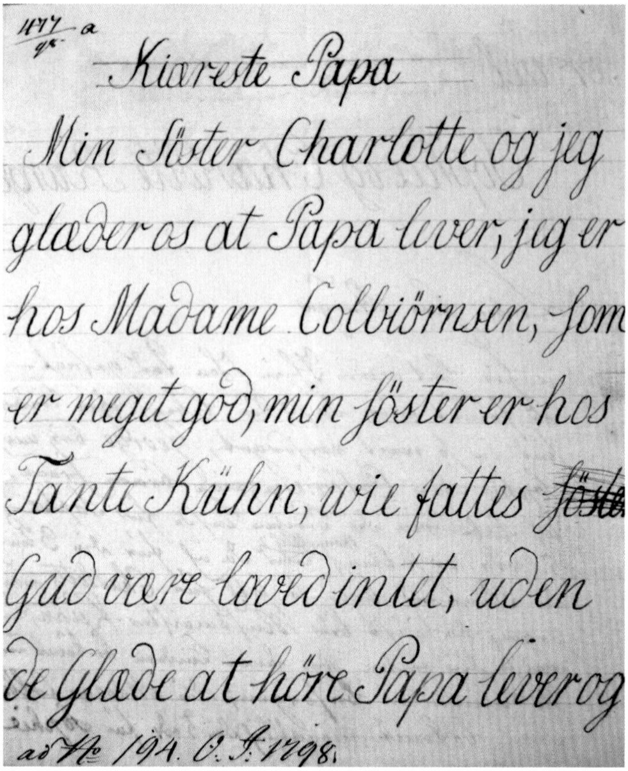
Kiæreste Papa
Min Söster Charlotte og jeg
glæder os at Papa lever; jeg er
hos Madame Colbiörnsen, som
er meget god, min söster er hos
Tante Kühn, wie fattes ~~föste~~
Gud være lovet intet, uden
de glade at höre Papa lever og
ad No 194. O. S. 1798.

Fig. 13.2: Letter from Sophie Magdalene Runge to her father when she was about 10 years old. Carl Ludvig Runge, her father, was sent back to Denmark as he threatened to shoot one of the missionaries in the Zion Church (RA: Kommercekollegiet – Ostindiske Sekretariat – Journalsager (1798) (Løbenr. 2015) #194) (Photo: P. S. Ramanujam).

Captain Schlimmermann and schoolmaster Sorgenfrey were the other witnesses. The latter testified that he had heard Runge say, in his house as well as Runge's own house and in the street, that he would shoot König if he did not get the 30 rdl that Madam Martini owed him.

While the court was in session, Runge sent a letter to the governor asking that the case be withdrawn and said that he would leave the Coromandel Coast, never to return within some 70 kms of it while König was alive. He wanted to be exiled to Denmark and be released from his work. While Runge was in prison, his wife, Anne Elisabeth Tannen, died.[493] Runge was paid the widow's pension of 55 rdl as well as his inheritance of 565 rdl and was to leave for Denmark as soon as possible. It was also decided that his children were to leave with him into his exile – however, guardians were found in Tranquebar to rear the children there.

Runge came back to Denmark and was placed under the care of town musician Ditlevsen in Roskilde. His life was miserable because he had become mentally deranged. He started complaining about small things. The only letter he received from his children in Tranquebar was written in 1797: 'Dearest papa, My sister Charlotte and I are glad that papa is alive. I am staying with Madame Colbiörnsen who is kind to me, and my sister lives with aunt Kühn. We are happy to hear that Papa is alive and well – (signed) Sophie and Charlotte Runge'.[494]

In the accompanying letter, Dr. Folly wrote that Sophie was living with Mdm. Colbiörnsen, Charlotte with armourer Kühn and George with himself, that he was paid 5 rdl by the church for bringing up the three children, and Mad. Colbiörnsen received 5 rdl for Sophie.

Runge wrote almost every year to the authorities in Denmark, asking them to let him return to Tranquebar to be with his children. On 28 August 1803, he appealed to the government: 'As I have received news from Tranquebar from my son-in-law, Wodschow, that it is impossible (for them) to subsist on the meagre income, please let me come back to my profession as a cantor or, in the worst case, let me support them with the 100 rdl granted me as pension'.[495]

Unhappy living under the care of Ditlevsen, he kept on changing his residence. In 1812, he pleaded to the government: 'I am living here in the greatest sorrow and concern in sadness over not being able to see my children in Tranquebar from whom I have been separated for twenty years. I am a very sick and miserable person without my children. Please let me come to my children on the first ship from Copenhagen to Tranquebar'.[496] In August 1803, he wrote: 'I have received information from Tranquebar from my son-in-law, who is married to my eldest daughter, that it is impossible to subsist on the meagre salary that he receives. I request the authorities to permit me to return to my work as a sexton in Tranquebar or at least support my family with my pension of 100 rdl. I do not understand why I should be refused the right to earn my living in Tranquebar. To put it plainly, an innocent man has been ruined, and my opponent, Missionary König, has been dead for six years'.[497] Runge died a wretched man, on 2 April 1819, 70 years old.

Through church records and census documents, we can follow his family up until 1843. His eldest daughter, Sophie Magdalene Runge, married Jens Jacob Wodschow at the age of 17 in 1802 and had 13 children (11 girls and 2 boys). She died the day after her last child – Johanne Mette Magdalene – was born on 13 April 1823, only 38 years old. Her husband,

Jens Jacob Wodschow, died on 2 September 1832. Of her many children, Sophie Elisabeth Wilhelmine Wodschow was married to a Georg Alexander Thaae; they had three children. Runge's younger daughter, Charlotte, who was brought up by armourer Kühn, married a man named Jacob Jahnsen. Most of the family seems to have died in Tranquebar in abject poverty.

*

We walk a few metres more. In the last house on the street lived Gowan Harrop with a daughter of his in 1790. Gowan Harrop may also have lived at the other end of the street, close to the cemetery – it is not easy to guess from the census of 1790. I have chosen to place him here, because I have decided that the chapter about him will be the last and the longest chapter of the book.

14

Plunder in Porto Novo

Harrup is a common name in Yorkshire and is also the name of a hamlet in Prestbury Parish in Cheshire. It has not been possible to trace the ancestry of Gowan Harrop. According to a search through the India Office Family History in the British Library, London, two Gowan Harrops are registered as having died in Calcutta: one is Gowan Harrop, buried 20 April 1761 in Calcutta, son of Mr. Gowan; the other is John Gowan Harrop, buried 16 December 1764 in Calcutta. Was the Gowan Harrop of this chapter related to the other Harrops of Calcutta? We do not know. The literature mentions a Harrop who was around Atchin (Aceh) as early as 1766.[498] He was an English merchant and came to Tranquebar in 1774, working for the Asiatic Company. In 1775, he wrote to David Brown, Governor of

Fig. 14.1: A view of the Bangalore fort, painted by Peter Anker (photo: Kulturhistorisk museum, UiO).

Tranquebar, saying: 'I would be extremely happy, if you would be pleased to grant me the post of Danish resident and factor (business agent) at Porto Novo',[499] which was a small coastal town north of Tranquebar. Denmark had a small trading post (factory) in Porto Novo. David Brown with Scottish ancestry became governor of Tranquebar during 1775-1779.[500]

During December 1775, he applied for money to construct and repair the factory's premises. Apparently, the construction was more expensive than he expected:

> 'I now have the honor to transit you Accounts of the expence of repairs, building a new ware house & new dwilling house for the residence of the factor of this place – I must confess, gentlemen, the expence runs much beyond my own ideas when the work was begun, but I have been insensibly led into it untill it went so farr, that I could not relinquish or alter the plan, I know also, gentlemen, it was never your intention to put the Company to such great expence nor was it mine neither at the beginning, & am affraid to have thereby incurred your displeasure, & which may draw upon you that of the Company at home, but rather than it should give you any uneasiness, & reflecting I am greatly the cause of this expence, as it was only your intention to build a new ware house on the spot of ground which was purchased for that purpose by the connakoply[501] some years ago and to repair the old factory house & warehouses & only add a room or two to it, for to make it habitable for an European, I say for all these reasons I should think it hard you should suffer any reproach or disapprobation from the Company, I am willing if the Company so pleases to pay yearly whilst I am their resident & factor at this place the sum of five hundred /500/ Pagodas until the whole is paid of I mean for what I reckon the extra dwilling house may have cost & which I think cannot exceed two thousand Pagodas the rest being laid out in building the ware houses, & other repairs which it is worth, & will make therewith a beginning at the close of this present year.

> I beg leave to observe to you, Gentlemen, that it is my opinion, this post of factor should never be put into the hands of black people, but give to one of the Company's European servant as a reward for his diligence & good behavior in the Companys service, because I am informed you have very few posts to give to your servants that is worth acceptance of. But this place may be very beneficial to an active understanding man, as many Commissions from foreigners for cloth of all kinds go through my hands & which will be continued after me, if care & diligence is observed – he will not only gain much by it himself, but it will also enable him to serve the Hon'ble Company the better with their own investment. – Excuse this freedom, I mean nothing more by it, than the good of this service in general and wellfare of the company's servants in particular.-'

He was appointed 'resident' (representative) and agent in Porto Novo by the board of directors of the Asiatic Company, Denmark, in 1778. In addition to being an agent, he was also allowed to conduct private business. He bought and sold textiles, both for the Company and for himself.

However, his comfortable world collapsed during the Anglo-Mysore Wars. Porto Novo was plundered by Heider Ali's troops in 1780, and Gowan Harrop was taken a hostage in July 1780. He was released in September 1781, having been kept hostage for more than a year and tortured in the attempt to extract a ransom from him. In 117 meticulous pages, he recounts his period as a hostage in a matter-of-fact, yet moving, way;[502] and it is reproduced here verbatim, complete and in his own wording. The only modifications that I have made are to omit the excessive use of capital letters in the original. I have kept the original spelling and only have made 'mild changes' in punctuation to make reading easier:

> A memorial of the capture of Porto Novo or Mahomed Bunder, a sea port town, belonging to his Highness the nabob Moahomed Ally Cawn, of the Carnatic on the coast of Coromandel; by a detachment of Heyder Ally Cawn Bahaders troops.

Containing an account of the plundering of the Danish and Dutch factory and other unhappy events, together with a particular account of the sufferings of Mr. Gowan Harrop, who at that time was employed and personally acting as factor and contractor for the honorable Danish Asiatic Company at the said place, and residing in the said Danish factory, and also one of the principal merchants and an inhabitant of Tranq. (Tranquebar)

On the 22nd July 1780, in the forenoon about 11 O'Clock a report was brought into Porto Novo by a cooly man that he had been plundered about 8 or 10 miles to the westward of the said place, by a party of horsemen, but he could not tell whether they belonged to his Highness the Nabob Mahomed Ally Cawn or to Heider Ally Cawn, however, the account was sufficient to give me the alarm, & put me upon my guard as I suspected the horsemen to belong to Heider Ally Cawn. I therefore began immediately to prepare to embale such of the piece goods as was ready for embaling, and of which there was a large quantity in the factory, belonging to the Danish company Captain Peter Dahl;[503] and others as well as my own as will appear by the several estimates of losses. These as well as my family & valuable I intended to have embarked on board the country vessels in the road for which purpose I had engaged four boates and thirty cooleys & advanced them money. I likewise, the moment I heard the report, sent peons to the washers and dressers of cloth, to bring in all the cloth they had belonging to the factory at the bleachery, wash'd or unwash'd. The whole town took the alarm as it were instantaneously and language is too feeble to express the terror; and amazement visible in every countenance. The Amildar Cooty Iyan himself and his brother, Narain Iyan endeavoured to pacify the people by assuring them that the horsemen belonged to their master, the Nabob Mahomed Ally Cawn, and that they therefore need not give themselves any concern or be under any fearfull apprehensions. But alas! We soon found their assurance was not to be depended on for to our utmost grief, and astonishment in a few minutes we had the disagreeable prospect of viewing the horsemen galloping in every street of Porto Novo, and one party of them passing by the north gate of my factory. I thought it most prudent to desist from embaling the cloth & endeavour as well as I was able to secure the gate of the factory which I accordingly did – The town was now in an uproar, and nothing but scenes of confusion, horror & dismay was to be seen or heard. Men, women and children all flying from their habitations made the best of their way towards the river mouth, in order by crossing the river to escape from, and avoid the wanton cruelty of those merciless ravagers who regarding neither sex nor age made all that were so unfortunate as to fall in their way a prey to their ungoverned rage and fury – About 1 O'Clock a message was sent to me from Mr. L. C. Topander / Resident of the Dutch factory which is situated on the bank of the river that several dead bodies of men and women had been seen floating down the river .

This melancholy news redoubled / if possible/ my exertions for the security of the factory; I get ready the few stan of arms I had in the factory belonging to me and what ammunition I had (which was but very little) consisting only of one bottle of fine powder, and some small short musquet balls I had none, nor any other weapons offensive or defensive.

A few minutes after this the enemies musquetry began to fire in the streets, and into the houses round the two factorys; many musquets were fired at the Dutch factory, and at the boats crossing the river with people and wounded several, one man and an old woman each received a ball from the enemy / which proved mortal to both / under the walls of the Dutch factory, & about 2 O'Clock a full company of seapoys consisting of one hundred men with their black officers, all dress'd in red jackets, and arm'd with English Company's musquets and bayonets fix'd appear'd before my factory, and summoned my appearance, I went upon the terras or roof of the factory, and spoke to them in the moorish language to the following purpose That I hoped they would be pleased to observe the good understanding subsisting between their Nabob Heider Ally Cawn Bahadur and the Danish Nation; whose colours they saw flying on the flagstaff in the factory, I likewise observ'd to them that our nation held this factory by a grant from the ancient Nabob that it was govern'd entirely by the directions of the Governor of Tranquebar and that I was placed in it in order to contract for and purchase goods to supply the annual ships of the Danish Company from Europe. The commanding officer of this Company a(n)swer'd and said that his Nabob Bahadur had sent the Chutta Nabob (or young Nabob) Carrim Saib[504] for to plunder the town of Port Novo and that he (the young Nabob) was encamped just without the bound hedge of the town, that he had no intention of commiting hostilities against or disturbing the peace of the Danish factory but that he would do us favors, if I would go & pay my respects to him as a friend – This (continues he) he expects from you and I desire you will obey the summons I have brought without loss of time. I then enquired if there was any European commanders in his army. To which he reply'd that there was 500 Europeans under the command of Monsieur Lally.

I then considering my feeble situation and that the least resistance or obstinacy, would most probably involve me and my employers into the greatest danger and trouble as it was in their power to force open the gates of the factory, and that to deal mildly with an enemy of such superior force was certainly the most probable and best method that could be took to bring them to reason, especially as I should thereby avoid giving them the least cause or plea to insult the Danish flag and moreover, that as I could talk pretty fluently in the moorish language, and by paying my personal respects to the Nabob, I might perhaps be able so to expostulate matters with him as to divert him from his purpose, should he have form'd an intention of plundering the factory – From these considerations I resolved to wait upon the Nabob as it was the only prospect I could trust to, of rescuing the Danish flag from insult and the factory from being sack'd & plunder'd – accordingly about half past 2 O'Clock in the afternoon, I deliver'd myself into the charge of the black officer and his Company and by them I was conducted to two chubdars (belonging to the Nabob Heider Ally Cawn) to whom I addressed myself & spoke in the same manner as I had before done to the officer commanding the company of seapoys. They gave me very favorable hopes that the Danish factory would not be molested; and then order'd a guard of 12 seapoys to conduct me to the young Nabob, who they repeated to me was encamped just without the bound hedge – I was conducted by this guard to one of the limit gates on the west side of the town and there was desir'd to sit down for the nabob was not dispos'd to see me yet – I was detain'd there until 6 O'Clock in the evening when a seapoy came & acquainted the guard that the Nabob was at the Dutch factory, where I was desir'd to be brought. I was conducted there accordingly and introduc'd to one Soyad Saib / a relation of the great Nabobs who I have since been made to understand had the command of this ravaging party, and not the young Nabob he being employ'd with another party of horsemen plundering the country about Mannar Goody[505] &ac. He however made no reply to the compliments I gave him being deeply engaged in taking an amount of the merchandise and effects which they had forced Mr. L. C. Topander to deliver.

 Having took all that they thought worth taking they loaded 50 camels therewith having for this purpose brought upwards of 200 camels with them – about ½ past 6 O'Clock having finished their business at the Dutch factory, Soyad Saib got up and desired me to – walk with him to the Danish factory. I made use of every expostulation I was master of to dissuade him from the action he was going to commit I laid before him the impropriety of it by urging to him that our nation to my certain knowledge were upon the best of terms with the nabob Heider Ally Cawn Bahadur in whose country / at Calicut / our nation had a trading factory as well as at this place, & that it was well known that the Danish merchants are the poorest of all the Europeans trading to India –

That we had always kept up a good understanding with all the European and country powers in India & therefore if he means to plunder or any ways molest our factory, he would thereby not only be guilty of an act of the highest injustice, but likewise by insulting the flag of his Danish Majesty in such a manner would draw upon his master the most odious epithets calumny and reproach from all the world, as his conduct in so doing was incapable of justification, having no just cause, plea or reason for committing such an act.

I begd him also to reflect for his own sake how dear the honour of so powerful and great a prince as his master must be to him and that any person under him conducing by any act based & unworthy to sully that honour, must consequently incur his heavy displeasure.

I endeavour'd to illustrate this argument more fully to him by intimating how great a fame, for value & generosity his master, the Nabob Heider Ally Cawn had acquired not only all over India, but likewise throughout Europe, which fame, would lose all its luster if he persisted in so unjust so unprecedented a design, which would not only render him as the instrument, but likewise his master as the author universally hated and detested.

Thus did I argue but it was all to no purpose I might as well have endeavoured to have affected the heart of a statue, deaf to every remonstrance, dead to every call of honour and justice he still persisted and peremptorily ordering me cause the gates of the factory to be open'd, told me at the same time (with an haughty and imperious air) that he was sent to plunder the two factorys / Danish and Dutch / as well as Porto Novo and that he both must & would execute his orders at all events (adding) that if the gates of the factory were not immediately open'd he would cut me down, and force them this. I order'd the south gate of the factory to be open'd at which we enter'd and Soyad Saib order'd me without hesitation to deliver up to him, all the ready money, gold, jewels, toys, silver plate, merchandize and all other valuables that I had in charge – I then made an apology for making a necessary observation and spoke to him in the moorish language as follows viz:

I have hitherto looked upon the Nabob Heider Ally Cawn Bahadur in the light of a firm friend to his Majesty the King of Denmark, and my masters the Hon'ble Company of merchants trading from Denmark to this country, but if I have been deceiving myself, if to the reverse he is an enemy to the said King & Company, and if by his order you are forcing me to deliver up to you the valuable merchandize and properties in this factory I must do it.

But I protest in behalf of my masters and myself against your master, and yourself, that you shall both and each of you, be accountable for all losses, damages & injuries whatever that the King of the Company, myself & every individual shall, or may sustain on your accounts by this act of violence and arbitrary power. As it was impossible for me to express myself in this manner without shewing some visible emotions of my feeling, Soyad Saib with apparent indignation in his countenance put a stop to my speech by threatening to deprive me of life giving me at the same time all manner of vile, and abusive language, and orderd several of his people to shove me along into the several chambers and warehouses of the factory and to make me deliver all the money, jewels, merchandize & valuables, that I had in possession. I desir'd him to suspend his anger, assuring him that I meant to obey his orders, and that what I had spoke was no more than what my duty to my employers requir'd of one, and that had he been so unfortunate as to have been in my place I made no doubt, but the same motives would have excited him to the same behaviour. Seapoys & centrys being plac'd in every part of the factory within and without, I was conducted by eight of his people first into my writing room, and opening my bureau. I delivered to them all I had valuable in it viz. three bags containing two thousand Porto Novo Pagodas, which I had in readiness to pay to the cloth merchants that same day, one bag containing 700 Star Pagoda for current expenses, & ready to be exchang'd into Porto Novo's for that purpose, a gold head for a cane with a watch and a spring in the top of it, sett with diamonds to the value of 500 Pagodas the property of the owners of the ship Grand Basilius – a large silver beetle (betel) box of 50 Pagodas value belonging to myself; & a small purse the property of Padre Caitans Viages of Porto Novo Containing 150 Porto Novo Pagodas.

My iron treasure chest standing close to the bureau I was obliged to open that next, and deliver'd from thence four bags containing 3600 Spanish Dollars – three bags containing 1500 Rupees and also a parcel of Manilla gold, jewels and trinkets to the value of 600 Pagodas / which as well as the Dollars I had receivd in barter from some Manilla traders about a month before in return for piece goods which I had given to them.

I had four thousand Star Pagodas in four bags & 5 parcels of gold dust weigh(ing) 4 Cattys[506] & B. 15 in the same chest under some books and papers, but the bulk of the booty they had already got took up so much of their attention, that they made no more search in the chest. This rich capture being brought before Soyad Saib, he assum'd a milder countenance, and addressed me in a more gentle manner than he did at my departure – He asked me if I had no more money I reply'd no, he then orderd me to open all the chests and presses that were in one of the rooms adjoining to the little hall, where he was then sitting, which being done, they took all the silver plate, and sundry other valuables which were kept in a press for daily use, he then demanded the jewels & toys of my family; I told him that I had deliver'd to him all that I had.

He did not insist to look into the two rooms occupied by my family, one of which being Mrs. Harrop's apartment contain'd the best part of my plate nor did he middle (meddle) with my apparel or linnen : I then by his orders open'd the doors of the two warehouses, and one chamber which were full of cloth already dressed, from whence some of his people took all the cloth, and laid it down on the floors of the two halls whilst others were employ'd lashing it into corges[507], two of which were a load for a camel. They likewise open'd all the ready pack'd bales that were strew'd up and down the verandas & loaded 150 camels with the choicest goods in the factory.

Report being brought to Soyad Saib that the whole 200 camels were fully loaded that is 50 with the goods taken out of the Dutch factory and 150 with those taken out of the Danish factory / and more goods still being in the factory. Horsemen, seapoys, horsekeepers, peons, and robbers of every denomination, were then permitted to take as many pieces of cloth as the(y) pleased and in a very short time cleared the warehouses of all the goods – My banksall or private warehouse, which stood opposite to the south gate of the factory, contain'd a large quantity of goods mostly my own property, such as coarse long cloth 8 and 9 kall blue cloth and other assortments for India marketts not for Europe of which I generally had a pretty large stock by me ready for any sale that might offer, and to send away in my own vessels to the eastward; this warehouse likewise receiv'd such cloths of the company and others as was not dress'd, and prepar'd for embaling, no goods being admitted into the warehouses within the factory, but such as was bleach'd dress'd and properly prepared to be embaled when convenient so that this warehouse at the time of the plunder contained besides my own some of the Companys 8 and 9 kall long cloth[508] brown and undress'd, half wash'd, and wett as they were brought in / on the first report of the enemy / from the bleachers and dressers houses, as likewise some chequer'd coarse goods belonging to a Mr. Felise super cargoe of a Portugueze Europe ship, the enemy having no more camels or other carriage to load with cloth, and finding these not to their liking they were indifferent about them, and only took some of the finest of the blue and white goods out of this banksall with a large quantity of coir rope, coir and gunny bags belonging to me, for to lash the packages they made up and for the use of their camels, eliphants & horses.

About 2 O'Clock in the morning on the 23 July, Soyad Said orderd a guard of a seapoys to conduct me to his camp, and told me that he was under the necessity of taking me to the Nabob, I remonstrated but to no purpose, I entreated but to no effect, that he would not take me from my family.

Soyad Saib had with him on this expedition one Meer Said, whom I had seen at Porto Novo about two years before purchasing eliphants for the Nabob Heider Ally Cawn this man told me that if I would give Soyad Saib and him one thousand Pagodas he could procure me my freedom but knowing him to be a man of no confidence I reply'd I had not a fanam left but if they would indulge me with a day or two, I could borrow that sum from Tranquebar, or Cuddalore. At this the guard was orderd to hurry me along. I entreated Soyad Saib to let me see my family before I went, and take a little linen with me but he would grant me neither one nor the other saying that at day light, he intended to return to the town again when I should go with him and have an opportunity of seeing my family and getting what necessarys I wanted for the journey upon this the guard pushed me along and would not suffer me to speak another word.

About 3 O'Clock in the morning we arriv'd at the camp where I found Mr. L. C. Topander / the Dutch Resident / Messrs. Villock and Herst / the two writers under him / Mons. De Close, an inhabitant of Porto Novo, my bramney[509] writer Lutchmenarain and his younger brother Pearaya; Vanketrow bramney Cotuwal[510] of Porto Novo, who pass'd as a vacheel[511] to Mr. Topander, Varabadrepulle formerly a dubash of Madras, with his 3 Servants, Arnachillum Pulle a broker of Porto Novo; a brahmney of Karical, two servants and a peon belonging to Mr. L. C. Topander and six servants and slaves belonging to Mr. Villock, all captives as well as myself.

I likewise saw there Irlapulle, the Governor of Negapatnams dubash, Shatooraw his bramney writer, and a peon of the said Governors with his badge on, seemingly as prisoners, with this distinction that the said dubash lay on his palinquin, and all the other prisoners lay on the ground / I here mention this particular circumstance because I shall have much to say before I conclude this memorial regarding the strong suspicion every person of Porto Novo entertained of his being greatly conducive and instrumental to the capture of that place.

Being very much fatigued, and having had no kind of sustenance the preceeding day, I laid me down on the ground waiting very anxiously for day light, hoping then I should be permitted to see my wife and family but to my unexpressive grief, sorrow and disappointment, I found at the dawn of day, that the horsemen and all the rest of the banditte of the camp was orderd to go and plunder the town and the factorys a second time, and that notwithstanding the promises of Soyad Saib, there was no possibility of my being able to procure leave to go, so that I should have most probably remain'd entirely ignorant until my release from captivity of the havock and injury they at this time did in and to the factory had I not sent a peon to bring me some refreshment from the house and to bring me some account of my family.

The peon / whom I sent / returning brought me word, that the north gate of the Danish factory was burnt down, and demolished by the horsemen & who enter'd and plundered every room in it, breaking open all the chests, bureaus, presses, & whatever else was likely to contain any thing of value in every quarter plundering & taking thence all the contents, especially the money & gold dust, which had been left in the treasure chest at the first plundering of the factory and now knowing what the parcells contain'd they was curious to know, and cut open one of them when the gold dust all ran out amongst the sand in the veranda, at the north gate of the factory, the larger particles of gold that were interspers'd amongst the dust they picked up again, but left the dust itself which was afterwards gather'd up by the peria[512] people of the town. He likewise informed me, that the floors of the chambers were all cover'd with blood occasioned by the plunderers who not agreeing about the sharing of their booty / which not withstanding the quantity that was took away before was very considerable / quarreled and sought for it. He also acquainted me that Mrs. Harrop and Family & Mrs. Karr, Mrs. Byrne, Mrs. Du Close, Mrs. Bento & several other women and children that had taken shelter in the factory / being first robbed & stripped of all they had about them / fled from the inhuman wretches, and in order to avoid any other insults or injuries from them ran into the river & there stood up to the chin in water, chusing by so doing rather to expose themselves to the danger of drowning & to the mercy of sharks & alligators than to the brutal disposal of those monsters in human shape.

In this situation he informed me they continued until a cloth broker of my house named Mootiapooley / and who was in the same distressed condition / ascerting himself swam across the river, and obtained a fishermans canoe with the assistance of which he put mistress Harrop and all the other distress'd families safely across the river, out of the reach of the enemy, & that they proceeded directly to make the best of their way to Patcheswaram[513] for shelter / which is a thick woody Country surrounded with the branches of the rivers Callatong and Devicotah.

The said peon also told me that nothing was left in the factory but broken furniture and some few stores that were of no use to the plunderers; such as china ware, glass ware and liquor. That a great part of my linnen and apparel were seen in the streets, and likewise some of my books and papers, a part of which was burnt in the middle of the factory by the enemy.

These accounts representing to my view my dear, loved wife & family exposed, insulted and distressed, forced away from home and abandon'd to the mercy of the world, nothing remaining in my power whereby to assist them, together with the thought that all my affairs must from their distracted and imperfect condition be entirely ruined thro' the loss of my books and papers, should I be able to procure my liberty, of which I now had scarcely a glympse of hope. I say, these thoughts, these ideas, added to the weight of what I already endur'd, renderd my situation at that time deplorable beyond description, and death would almost have been preferable to the load of suffering life obligated me to bear.

But my sorrow was not even yet half ripe, Heaven had for me greater and still, if possible, severe trials in store as the sequel of my narrative will show; and as it is impossible for me to describe my feelings in a proper manner, I humbly refer them to every human reader; let him but take home to his own breast my misfortunes, my griefs and my sorrows, and I am persuaded he cannot but feel the effects of pity & commiseration as advocates in his bosom for my unhappy condition.

The peon having brought me a little biscuit I distributed it amongst my fellow captives and dispatch'd him away again, with strict orders to go and find Mrs. Harrop and desire her from me to proceed as soon as possible to Tranqr.(Tranquebar) enjoining him to return to me as soon as he had deliver'd this message and to bring me some accounts from Mrs. Harrop of her state; but by no means to make any delay as I had no other servant with me but him – At this time, the camp was preparing to march and the peon left me, promising to join me in a day or two, but I never saw him afterwards during the whole time of my captivity.

On the 23rd day of July in the forenoon, the camp being in readiness for marching, the principal prisoners were ordered for to mount the loaded camels and the rest to walk. We were all safely mounted except Mr. Villock who, being a very corpulent man and not being able to hold himself fast, at the sudden motion of the camel, at its rising from the ground, he fell off its back, and the fall proved dangerous to him for, as he fell upon his head, his nose and mouth bled excessively, the wrist of his right hand was dislocated, his head, neck and shoulders much hurt and bruised and, notwithstanding all this tho' he was so hurt as not to be able to move, yet they set him upon a horseback and lashed him with ropes to prevent his falling, and he was not able to hold himself steaddy several seapoys walk'd along side of the horse to keep him so.

We march'd this day from 11 O'Clock in the forenoon to 4 O'Clock in the afternoon, thro' paddy fields and bye-roads and then halted at a village – The next morning, which was Monday the 24th Day of July, we proceeded on our march and about 4 in the afternoon halted at a village called Kistnaparam.[514] During this day's march, the horse on which Mr. Villock was mounted not being able to bear him any longer, he was dismounted therefrom and put upon the back of an eliphant and lashed on, after he had been sometime on the back of this beast he became faint with excess of fatigue and unable to support his body, he therefore dropped, hanging only by the lashings wherewith he was lash'd on. The seapoys were obligated to cut him loose in order to save him and, putting him upon a horse, he continued the march of the day; it was night before he joined us, and when he did, we had every reason to imagine he could not survive the fatigue of another day's march. We therefore applyd to Soyad Saib, acquainting him with the condition Mr. Villock was in and that it was next to an impossibility for him to survive another day's fatigue, we therefore requested that he might be left behind us at that village together with his servants to which he /Soyad Saib/ reply'd that if he could not take him alive to the Nabob, he would take him dead; however, the next morning cooleys were press'd and Mr. Villock was put into a palinquin. The day following, being the 25th in the morning, we marched and came in sight of Verdechellom,[515] a fortified pagoda at the distance of half a mile from it. Here the camp made a halt of three hours behind a large grove of trees / the motive for which was best known to Soyad Saib. When the three hours was elapsed, we proceeded on our march and had no sooner got into the open field and in sight of the pagoda, but they began to fire at us, aiming chiefly at the eliphants and camels, being the largest objects, many of the shells pass'd near us, but providentially none of the captives were hurt. In the evening we halted.

Thus we continued marching thro' the day and halting as night drew on continually, without any thing else material occuring untill Saturday July 29th. The army did not march on this day, Soyad Saib was employ'd in plundering the plunderers, or in other words in searching the troops & taking from them all the valuables they had concealed; at least so much of them as he could find, which consisted not only of jewels, toys, gold and silver plate, but likewise silks of all sorts, fine cloth of allmost every kind, apparel and fine linnen belonging to ladies and gentlemen, which had been took in the plundering of Porto Novo; but it appears to one that these troops were used to and consequently apprehensive of such searches, for notwithstanding the strictness of Soyad Saib and his attendants, they found means to secrete away from him great part of their booty, as I shall shew hereafter; besides I obser'd that from the time we left Porto Novo the whole army continually cutting up fine silks and cotton piece goods & making up dresses for themselves in the greatest hurry – I was also so particular as to note that of a whole piece of fine long cloth they made but one trouser, a whole piece of Suckertoon or long cloth went into the making of a long gown, so that the whole army from a most ragged & despicable appearance now form'd a most superb one, every individual being appareled in silks or fine long cloth, mouslins, chinzes or other valuable piece goods, and those cloths which they had on them were not molested.

This detachment, by every information and what we could observe ourselves, consisted of about 5000 horsemen, 400 seapoys or regular infantry, 200 camels, with about 4 or 500 bullocks and baggage horses of the followers and robbers belonging to the camp, besides 54 elephants which they took at Porto Novo.

Men of every rank & quality in this army were liable to and underwent the same search, both of themselves & baggage without distinction, and immense quantities of money, jewels, gold, toys, silver plate and fine silk and cotton goods weaving apparel and linnen were taken and collected from them and, an account taken of the same, this extraordinary booty was packed and elephants and bullocks laden with it, in sight of us captives; & we had the mortification to behold great part of our respective properties intermingled amongst the various packages.

Carrim Saib, the young nabob, with his party join'd us this day. He came into our camp about 3 O'Clock in the afternoon & received all the plunder of elephants and horses brought from Porto Novo and likewise us captives, to whom he spoke, giving us some hopes of relief when we saw his father and made him acquainted with our several historys. We mentioned to him that we were brought away in such a manner that we had not leave to procure any apparel or necessarys than what he saw on our backs and therefore desir'd he would order us some linnen in compliance with which requests he orderd us a piece of damaged brown long cloth of 9 kall, and a little old linnen of our own, such as was tore (torn) unfit for sale and consequently almost unserviceable. He also ordered us 5 brass dishes to eat our rice out of, we having no kind of vessel before for that purpose but the black earthen pott in which it was cooked. The provision allow'd us was rice, tamarin,[516] and salt & of these articles but a very scanty allowance, especially for the last two days, for no bazar / as is customary with almost all other camp / followed us, so that the whole detachment was obligated to subsist on the grain they procur'd by plundering the country we pass'd thro'. On the Morning of the next day, being July 30th, Soyad Saib dispatched all the plunder & captives under the guard of a detachment consisting of five hundred horsemen and one hundred seapoys for Commenalore,[517] a small town defended by a little mud fort, thereto be delivered into the charge of one Porney Oyan,[518] a bramney who had the charge of the baggage camp at this place; Soyad Saib himself and the rest of his party followed Carrim Saib / the young nabob / who was going to join the grand army then laying near Arcott.

The plunder, which Carrim Saib's party brought with him, consisted of brown long cloth of different qualities, silk clothes, brass and copper wares with which a great number of camels and bullocks were loaded, besides these the number of cattle of different kinds such as bullocks, cows, buffaloes, horses, sheep and goats that they drove out of this country and sent into Bahadur country, to be sold, amounted to at least four lacks / or four hundred thousand heads.

'Twas early in the morning when we began to march from this place, under the command of Gopalrow, a bramney writer, and one Peer Mohamed, a chubdar, and for two days these men kept us without food, and when we sent to them requesting a little piece that we might not die with hunger, they returned for answer that if we wanted food we might subsist ourselves on our own excrement for they had no rice or any thing else to give us; indeed, the country and villages thro' which we were then passing had been all plunder'd and burnt by the ravaging party under Carrim Saib & of course was entirely desolate and dispeopled so that no rice or other provision was to be procured in them.

This escorting party with their baggage was searched again on our entrance into the confines of the Bahadur Country, and notwithstanding the quantity of gold and silver jewels and other valuable that had been took from them when searched by Soyad Saib, there was now found amongst them and took from them no small booty of the same kinds.

As we proceeded in our travels into the territory of Bahadur we saw many small mud forts, slightly built, some of them in a ruinous situation with no guns in them & some entirely abandoned; the country itself indeed had a pretty fertile appearance, but was very thinly inhabited. The fort of Anundgary was the first we saw worthy calling a fort, it is built with stone and brick and is in a pretty good condition, but without any guns mounted (it is situated on the side of a river), and has a pretty good appearance. The next fort we saw in a tolerable condition was Kingree Kotta. After a fatiguing journey of 17 days from the time we left Porto Novo, we arrived at Commenalore on the 8th Day of August 1780 about noon, where near an old ruinated mud fort the bramney Porney Oyan[519] was encamped who came forward and met us about half a mile from his camp where the seapoys horsemen & etc were again search'd and a considerable quantity of plunder took from them, many things of great value having been concealed in the packsaddles on the camels' backs, which had not been discover'd in the two former searches and for which the camel keepers were severely punished.

When we entered this camp, the said Porney Oya[520] seeing that all we who were captives were in an ill state of health / occasion'd by want of provision and what we had being excessively bad, with the fatigue we had undergone, drinking bad water, laying all night in the open air expos'd to rain, dew and bad weather, together with the scorching heat of the sun upon us all day; all which concurred in destroying our health and had thrown the generallity of us into a violent fluse[521] and fever, of which number I was one / He, the said Porney Oya, thereupon ordered us to be placed under a tent, with a guard of about 25 seapoys over us within the tent and a number of peons round about us without the tent. Having frequent squalls and heavy rain every night, and the tent we had over us not being sufficient to protect us from the weather, Porney Oya sent us four coarse blanckets to cover us from the damp and cold. In the course of our travel from Porto Novo to this place I had frequent opportunity of conversing with the seapoys and black officers as likewise with many horsemen of different casts or nations, such as Moors, Maratta, Bramneys &ac, amongst which I found some endowed with tender bowels of compassion for the sufferings of their fellow creatures and by many of these I was assur'd that it never was the intent of their master Bahadur to cause either the Dutch or Danish factory to be molested, nor had he, they affirmed, any the least knowledge of such a thing untill it was executed. How possitive orders extending no farther than the plundering and sacking of the town of Porto Novo and the capture of all its rich inhabitants, Moors, Gentoos &c &c –

But that the havock and devastation that had been made in the factorys was entirely owing to the instigation of Irlapulle, the Governor of Negapatnam's dubash, who had not only wrote to the Bahadur of the riches these two factorys contained, but had likewise sent him a particular list of the names of every rich black merchant in the town, and how much each of them was re(s)pected to be worth, as likewise of the number of elephant and Acheen horses there was in the place, which induced the Bahadur for to order a general plunder of the town and inhabitants. But the black merchants having all made their escape, Irlapulle and the commander of the party were apprehensive of incurring the Bahadur's displeasure; in order as much as possible therefore to prevent it, they resolved that the factorys should be plundered and, if the Bahadur should disapprove of it, excuse themselves by pleading ignorance of the particularity of his order, that they held it to be general and had acted up to that opinion, which they thought would be most implicitly answerable to his command – This excuse gilded with the vast quantity of treasures that they should procure, this they thought would be the only probable means of reconciling the Bahadur to the escape of the black merchants.

The same people also aver'd to me that, notwithstanding Irlapulle's concurrence to and approbation of the above scheme, yet he had more than once mentioned his dissatisfaction at the conduct of the officers commanding the party, respecting the escape of the above said merchants & said he would acquaint the Bahadur of their misconduct as, by not paying due attention to his advice and instructions, they had given the said merchants an opportunity of getting away when they might, had they acted up to his directions, have secur'd them #

The account was confirmed to me by different people and at different times and, more especially, to the account of my bramney writer Lutchemenarain and his brother Paroyan, with several other Malabar captives, whose credit I had every reason to depend on. They informed me severally and jointly that they heard him / Irlapulle /express the above declaration to Tremeloya[522] a Bramney hercara[523] of the Bahadurs on our first setting out from Porto Novo, besides, as soon as we arrived at this place, Irlapulle had a separate tent given to him and his bramney writer, and had very particular marks of attention shewn him from Pornioya and was constantly in his company, except at the necessary times for victuals and sleep, and neither he nor his writer had ever been treated as the rest of the captives were.

On the tenth or eleventh of August Pornioya sent for me, Mr. Topander, Venkatrow bramney and Verabadra Pulle captives, to a private tent by our desire, where being present with us Pornioya himself, Peer Mahomud a chubdar and his son in law, likewise a chubdar, we was desir'd to speak what we had to say – I thereupon addressing myself to Pornioya and represented to him the injustice done to the two European nations, Danish and Dutch, by insulting their colours and plundering their factorys at a time when the two powers were observing a strict and impartial neutrality with respect to the contending powers of his Highness the Nabob, the Mahomed Ally Cawn & his master, the Bahadur, and at the same time holding a firm opinion of the security of these factorys from the tyes of amity, which they had every cause to believe subsisted between his master and each of these respective power, the Danes especially being allowed a factory in his country on the coast of Malabar. I therefore told him that I could not bring myself to imagine that the Nabob Heider Ally Cawn Bahadur had ever given any such orders, that from my opinion of his sensibility of what was & what was not political as well as just. I thought him incapable of entertaining such a thought as committing hostilities against two nations entirely free from war and only carrying on peaceably and honourably such a commerce as is allowed them by the country's powers, without interfering in any thing whereby they might give cause of disgust to any, but on the contrary the Danes especially had always paid the greatest respect to his master.

I reminded him also how much the Nabob his master's fame would be tarnished, & how little any power would for the future be able to rely on his friendship or alliance, unlike a speedy restitution was made to the suffering nations, their merchants and subjects – From which considerations I told him I was fully persuaded that, when our grievances were laid in a proper manner to the Nabob, then he would take the matter into consideration and redress them.

Pornioya reply'd that Soyad Saib had certainly acted wrong and so dismissed us on account of other business, which required his presence at that juncture.

On the 12th August in the evening, Mr. Topander myself and those who went with us the day before were sent out for by Pornioya, we waited on him accordingly at his publick tent / for cutchery[524] / where, being seated on the ground, he began to enquire what number of forces the English had in Madras, the Dutch at Negapatnam and the Danes in Tranquebar. We exaggerated as much as prudence would admit this number, which however he seemed disappointed with. On his dismissing us to our tent, we requested his leave to lay forth our grievances to the Nabob, either by writing to him or by being sent to his presence. He reply'd that he could not comply with either without orders from his master, but that he would write to him himself concerning it. We was then desir'd to return to our tent and shortly after orders came to the officer of our guard to admit no pen, ink or paper into the tent and to prevent our conversing with any but those within the tent.

On the 14th August 1780 the horsemen and seapoys that guarded the plunder and captives to Commenalore were sent away to the grand army, with whom Irlapulle / as we was informed by an order from the Nabob / was sent; he was equipped with a good horse and had two servants allowed him by Pornioya, with whose permission he called at our tent to tell us that he was going to the Nabob, and that he should sett off immediately, whereupon we who were captives, one and all of us in the most earnest manner, beg'd him to lay before the Nabob our heavy grievances and to do all in his power to procure redress & liberty, which we told him we made no doubt the nabob would comply with if we stated to him in a just and proper manner. He promised faithfully to excert himself and do the utmost in his power to procure us our liberty & restitution of damages sustain'd, and so saying rode off on his journey.

About a week after the departure of Irlapulle, whom we were all anxiously and ardently expecting to hear of some happy accounts of our liberty &ac Pornioya sent for Mr. Topander and me, and to our utmost grief and surprize inform'd us that he had just receiv'd an order / or parwannah / from the Nabob to demand four lacks of Pagodas from each of us for our ransom, and that in case of our non compliance he was strictly enjoined to inflict corporal punishment on us. He therefore bid us fall upon some very speedy method to cause these requir'd payments to be made as otherwise he must unavoidably inflict upon us the punishment orderd by the Nabob.

Our astonishment and agitation of mind on hearing this was so great that it almost bereaved us not only of the power of speech, but almost of life itself for a few moments. When we had somewhat recover'd ourselves, we reply'd that nothing in nature could have given us more surprize than the present demand, that we were ruin'd in the utmost extent of the world, not only having lost all the properties and valuables belonging to ourselves, and the properties of the respective companys whom we serv'd to a very large amount, but likewise those of many private merchants which at the time of the plunder was in our expected charges, that we were only servants acting for the respective companys to whom the factorys belonged, at the low salary of 8 or 10 Pag. (pagodas) per month; our employ being to purchase and collect piece goods for their annual shipping bound to Europe – We beg'd of him to consider how unreasonable it was to suppose us rich and employ'd in so low a way; that if we really had been so we should have employed servants to transact our business & not have done it ourselves, as was the constant custom of all European traders of affluence; that on the contrary it was well known that we never were so, but that all we had was deposited with us in our factorys; so that in the plundering of them we were entirely ruin'd and reduced to a state of indigence and want, and by the loss of other people's goods in our charge we were involv'd in very heavy debts so that it was not in our power to raise a single fanam for our ransom – Pornioya, after hearing what we had to say, order'd us to retire to our tent and to consult within ourselves a means to procure the money demanded to be paid. We left him with visible marks of derution painted in our countenance, and our hearts almost sunk within us by the weight of our griefs.

The day following, Peer Mahomed chubdar and some others being ready to depart for the grand army, Pornioya sent them to us to tax us about the ransom, in order that they might mention to the Nabob what they heard us say in answer to the demand for it. It was about midday when they came before our tent and, calling Mr. Topander myself and all the captives out of it, they repeated the Nabob's orders that severe threats of corporal punishment if we did not promise to pay the four lack (lakh) of pagodas set for our ransoms; we reply'd to them in the same manner as we had done the day before to Pornioya. They kept us two hours exposed to the scorching heat of the sun / which is no small punishment in this country / hoping thereby to be able to draw from us some satisfactory answer to deliver to the Nabob, but finding us inflexible and firm to our first protestations, they then told us publickly and without reserve that Irlapulle was the man that had declar'd to the Nabob that we were men of great property, and he / added they / undoubtedly must know in a great measure your circumstances and connotions, and certainly too knows that they are as he had reported, or he would not have presum'd to have told the Nabob.

To this I reply'd that we thought it impossible he / Irlapulle / could act so vilely and so contrary to truth, he knowing too well our present poor and ruin'd condition. They prevented me from saying any more by giving us to understand that nothing but the alternative of death or paying the sums requir'd could free us from the bondage and torture of their master, then ordering the guard to conduct us back to our tent, they return'd to Pornioya.

On or about the 22nd day of August, Pornioya sent for Mr. Topander and me again and acquainted us that he had receiv'd another pervannah from the Nabob concerning us, whereby he was orderd to lash us to elephants' feet and cause us to be dragged thro' the streets untill we died if we did not immediately promise to pay the sums demanded of us: I am, says he, very sorry to be obligated in compliance with my orders to cause this punishment to be inflicted on you, it is a serious matter and I desire you will look upon it in that light many princes and great merchants who have had the misfortune to fall into the power of my master having undergone most cruel tortures & in the end death itself, so that you must not think of escaping their fates, if you do not find some means whereby to comply with his demand for your ransom. However / continued he / I will so far befriend you that, if you will but mention a sum that you are able to pay, I will make the sum known to the Nabob & use my utmost endeavours hereby to procure you your liberty. We told him that all proposals of that kind were entirely useless; not from an obstinacy or perverseness in our natures, or the desire of keeping back the money requir'd at the expence of our liberty, but on account of our entire incapacity to advance it or any part of it, that we had already told him so more than once, and laid our miserable case open to his view; that we had it not in our power to raise the least trifle to save our lives, or we would not thus stand altercating on the brink of the precipiece [sic] of eternity, that we would with the utmost pleasure offer a sum had we a sum to offer, for in comparison to our lives all the gold in the world was nothing worth.

We further / tho' with much difficulty / added that if all our preceding endeavours to convince him of our utter inability to comply with the sums demanded by the nabob were insufficient, we beg'd that he would be convinc'd by this, which was attended with a flow of tears occasion'd by the oppressive weight of our sufferings obligating us to declare that, if the Nabob Bahadur still remains unmov'd at our miseries and still persists in branding his name with cruelty, reprieve and injustice, if he still continues to demand of us impossibilities and unreasonable exactions, we in such case have no resource but to the almighty and must therefore resign ourselves to the punishment, which the Nabob may have been pleas'd to order, and therefore beg'd of him / Pornioya / to look upon this as the only answer we could ever give to the demand, tho' death itself should be the consequence. Pornioya hereupon told us that he must have another answer from us on the morrow, desir'd us to prepare to give it so dismissed us to our tent. The next morning Pornioya sent for Verbadro Pulle / one of our fellow captives, formerly a dubash of Madras / and read unto him the contents of a fresh perwannah from the Nabob, in which he / Pornioya / was orderd to punish us in the severest manner, if we did not immediately offer a heavy ransom. Verabadrapulle expostulated with him and assured him that we were actually in the distressed circumstances we had represented to him, that he knew our friends and connections very well, and he did not think they would advance one hundred pagodas even to save our lives at this critical juncture. On being asked the motive for his thinking that our friends would not advance a sum to ransom us, he reply'd that it proceeded from the knowledge of what they had already suffer'd by the life of their goods in our charge, and there being no likelihood of their being ever paid again in case they should advance a sum to set us at liberty.

Pornioya then shew'd him a letter wrote in the Malabar language, which he had als (?) receiv'd from the grand army; it was signed by Irlapulle and directed to Pornioya, setting forth that if he / Pornioya / would be hard & pressing upon the fringeys[525] / or Christians / of Porto Novo, the sircar or treasury of the Nabob Bahadur would find a considerable benefit thereby.

The contents of this letter struck Verabadrao Pulle with astonishment and surprize, Pornioya desir'd him to acquaint Mr. Topander and me with what he had seen and read and likewise to inform us that it would be out of his power shortly to prevent the punishment / order'd by the Nabob on our non-compliance / from being inflicted on us – it was therefore his advice to us not to make so light of the matter; but to give him a promissory note, at least for forty thousand pagodas each; with which he would befriend us as far as to procure our liberty – Verabadrao Pulle came and told Mr. Topander and me all that had been seen and read by him, and likewise the message that Pornioya sent us. This account serv'd but to confirm us in our opinion concerning Irlapulle and, holding a consultation with all the rest of the captives, we concluded it would be best to send Verabadro Pulle to Pornioya with the following answer:

That with respect to the sum demanded, we had repeatedly given all the answer we could to it; but, as we found, that the

Nabob had been actually led to believe us rich, by the false insinuations of a man wanting to ingratiate himself into his favor at the expence of our lives. We therefore beg leave to acquaint Pornioya, that if he will cause Irlapulle to be sent to Tranquebar, and Negapatnam, we will furnish him with power to ask, claim, receive, and demand, in our names and for our use, all the properties of whatever kind that we have in these places, and the same to be apply'd to the payment of our ransom.

As to giving a note for forty thousand pagodas, we could look upon the proposal as little better than a decoy of the Nabob whereby to ensnare our lives by having then a plea to make to the world, that he put us to death for imposing upon him in such a manner.

If the Nabob's demands were confined to a few hundreds indeed instead of forty thousands of pagodas, there might be a possibility of our friends collecting such a sum for us; but even of this we were so dubious that we durst not promise it for a certainty – Verabadro Pulle went with this to Pornioya, who return'd us no answer to it.

On the 24th August, Pornioya sent for Verabadraopulle and inform'd him of the contents of a purwannah he had just received from his master, ordering him to demand the respective sums of money from each person in the following list.

Verabadro Pulle......................	pagodas	20,000
Lutchmenarain Bramney.............	Do	10,000
Arnachillam Pullea a Booker	Do	10,000

and of Venkatrow Bramney and others, Pornioya was to exact such sums as his discretion should judge fit.

Pornioya told Verabadropulle to acquaint us of this order and to desire the respective persons mentioned, to fall upon means speedily to pay the sums specified, or they should be punish'd to death.

Verabadra Pulle came and made the orders known to every one of the captives. All were most affectingly afflicted with the news, especially Arnachillam pulle, who judging Irlapulle to be the cause of this demand on him exclaim'd against him in the bitterest manner and informed us all of what service he had been to him at different times, one time especially, on our journey from Porto Novo, Irlapulle not knowing how to write well, and being in a great measure ignorant of the names and worth of the principal inhabitants of Porto Novo, after making numberless protestations of friends life and promising great benefits to Arnachillam Pulle persuaded him to write him down upon an olla[526] the names & work of every person of note in Porto Novo, and likewise an amount of what houses were and what were not plunder'd, in which list he inform'd us that Mr. Topander and my names were inserted and our worth, with also the computed value of the factorys at the time of plunder. This he told us he wrote & deliver'd to Irlapulle on the road between Porto Novo & Commenalore.

I ask'd Arnachillam Pulle if he could inform me what Irlapulle intended to do with that list, he told me that he had the curiosity to ask Irlapulle the same question who answer'd him that, if the nabob should ask him any thing concerning those affairs, he should thereby be enabled to give him a particular account.

In the evening of this day, Mr. Villock alone was sent for by Pornioya and ask'd by him what loss the Dutch Company might have sustain'd by the plundering of their factory at Porto Novo. He answered at least 50,000 pag. – Then he was asked what the loss sustained by the Danish Company might amount to, to which he reply'd at least as much as the Dutch. He was then ask'd what loss Mr. Topander and me might have sustained by the plunder. He reply'd he could not tell but that we both transacted much business both for the Company, ourselves and other merchants and consequently had large quantitys of goods in the factory at the time of the plunder; which as well as our valuables and effects of every kind were to be certain knowledge all plunder'd & brought away, and that we had nothing now left. Purnioya, interrupting, ask'd him with some emotion how he could say so? When Irlapulle, who certainly know our circumstances very well, affirm'd the contrary to the Nabob and acquainted him that both me and Mr. Topander were yet both worth a great deal of money? Mr. Villock, being a very rough and blunt man, told Pornioya in plain terms that Irlapulle had told a great falsity in so saying – Pornioya then ask'd Mr. Villock how much he was worth before the capture of Porto Novo; to which he reply'd 800 pagodas, including his house and effects, at which Pornioya laughingly told him he was certainly worth more than that, and that the Nabob had order'd 1500 Pag. to be demanded of him – Mr. Villock, in his blunt manner, told Pornioya that he was master of so many cash, so the Nabob might do what he pleas'd with him. He was then desir'd to return to the tent.

On the 25th of August, in the morning early, a subahdar / a black officer / of the guard of seapoys over us, with about a dozen ill-looking fellows, by order of Pornioya came to extort a written promise from Mr. Topander and me for 40,000 pagodas, for which purpose they brought with them several instruments of torture, viz. two long and thick leather whips for corporal punishment, four musquet locks for to pinch and torture the ears, four bamboo pinchers made so as to fix upon the joints of any person and being press'd together cause the most exquisite torture – Mr. Topander and myself were called out of the tent and the implements of punishment shewn to us, the subhadars telling us at the same time that if we desir'd to escape the tortures these instruments were meant to inflict, we must immediately give him a written promise for 40,000 pagodas each for our ransom.

We / as we had repeatedly done before to Pornioya and others on the same occasion / told the subhadar that we had already lost all we had in the world and were thereby render'd entirely unable to make any such promise; as it would be entirely out of our power ever to perform it. Necessity therefore compelled us to resign ourselves patiently to the disposal of the Nabob so far at least as the almighty should ordain from whom we implor'd mercy and protection. The subhadar went & acquainted Pornioya with what we said; when he sent for Venketrow bramney and enquir'd of him our circumstances, Venkatrow told him exactly the same as we ourselves, Mr. Villock and Verabadropulle had done before, and which therefore it is needless to repeat in this place. After hearing what Venkatrow had to say, he order'd him to acquaint us that he would give us another day to consider on and, if before the expiration of that time we did not comply with the Nabob's demand, he could no longer delay the execution of his orders, but agreable thereto must compel us to comply by hunger and tortures. On Venkatrow's return, he deliver'd to us the message sent us by Pornioya, and the instruments were taken away for this time.

Thus we were again reduc'd to the greatest agonies of mind, our sorrow not permitting us to take any sustenance or rest; all our thoughts were bent on our impending fate; as we now expected nothing less than to experience the cruel tortures of those instruments, which had been shewn us, on the following morning.

As we had no means of ending the torture, Mr. Topander and myself took a firm resolution this day and promis'd each other in the solemnest manner not to make any promise of money but such as we could rely on our friends for the advancement of, and which upon computation we found could not exceed 2000 rupees or about seven hundred pagodas each, and that no torture or death itself should induce us to exceed in our promise to the Nabob that sum.

On the 26th August, early in the morning, orders were sent to the havildar of our guard for to deprive us of victuals and water, until further orders from Pornioya, and to search us and our little baggage and take from us all knives and every kind of sharp instruments we might have, which was done immediately.

After Mr. Topander, myself and all the other captives had been kept in this manner without food for 48 Hours, the same subahdar above mentioned, with his horrid gang and the aforesaid instruments of torture, appear'd before our tents; and with the most horrible threats and abuse call'd Mr. Topander and me out of it. We obey'd the summons immediately &, with tears in our eyes and our hearts ready to burst with grief, we stood before these executors of cruelty. The subahdar put the question to me whether or not I would give a promissary note for the sum of 40,000 pagodas demanded by the Nabob? I reply'd that I had repeatedly answered on that head in the fullest manner I was able and further told him that, were I to give such a note, which I knew I could not perform, I should only thereby justify the Nabob to the world for any further cruelty he might think proper to inflict upon me, and by deceiving him render myself unworthy of any clemency.

 He would hear no more, but ordering his attendants to proceed in inflicting the tortures; they in the roughest manner seized hold of my right hand and applied the bamboos pincers to the lower joints of my fingers and pressing them together compelled me in the most lamentable manner to implore for mercy. The pain I felt was inexpressive such as God forbid my worst enemy should undergo; yet were my crys of no effect with these people, but deaf to all my entreaty; and dead to every thing but the compliance of their cruel orders, they still persisted in punishing me, until what with the agonizing tortures I endured, and the weakness of any body thro' illness and want of sustenance for two days and nights, my senses failed me and I fell down on the ground motionless – Mr. Topander and all the rest of the captives on being spectators of my sufferings began to lament and cry aloud for mercy of the Nabob & Pornioya – which together with the state I was in / which had the appearance of death / struck the subahdar with some compassion and he caused Pornioya to be acquainted therewith, who thereupon order'd my hand to be released after it had been press'd for about 10 minutes – But I did not recover my senses for full half an hour afterwards when I found my hand very much swell'd, and it had receiv'd so much hurt that I had not the proper use of it for a month afterwards – I was put into the tent and immediately orders were sent to the officer of the guard to let us eat and drink, but not to allow us any knives.

It was 3 O'Clock in the afternoon before any thing could be got ready for us to eat, the rice & gram not being boil'd before that time – As to myself, I had not the least appetite to eat, nor really the least inclination to live; all my former sufferings came fresh into my mind, which added to the weighty thoughts of others yet to come, made me think of death rather / in my circumstances / as a friend than an enemy, as it would ease me of the insupportable load of sorrows I now bore; I therefore rather wished ... than dreaded it, and would much

Fig. 14.2: A portrait of Purniah. Purniah (Purnaiah, 1746-1812), a Hindu administrator, had the distinction of serving under Heider Ali, Tippu Sultan and Krishnaraja Wodeyar of Mysore. He served as a military commander under two Muslim rulers, Heider Ali and Tippu Sultan. At the end, when Tippu Sultan's power was on the wane, the English bought him off. He was very skillful with finances and a respected administrator. He became the first Diwan (Prime Minister) of the erstwhile Mysore state (Yale Center for British Art, Paul Mellon Collection).

sooner have at that time … encounter'd it than another such punishment as I had just undergone.

It may perhaps be necessary for me to observe why I was so particularly address'd and the tortures apply'd to me alone, lest I should be deem'd partial in the relations of my own sufferings.

This proceeded from my being acquainted with the Moorish language, which none other of the Christian captives were, so that I being obligated to speak for us all was only deem'd culpable in such answers and observations of our state as gave umbrage to the different people we had to deal with.

This was the motive for their pitching upon me as the first and, indeed, only person amongst the captives that the torture was practiced upon.

In the evening, the havildar of the guard reported to Pornioya that I was very ill & had eaten nothing at all, when he sent for Verabadropulle and desir'd him to come to acquaint me that he was excessive sorry for having put me under so much torture, that nothing should have induc'd him to it but the Nabob's possitive orders, & that he would now write to the Nabob of the punishment he had inflicted upon me and of the condition I was reduced to thereby, and that I might rest easy until the Nabob's further pleasure was known.

Verabadro Pulle informing us of the same, it gave some trifling relaxation to our troubled minds; and by Mr. Topander's tender persuasions, join'd to those of all the other captives, I was prevail'd upon to take a little food.

On the 3. of September 1780, Irlapulle return'd from the Nabob and dismounted from off his horse near the tent of Pornioya who being gone to his prayers and dinner. He was obligated to wait some hours, during which time, tho' the distance between him and us did not exceed 40 yards, yet he would not come to see or speak with any of us, from which behaviour we concluded no good tydings had come from the Nabob for us.

However, we, as the reader may imagine, was very anxious to know if any orders had come by him concerning us, in order to acquire a knowledge of which Mr. Topander stood at the tent door & calling to Irlapulle told him he should be glad to speak a few words to him, to which he reply'd that without Pornioya's permission he could not talk with us. However, on Mr. Topander's pressing him to stand a little where he was / which was then about 30 yards distance / and inform him if any letter had been receiv'd by the Nabob from the Governors of Negapatnam or Tranquebar regarding us, he answer'd yes, that he himself had introduc'd the peons with letters to the nabob after they had been sometime in the camp without being able to gain admittance, on account of the letters not being made up nor sent in a more respectful manner, that thro' his intercession the Governor of Negapatnam's letter was read, but the Governor of Tranquebar's letter was thrown aside unnotic'd – Whether it has been open'd and read since he knew not. But the Governor of Tranquebar's peons were still waiting for an answer when he left the camp – Mr. Topander ask'd him if the Nabob had given any answer to the Governor of Negapatnam's letter; he answer'd: No, instead of which he heard that the Nabob intended to go and visit Negapatnam and Tranquebar soon in order to take and plunder those settlements. He likewise told Mr. Topander that the Nabob had order'd ten thousand men, horses and regulars to march against Sadras in order to take it. But that thro' his / Irlapulle's / intercession, that order was countermanded – and / says he / I am going to Negapatnam to execute a commission for the Nabob, which is to procure him ammunition and men from Negapatnam, which he wishes much to have.

 He likewise told Mr. Topander that he had used any means in his power to procure his / Mr. Topander's / liberty as well as the liberty of all the captives, but that the Nabob would by no means give ear to any application on that head, farther than assuring him that none of the Porto Novo captives should be hurt till he return'd from Negapatnam. Mr. Topander, observing him very richly dress'd, ask'd if the Nabob had given back to him his gold toys that Soyad Saib had taken away from him at Porto Novo; he reply'd: Yes, & that he was very well receiv'd by the Nabob and that all his things were deliver'd back to him again, and that he had moreover receiv'd several presents from the Nabob, as a pair of large gold bangles, a pair of gold earrings with large pearls, a gold solitaire sett with rubies and diamonds with a gold chain and 200 Rupees for his expences; after saying this, he took his leave of Mr. Topander and promis'd to see him again as soon as he got leave from Pornioya to do so. Mr. Topander reply'd that he should be much oblig'd to him for so doing as he had matters of much moment to communicate to him.

The two servants that I mentioned were allowed Irlapulle by Pornioya on his departure to the Nabob had been formerly servants to Verabadra Pulle, when he was took captive, and on their return with Irlapulle from the Nabob came to see their old master from whom we learnt / as also by Irlapulle's Bramney writer / that instead of 200 Rupees, it was two hundred Pagodas that the Nabob gave him and 2 shawls with a rich turband, besides all the toys and jewels mention'd by himself.

The next morning, we expected Irlapulle would come to our tent, agreeable to his promise, and kept a strict watch for him accordingly. He pass'd & repass'd several times, and Mr. Topander call'd to him, but he always evaded speaking to him by pretending to be always in a hurry. Suspecting that he would go away without giving us an opportunity of talking to him, & Mr. Topander & me judging it necessary that we should – before Pornioya – ask him concerning the information that he had given the Nabob of our being men of much property and riches, & likewise as he was now going to Negapatnam, whether he would undertake to collect what property we might have remaining in Negapatanam and Tranquebar for our ransoms, by virtue of any writing he should require from us for that purpose – We therefore beg'd of the subahdar of our guard to acquaint Pornioya that Mr. Topander, myself and several others of the captives solicited his permission to come before his presence & there to talk with Irlapulle, who, we understood, was to set forwards on his journey to Negapatnam that day. The subahdar went & made our request known to Pornioya and soon after return'd with an answer from Pornioya that he could permit of no such thing without an order from his Master, from which refusal many disagreeable reflections occur'd to us.

In the evening, Mr. Topander seeing Irlapulle near his own tent called out to him and told him that he was very sorry to find Pornioya would not give us leave to talk with him, even in his own presence. He answer'd and said that he was sorry too, and that he had been refus'd by him likewise to visit us.

Mr. Topander then told him that we had been inform'd by Pornioya and several others that he had given a particular account to the Nabob and his principal people of our worth & connections, and that in so exaggerated a manner that we had every reason to believe our cruel oppressions and my particular torture / of which he had no doubt heard / was occasion'd thereby.

He with seeming surprize reply'd that God knew the innocence of his heart in this & that he had not done any such thing; but on the contrary had used his utmost endeavours to procure our liberty by speaking to the Nabob and the principal people about him in our behalf the truth of which he said we should be convinc'd of by and by.

We thinking it not prudent to enlarge upon this subject at this time, Mr. Topander wav'd it and began to represent to him our situation & ill state of health for want of proper necessaries of life and desir'd him to advance us some money for our bazar expences which he might be sure our friends at Negapatanm & Tranquebar would repay him on his arrival at either of those places. He answer'd that he would let Mr. Topander have some out of the trifle he had, but that it was not convenient to him to oblige any person else. On hearing him say so, we desisted from importuning him for money and began to recommend ourselves to him, praying his kind endeavours to procure us our liberty. We told him that we depended on him next to God for our release, & entreated him therefore to leave no means untry'd with our masters and friends at Negapatnam & Tranquebar to induce them to excert themselves in our behalves with the Nabob, and to bring letters with him from the Governors / of these places / when he returned to the Nabob – He, promising to do for us all that lay in his power, left us with an assurance that he would visit us in the morning before he sett off, which he told us would be about noon.

This evening, Arnachillam Pulle / the person whom I have mention'd gave the accounts to Irlapulle of the names and worth of the inhabitants of Porto Novo / was sent for by Irlapulle and had liberty given him to return to his own country with Irlapulle, which he did accordingly. About eight O'Clock, Irlapulle sent Mr. Topander three Porto Novo pagodas with an apology that he could spare him no more on account of his heavy expenses in travelling.

On the 5th of September, Mr. Topander sent one of the seapoys of our guard to acquaint Irlapulle that he had receiv'd the 3 pagodas he had sent him, begging at the same time if he could possibly spare any more to be favoured with it, upon which he sent three pagodas more. About 10 O'Clock in the forenoon, he departed from the camp for Negapatnam without visiting us as he had promised. He was accompanied with a large equipage and retinue consisting of peons, chubdars, servants, horses, palankens, bullocks &ac.

On the 6th September, Pornioya finished sending off to their respective destinations the different kinds of plunder that were deliver'd into his charge by Gopalrow and Peer Mahomed, the elephants he sent to Seringpatnam, the cloth, gold, jewels & silver he sent to Benglore. All the Acheen & other horses fit for the purpose he sent to the grand army, the other cattle such as bullocks, cows, buffaloes, sheeps, goats, baggage horses and even asses were all sold in the camp and the amount of sales collected.

On the 8th September in the morning, Mr. Topander and me was sent for by Pornioya, when we came to him was desir'd to sit down, being seated, he began to talk to us, saying that it was impossible we should escape further torture & punishment if we did not fall upon some measures to pay the sums demanded for our ransoms – To which we reply'd that it was neither in our powers nor that of our friends to pay such a sum.

He then told us that he would send us to the fort at Benglore, where we must remain prisoners untill we or our friends would pay it.

We reply'd that he must do what he thought proper with us, for we had no alternative left for remedy to help ourselves. Hearing this, he told us to hold ourselves in readiness to march for Benglore the next day, we told him we was not able to walk that distance, whereupon he order'd six bullocks for us to ride on and one for our baggage, with twenty coolies to carry. Mr. Villock, in the same manner as he was brought to Commenalore we was then order'd to retire to our tent. The same evening he sent for me again and informed me that he had, the moment he sent for us, received a purwannah from the Nabob in which he was order'd to direct us to write to our governor, employer and friends to acquaint them that the Nabob demanded 40,000 pagodas from each of us for our ransoms, and that if such sums were not sent, we must not expect our liberty, and likewise that the people whom we did send should return with money or an answer within sixty days from the date of the letters, otherwise we should be tortur'd and punish'd to death, which was, he said, the common practice of the Nabob with his captives. We told him that we was positive our governor and friends had already suffer'd so much by the loss of their goods in our respective charges that they would not pay such a sum for us, especially as they had many such servants as us, so that our places would be easily supply'd and we, on account of the exorbitant sum demanded for our ransom, be left entirely to the Nabob's mercy. All we said made no impression on him, but he commanded us to write what the Nabob had order'd, telling us at the same time that we might return to our tent & prepare such of our people amongst the captives to go with our letters as we could depend upon, returning within the limited time, as we in case of their nonappearance should be answerable for them. That in the morning we should be furnish'd with pen, ink and paper for that purpose. After our return to the tent, we began to consider who we should send that we thought would not deceive us, but return again with letters to the Nabob from our governors, employers & friends. Mr. Topander pitch'd upon Venkatrow Bramney and his peon Mootia, & I could have no person more proper than my own writer Lutchmenarain. On proposing the matter to them, they told us that they would willingly go and faithfully return as required with letters from the Governors of Negapatnam & Tranquebar to the Nabob Bahadur. The next morning, being September 9th, Ponioya sent for us and gave us pens, ink and paper, sealing wax and our seals / the latter we ask'd for, as we knew he had them / We mention'd the people we had appointed to send with our letters, he approv'd of them and order'd us to finish the letters by evening as we should depart for Benglore early next morning. We promised to do so & took our leave. We made the best use of our short time in writing letters to our friends & superiors, but as I was not able to take copy of them I can only insert them at the charge of my memory so that tho' they may perhaps differ in some few words from the originals the purport of both is exactly the same.

To Messrs. Ottison, Halkier & Lÿcke, Agents for the Honourable Company of Denmark Merchants Trading to the East Indies in Tranquebar

Gentlemen

You have no doubt long ere this been made acquainted with the plundering of your factory in Porto Novo / on the 22nd of July last / in a more perfect manner than I at present am able to give you by a party of horsemen & regular seapoys belonging to Nabob Heider Ally Cawn Bahadur, who have brought me captive to this place with all the merchandize valuables & properties contain'd in the factory & my warehouses belonging to the Company, myself and others, which was under my charge.

The Dutch factory and town of Porto Novo shar'd the same fate with your factory & the Dutch resident / Mr. L. C. Topander / with his two writers – Mr. Du Close, an inhabitant of Porto Novo and many others, Mallabars & Bramineys are brought here with me, by the same party and remain here my fellow captives. The ill treatment and torture I have undergone already to extort from me a promise of 40,000 pagodas for my ransom is inexpressible, but has been hitherto in vain as I am sensible that I am not able to raise such a sum, nor do I think myself at this time worth one pagoda.

I am now commanded by the Nabob / as I am informed by Pornioya, the person under whose charge I am at present / to write to the Governor, my employers & friends and to acquaint them that he demands forty thousand pagodas for my ransom, and that if this sum is not sent within sixty days from the date hereof, that I am to be punished & tortur'd to death. In the mean time, I am to be sent to Benglore with the other captives there to remain untill that period arrives.

I have repeatedly assur'd Pornioya that I have no reason to imagine that my employers would send me any money for my ransom, as they have been such sufferers already by the plundering of their factory at Porto Novo that my friends are not in a situation of life capable of assisting me in this matter.

But he is deaf to all I say on the subject and I am compelled to write this letter to you to acquaint you of the Nabob's demand.

I beg leave to refer you gentlemen to Lutchemenarain & Venkatrow Bramneys / who were took captives with me / for further particulars as they have leave given them to go with letters to Negapatnam & Tranqr from Mr. Topander & me, who are to be answerable for their appearance within the limited time of 60 days, when they are to bring the money or a letter to the Nabob.

The only trust I have in this case is that the Governor in his representation of the affair to the Nabob will demand me in a proper manner thro' your kind intercession on my behalf.

I am therefore to pray you will use your utmost care & activity in sending back the messenger with letters from yourselves and the Governor to the Nabob, using every force of words needfull to procure my liberty &, if a present is requir'd to be sent with the letters, I humbly hope you will not let it be wanting.

 I take the freedom to recommend my poor distress'd family to your kind care and
>I remain with the most
>perfect respect
>Gentlemen
>>Your most obedient
>>humble servant
>>Gowan Harrop

Commenalore
9th Sept. 1780

To the Hon'ble Herman Abbestee Esq.
Hon'ble Sir
I make no doubt but my misfortunes have long ere this reach'd your ears, but in case they should not, for the particulars I am obligated to beg leave to refer you to the bearers hereof & my letter to my employers, Messrs. Ottison, Halkier & Lÿcke.

 I humbly beg you will be pleased to give ear to their intercession with you on my behalf and write to the Nabob in a proper manner for my release, and I doubt not but it will have a good effect.

 I have no one on earth to trust to but yourself and am threatened with tortures & death. I have no more time allowed me than to subscribe myself.
>Hon'ble Sir
>>Your most obdt.
>>humble servant
>>Gowan Harrop

Commenalore
9th Septem. 1780

In the evening, having finish'd our letters, we waited upon Pornioya with them, the two Bramneys and a peon – He, taking the letters into his sure hands, enquir'd who they was directed to, which we told him. He then ask'd what was the contents of which the Governor's letters, & I told him, repeating the words he had order'd us to write. He then deliver'd the said letters to our respective Bramneys, strictly charging them to return in the time limited. He then told us that, agreeable to his master's orders, he should dispatch us away to Benglore on the following morning and write to the Killedar / or Governor / of the said place to put us under torture & punishment if, agreeable to their promise, the Bramneys did not return on the limited time – On which the Bramneys repeatedly protested that nothing but death or some unavoidable accidents should prevent them from returning. He then ordered a passport to be made out and given to them to enable them to pass thro' the Bahadur's country unmolested, which being done we were all dismiss'd from his presence with orders to be in readiness to proceed on our journey in the morning.

We spent best part of the night in giving such necessary orders & instructions to the Bramneys as seem'd most requisite & need full to enable them to recommend in most strongly to the consideration of the people to whom they were sent.

Morning being arriv'd, we were hurried to sett off, but thro' unavoidable delays it was ten O'clock before we were in readiness to proceed, when our provision of rice for the days being given us we began our march for Benglore under a guard of 12 seapoys & 20 peons – the number of us captives being 16, viz.

Mr. Harrop / myself	1
Mr. Topander & 2 servants	3
Mr. Villock his 3 servants & 3 slaves	7
Mr. Herft	1
Mr. Du Close	1
Verabadra Pulley & servant	2
Peroya Bramney, younger brother To Lutchmenarain, my writer	1
In all	16

We saw nothing in our way worthy notice untill we came to Hoosare Cottah,[527] which was on the 14th September.

This fort[528] is built with brick & stone, has a pretty formidable apperance and is pretty regularly fortified, but we saw no guns mounted. We was inform'd that this fort was took in the last war by General Smith. The night before we arriv'd here, we heard the report of several guns, which we was made to understand was a rejoicing salute fir'd at Benglore on the arrival of the news of the defeat of the English army under Colonel Bailey.

We the next morning proceeded forward on our journey & receiv'd daily our allowance of rice &ac at the villages where we halted to rest. On the 17th of Septr., we arriv'd at Benglore & were detain'd at one of the limit gates untill orders came from the killedar for our admittance into the fort, which we enter'd about 6 O'clock in the evening, having pass'd thro' five gates before we got into it. In passing the last gate, we saw the killedar[529] Mizza Heider Hossen descending from a bastion of new works in the fort in order to see us, at the foot of which he stood, receivd and return'd our complements very politely & enquir'd of our healths very kindly; seeing that we were much fatigued with travelling he desir'd us to go and take some rest in a choultry in the middle of the fort, which was then in our sight. We went into it, & soon afterwards a basket of fruit was sent us by the killedar, which we eat for our supper that night, and then laid ourselves down to sleep under a roof for the first time since our captivity.

The next day about 8 or 9 O'clock, we were all sent for by the said killedar / Mirza Heider Hoossen / into the Nabob's palace where he held the cutchery for the place where he transacted the government business / this place is a large building in the Moorish taste, the appartments of which was richly ornamented with paintings & gildings, all in the same taste / we were desir'd to sit down being seated, the killedar ask'd our names, which we told him. He then enquir'd very minutely of our respective disorders, troubles & losses, and, as I was the only person that could speak the Moorish language amongst the Christian captives, I was obliged to interpret for them all, having related my own.

I concluded the account of our respective sufferings with some remarks on the injustice of the Nabob's behaviour towards the Dutch & Danish factorys & the insults he had given to both these powers, as likewise of his cruelty to us in not being content with having ruin'd us by taking from us all we were worth in the world, but still persisting in persecuting us for to comply with such demands as was not in our power, especially Mr. Topander & myself, from each of us demanding a ransom of 40,000 pagodas and, on our repeated asserting our incapacity to pay such a sum, he had given orders to Pornioya to put us to torture, and that I was tortur'd accordingly in order to exact from me written obligation to pay such a sum.

I then complain'd to him / the killedar / of our ill state of health, which I told him was occasion'd by our cruel treatment and bad provision, & that it was impossible we could live much longer if such treatment was continued toward us.

The killedar paid a more than ordinary attention to my recital & remarks and gave us every reason to believe that he was convinc'd of the truth of our sufferings & the justness of my observations and, expressing himself very feelingly affected thereby, told us that we might rest satisfied of being treated in a much better manner whilst in his charge than what we had hitherto experienced during our captivity. He beg'd of us to be cheerful and to compose our minds by reposing our confidence in God, the only deliverer from all troubles & afflections. He then desir'd us to return to the choultry, saying that it was the best place for us to be in at that present time, as the sight of the different objects that would present themselves to our view in the publick streets would afford us amusement to our minds & direct us from melancholy thoughts, whereas was he to put us into a house walled ground, it would have more the appearance of a prison & thereby render us sorrowfull & dejected. We thanked him for all his kindness &, praying him to continue his favor towards us, we took our leave and return'd to the choultry with hearts more lightsome & easy than they had been during our captivity.

The escort that came with us to Benglore being order'd away, a fresh guard was put over us, consisting of a havildar, six seapoys and six peons.

On the 19th Septemr, the killedar sent us another basket of fruits when we were made to understand that he had sent to acquaint the Nabob of our ill state of health and what it was owing to, & that he did not expect Mr. Topander & me to live but a little while longer as we had not a cash whereby to help ourselves with the least refreshments.

This information gave me some comfort & hopes at least of a continuance of the killedar's kindness towards us.

On the 29th Septemr, the killedar sent for me & Mr. Topander & gave five pagodas to each of us, saying that the Nabob had sent it in consequence of a petition he had addres'd to him in our behalves. We thank'd him for his goodness & took our leaves.

On the 5th of October, a barber was allowed to come and shave us. This was the first time we were allowed one since our being made prisoners, neither was herman or barber being allowed us before.

On the 10th of October, Mr. Topander and myself were sent for by one Balagerow[530] / a Bramney in power here, next to the killedar / we were conducted into the store magazine where he was, and after returning our complem(ents) desir'd us to sit down. When we were seated, he acquainted us that the Nabob had order'd the killedar in a purwannah receiv'd the preceding night for to press each of us for the ransom of 40,000 pags. (pagodas), which / he said / we had promis'd Pornioya & of which Pornioya had likewise acquainted the killedar by a letter. We express'd our astonishment at hearing this and told him that we never had promis'd any such things, but so far from it, that altho' I had been tortur'd by Pornioya in order to extort from me such a promise, I had still persisted in not making it from a consciousness of my incapacity to pay it, & that I was sensible our Company were already too heavy sufferers to be induc'd to pay such a sum for me, and consequently that their agents in Tranquebar could not be answerable for to make any advances of consequence on my account.

I could not therefore with any truth or certainty make such a promise and I would sooner have suffer'd death than sign'd a paper, which would not only have brought a reproach on me all the remainder of my life, but would in some measure have justified the Nabob in taking my life from me.

This / says I / I told Pornioya & it was then he order'd Mr. Topander & me to write to our superiors at Negapatnam & Tranquebar, acquainting them of the Nabob's demand from each of us, and that if the money was not sent in sixty days from the date of our letters, we should suffer death by a torturer — And this much we wrote accordingly.

Balagerow, on hearing what I said, saw clearly & express'd it to others sitting near him, that Pornioya had played us a trick, & in order to ease himself of the burthen of compelling us to a compliance had forg'd one, and thereby thrown the trouble on the head of the killedar — We were now dismiss'd and, shortly after, the Bramney Paereoyan was sent for in order to read Pornioya's letter to the killedar, and then was ordered to acquaint us with its contents, which directly corresponded with what we had been told by Balagerow himself.

On the 12th of October, we were sent for again by the killedar who spoke to us in the same manner that Balagerow had done / who was then present / and I recited the same particulars as I had done to him and beg'd of the killedar to write to Pornioya to know the truth of what I then asserted.

The killedar reply'd that all we could say now was to no purpose, Pornioya having wrote to the Nabob the same as he had done to him, in consequence of which the Nabob had now order'd him to press us for the money, and if it did not come soon he was much afraid the next order would be a very disagreeable one, no less than that of putting us to torture. He therefore desir'd & advised us to write to our Governors again, the sooner the better, and to send some trusty people with the letters whose return we could depend on.

I reply'd in answer that we had no person we could send, and that it would be entirely unnecessary if we had, as the letters we had already wrote would answer the same purpose to the full as twenty others would, we having in them set forth our situation in the openest point of view possible, so that, if it was in the power and intentions of our Governors and employers to serve us, they would certainly do it without any further solicitation. I therefore beg'd he would be pleas'd to permit us to wait 15 or 20 days, in which time I told him we had great reason to believe that the Nabob would hear from our Governors, if he had not already. Should we receive no accounts in that time to our satisfaction, we should fall upon some method of sending letters again.

The killedar & Balajerow were satisfied with this and permitted us to retire to the choultry.

Sometime in this month the unfortunate officers & European soldiers taken by Heider Ally Cawn's troops at the defeat of Colonel Bailey were brought prisoners to this place. The number of officers amounted to about 25, the number of private men about two or three hundred, the former were all kept prisoners in the fort, the latter kept in the pettah or town, excepting a part that were sent to Seringapatnam. About 20 or 25 days after the arrival, the officers as well as men put in irons by order of the Nabob.

The 2nd of November Mr. Topander's peon, Mootia / who went along with the Bramneys with letters to Negapatnam & Tranquebar on the 9th September last / arrived here with another of Mr. Topander's servants who brought a few shifts of linen cloths & necessarys for his master, with two letters from his friends, acquainting him that the Governor of Negapatnam's letter & present for the Nabob was preparing, with which Irlapulle & the Bramneys were to have sett off from Negapatnam a few days after the departure of this peon & servants.

The peon was first carried before the killedar who examin'd him with respect to the news he had brought and then sent him to Mr. Topander. The peon left Negapatnam the eleventh day of October, so that he was 21 days on the journey to this place from thence; the passport which was given by Pornioya to the Bramneys serv'd to bring him & the servants without molestation to Bangalore. My family & friends had no tydings at Tranquebar of this peon's returning to this place, so that I – receiving neither letter nor any thing else – must have suffer'd much from want of necessarys, had not Mr. Topander been kind enough to have shar'd his with me. All I could learn from this peon was that a letter & present was preparing to be sent to the Nabob from the Governor of Tranquebar by the Bramneys & Irlapulle, & that my family was safe at Tranquebar.

On the 8th day of November, about 9 O'clock at night, a rejoicing salute of great guns was fir'd from every bastion in the fort for the taking of Arcott. On the 12th day of November, the killedar sent for Mr. Topander & me and enquir'd what accounts we had receiv'd from Negapatnam & Tranquebar concerning the money for our ransom. We told him that our Governors had receiv'd the letters we wrote them, and that this peon was dispatch'd to acquaint us that the Governors' letters & presents for the Nabob was to proceed on their passage to Benglore by Irlapulle and the two Bramneys that we had sent from Commenalore. The killedar reply'd that he, agreeable to his last orders receiv'd from the nabob, was not to be satisfied with this information above, but that we must find a means to write to our masters again on the same subject and in the same supplicant manner as before. We beg'd his patience for a few days more in which time we had every reason to hope that he would hear from the Nabob concerning us. The killedar seem'd satisfied with our request, made some kind enquiries after our health and & manner of living & desir'd us to retire. On the 9th of December 1780, Verabadra Pulle departed this life with a putrid fever of two days, & his linnen with the few necessarys he had were by the killedar's orders given to his servant Tondroy.

The money which was given to Mr. Topander & me on the 29th of September having been all expended sometime / by reason of us having all our unhappy fellow captives to supply as well as ourselves / we made several applications and presented several petitions to the killedar of our being again distress'd for a little money for to defray our bazar expenses. He took the pains to write repeatedly to the Nabob concerning it and at last obtain'd leave to give us a supply equal to that we had receiv'd from him before, That is five pagodas each to Mr. Topander & myself, which was sent us on the 24th of December. Shortly after, the killedar passing near the choultry in which we were, we all stood up to pay our compliments to him whereupon he call'd me to him & ask'd me why we did not write to our employers & friends again regarding the ransom money in order to get our liberty.

   I reply'd that it was needless to write again before we heard the result of our first letters, that we expected our Governors had certainly wrote to the nabob concerning us long before this, and we imagin'd that matters must at this time be set on foot between the nabob & them for our liberty – which we trusted in God he would soon be inform'd of – On hearing which he smil'd & left me.

   In this anxious state we waited, expecting every day to hear some news from Negapatnam & Tranquebar, but every day brought forth nothing but disappointment untill the 31st day of January when we were agreeably surpriz'd by an information given us by several people that the killedar on the preceeding night had recd an order from the nabob to send all the Porto Novo prisoners to him at the camp. We were all inexplicably happy to hear this news, especially when as a confirmation of it we saw a dooley preparing for Mr. Villock which induc'd us to make what little preparation we were able for our journey.

Here I think it proper to remark that not only on our passage from P(orto) Novo to Commenalore, but likewise at that place, on our journey hither and during our stay here, we were inform'd by different people / entirely uninterested in our affairs, such as Bramneys, Moors Mallabars &ac who were moved by our sufferings / that Irlapulle was the cause of the army being sent to plunder Porto Novo.

On the 2nd of February 1781 in the morning, the killedar sent the Mayor / a black officer / to inform us that, as the Nabob had sent orders for all the captives from Porto Novo to be sent to him, we were to hold ourselves in readiness to depart for the grand army.

About 11 O'clock in the forenoon, a couple of tattoos or small country horses, five bullocks & a dooley with eighteen cooleys were brought before the choultry with orders from the Mayor to depart with us under the escort of one Hossen Mahomed with 12 seapoys & 40 peons.

The good usage & many civilities we had receiv'd from the killedar during our stay in Benglore merited our greatest attention & gratitude: we therefore requested leave to pay our respects to him before we departed. The Mayor inform'd the killedar of our desire & he sent for us accordingly. Mr. Topander, Mr. Villock, Mr. Herft, Mr. Duclose & myself waited upon him, and he recd us with great complaisance & civility and express'd his satisfaction at our going to have our liberty / as not only he but every person about him expected that it was for that purpose we were sent for / and congratulated us thereupon, wish'd us a happy sight of our friends & families and / as is customary in India as a mark of favour / he gave us some beetle nutts and leaves at parting. We took our leaves of him & all the mutchedys[531] in the palace and return'd to the choultry where the escort of guard were waiting for us; we sett out immediately, Mr. Topander & myself on horsebacks, Mr. Villock with dooley & the rest some on foot & some on bullock, walking & riding by turns as they grew tir'd of either.

We were conducted out thro' the same gates as we enter'd – after which at a small distance from the outer gate was the pettah / or town / thro' which we pass'd. I observ'd it was surrounded by a thin mud wall with small bastions at regular distances from each other and a thick chiakoy hedge within the wall; we saw no guns in the bastions, & indeed they had not the appearance of admitting any larger than one of two pounders being put in them. We likewise understood by enquiry that the inhabitants were oblig'd to defend it with small arms in case of an attack by an enemy.

We travell'd untill night came on and then halted at Kistnaparam. The next night we halted at Hoosare Cottah[532] – the next at Nursapuram[533] & the next at Colar[534] where an express from the killedar of Benglore arriv'd with an order to the escorts to avoid going thro' the Sautguru Pass, as he had order'd before, and directing them to go thro' the Chingernow Pass as the former had lately receiv'd some very disagreeable visits from Colonel Lang, who had made free with a vast number of bullocks laden with provision for the use of the Nabob army. We, accordingly, the next morning began our march towards the pass last order'd, which occasion'd us a rout of 4 days thro' woody & mountainous countrys before we could fall into the proper road., the first night we halted at a village called Coopom,[535] the next night at Boody Cottah,[536] from which place we marched the next morning and went thro' the Pass of Singrepelly & put up at night in the village Manarlapally. The next night we halted at Boodapally, next at Kistna Gurry,[537] next at Mottoor,[538] & the next at Chengamow; we got thro' the pass & arriv'd at Trenamally,[539] where we rested one day having had a forc'd march the day before. Here we got our linnen wash'd. The next day we march'd & at night, put up at Avalloor, from thence to Gingee where we was conducted to the baggage camp of Pornioya, again where we remained one night & the next morning halted at a fakeer's house; next night we put up a satrum or a Bramney cottage from thence we arriv'd at Panoratty[540] the following evening and halted, the next morning we march'd again & after passing Venketram Pettah we arriv'd at Mangalam.[541] Here the grand army was with the Nabob Heider Ally Cawn Bahadur in person. This was on the 22nd of Febry 1781. About 6 O'clock in the evening, we were conducted to a tent called in the Moorish language Toshakannah / or the treasury tent / under the care of a Bramney nam'd Kissengrow,[542] the Nabob's treasurer a man in great power & esteem with the Nabob Bahadur.

This man order'd our names to be took and that we should remain under the same guard that conducted us hither, at a little distance from the said tent, where we was kept at only half allowance of provision & exposed to the sun & rain. We now began to lose the sanguine hopes we had entertain'd of gaining our liberty, finding that the Nabob had order'd us to be brought to the camp in consequence of something, which Irlapulle had promis'd, but what was I have not been able to learn. My Bramney Lutchemenarain & Mr. Topander's Bramney Venkatrow were both in the camp, as well as Irlapulle, but they were not permitted to see or speak to us / the guard being strictly order'd to let nobody come near us / when we had been kept three days in this manner on the evening of the third day Irlapulle came to visit us, having obtain'd the Nabob and Kissenrow's leaves so to do and brought with him the two Bramneys Lutchemenarain & Venkatrow.

We ask'd Irlapulle what he had done regarding our liberty. He told us that the Nabob, well satisfied with the letters and presents which he had brought him from the Governors of Negapatnam & Tranquebar had in consequence thereof sent for us from Benglore, but he was sorry to find the nabob deviate from his first purposes (which certainly was to release us), but on some advice given him by Kissenrow the Nabob had order'd us all under his (the said Kissenrow's) charge. We then ask'd him his opinion with respect to Kissenrow's intentions towards us, to which he reply'd he could not tell; he only knew that Kissenrow had overturn'd all that he had done with the Nabob in behalf of us; but that he would go and try if by offering him a fee he could work upon him so as to be able to bring matters about again. We beg'd of him earnestly to use his utmost endeavours on behalf of us, & that as soon as possible as our present situation render'd our lives very miserable.

While Irlapulle was busy talking with Mr. Topander concerning affairs at Negapatnam, my Bramney deliver'd me several letters, two of which being from the Governor & one from the Company's factors. I here insert copies of them by which the reader will be the better enabl'd to judge how far these gentlemen excerted themselves in my behalf.

Tranquebar 10th Nov. 1780

Sir

By the letter, which you did me the honor to write me, I have learn'd your sad situation, which has given me much uneasiness & more so that in the present circumstances I see no remedy but to wait the Nabob's generosity & have patience.
I am most Sincerely
Sir
Your most Humble Servt.
/signed/ Abbestee

Tranquebar 30th Novemr, 1780

Sir

I have learn'd by your letter & that of the factors your bad situation, which has given me a great deal of uneasiness & I pity your fate. I wrote you by La Valiere. I have also wrote several times to the Nabob I see no remedy all circumstances consider'd. You must have patience & wait the Nabobs generosity who perhaps will be inform'd of your innocence and change his mind.
I wish you good health that you may be able to support your misfortunes. For the rest, be assur'd I shall do every thing in my power to be usefull to you & that I remain very sincerely

Sir
    Your most Humble Servt.
    {sign'd} Abbestee

To Gowan Harrop Esq. Tranqr. Novemr. 7 1780

Sir

Sometime ago we were favor'd with your letter dated Commenalore 9th Septem. by which we with the greatest concern are inform'd of the pityfull treatment, which you are oblig'd to subdue under in your confinement with Nabob Heider Ally Cawn Bahadur. We are, however, in the sure hopes that when the Nabob is better acquainted of your not being an English subject, but a Danish servant & inhabitant, that he then will be so gracious generously to see you releas'd of your disagreeable & melancholy situation, which you may depend upon will not occasion us lesser joy to learn as your imprisonments has occasion'd us sorrow.

To think of seeing you releas'd by paying 40,000 pagodas, as is demanded, you will easily judge yourself to be unnecessary, for if we even by ruining ourselves would join all our properties together, we then scarcely should be able to make up a third part of that sum. We wish to God that you was here, that we might get some account of the Company property at Porto Novo as the considerable loss, which it has suffer'd by the plunder of said place, has distressed us a great deal. Agreeable to your desire, we have spoke to Governor Abbestee for to do all in his power to get you out of confinement &, as he has wrote to the Nabob concerning you in the best manner, we are also in hopes that will have some good effect.

As we have no more to say at the present, we wish that God, who is our only & best comforter, will grant you patience in your pityfull situation and that we may soon have the happiness of seeing you free from further trouble and disagreeable manner of living.

We are with perfect esteem

Sir
Your most Obed(ien)t.
Humble Servt.

N. Ottisen, F. C. Halkier, I. Lÿcke

Lutchmenarain, after having given me the above letters, embraced an opportunity when Irlapulle was engag'd very seriously in discourse with Mr. Topander to whisper the following intelligence into my ear:

That Mrs. Harrop and Mr. Ottison had agreed with Irlapulle to give him two thousand pags. (pagodas). On his promising to procure me my liberty, 500 pag(oda)s of which was paid down to him them, the conditions between the parties being that, if he succeeds, the remainder should be paid on demand; but if he did not succeed, he should repay the sum advanc'd on his return from the army.

Irlapulle left us, giving some faint hope of his being able to yet to procure our liberties, but we never saw him afterwards during our stay at the camp.

Kissenrow,[543] a day or two after we had seen Irlapulle, sent for us & signified to us that we must pay the 40,000 pagodas that had been demanded of each of us for our ransom, that untill such sums were paid we need not flatter ourselves with any hopes of liberty unless by death, which would be administered to us by slow & lingering tortures. I reply'd for Mr. Topander & myself (as I had always done before) that the Nabob must use his pleasures with us, for that we were entirely ruin'd & reduc'd to poverty, & moreover involv'd very heavily in debt by the plundering of our factorys & therefore have no means whereby to raise the verriest trifle, much more the sum of 40,000 pag(oda)s for ransoms. He then told us that we should be kept in the heat of the sun and be secur'd with iron shackles, immediately upon which he gave orders accordingly & two pair shackles were brought and the blacksmith sent for; but he not being to be found, we after being kept two hours in the sun was remanded back to the guard from whence we came & the shackles with us – the same evening my Bramney Lutchmenarain convey'd intelligence to me that European ambassadors were expected shortly from Tranq(ueba)r as well as from Negapatnam. This news in some measure raised our drooping spirits, as we expected to hear of something by them to our advantage. On or about the 2nd day of March 1781, Mr.

Thomas Christian Walter & Mr. Stricker, a Lieutenant in the Danish service, with Daniel Pulle, a translator & interpreter, and a bramney vackeel arriv'd in the camp on an embassy from Tranquebar where tents were pitch'd near the treasury tent at the distance of about 60 English yards or 120 cubits.

By means of Pearoya bramney, I found means to convey any thing I had to say to his brother my bramney Lutchmenarain & receiv'd from him such news as he could learn without suspicion.

By this means I sent to him, desiring him to wait upon Mr. Walter with my best respects and request the favor of him to let me know if Brigadier General Abbestee had made any mention of me in his general letter to the Nabob and likewise to acquaint him of the misery I endur'd and the threats I had receiv'd from Kissenrow & such other matters as in the course of conversation might occur to him as necessary to display to him my situation. Lutchmenarain waited upon Mr. Walter and deliver'd the message according to my directions & return'd with the following message in return from Mr. Walter to me:

That he was exceeding sorry and very much concern'd at my misfortunes & troubles, and tho' the Governor had not made any mention of me in his general instructions to him, he was desir'd verbally by the Governor to speak to the Nabob about me, as soon as the business he came upon was settled, and that I might rest assur'd of his using his utmost endeavours for to assist in procuring my liberty.

On the 4th or 5th of March, Mr. Walter got audience of the Nabob when the Governor's letter & presents were received by him and, after that time, Mr. Walter had one or two more audiences with the Nabob that came within my knowledge, in one of which (I was inform'd after the matters of Tranq(ueba)r as far as Mr. Walter's instructions tended) was explain'd to the Nabob. Kissenrow ask'd the interpreter (Daniel Pulle) if they had anything else to say, and was answer'd no, they had not. Kissenrow then with surprize (as not only he but all the Durbar knew but too well that I had serv'd the Danish Company for several years at Porto Novo, which was the cause of my being thought of much importance to the Company, & so large a ransom in consequence demanded of me) ask'd him again if they had nothing more to say, adding withal: 'pray, who is Gowan Harrop, was he not in the Danish Service at Porto Novo?' To which Daniel Pulle reply'd that I was a servant of the Company and not the King's, for which reason they had nothing to say concerning me.

This circumstance being only intelligence that I receiv'd from my servants and other bramneys, I cannot positively affirm it for fact altho' the next days' occurences gave me but too much reason to believe it true.

On the 7th day of March 1781, Kissenrow order'd a guard of seapoys to bring me to him alone. It was between 4 & 5 O'Clock in the afternoon when I came before him and he, in the most tyrannic tone of voice, order'd me to go and prostrate myself at the feet of the Danish ambassador and beg of him in the most suppliant manner to be accountable for the ransom demanded of me by the Nabob. I reply'd that the ambassador knew the deplorable situation of my affairs too well for to advance the least sum for me; therefore, it was in vain for me to ask it of him.

Kissenrow then order'd two jellibdars[544], or whip bearers (whose business is that of flogging people), who no sooner came but he order'd me to be stripp'd, whereupon four fellows immediately seized me with an intent to strip me and lash my hand. I struggled much in order to prevent them from stripping me, & they gave me several blows in differ'nt parts of my body for resisting, untill they were tired with endeavouring to overcome me, I calling out as loud as I was able to them to shoot me, or put me to death any other way rather than punish me with them whips. Kissenrow then order'd the two jellibdars to begin to flog me as I was standing, which they did in a most unmerciful manner, fetching blood with every stroke, one standing on my right & the other on my left side; I called out begging leave to speak to Kissenrow one moment, upon which they stopped and I, addressing myself to the inhuman monster, told him that money was far from being so valuable to me as my life, that if I had'd I would most assuredly give it were the demand ten times as great as it was at present, I therefore beg'd of him to desist from endeavouring to extort from me such an impossibility. He turn'd a deaf ear to all I said and ordering his butchering myrmidons[545] to proceed on their bloody work, they laid on me with redoubled fury, my banyan (or open shirt), which they had in vain attempted to take off from me, was the only thing I had on my back, & it was soak'd in blood: my body all round being cut & mangled in a most shocking manner with their whips & bruis'd inwardly with the blows I had received from the ruffians that attempted to strip me.

They continued to flog me & I in vain to call out for mercy untill what thro' excess of pain and weakness from loss of blood, which ran in streams from all parts of my body, I dropp'd down senseless, & when I recover'd I found myself convey'd to the ground where my unhappy captives lay.

Messrs. Walter's, (and) Stricker's tent not being above sixty yards from the place where I rec(eive)d. this punishment (which was, I have good reason to believe, inflicted upon me in order to induce them being spectators of what I suffer'd to treat with the Nabob for the sum demanded or at least on their return to Tranquebar by reciting what they saw to induce the Governor and my employers to it) I take the liberty to call upon those gentlemen for to testify the verity of this account of my punishment, which is here related without the least deviation from truth.

Mr. Topander and others of my fellow captives procur'd some aloes from the bazar with which, mixed with lime juice, they anointed my wounds & cuts. In this condition, enduring the most exquisite pain & torment, I was oblig'd to remain always setting for some days & nights being unable to lay down & my sufferings not permitting me to sleep.

On the 9th of March 1781, about 12 O'Clock at night, I was suddenly sent for by Kissenrow, order'd away for Benglore with my bramney Pearoya, to whom Kissenrow offer'd his choice either to go with me or to take his liberty, but he was so generously grateful as to chuse to attend me to Benglore again.

The guard that escorted me from Benglore hither was now ready to return with 100 camels & 200 bullocks laden with plunder of various kinds, said to be took from the country about Negapatnam, and had receiv'd orders likewise to take charge of me & my bramney Pearoya, and they apply'd to Kissenrow for a bullock for me to ride on as I was not in a condition to walk. But this cruel man denied them, saying he had no bullock to spare, so I should walk. In this distressed situation, and not a rupee to help myself withal, I found means to send Lutchmenarain at that time of night to Mr. Walter & acquaint him with my distress & to request him to send me 15 pag(oda)s, if he possible could spare so much. It was sent immediately & I had just time to receive it before we began to march.

In passing the ground where the other captives lay I had an opportunity to embrace and take, as we both thought, my last farewell of my friend Mr. Topander. I walk'd in unspeakable anguish untill the morning when, overcome by fatigue, I could not walk or stand; but was obligated to lay myself down on the ground, my body being so decay'd with grief & the bloody fluse as well as the smarting pain of my yet open sores that I really once more wish'd for death, rather than live in such agonizing torments, especially as the fluse was more violent than it had been ever since it first came upon me, which was then eight months back.

The havildar of the guard seeing my distressed situation kindly gave me a baggage bullock to ride on, & I continued to march with them on this creature, tho' with the utmost difficulty, my faithful bramney sometimes supporting me on the bullock and sometimes leading it into the most easy parts of the road. Indeed, I cannot say too much on the kindness of that poor fellow towards me, for in my state on account of my disorder, being obligated to alight very frequently, I should never have been able to have liv'd to the end of our jour(ne)y had it not been for his assistance.

On the 30th day of March 1781, I arrived at Benglore about noon and the killedar order'd me to be kept at choultry opposite the Nabob's palace, under a guard of 6 seapoys, untill the next morning when, on his going to view the works, I had the pleasure to see and pay my respects to him. He called me to him and expressing the most friendly sorrow for my ill fate kindly beg'd me to support myself under it in the best manner I was able & put my trust in God – ordering me at the same time to be put into a house along with one Capt. James Hoddel of his Highness the Nabob Mahomed Ally Cawn's cavalry, who was taken by the Bahadur's troops at a place call'd Caleskpeak,[546] & kept prisoner in the said house under a guard of 6 seapoys, the killedar telling me that it would be much better for me to be with this gentleman than alone, as we should be company to each other and I would have the benefit of his servants & medicines. I thanked him for kind attention towards me & was conducted to that house & put under the same guard as Captn. Hoddel, who was happy in having my comp(an)y & express'd it by every attention to my welfare, so that by his kind care & medicines I soon began to find relief both in my body & mind by degrees.

On the 5th April 1781, Colonel Bailey under a strong guard of seapoys & peons in their way from Arcott to Seringapatnam stop'd at the pettah of this place when one of our guard (who had been a seapoy in the English service and knew Colonel Bailey) told us he saw that gentleman laying in his palankin with both his legs & hands in irons, and that he had seen Captain Rumley and two other Gentlemen likewise in palankins with but only their legs in irons.

On the 9th of April, Lieutenants Malvila and Dalrymple were brought to this fort from Arnie[547] & put in the prison along with the following gentlemen, viz.

Captains Jones & Gowdie	2
Liutenants Muit, Smith, Campbell, Forbes, Read Mr. Neile and Halliburton	7
Ensigns Forbes, Conner, White, Mackey, Innis, Lang, Frank, Cuthbert, Gorey, Hodges, Nash, Doing and Lathom	13
Doctors Ranu & Ogleby	2
Oficers in all	24
Sarjeants and private Europeans kept in the pettah of this place	74

On the 16th April, Lieutenant Malvile and Dalrymple sent Capt. Hoddel & me seven pag(o)d(a), which, as I had money & Capt. Hoddel being scant, I gave up my part to him.

On the 19th of April, 506 bullocks laden with brass & copper wares & 200 bullocks laden with white & brown cloths, which had been plunder'd from the country about Tanjore – and on the 30th of April, 150 bullocks more arriv'd laden with carpets, cloth, and brass wares from the same country.

On the 7th of June, 500 bullocks laden with cannon shott and horses were sent from this place to the army, and on the 20th of the same month, 400 bullocks laden with powder and musquet balls were sent to the army, and 300 more order'd to be got in readiness to go in a few days.

On the 23 June, a rejoicing salute was fir'd here for cutting off a party of English troops near Trichenapolly.

On the 28th June, an old bramney came and spoke to Pearoya, my bramney, at the place where he was dressing his victuals in the fort & acquainted him that he was sent by Mr. Robert Holford, a merchant lately arriv'd from Denmark to Tranq(ueba)r, & Moota Combra Mudliar, my dubash, to acquaint me of that gentleman's return to India, that my family was all well & also to acquaint me that my friends were all labouring to procure me my liberty and that, in a short time,

I might expect it, recommending to me in the mean time to keep up my usual spirit.

Pearoya then ask'd him if he had brought any letters, to which he reply'd no, that he durst not bring any.

Then being ask'd if he could take one with him on his return, he said no, that he did not chuse to run any hazard of his life.

Pearoya, enjoy'd at the news, came & told it me, and I, the reader may imagine, was not less so as I had great reason to depend on the truth of it, from the known good will of that worthy friend (Mr. Holford) towards me.

On the 2nd day of July 1781, the killedar sent a black officer to acquaint me that, by the nabob's commands, I was orderd back to the camp, and in consequence of which I was desir'd to hold myself in readiness to march the next morning. I return'd my most respectfull acknowledgments of the favors I had receiv'd at the hands of the killedar and beg'd the officer to request of him on my behalf that I might be allowed a horse to ride on and a bullock to carry my provision & little baggage. The officer acquainted the killedar with what I had desir'd him and soon afterwards return'd with an answer & ten fanams as a present from the killedar, which he said was to furnish me with provision on the road, the Nabob not having order'd any to be allowed me. A horse, he told me, he would allow one, but as to a bullock he was sorry to say he could not safely grant me one as he should thereby be liable to be taken notice of when I am to the camp – I thereupon requested of the officer to present my best thanks to the killedar, for all he had done me, and to ask him to be so kind as to suffer him (the black officer) to hire one for me, which I would pay the expence of. My request was granted immediately, & the next day about noon a little horse was sent me to ride on. About 3 O'Clock the same day, the guard being ready, we began to march without my being able to take my leave personally of the killedar, he being asleep. Nothing material occur'd untill we arrivd at the camp, which at that time was near Catmadoo. Here, we arrived on the 15th day of July in the evening, and I was conducted to Kissenrow who order'd the havildar of the guard to take care of me untill he got an answer to a letter, which he had wrote the Nabob's vackeel at Tranq(ueba)r. Thus, I was again expos'd entirely to the weather, not having the least shelter of any kind.

The camp mov'd often from place to place and, now going to march towards Congee Varam[548] & Arcott, I was obliged to walk with my guard. I was three days in the camp before I could get the least tydings of my bramney Lutchmenarain, who I expected would have been waiting for me.

On the 19th day of July 1781, early in the morning when the camp was marching, Lutchmenarain by chance saw me & ran to me, as did also a servant belonging to my family named Mahomed, who had been waiting in the camp for me some months.

I receiv'd by Lutchmenarain a letter from Captain Holford, full of the most friendly advice and affectionate expressions of sorrows for my misfortunes and begging me to keep up my spirits, as he hop'd soon thro' the blessing of God to have the pleasure of embracing me in Tranquebar.

I was acquainted by these two men that my family & friends were all well and that Mrs. Harrop had signed a bond of ten thousand rupees and deliver'd it to Messrs Ottisen, Halkier & Lÿcke, the honourable company's agents. In consequence of which and Mr. Robert Halford passing his word for the said sum, Governor Abbestee was requested not only by the said agents, but likewise by Mr. Holford & Mrs. Stevenson, sister-in-law to the Governor,[549] to write on my behalf, which in compliance to their requests he did in the following manner:
That as I had nothing valuable left in Tranq(ueba)r but a house, which when sold would not fetch a sum exceeding 6000 rupees, but that my friends having made a collection amongst themselves, had raised 4000 rupees more which two sums making in all ten thousand rupees was all that could be rais'd for my ransom, he therefore hoped the Nabob would be graciously pleas'd to consider my miserable situation and accept the said sum for my ransom, and that he himself (Governor Abbestee) stood accountable for the sum to be paid to

the Nabob's vackeel on the safe delivery of my person into Tranquebar. This letter was receiv'd by the Nabob and I was to have been sent immediately on my arrival at the camp. But Kissenrow, judging that as the camp was now marching at some distance from Tranquebar, perhaps the Governor might be induced to refuse or dispute the payment, he therefore a few days before my arrival wrote to the Nabob's vackeel at Tranq(ueba)r for to acquaint the Governor that the Nabob as a security for the ten thousand rupees desir'd (a Sowcar) or banker's note for that sum for my liberty, and that I could not come to Tranquebar before such a note was receiv'd by the Nabob.

Having learned this, my mind was something more at ease and I continued with anxious expectation of the arrival of the note untill the 31st day of August 1781 when, it being arriv'd, an order was given for my liberty and a guard of 6 seapoys & two hirkarrahs to conduct me to Tranquebar, I was sent for before Kissenrow, who deliver'd me over in charge of the sowcar at his camp, who likewise sent two of the peons with me, & then I was desir'd to go.

I spent this day at the tent of Mr. David Simone in company with him, his brother Mr. Isaac Simone & Mr. Gekee (the Dutch ambassadors from Negapatnam), who treated me in a very kind & friendly manner and provided me with a dooley and boys to carry me to Tranquebar.

On the 1st of Septem(be)r early in the morning, I took my leave of my kind entertainers and sett for Tranq(ueba)r with my two bramneys under the escort of two hirkarrahs, two peons, six seapoys and a havildar; the latter were chang'd at every stage where we halted. We travelled all day and halted as night came on at different villages.

On the 7th of Septem(be)r, as we were passing Povengerry,[550] we met two dubashes of whom I enquir'd whence they came, they told me from Tranquebar, which they had left two days ago. My inclination leading me naturally to enquire of my friends, I was inform'd that they were all well. But on asking them particularly if they knew Mrs. Harrop and if they had seen her lately, they ask'd me (not knowing me on account of the alteration in my person in my captivity) if I meant the wife of Mr. Harrop that was at Porto Novo, I answering in the affirmative, they told me that they knew her very well when alive, but that they had attended her funeral some months back. I then address'd my servant and Lutchmenarain (as well as I was able, which was but in a very ill manner owing to the violent agitation of my spirits) if they knew of Mrs. Harrop's death, and they confirmed the fatal news, at the same time acquainting me that they had been enjoin'd to keep it a secret from me by the commands of Mr. Holford & Mrs. Stevenson, whose tender concerns for me induc'd them to it lest I should, by a knowledge thereof added to the weights of my other sufferings, be so overpower'd as to give way to some desperate act for redress, and so make the remedy worse than the disease: which I am apprehensive must have been the case, from my sufferings at the recital of it now when all my other miseries were no more. Judge but yourself, kind gentle reader, what must be my feelings on this occasion; Heaven, as I have before observ'd, kept this the heaviest of my misfortunes in store for me as a trial, the severest I am capable of undergoing on this side eternity.

As little winds finding entrance in at small cavities lose themselves in the intricate windings in the bowels of the earth, untill by frequent & repeated additions, they become too bulky for the space in which they are pent and forcibly breaking thence, rend with convulsions their dreary mansions and overwhelm every thing anear them untill dispers'd abroad amidst the wide concave of heaven they love their force and rest in sullen silence, or as a current course, which swell'd & enlarg'd with heavy falling showers, breaks from its bounds and with redoubl'd fury traversing across the plains o'erturns the face of nature untill it falls into the wide extensive ocean, and burying its rage in the bosom is heard no more – just so with me, all my former sorrows pent up within my bosom and now augmented by this more heavy than them all – bursting at once from their habitation – now are no longer able to contain them, rack'd & conceal'd my soul with inexpressive fortunes and ten thousand thoughts (if possible) rushing at once into my disorder'd imagination & with their overpow'ring force bearing down my reason so overcame me that I became stupidly melancholy and in silence, only without being any longer able to think at all, I pass'd on the remainder of the road untill we came to a sheally; where we lay on the night of the eighth of Septem(be)r at which place I found a letter from Mr. Holford for me wrote in such an affectionate & friendly manner that even my sorrows found some trifling alleviation therefrom.

On the 9th of September, about 5 O'clock in the evening, I arriv'd at Porriar (a small village very near Tranq(ueba)r) and was conducted to the house of Heider's vackeel where Mr. Holford & Mr. Daniel Stevenson had kept a servant waiting to conduct me on my arrival to the Governor's garden house. The vackeel in consequence of this order'd the guard to be taken off & the two hirkarrahs to attend me to the garden and deliver me up in charge to the Governor with his master's compliments, to which was done accordingly, and as soon as I came before the Governor, the two hirkarrahs were dismissed. The Governor received me very politely and my two friends embrac'd me with all the warmth of brotherly affection, and by them I was conducted to their house. I was likewise receiv'd by Messieurs Ottisen, Halkier & Lÿcke, in a very kind and obliging manner, as likewise by every gentleman of my acquaintance.

When I came to enquire concerning Mrs. Harrop's death, I receiv'd the following information from a lady who had liv'd with her during our residence at Porto Novo and continued to do so untill the day of her death. This lady told me that Mrs. Harrop, whose grief for me was excessive from the time of my departure from Tranquebar, had the additional misfortune to be acquainted with the punishment I had receiv'd by Kissenrow's orders, within a month after that period and that from the time of her hearing that news she never ceas'd to complain but refusing sustenance entirely gave up herself to grief and heart corroding reflections and, when press'd and advis'd by her friends to moderate her grief, all the answer she ever made was that she was confident I would never survive that punishment, and that she would not, she could not, think of living without me. In this languishing state, she continued untill the 18th day of May 1781 when she died, having a few days before sign'd the bond, which procur'd me my deliverance.[551] ... Think, O gentle reader, do but think what I must feel on this recital of her love towards me. And think not you are perusing a romance, for every word is strictly as true as truth itself can be. Judge then of my loss, in the loss of this the best of women, the best of wives & the best of parents – dear to me in life as my own soul & renderred still dearer to me in Death by despising Life without me – I have, thank heaven one child the namesake & image of the dear departed mother & 'tis for this child alone I wish to live, 'tis for her I wish to meet to redress in my unhappy circumstances, & if I live but to see her well settled in the world, let heaven call me when it pleases, I die contended.

At the time that my bramney Lutchmenarain was sent to Tranquebar with letters to the Governor & Company's agents, a particular circumstance secur'd to him during his stay in that place, which I think proper to insert separately by itself as follows –

My bramney Lutchmenarain inform'd me that, on his arrival at Tranquebar, having deliver'd the letters under his charge to the respective persons to whom they was directed, he was one day sent for before the justice of Tranquebar and interrogated before several gentlemen respecting what he knew concerning the commissioned goods belonging to Captain Dahl whether, at the time of the plundering of the Danish factory, these goods or any part of them was ready; to which he reply'd that they was all ready that were to compleat the Comp(an)y's contract for that season were ready also, being either pack'd or ready for packing, in the warehouses within the factory, excepting some corges of brown clothes belonging to the Company, which was part at the bleachery and part in my own private warehouses. They then ask'd him how he knew that, & insisted on his giving them an account of what kinds of goods were in the factory at that time, & to take his oath to that account.

He then told them that it was impossible for him to give an exact account of all the goods in the factory & that his religion would not permit him to take an oath, tho' he should suffer death by the refusal, but that he would give them such an account as he could with certainty charge his memory withal, & sign it if they thought proper.

He moreover told them that, to convince them of the certainty of all Captn. Dahl's goods being in readiness, he remembered that I had sent a letter sometime before my being took away captive to Tondevory Pulle, my conecople[552] at Tranquebar, ordering him (Tondevory) to acquaint Captain Kroger (commander of a ship belonging to Captain Peter Dahl) on his arrival, that the goods were all ready for him and to learn from him if he would have the goods sent to Tranquebar, or call at Porto Novo to receive them on board, (as) Captain Dahl had given me no orders in that respect.

Upon hearing which they sent for Tondavary and question'd him with respect to the letter and account Lutchemenarain had given them, & he confirm'd the same.

They then took an account of the different kinds of goods contain'd in the factory from Lutchmenarain's mouth, which they wrote down as he utter'd & then made him sign.

I must here add (and I dare say it appears most probable to those who peruse this memorial) that Irlapulle was certainly the instrumental cause of the plundering of Porto Novo and the two factorys ... But I must add moreover my opinion that Irlapulle was not the first proposer of his own transactions in this affair. I wish I could say with a certainty who was, but alas, from the want of direct positive proof in some particulars, I am not able to do it with security. I therefore do not particularize the person, but I shall give such intimations as shall point him out to most, and as I am certain none can with propriety apply this reflection to be levelled at them, but he when it suits. Let him only ward it off.

When the actions of men in power and trust will not bear scrutinizing, they generally endeavour to block or obliterate them from publick view & never fail in finding creatures to answer their purpose, be it ever so black, and it often happens that these very men who deserve the worst of treatment from their master receive the greatest honours & employments from them.

There have been repeated instances of men who, having squander'd away or embezzled to their own private purpose the properties of others committed to their charge, have set the places in which they were deposited on fire in order to prevent detection: Yet with all their cunning, many of those people have been in the course of time found out, and their villanies detected & expos'd to view... And if there has been any intention any way answerable to or similar to this in the plundering of the Dutch & Danish factorys & town of Porto Novo, I hope the author of it will not escape the reward of his deserts.

My own bosom urges to me that such has certainly been the cause in this affair... And some thing more than shadowy conjecture assures me that Heider had an invitation into this country by a man of much greater consequence than Irlapulle, in order if possible to obscure in oblivion his dark & villainous transactions.

Should time & future events prove my conjectures true, it will appear that this very man has since that period receiv'd a greater extent of power & advancement in the employ of these people, whom he intentionally injur'd in the most vile manner.

As to Irlapulle himself, he was sent to Negapatnam (a second time) by the Nabob to demand a lack[553] of pagodas from the Dutch Company and did not return again to camp, having fallen under the Nabob's displeasure ... Soon after his arrival at Negapatnam, the Governor orderd him to be apprehended on suspicion of not having deliverd all the presents sent by the said Governor to the Nabob & was condemn'd to be hanged, but escaped on the English army's laying seige to and taking that place, and is now hiding himself in some part of the country.

It is thought that this man's death was much wished and that the charge against him was only a pretence to take away his life, for reasons almost too obvious to escape being clearly understood.

The Conclusion
I now beg leave to conclude my memorial by observing that I have acted very intensively in business, and ran very great risques by my enterprizing spirit, and my returns by such risques were generally answ(era)ble thereto.

I had the heartfelt satisfaction of looking round me with pleasure and finding myself esteem'd & respected by all ranks & degrees of people with whom I had any dealings or acquaintance, and was honour'd with very great trusts in the transacting of business for private merchants of all nations that traded to this country (as well as those of Denmark) and, had it not been for this stroke of Heaven's chastisement, I might perhaps in a little time have retir'd from business and... pass'd the latter part of my days in humble peace and quietness.

But since I must launch again into the vast ocean of business, I humbly hope all my former employers & friends will kindly assist in retrieving my (at present) embarass'd affairs, by honouring me with the favor of their command, as formerly.
For past favors I make this publick declaration of my most hearty and sincere thanks and high sense of the many obligations. I lay under to them and I beg leave to assure them it shall be my constant study to deserve a continuation of their favors, esteem and regard –

Gowan Harrop
Tranquebar
26th Janry. 1782

In the year one thousand seven hundred and eighty-two, the twenty-eighth of January, appeared before me, Thos. Christian Walter his Royal Danish Majesty's Councellor of Chancellary, Secretary to the Supreme Council of Tranquebar & Publick Notary of this Place, Mr. Gowan Harrop, who presented to me the before staying memorial of the capture of Porto Novo by the forces of Heider Ally Cawn Bahadur, and desir'd me to take his declaration by oath to confirm the truth of the same, which, having been granted by me, he made the oath prescribed by the Danish law in my presence of the undersigned witnesses, dated the same day & year as above.
Thos. C. Walter

Witnesses:
M. A. Fugl
T. Westerholdt

Here ends Harrop's own memorial of his captivity. Harrop's torture was witnessed by both Thomas Christian Walter and Daniel Pullei. Walter notes in his reports:

'I appealed to him (Krishnarayan) that Harrop had never promised to pay such a sum and that it was inhumane to torture a man who could not pay. In spite of this, Kistnaraien subjected Harrop on the same day, close to where our interpreter was, to 30 lashes from a Siambue,[554] /: a long whip with knots to rip off the flesh :/ had him bound to a camel and sent him in chains to Cheringapatnam for further torture'.

The presents to the Nawab on this futile trip included one diamond pendant necklace, a gold vessel and a dish for sprinkling rose water, a gold 'aigrette' with diamonds, rubies and emeralds, 28 French 'auner ponceaux', one Atchin horse with silver mount and several silver plates. The entire cost of the delegation was more than 83,560 rdl,[555] over twice the amount demanded for the release of Gowan Harrop.[556]

This is what another source of history writes about the plundering of Porto Novo by Karim [Mohammed]:

> 'Kureem (Karim) Shah, meanwhile, when he moved off to Mahmood Bundur, met with no resistance, and having by night marches arrived at the town, he surrounded, and, at the first assault, bravely took possession of it and plundered the houses of all the wealthy merchants, bankers and traders of bales on bales of merchandise, and bags on bags of gold and jewels. The next day, the whole of the wealth and commodities taken from all the merchants, who had expended millions of rupees in commissioning or procuring them from different parts of the world for the purpose of barter, were collected in one place. Amongst the rest was the whole of the property of a certain Muhammad Mokrim, a man of the Bohra tribe (the Bohras are a tribe of newly converted Mussulmans, residing mostly in the North Western provinces of India, they are chiefly merchants and traders), the chief of all the merchants, and the owner of three or four merchant ships, who about this time had purchased thirty-five young elephants of eight or nine years old, sixty taukun, or ponies of Manilla and Pegu, and also cloths of great value, and dresses of honour from the countries of Bengal, Bunares, China, Cashmere, Boorhanpoor,[557] Mutchliputtun[558] etc. All these articles were taken and laden on elephants, camels, bullocks and carts, and with the merchant to whom they had belonged, and his dependants, as prisoners were sent to Heider.'

After being plundered, tortured and treated miserably by Heider Ali, Harrop returned to Tranquebar where he had a house in Nygade. He continued to work in shipping, exporting and importing textiles.

By 1782, he seems already to have recovered enough from his experiences to concentrate on his business once more. In a letter from 1782 to the Government of Tranquebar, he is pleading for a reduction of the excise duties.[559]

Gowan Harrop was married to Margurite La Valiere, who died, as narrated in his memoirs, during May 1781 and was buried at the Catholic Churchyard in Tranquebar on 19 May. Gowan Harrop and Margurite La Valiere probably had a daughter, Anna Ignate Harrop, in 1775, but she must have died soon after birth.[560] Probably, they also had a son, John Harrop, who died on 30 May, 1776 and was buried at the Roman Catholic Church in Porto Novo [Cotton, serial number 1267].

Their surviving daughter, Catherina Harrop, 'the child for whom alone I wish to live', married Johann Carl Wilhelm von Braun on 26 September 1786, at Zion Church in Tranquebar [Heiberg]. During the Suppremania conflict, Braun was dismissed from work in 1790 and he died a year later. At the same time, their one-year-old daughter, Lovisa Augusta, also died. According to the Church Registry, she was baptised on 23 September 1789, died a year later and was buried on 1 October 1790. Their son, Carl Govan, who was born just a month before Carl Johann von Braun's death, was later educated in England, but he then returned to India and died in Madras at the age of 23 (http://www.trankebar.net/history/tranquebar-persons/braun-uk.htm).

Their eldest daughter, Catherina Elisabeth Braun, who was four years old at the time her father died, married Hans Jacob Fjellerup at the Zion Church on 13 April 1807. This pair produced five children, four daughters and one son. The eldest daughter, Angelique Wilhelmine, and the son, Charles Brown, both died on 11 May 1817. The middle daughter, Louise Augusta, was born on 11 May 1811, and it was probably her birthday that Rasmus Rask attended (see the chapter on Rasmus Rask). However, the second daughter, Helena Maria Elisabeth's family continues to thrive until today in various parts of the world. Catherina Elisabeth Braun must have visited Denmark sometime in the 1820s. A lovely portrait of her painted by the famous Danish painter, C. W. Eckersberg, was recently put up for auction in Denmark.[561]

Catherina Harrop, the daughter of Gowan Harrop, seems to have been married for a second time to Edward Swale Portbury, also at the Zion Church, on 22 May 1794. The Zion Church's list of marriages holds another entry for Portbury, who married Harriet Teler (or Taylor) two years later, on 9 October 1796 [Heiberg]. This seems to indicate that perhaps Catherina Harrop died between 1794 and 1796, probably in her late twenties (unless there was more than one Portbury). Gowan Harrop ran a

Fig. 14.3: Portrait of Catherina Elisabeth Fjellerup painted by C.W. Eckersberg. Catherina Elisabeth Fjellerup was the granddaughter of Gowan Harrop, was married to Hans Jacob Fjellerup, and was the mother of Harriet Anna Fjellerup (photo: www.lauritz.com).

business, 'Harrop & Stevenson', for a few years. Gowan Harrop died on 5 September 1799 in Tranquebar[562] and was buried at the Zion Church on 9 September.[563] After his death, Harrop & Stevenson[564] collapsed.

Browsing through the church books, there was one more surprise in store. A woman named Elisabeth Harrup was married to Charles Edding in Walter's garden on 9 March 1801. On 10 August 1803, a boy, John Gowin, born to Captain C. Edding and his wife Elisabeth was baptised in the Mission Church.[565] There is no information about how she related to the Harrop family.

L. C. Topander, who was responsible for the Dutch factory in Porto Novo, died on 28 January 1816. Captain Bailey, who is also mentioned in this memoir, was poisoned at Seringapatnam in 1782; Captain Rumley was murdered in Mysore on refusing to take poison. Dalrymple, probably James Dalrymple, likewise mentioned in the memoir, had an illustrious career.[566]

Journey's End

We have come to the end of our tour. Just a few feet down Athangarai Street towards the west, then turn to the right towards the north and we are at the town entrance. The only entrance to the town is through this gate (Landport), which was part of a defence wall that once surrounded the town. This defence system was established during the time of Eskild Andersen Kongsbakke in the 1660s, and a small part of the wall can still be seen to the north as well as south of the town gate.

The town gate was responsible for the preservation of the town as it was. All traffic in and out of town passed through this gate. The position of the

Fig. 15.1: The town entrance seen from the east, showing the monogram of Christian VII (C7) as well as the year of construction, which was 1792. This was designed by Peter Anker and constructed by Mathias Jürgen Mühldorff. In the 1660s, Eskild Andersen Kongsbakke constructed a defensive wall around the town, it had several entrances and one of them was at this point. This can also be seen in Trellund's map of the town. In 1791, this entrance was in danger of collapse. The present entrance symbolises the power of the king, displaying stacks of cannon balls. This solid brick construction was designed to resist attacks from passing armies (photo: P. S. Ramanujam).

gate can be seen on the Trellund map. In 1791, during the governorship of Peter Anker, engineer Mathias Mühldorff decided after surveying the old gate to establish a new one. The foundation was laid on 3 October 1791 by the governor. Missionary König wrote:[567]

> I began the ceremony with a hymn, prayer and a speech. The entire colony was invited on this occasion, and the troops were to parade in their new equipment. Early in the morning, at 7, the troops marched to the gate to the accompaniment of music, and when the general (Peter Anker) arrived, I started the service… After the general had laid the foundation stone, on which a silver plaque was set with some inscriptions and coins from Tranquebar, I came up to the stone, said a short prayer and speech, finished with a short prayer and concluded with the singing of the third verse of the psalm. The artillery then fired 27 rounds to the accompaniment of drums and trumpets, and the regiment presented arms; the troops marched back to town. The important people went into a large tent to enjoy their breakfast, and the function finished by 9. It is difficult to believe that everything went so well considering the crowds [Colding, Architectura 9].

The town entrance is constructed from bricks and is about 8 metres thick. The top of the side facing east shows the monogram of Christian VII, who was the king of Denmark at that time. This monogram, incidentally, can also be seen on the cannons outside the Chennai Museum.

At this juncture, take a bit of time to reflect on the life in the colony. The question waiting to be asked is: What was the relationship like between the Danes[568] and the Indians? What did the Danes think of the Indians?

Hans Mesler travelled to Tranquebar several times during 1708-1711.[569] He followed Ziegenbalg in his religious discourses around the country. He describes Tranquebar as a pretty citadel, with three pretty churches, a Muslim Mosque and five temples. The territory of Tranquebar included 15 villages. Describing the Kingdom of the Nayak, Mesler says that this part of India has the most elegant temples. There were resthouses every mile where weary travellers, be they Christians, Muslims, Hindus, blacks or whites, could rest and slake their thirst. The Malabarians ate rice with junket and drank arrack with their food. Poor people built their houses from clay and covered the roof with straw, whereas the rich and middle-class had houses built from bricks. Some Malabarians were merchants, some worked in the fields and others earned their living by servicing the whites. Anyone who wanted to work could easily find employment within the territory of Tranquebar. There were no poor people in Tranquebar, except for the fakirs, who were always given alms in the form of rice. Their (inhabitants') craftsmanship was very subtle, and they could make anything that the eye could see. The women in the house made their living spinning and weaving, selling milk, butter and pancakes and fetching water or selling fish. The Malabarians wrote on palm leaves with an iron stylus, which they held in their right hand. The palm leaf was held and moved with the left hand. The stylus was held between the thumb and the other four fingers when they wrote. On the question of whether the pagans were fickle-minded, Mesler says that they were true to their own religion. But they did not have a high opinion of the Christians; rather, they believed that there were no people more foolish and harmful than Christians. However, when they found an honest European, they would show that person the utmost favour and fidelity. They were very perspicuous and dextrous. Their medicine was made from plants and metals, such as gold as well as pearls. The pagans[570] had a habit of fasting on certain days of the week, viz. Sunday, Monday, Tuesday, Friday and Saturday. On Sunday to honour the Sun, on Monday for the god Sivan, on Tuesday for Waiddianada Schwamy, son of Ishwara, on Friday for Mahalakshmi (for wealth) and on Saturday for the planet Saturn for whom there is a temple close to Tranquebar (at Dirunallaru or Thirunallar). Saturn was the mightiest of devils. Mesler goes on to describe the religious practices of the pagans, the fate of the people, who converted to Christianity, diseases one could get, the sacredness of the Ganges, belief in ghosts, education of women, widow burning, penance, marriage ceremonies, offerings to god, and the creation of the universe.[571] Mesler was not alone in his opinions. Some of the the missionaries who came later commented about the behaviour of the 'Malabarians'.[572]

What, then, did the Indians think of the Danes? The locals had misgivings about the 'strange' behaviour of both the Europeans and the local Christians. Irschick, citing Fenger, notes: 'One commentator, Alleppa, possibly the author of many of the responses to the missionary inquiry that came to make up the 'Malabarische Korrespondenz', wrote that Christians: 'perform very few good works, give very few alms, have no penitences, willingly accept presents, drink strong drinks, ill-treat animals and use them for food, care very little about bodily cleanliness, look down upon all others as inferiors and are very avaricious, proud and passionate; indeed, our Brahmans say that the white people are descended from the giants, that they do not know the difference between good and evil, but sin continuously'.[573]

Having led a quiet life for the last 150 years or so, Tranquebar is once again attracting interest – mainly because of the foreign tourists. Danes who want to learn more about the history of their colonies in the East and West are regular visitors. 'Trankebar Forening' (Tranquebar Society) is a private organisation that has been restoring the Dansborg Fort, the old churchyard, and other buildings with means from private funds. The National Museum of Denmark has provided the funds with which the governor's residence has been restored. No doubt the interest will increase much more in the future.

On 16 April 1990, Queen Margrethe II of Denmark turned 50. In her honour, the famous Danish artist Bjørn Nørgaard designed sketches for 17 large tapestries depicting Danish history through the centuries. These were then woven at the Beauvais tapestry manufacturers in Paris and presented to the queen by the Danish business community. They are on display at Christiansborg Palace, which houses the Danish parliament. The fifth tapestry, which represents the aristocratic rule, Christian IV together with the Dansborg Fort and Raghunatha Nayak occupy a prominent place. Tranquebar still holds a place of distinction in Danish history.

It is remarkable that a town of barely two square kilometres contains so much history. Numerous other people than those described in the previous chapters have contributed to the history of the town; some examples are Coja Petrus Uscan,[574] an Armenian merchant, who was captured by the French in 1746 for supporting the British and taken forcibly to Pondichery, escaped on a Danish ship and probably came to stay in Tranquebar;[575] Carsten Niebuhr who was sent out to investigate the area around 'Arabia Felix' (Yemen) and who reached Surat in India, while his treasure chest was sent to Tranquebar to be returned to Denmark by ship; Einar Mikkelsen, one of the great Greenland explorers, also visited Tranquebar in his early life. On the Indian front, we have Tharangambadi Panchanada

Iyer who lived between 1824 and 1874 and who composed some wonderful classical South Indian music following the Tanjore tradition set by Raghunatha Nayak himself.

Obviously, this book is not an exhaustive history of Tranquebar. There are many more documents to be investigated. We do not know much about the history of the town during the late 17th century and the first half of the 18th. There are several questions to which I would like to know the answers:

1. Slavery: How big was the slave trade in 17th and early 18th centuries? According to Asger Svane-Knudsen, there are several badly damaged documents from this period. Was slavery as bad as in the Danish West-Indies? Were slaves punished when they ran away? Did they get their hands or legs chopped off?
2. The Black Court: Several of the proceedings of the Black Court (both in Danish and Tamilnadu archives) are not available for study. They may be able to tell us more about the types of judicial proceedings that were used.
3. John's House and his astronomical observations: It is said that Christoph Samuel John sat in a tower and made astronomical observations. It is true that John moved to Pingel's house, 22 King Street, according to the title of a deed found in the Tamilnadu Archives. But did he build the tower onto the house or was it there already from Pingel's time? Did he take over the astronomical apparatus after the demise of Engelhart? What sort of observations did he make?
4. The Moravian Brothers: What happened to the Moravian Brothers? Was it really their sole intention to settle and convert people from the Nicobar Islands? Where are their graves?
5. Tranquebar after 1845: We have no records of Tranquebar during the British period from 1845 until 1947. Did the British neglect the town entirely and let the cultural legacy of the Danes disappear?

Unfortunately, the town suffered a severe setback when it was hit by the tsunami of 26 December 2004. More than 300 people lost their lives, and the fishermen who lost their dwellings and living are still struggling to get back to normal life. Looking on the bright side, several improvements have been made to the living conditions of the citizens. It is a pity that a town with such an extensive heritage is slowly fading into oblivion. It is my sincere hope that the town will preserve its monuments for the future – not to serve any nostalgic longings for the past, but to remind us that history is a great teacher, if we are prepared to listen to it.

Glossary of Indian Terms

amildar, havildar: A manager who collects revenue.
areca: Nuts of a palm tree, *Areca catechu*, chopped and chewed with betel leaves.
arrack: fermented palm juice.
banian: an undergarment used by men.
betel: leaves of a creeper, *Piper Betle*, said to aid digestion.
Beri Chetti: traders belonging to a left hand Caste.
Brahmin: a member of the Indian priestly caste.
calico: cotton material of exceptional quality.
Caluppan (also known as Saluppan): A caste that makes clothes from linen or jute. The name comes from *Chanal*, a Tamil word for jute.
Cetti, Chetti, Cetty, Setti or Setty: A person belonging to trader caste.
choultry: A resting place; similar to a caravanserai.
chowltry, see choultry
chubdar: see subedar: a provincial governor.
cooly or cooley: labourer.
cotuwal, kottawal: chief police officer.
dal: a lentil dish.
darbar, durbar: Indian royal assembly.
dargah: a Sufi shrine.
devadasis: dancing girls associated with temples.
diwan: A high-ranking official.
dubash: A bilingual translator or interpreter; the term came to denote trade agents as well.
fanam: from Sanskrit, coinage.
firangi: a foreigner.
firman: A royal grant or permit.
harkarra, hirkarrah, hurcar: A messenger, sometimes a spy.
havildar: non-commissioned officer.
itangai or idangai: left hand castes.

killedar: from the Hindi word kiladar, denoting a person in charge of a fort (kila = fort).
Komati Chetti: south Indian merchant who speaks Telugu.
kovil: a South Indian hindu temple.
Lakh, lac, lak: One hundred thousand.
malabar: Literally means hill country; refers to the Tamils, as the south-west of Tamilnadu is hill country.
maniyakkaran: village head-man.
Morador: a mirasdar; landholder.
nawab or nabob or nabab: a Muslim ruler.
nayak: Leader or king.
nellu: rice with husk.
olai (ஓலை) or ollis: leaves from a palm tree used for writing.
overmaniagar: senior accountant.
palanquin: A litter carried by four to eight people.
palayakkarar: A local commander.
pandal: a shamiana or marquee.
paraiyan: a person belonging to the untouchable caste.
peon: an unskilled worker.
peshcash: present given by a subordinate to a superior.
pir: a Sufi holy man.
polygar or poligar: a south Indian local chief (Palayakkarar).
providiteur: provider.
raja or rajah: local king; both forms are used in the text interchangeably.
Raudra (or Raudri): name of a year in the Tamil almanac.
sati: self-immolation by women.
sellappa: see caluppan.
selling (salangu): a coastal boat in Tamilnadu, used to transport goods and people.
sepoy: an Indian soldier.
subedar: a provincial governor.
topas or topaz: an Indian lascar of Portugese descent. A lascar was a militiaman from the Indian subcontinent.
vakil, vakeel: Agent who acts on behalf of someone, ambassador.
valangai: right hand castes.
vellalar: a caste, primarily dealing with agriculture.
zamin: land.
zamindar: landowner.

Bibliography of Principal Sources

Abd-el Dayem, Torben. 'Det Ost-indiske eventyr – Ove Geddes rejse til Ceylon og Indien 1618-1622', Fiskeri og Søfartsmuseet (2006).

Andersen, P. B. 'Processions and Chariot festivals in Tharangambadi and Velankanni as instances of cultural exchange and marking', http://asiandynamics.ku.dk/pdf/Processions_and_Car_festivals_PA_v2.pdf/ (2009).

Architectura vol. 9, 'Tranquebar', Selskabet for Arkitekturhistorie, Copenhagen (1987).

Architectura vol. 29, Arkitekturhistorisk Årsskrift, Copenhagen (2007).

Baldæus, Philip. 'A true and exact description of the most celebrated East-India coasts of Malabar and Coromandel as also of the Isle of Ceylon', Vol. III, p. 700, Asian Educational Press (2000) (translated from 1672).

Bes, Lennart. 'The heirs of Vijayanagara: Court politics in early-modern South India', Ph. D thesis, Radboud University Nijmegen, The Netherlands (2018).

Bredsdorff, A. 'Willem Leyels liv og farefulde rejse til Indien', Museum Tusculanum, Copenhagen (1999); 'The trials and travels of Willem Leyel', Museum Tusculanum, Copenhagen (2009).

Brimnes, Niels. 'Constructing the Colonial Encounter – Right and Left Hand Castes in Early Colonial South India', (1999) Curzon; 'Konstruktion og beherskelse af Indien', Master's thesis, Aarhus University (1991).

Brimnes, Niels. 'Herredømmets svære balance – den danske koloniadminsitration i Tranquebar under kasteurolighederne 1787-89', Historie/Jyske samlinger, Bind Ny række, 19 (1991).

Brimnes, Niels. 'Danmark og Kolonierne: Indien – Tranquebar, Serampore og Nicobarerne', vol. 1, Gads forlag (2017).

'Det begyndte i København – Knudepunkter i 300 års indisk-danske relationer i mission', Editors: K. E. Bugge, H. R. Iversen, N. Kastfelt, L. Malmgart, H. Nielsen, A. Nørgaard and G. Oommen, Syddansk Universitetsforlag (2005).

Cotton, J.J. 'List of inscriptions on the tombs or monuments in Madras possessing historical or archaeological interest', Madras (1946) (available at Digital Library of India).

Dalrymple, William. 'White Mughals', Penguin Books (2002).

Dalrymple, William. 'The Anarchy – The East India Company, Corporate Violence, and the Pillage of an Empire', Bloomsbury (2019).

Diller, Stephan. 'Die Dänen in Indien, Südostasien und China (1620-1845)', Harrosowitz Forlag, Wiesbaden (1999).

Dübeck, Inger. 'Herrefolket og hedningen', Krøniken i Politiken, 26 March 1988.

Dubois, Abbe J. A. 'Hindu manners, customs and ceremonies', Rupa Publications (2006).

Eliassen, Finn-Einar. 'Peter Dahl (1747-1789) in the Oldenburg Empire: The Life, Career and Interests of a Norwegian shipmaster and Merchant in the 1770s and 1780s' in 'Der Dänische Gesamtstaat – Ein underschätztes Weltreich', Verlag Ludwig (2006).

Engelhart, Henning Munch. 'De Danske Ostindiske Etablissementers Historie' (see Groesmeyer et al.).

Erichsen, John. 'Brødrene Classen', Gyldendal (2017).

Ewing, J. Transactions of the American Philosophical Society, Old Series, Vol. 1 (1769-71) pp. 42-78.

Feldbæk, Ole and Justesen, Ole. 'Kolonierne i Asien og Afrika', Politikens Forlag (1980).

Fenger, Johannes Ferdinand. 'Den Trankebarske Missions Historie', Reitzel (1843); 'History of the Tranquebar Mission', translated into English by Emil Francke, Madras (1906).

Fihl, Esther. 'Tropekolonien Tranquebar', Gad (1989).

'The Governor's residence in Tranquebar', Ed. Esther Fihl, Museum Tusculanum Press (2017).

Forchhammer, Herluf. 'Missionærerne i Tranquebar i 1700-tallet', Master's Thesis, University of Copenhagen (1985).

Frendrup, W. 'Den Katolske Kirke i de Danske tropekolonier', Ælnoths Skriftserie nr. 15 (2008).

Gensichen, H. W. 'Tranquebar – Then and Now', Christian Literature Society, Madras (1956).

Goldingham, J. 'Of the geographical situation of the three Presidencies, Calcutta, Madras, and Bombay, in the East Indies', 'Of the difference of longitudes found by chronometer, and by correspondent eclipses of the satellites of Jupiter; with some supplementary information relative to Madras, Bombay, and Canton; as also the latitude and longitude of Pint de Gaulle and the Friar's Hood', pp.408-430; 431-436 (1822).

Gregersen, Frans. 'Introduction to the new edition of Niels Ege's 1993 translation of Rasmus Rask's prize essay of 1818', Editor's introduction, EFK Koerner (red.), Amsterdam (2013).

Gregersen, Hans. 'Trankebar', Wormianum (1987).

Groesmeyer, Lise., Jensen, Niklas Thode., and Ramanujam P. S., 'Videnskab, Oplysning og Historie i Dansk Ostindien: Udvalgte skrifter af Henning Munch Engelhart. ', Selskabet for Udgivelse af Kilder til Dansk Historie (2020).

'Halle and the beginning of Protestant Christianity in India, Vols. I-III', Edited by A. Gross, Y. Vincent Kumaradoss and H. Liebau, Verlag der Frankeschen Stiftungen (2006).

Harding, Georgina. 'Tranquebar – A season in South India', Sceptre (1993).

Harris, Jónathan Gil. 'The First Firangis', Aleph Book Company, India (2015).

Hastings, J. 'Encyclopedia of Religion and Ethics', 12 vols. (1908-1927).

Heiberg, K. 'List of Marriages Registered in the Danish Church Register of Zion Church, Tranquebar 1767-1845', Government Press, Madras (1935).

Hennings, August., 'Gegenwärtiger Zustand der Besitzungen der Europäer in Ostindien'(1784).

Henrichsen, R.J.F. 'Rasmus Rasks skoleliv (Rasmus Rask's school life)', Odense (1861).

Hobson-Jobson: see Yule, Henry and Coke, Arthur Burnell.

Hodne, Kjell 'Danske embetsmenn og indiske eliter i kolonien Trankebar: interaksjóner, 1777-1808.', Hovedopgave, Oslo (2007), in Esther Fihl (ed.), *Tranquebar Initiativets Skriftserie*, no. 5. Nationalmuseet. https://natmus.dk/fileadmin/user_upload/natmus/forskning/dokumenter/Tranquebar/Skriftserie/Tranquebar_Initiativets_Skriftserie_nr_05_2008.pdf

Holberg, Ludwig., 'Danmarks Riges Historie', Vol. V, (1810) pp. 410-420.

Ihle, A. 'Under sydkorset', Copenhagen (1894).

Jain, S. and Murthy, P. 'Madmen and specialists: The clientele and the staff of the Lunatic Asylum, Bangalore', International Review of Psychiatry, 18(4) (2006) pp. 345-354.

Jayaraman, R. 'Saraswati Mahal', Tanjore Saraswati Mahal Library, Tanjore (1981).

Jensen, Niklas Thode. 'The medical skills of the Malabar doctors in Tranquebar, India, as recorded by surgeon T. L. F. Folly, 1798', Medical History, 49 (2005) pp. 489–515.

Jensen, Niklas Thode. 'Laboratoriet ved verdens ende – om det naturvidenskabelige arbejde i den danske Halle-Mission i Tranquebar, cirka 1709-1813', Siden Saxo, Nr. 3 (2019) pp. 4-15.

Kochhar, T. K. 'Madras Observatory – the Beginning', Astron. Soc. of India Bulletin, V.13-2 (1985) p. 162.

Krieger, Martin. 'Some observations on life and death at Tranquebar around 1800' in 'Der Dänische Gesamtstaat – Ein unterschätztes Weltreich', Verlag Ludwig (2006).

Kryger, Karin. 'Kirkerne i Tranquebar i den Danske Periode 1660-1845', in Architectura 29, Selskabet for Arkitekturhistorie, Copenhagen (2007).

Kryger, Karin and Gasparski, Lisbeth. 'Tranquebar – Cemeteries and grave monuments', The Royal Danish Academy of Fine Arts, School of Architecture Publishers (2003).

Larsen, Kay. 'De Dansk-Ostindiske Koloniers Historie', Centralforlaget, Copenhagen (1908).

Larsen, Kay. 'Krøniker fra Trankebar', Nordiske Forfatteres Forlag, Copenhagen (1918).

Larsen, Kay. 'Guvernører, Residenter, Kommandanter og Chefer samt enkelte andre fremtrædende Personer i de tidligere danske Tropekolonier', Arthur Jensen (1940).

Lehmann, Arno. 'It began in Tranquebar', (Translated from the German by M. J. Lutz), The Christian Literature Society, Madras (1956).

Liebau, Heike. 'Indische Angestellte in der Dänischen kolonialadministration während der sozialen unruhen in Tranquebar und umgebung im Jahre 1787', Asien Afrika Lateinamerika, 25 (1997) pp. 111-126.

Liebau, Heike. 'Tamilische Christen im 18. Jarhundert als Mitgestalter sozialer Verändrungen. Motivationen, Möglichkeiten und Resultate ihres Wirkens', in Akteure des Wandels. Lebensläufe und Gruppenbilder an Schnittstellen von Kulturen', Zentrum Moderner Orient, Studien 14, Verlag Das Arabische Buch (2001) p. 31.

Liebau, Heike. 'Cultural encounters in India – The local co-workers of the Tranquebar Mission, 18th-19th Centuries', New Delhi: Esha Béteille (2013) – translated from German by Rekha Kamath Rajan.

Madsen, Verner. 'Peder Hansen', Odense Universitetsforlag (1984).

Markey, T. L. 'Rasmus Kristian Rask: His life and work' (1976).

M. M. D. L. T., (Revised and corrected by H. H. Prince Gholam Mohammad) 'The history of Heider Shah alias Heider Ali Khan Bahadur and of his son Tippoo Sultaun', W. Thacker & co, London (1855), reprinted by Asian Educational Services (2001).

Mohanavelu, C. S. 'German Tamilology', The South India Saiva Siddhanta Works Publishing Society, Madras (1993).

Muthiah, S. 'Madras Rediscovered', Eastwest Books, Madras (1999).

Nagaswamy, R. 'Tarangambadi'(1987).

Narasiah, K. R. A. 'Madras', Oxygen Books (2008).

Niebuhr, Carsten. 'Beskrivelse af Arabien ud fra egne iagttagelser og i landet selv samlede efterretninger', Forlaget Vandkunsten (2003) p. 155.

Nielsen, Sandra Østervang. 'Sorteretten i Tranquebar', Graduate thesis, University of Copenhagen (2009).

Nielsen, Y. 'General-Major Peter Anker – Guvernør i Trankebar', Historisk Tidsskrift, Vol. 1, Oslo (Kristiania) (1870).

Olafsson, Jón. 'Memoirer og breve', Translated by S. Bløndal, Gyldendal (1905).

Olsen, Gunnar. 'Vore Gamle Tropekolonier' vol 5, Fremad (1967).

Olsen, Poul Erik. 'Tamilsager', Siden Saxo (1992) pp. 8-14.

Paludan-Müller, Astrid. 'General Major Classen 1725-1792', Det Classenske Fideicommis (1923).

Pandian M.S. 'Aavanangal pesinal' (ஆவணங்கள் பேசினால்), Thirukkural Publishers, Chennai (2003).

Pearson, Hugh. 'Memoirs of the Life and Correspondence of the Rev. Christian Frederic Swartz' (1835) (available on the internet as a digital book from Google).

Petersen, N.M. in 'Samlede tildels forhen utrykte afhandling af R. K. Rask udgivne efter forfatterens død af H. K. Rask – vol. 1' (1834) (available as a Google book).

Prahl, Bendix. 'De Nicobariske Øers nærværende Tilstand samt Nytten for den danske Handel at befolke samme', Copenhagen (1804)

Ramachandran, S. 'Tharangampadi Olai Avanangal' (தரங்கம்பாடி ஓலை ஆவணங்கள்), State Department of Archaeology, Chennai, India (2005).

Ramanujam, P. S. 'Tranquebar Registers', ebook, Saxo, Copenhagen (2013); 'Tranquebar Registers – Version 2', www.saxo.com (2016).

Ramaswami, N.S. 'The political history of Carnatic under the Nawabs', Shakti Malik (1984) (available on the internet as a digital book from Google).

Rasch, Aage. 'Vore Gamle Tropekolonier' vol 7, Fremad (1967).

Rask, Kirsten. 'Rasmus Rask', Gad (2002).

Rask, Rasmus. 'Dagbøger 1816-1832', NKS 389 ek oktav, The Royal Library, Copenhagen [abbreviated RR, in the text].

Rasmus Rask. 'Erasmi Raskii Collectanea & Commentationes argumenti philologici, qvæ continent, præter lineamenta grammatica et indices vocabulorum, etiam apparatum observationum de origine & indole lingvarum scandinavicarum, germanicarum, celticarum aliarumque Europæ occidentalis, slavicarum, fennicarum, caucasiarum, persicarum, indicarum ex utraque Indiæ parte, semiticarum, Asiæque insuper tam borealis quam orientalis', NKS 149 c kvart , Royal Library, Copenhagen, Manuscripts, vol. 73 and 74.

Reid, Col. D. M. 'The story of Fort St. George', Diocesan Press, Madras (1915), Reprinted by Asian Educational Services, New Delhi (1999).

Rönning, F. 'Rasmus Kristian Rask', Copenhagen (1887).

Richards, Annette. 'Carl Philipp Emanuel Bach, Portraits, and the Physiognomy of Music History', Journal of the American Musicological Society, vol. 66 (2013).

Schlegel, Johan Heinrich. 'Samlung fur Danischen Geschichte, Munzkenntniss, Oekonomie und Sprache', Copenhagen (1774).

Seth, M. Jacob. 'Armenians in India', Calcutta (1937), republished by Asian Educational Services (2005).

Schönbeck, O. (Andersen, P. B.) 'All religions merge in Tranquebar – Religious coexistence and social cohesion in south India', NIAS (2012).

Silén, Elin. 'Christian Freidrich Schwartz', Svenska Kyrkans Diakonistyrelses Bokförlag (1924).

Singh, Brijraj. 'The first Protestant Missionary to India', Oxford (1999).

Sobel, Dava. 'Longitude', Walker & Company, New York (1995).

Stansfield, H. 'The Missionary botanists of Tranquebar', Liverpool Bulletin, Vol. 6, (1957) pp. 18-42.

Strandberg, Elisabeth. 'The Modi Documents from Tanjore in Danish Collections', Franz Steiner Verlag, Wiesbaden (1983).

Struwe, Kamma. 'Vore Gamle Tropekolonier' vol 6, Fremad (1967).

Swamikannu Pillai L. D., 'An Indian Ephemeris A. D. 799 to A. D. 1799', Government Press – 6 vols.

Swamikannu Pillai, L. D. 'An Indian Ephemeris A. D. 1800 to A. D. 2000', Asian Educational Services (1994).

Søndreholm, Erik. 'Jacob Worm', Munksgaard (1971).

The Lifco Tamil-Tamil-English Dictionary, The Little Flower Company, Tiruchi (1986).

Thestrup, Poul. 'Mark og skilling, kroner og øre', Statens Arkiver (1999).

Thestrup, Poul. 'Pund og alen', Arkivernes Informationsserie (1991).

'Tranquebar', Arkitekten, vol. 23 (1979).

Tranquebar Initiativet – a complete list of publications post-2004 relating to Tranquebar published under 'Tranquebar Initiativet' can be found under https://en.natmus.dk/historical-knowledge/historical-knowledge-the-world/asia/india/tranquebar/publications-2004-2016/

Vridhagirisan, V. 'The Nayaks of Tanjore', Asian Educational Service (1942).

Waaben, Knud. 'Et sendebud fra Tranquebar – Sennapa Naik i København 1795-1801', Historiske Meddelelser om København (1995).

Wulff, Inger. 'Den dansende Siva fra Trankebar', Jordens Folk, p. 326-327 (1965).

Yule, Henry and Burnell, Arthur Coke. 'A glossary of Anglo-Indian Colloquial Words and Phrases', London (1886).

List of Archival Material from the National Archives (RA), Copenhagen (Translations by C. Rise-Hansen)

Asiatisk Kompagni – Asiatic Company
Danske Kancelli – Danish Chancery
Den Ledreborgske Dokumentsamling – Ledreborg document collection
Det kgl. Ostindiske Guvernement – Royal East Indian Government
Det Classenske Fideikommis – Classen's Fideicommis
General Toldkammer – og Kommercekollegiet – The Board of Customs and Trade
P. Hansens Embedsarkiv – P. Hansen's official archives
Højeste Ret – Supreme Court of Judicature
Håndskriftsamlingen – VII E – Manuscript Collection
Kommercekollegiet – The Board of Trade
Missionskollegiet – The Mission Board
Mourier, Familien – Family Mourier
Ostindisk Kompagni – The East India Company
Peter Ankers privatepapirer – Peter Anker's private papers
Tyske kancelli, Udenrigske afdeling – The Foreign Department of the German Chancery

Notes

Documents from the Danish National Archives are kept in packets, and each packet has a 'løbenr' (serial number).

Preface

1. Denmark refers here to Denmark-Norway, encompassing the double monarchy of Denmark-Norway as well as the German Duchies of Schleswig and Holstein. The persons described and discussed in this book come from all corners of this large kingdom.
2. Denmark also had a colony at Serampore (Srirampur) in Bengal and several trading posts in places such as Masulipatnam in Andhra Pradesh and Calicut in Kerala.
3. The Chola dynasty ruled the area around Tanjore in South India from the 3rd century BCE until the 14th century CE.
4. Muthiah, S. 'Madras rediscovered', Madras: East-West Books (1999).
5. According to Indian legend, Markandeya was a devotee of Shiva and was destined to live only until he was 16. When death came in the form of Yama, Markandeya embraced the lingam at the temple and was rescued by Shiva who granted him eternal life.
6. The cremation ground was located to the north-west of the town in the 1730s (Der Königl. Dänischen Missionarien aus Ost-Indien eingesandter Ausführlichen Berichten, Von dem Werck ihres Amts unter den Heyden, Teil 3, Cont. 29 (1730) p. 482).
7. Om Tranquebars natur: '…men når nyhedens interesse har tabt sig, finder man den sørgeligere end granskove' [Madsen], p. 22.
8. German missionaries record that 23 languages were spoken in Madras (Chennai) in 1734: English, Portuguese, French, Spanish, Italian, Dutch, German, Danish, Swedish, Russian, Greek, Arabic, Persian, Turkish, Armenian, Pegu, Grantham, Marathi, Tamil, Telugu, Malay, Chinese and Moorish (Der Königl. Dänischen Missionarien aus Ost-Indien eingesandter Ausführlichen Berichten, Von dem Werck ihres Amts unter den Heyden, Teil 2, Cont. 23 (1728) p. 944). This number increased to 34 in 1742, according to Benjamin Schulze (Der Königl. Dänischen Missionarien aus Ost-Indien eingesandter Ausführlichen Berichten, Von dem Werck ihres Amts unter den Heyden, Teil 5, Cont. 56 (1745) p.1372. Surely, this renders Madras one of the most cosmopolitan cities at that time. In all probability, more languages were spoken in Tranquebar than those listed in the text.
9. Nayaks were the principal rulers of the area around Tanjore in the 16th and 17th centuries.

10 The number of currencies and their inter-relations in the Danish territory is enough to leave anyone utterly confused. Apart from the Danish Rigsdaler (Danish Rdl.), the following were also used in Tranquebar: Tranquebar Rigsdaler (Trqb. Rdl), Pagoda/star pagoda, Porto Novo Pagoda (P. N. Pagoda), Dutch Gylden, Portuguese Piaster and Pardau, not to mention fanams and kas. This was so complicated that Governor Peder Hansen made notes about Weights and Measures, and Monetary values [RA, General Toldkammer- og Kommercekollegiet, Generalguvernør P. Hansens embedsarkiv]. Studying Peder Hansen's notes and documents from the National Archives [General Toldkammer – og Kommercekollegiet, Indisk Kontor (1821) #258: Placat af 27 dec. 1821 (Løbenr. 3266); Det Kgl. Ostindiske Guvernement, Kolonien Trankebar, Guvernementets Resolutionsprotokol 1808 jan. 14 – 1822 juli 4 (Løbenr. 1339-1341), Guvernementets Resolutionsprotokol, 29 apr. 1819 – 4 juli 1822, Kommercekollegiet, Ostindiske secretariat, Journalsager 1793 (Løbenr. 1011), and Julius Wilcke, Kurantmønten 1726-1788, Copenhagen (1927)], the following conversion factors are found for currencies around 1800: 100 Trqb. Rdl = 73 Danish Rdl. = 58.4 speciedaler = 140 Madras rupees = 40 (Star)pagodas = 48 Porto Novo (P.N.) pagodas =65.4 piastre = 112 pardaus = 195 gylden. These values are approximate and do not reflect the conversion factors for the entire 225 years of the Danish period; but they give an idea of what the cost of living was. In addition, Hansen notes that 100 Sicca rupees are equal to 116 current rupees. A sicca rupee is a freshly minted rupee, unworn. There were 42-45 fanams to a pagoda, and 80 cash (cas) to one fanam. Ove Gedde [Schlegel, Samlung zur Dänischen Geschichte, vol. 1, kap. 3, p. 88] also mentions that one piece of eight (stück von acht) was worth 10 fanams. What are these worth in the year 2016 in terms of buying power? The value of 1 Danish Rigdaler from the year 1620 will be approximately 60 US (2016) dollars (usd), 1 Rigsdaler from 1788 will be approximately 25 usd (2016), and 1 Danish rigsdaler from 1845 will be only 4 usd (2016). More accurate estimates can be obtained from the consumer price index list of the Danish National Bank ((http://www.nationalbanken.dk/en/publications/Pages/2009/02/Consumer-Prices-in-Denmark-1502-2007.aspx). The 2,000 Danish Rdl. that was paid as tribute for Tranquebar would be worth 80,000 usd per year in today's currency.

11 RA, Kommercekollegiet, Journalsager (1788) #207 (Løbenr. 992).

12 Heider Ali (1720-1782), de facto ruler of the Karnataka in South India – more on him and his son Tippu Sultan (1750-1799) in subsequent chapters.

13 A resident is a representative (see Hobson-Jobson); also meaning an envoy.

1. A Shipwreck and the Beginnings of a Colony

14 'Danmark og Kolonierne – Indien', ed. Niels Brimnes, Copenhagen, Gads Forlag, (2017).

15 Journal of the Asiatic Society of Great Britain and Ireland (1898) p. 625. However, in his detailed report 'Ausführliche Relatio von der Reise, die die Jacht gethan auch wie sie genommen undt endtlich das Contor undt Fort vff Trangebary gebauet von Rolandt Krappe eingeshicket', on the fate of the cutter *Øresund*, he does not mention the name of Andre Botelho da Costa. This report can be found in the National

16   Archives, Copenhagen. (RA, Tyske Kancelli, Slesvig-Holsten-Lauenborgske Kancelli – Diverse akter vedr. det Ostindiske Kompagni og Guinea, (Løbenr. A171)).
16   Crappé himself signed his name Roelant Crappé, even though he is called Roland or Roeland Crappe (RA, Danske Kancelli, Akter vedr. Ostindiske Kompagni (Løbenr. B169)).
17   'Cutis moeder, en Quinde hvis mand haffer bierget Generalen Crappes liff dend thid hand forloer skibet Øresund for Carical' (RA: Danske Kancelli, Rentekammerafdelingen, Willem Leyels Arkiv, Løbenr. B246C). Asta Bredsdorff in her book 'The trials and travels of Willem Leyel' interprets 'Cutis moeder' as a proper name; however, it seems more likely that it should be interpreted as Cuti's (or Kutti, which is a common name in Tamilnadu) mother, 'moeder' being 'mother' in Dutch, the language of Crappé. Perhaps, Cuti's father died trying to save Crappé's life, and hence the money was paid to his widow.
18   Archaeological News, American Journal of Archaeology, vol. 7 (1891) p. 111.
19   South Indian Inscriptions, Vol.IV, No. 399.

> **No. 399.**
> (*A.R. No. 75 of 1890*).
> ON THE WALL OF THE MASILAMANISVARA TEMPLE AT TARANGANPADI (TRANQUEBAR), MAYAVARAM TALUK, TANJORE DISTRICT.
> 1 உ ஸ்வஸ்தி ஸ்ரீ [॥*] ஸ்ரீஸ்திதிக்குமேல் கொமாற(ர்)பங்மா திருபுவசச -
> 2 க்ரவத்திகள் ஸ்ரீகுலசெகரதெவற்கு யா[ண்*]டு டிள்ள வது சித்திரை
> 3 மாதம்முதல் சடங்கன்பாடியாக குலசெகன்பட்டிகத்து உடை -
> 4 யார் மணிவண்ணஞ்சுரமுடையார்க்கு வீரகம்பகன் [ச]ன்தி[ய]முது செய் -
> 5 தருள [ப]ணிணென்¹ மிஷயத்தாரும் கரையாரும் சிச்சயித்தபடி இ -
> 6 வ்வூர் நாடுவெலிக்கும் உன்பட்ட மஞயால் மாதம்தொராம் இரு -
> 7 நாழி அரிசி தண்டிக்கொள்ளக்கட வதாகவும் தண்டம் இடத்து இ -
> 8 துக்குத் தாழ்வு சொன்ன ருண்டாகில் பதினென்மிஷயத்¹-
> 9 க்கும் கரையார்க்கும் துரோகியாக[க்*] கடவ[ர்*]களாகவும்
> 10 இ[ப்*]படிக்கு பதினென்¹[மி]ஷயத்தாரும் கரையாரும் ஒழ் ஸ்வஹஸ்த உ

20   'Tharangam' in Tamil means 'waves' and 'Padi' is a village. It is unfortunate that people try to romantically associate the town with singing waves on the basis of a false etymology.
21   'Pattu' in Tamil means 'song'.'Padi' is the verb, and could mean the singer. In the present context, 'Padi' refers to an old Tamil word meaning 'a place where troops stay' (see The LIFCO Tamil-Tamil-English dictionary).
22   'Alphabetical list of villages in the taluks and districts of the Madras Presidency', Asian Educational Services (1992).
23   http://www.kb.dk/maps/kortsa/2012/jul/kortatlas/object79148/da/
24   Faarborg, Birte. 'Trellunds Trankebarkort 1733', Arkiv, vol. 3, Copenhagen (1970-71) p.242-270.
25   செக்கு
26   Portrait in the Royal Library, Copenhagen.
27   'Danmarks Historie – Reformation og Renæssance 1533-1596', Politikens Forlag (1963), Bind 6.

28 Alastair H. Thomas. 'Historical Dictionary of Denmark'. Maryland : Rowman & Littlefield (2016) p. 361
29 Angus Maddison. 'The world economy – A millennial perspective'. Development Centre of the Organisation for Economic Co-operation and Development (2001) p. 75.
30 Gunnar Olsen. 'Vore gamle tropekolonier'. Copenhagen : Vol. 5 (1967) p. 35.
31 An extensive account of Boshouwer's association with Ceylon can be found in an article by Kåre Lauring, 'Marchelis Michielsz Boschouver – imperiebygger eller svindler', Handels- og Søfartsmuseet på Kronborg, Årbog 1988, pp.71-114.
32 RA, Tyske Kancelli, Udenrigske afdeling, (1454-1699), E1 Traktater.
33 Negombo [www.jmarcussen.dk/historie/reference/person/gjedde.html].
34 Traktaten af 30. Marts 1618, Gunnar Olsen. 'Vore gamle tropekolonier'. Copenhagen (1967) p. 39.
35 There was a fifth vessel, which was sent back from Africa as the expedition managed to capture an extra vessel.
36 One last was approximately 20 barrels or 2 tons. Last or Læst was an old Dutch measure (Thestrup 1991).
37 One amme (Ahm, Ame, Amme or Ohm refer to old German measures) was approximately 150 litres (Thestrup 1991).
38 One pound corresponds to 0.5 kg.
39 Journal of the Royal Asiatic Society Ceylon Branch, vol. 30 (1926).
40 Possibly Verhagensbaai in south Mozambique (see Groesmeyer et al.).
41 Mich. Henrichsøn [Tistorf]. 'Præd. udi Offve Gieddes til Thommerup, hans Liigs Begiengelse 5. Febr. 1661 udi St. Nicolai K. i Kbh. Haabet, aff Psalme 31', 1-7. København.
42 It is difficult today to find the route taken by Ove Gedde to Tanjore, as there are several Tamilian towns with similar names. My proposal is that Ove Gedde went from Tranquebar (Trangebari) to Akkur (Aktiur) to Thirumailadi (Trimulavarde) to Tiruchitrambalam (Trissipal) to Darasuram (Pette) to Tanjore. The reason for this suggestion is that Roelant Crappé mentions in his letters specifically 'Pætte – Darasurapætte'. Crappé notes in his letters that he himself bought pepper from 'Darasuripette'. 'Pettai' is common ending in names of small towns. The temple in Darasuram is from the Chola period and has several chambers for storage. Crappé's letters, written in 17th-century Dutch, can be found in the National Archives (Tyske Kancelli, Slesvig-Holsten-Lauenborgske Kancelli, Diverse akter vedr. det Ostindiske Kompagni & Guinea (Løbenr. A171)). I am grateful to Asger Svane-Knudsen for kindly sharing a copy of the Danish translation with me. The other possible route is from Tranquebar to Athiyur to Thirumalapadi, on the northern banks of the river Kollidam, and thence to Tanjore. This will directly lead through the town of Ammanpettai. I do not know whether there is a large enough temple there for the storage of spices. This alternative route moreover makes it difficult to explain the name 'Trissipal'. Other routes may also be possible.
43 'Den 19 lod jeg Contracterne paa ny udskrive, og tegned min Haand under den eene, hos mit underhængende Segl, og gik dermed op til Hove' (Schlegel).
44 This parchment treaty is held in the National Archives, Copenhagen (RA, Tyske Kancelli – Udenrigske Afdeling: Pergamentsbreve). The treaty carried only the

signature of Raghunatha in Telugu, with no counter-signatures from Ove Gedde. After the return of Gedde, Christian IV ratified the treaty on 5 April 1622. This treaty is neither signed, nor given a seal. The ratified treaty was probably not sent to Raghunatha. This treaty is also held in the National Archives (RA, Tyske Kancelli – Udenrigske Afdeling, E1 Traktater #6a).

45 'Den 29 December var de Sortes Nyaarsdag, som kaldes Pungelen, som er deres fornemste højtid, paa hvilken de lode deres Afgud ombære i Byen den ganske Nat. Og den 30 var deres anden Højtidsdag, paa hvilken de bare deres foreskrevne Spøgerie ud paa Marken for deres Køer' (Schlegel).

46 The fact that it is now celebrated on January 15 is due to the change from the Julian to the Gregorian calendar, which took place in India in 1752, and as a result of the precession of the equinoxes.

47 Constructional details of the Dansborg Fort can be found in Architectura vol. 9 (1987) and Architectura vol. 29 (2007), Selskabet for Arkitekturhistorie, Copenhagen.

48 Engelhart, Henning Munch. 'De Danske Ostindiske Etablissementers Historie'. Handwritten manuscript, The Royal Library, Copenhagen (see Groesmeyer et al. 2020).

49 Der Königl. Dänischen Missionarien aus Ost-Indien eingesandter Ausführlichen Berichten, Von dem Werck ihres Amts unter den Heyden , Teil 1, Cont. 11 (1719) p. 883.

50 Ove Gedde was perhaps the first one to bring a tamilian to Denmark. 'With him, he had a Moor, Peder, who found and retrieved pearls in the large river at Nørholm in the Skads district' in the Varde River in Denmark. Unfortunately, the Moor, Peder, seems to have died the same winter, unable to bear the cold' http://geltzer.dk/artikler/sgflen.php. I am grateful to Karl Peder Pedersen for this information.

51 Johann Heinrich Schlegel (1726-1780) was a German-born Danish historian.

52 https://en.wikipedia.org/wiki/Farang.

53 This could refer to a firangi, also known as 'Frank' (see Hobson-Jobson – Firinghee').

54 L. D. Swamikannu Pillai, 'An Indian Ephemeris – A.D.700 to A.D. 1799', Vol. VI (A.D. 1600 to A.D. 1799)'. In the British system, which was adhered to by Swamikannu Pillai, the change from the Julian to the Gregorian calendar occurred in 1752.

55 Ove Gedde is called 'Gule de Gedde' in the reports of the German Missionaries (Der Königl. Dänischen Missionarien aus Ost-Indien eingesandter Ausführlichen Berichten, Von dem Werck ihres Amts unter den Heyden , Teil 1, cont. 11, p.883 (1720)).

56 'Das Datum dieses Briefs ist ins Jahr 1621 zu setzen, weil darin von dem bereits geschlossnen Tractate die Rede ist, und Gieddes al seines noch Inwesenden gedacht wird. Giedde war im April 1621 noch unter Ceilon. Warum er in diesem Briefe Ulandisa gennant wird, muss sich wohl aus dem Malabarischen erklären lassen. Baldeus nennet den Dänischen Befehlhaber immer Gule Giedde, ich weis nicht, ob aus blossom Irrtum, oder in einer Beziehung auf diesen namen Ulandisa. Roelant Crappe wird hier Rulangalappei genannt, welches wohl nur eine Verdrehung seines namens ist.', J.H. Schlegel, 'Samlung fur Danischen Geschichte, Munzkenntniss, Oekonomie und Sprache'. Copenhagen (1774).

57 'Han discurrerered meget om vores Lande, og spurgte, om vores Lande vidt paa hin Side Portugal liggendes? Om min Herres, de Engelskes, Hollænders og Portugisers Lande? Hvem af de Herrer den fornemste var?' (Schlegel 1774)
58 Engelhart, Henning Munch. loc. cit.
59 Rigsarkivet: Ostindiske Sekretariat, Journalsager (1791) (Løbenr. 1004) #245.

Translat
Af en Mallabarsk skrift, som er indhugget
Paa en Guld Flade.-
Udi Aaret Nala /: det er efter den Danske stiil Anno 1621/ den 22de April, Vi Regunada Naiker önsker alt velgaaende til Hands Majestate Kongen af Dannemarks Æmbedes Mændene, og lader dem hermed naade, Vi ere vel og anmoder Vi at tilskrive os om Hands Majestæts Höye Navns og Rygtes forfremmelse; Vi glæder Os meget over det som Vi har erfaret om Nyeheder derstæds, som blev Os underrettet af den Hollandske General og Capitain Roelant Crabbe, som ere her ankommen; Da Vi haver i sinde, at leve med Hans Majestæt i Eevighed og Venlighed uden nogen forskeel, saa have Vi forundet bemeldte General og Capitainen, at gaae med Pallankin, foruden den Domme, som Vi have foræret dem og overladet dem, en Bye som Tranquebar kaldet, nær ved Söe Stranden for at Beboes af Hiinlandske Folkene /: det er Danske Nationer :/ forskaffet dem mod Betaling nogen Peber, da samme er rart i Deres Land, straffet de Europæer som har giort fortræd til bemeldte Capitainen, ved 12,000 Pardouer, som er bleven fordret af dem i Mult, forbydet at have noget at bestikke med det Danske Nations skiib, expederet bemeldte General herfra, og befalet bemeldte Capitainen, at han skulde forblive her i Landet, til hvilken er de forbliver ogsaa bemeldte Capitainen herpaa stædet. – Vi vil have gierne at Vores Landmann være anseet af Dem uden forskiel ligesom Deres derfore behager De at sendes Deres Landets folkene her til Stædet, med Oversendning af alleslags Raritæter derfra, som skulde skee oftere paa det at bemeldte folk kunde etablisere dem her i Vores Land. Fordringen bestaaer af 2d Cavay Pidambaram kaldet, 1 Lencol, 2. stk af en slags Lærreder Pattan Kapatzeiwadam kaldet, 4 stk senge duug af Sirtzer, alt dette forestaaende ere forvarede i en pakke; hermed följer 2: Dolg 1 Kniv 1: Ditto af en anden slags, 4 Piile; de vilde imodtage alt dette, hvilket Æmbeds mændene reporterer til Hands Majestæt Kongen af Dannemark –

  Regunaden
  Dette Navn staar skrevet
  Paa det Tellunkiske Sprog
  Translationens Rigtighed testerer
  Daniel, Piragasam: Kongl. Tolke

  Copiens Rigtighed vedgaar
  JHKoefoed

60   Hallesche Berichte, vol. 1, Cont. 11 (1720) pp. 907-910.
61   Schlegel, Johann Heinrich. 'Samlung zur Dänischen Geschichte, Münzkenntniss, Oekonomie und Sprache'. Erster Band, Viertes Stück, (1771), p. 162-163.
62   Rigsarkivet, Den Ledreborgske Dokumentsamling, 11 April 1631: 'Den stormechtige hoybaarne Fÿrste Herr Rambadro Naico, Konge till Taniura, voris sÿnderlige goede ven'.
63   Srinivasan notes that Tamil copper plates from the Maratha period mention the era of Ramabhadra Nayakar between those of Raghunatha Nayak and Vijaya Raghava Nayak. (Srinivasan, C. R. 'Some interesting aspects of the Maratha rule as gleaned from the copper plates of the Thanjavur Marathas', Jour. Epigr. soc. India, vol. 11 (1984) p. 45.)
64   According to reports of the Dutch East India Company (VOC), Ramabhadra seems to have died on 24 January 1631 [Bes] p. 97. Achyutha Vijaya Raghava Nayak and Vijaya Raghava Nayak refer to the same person.
65   Velcheru Narayana Rao, David Shulman and Sanjay Subrahmanyam. 'Symbols of Substance. Court and State in Nayaka Period Tamilnadu' (1992), p. 311. I am grateful to Lennart Bes for pointing out this reference.
66   Loc. cit.; Jacob van den Meersche, ARA, OB, VOC (1673)
67   RA, General Toldkammer og Kommercekollegiet, Indiske Kontor, Journalsager(1836) #34 (Løbenr. 3284). There are several documents relating to the correspondence between the Danish and the British governments.
68   Olai is a palm leaf (a leaf of Corypha umbraculifera or the talipot palm).
69   RA, Ostindisk Kompagni, Afdelingen i Trankebar, 1670-1778, Løbenr. 2183a.
70   Translation from the Treaty of 19 November 1620 in 'The Life of the Icelander Jón Ólafsson', vol. II (1931) p. 23.
71   For a detailed discussion of this, see Rastén, Simon. 'The Tranquebar Tribute – Contested perceptions during the reign of Rajah Serfoji II' in 'Beyond Tranquebar: Grappling across Cultural Borders in South India', Edited by Esther Fihl and A. R. Venkatachalapathy, Orient Black Swan (2014) p. 257.
72   Der Königl. Dänischen Missionarien aus Ost-Indien eingesandter Ausführlichen Berichten, Von dem Werck ihres Amts unter den Heyden , Teil 1, Cont. 11 (1710) p. 883.

2. Jón Ólafsson's Saga

73   'Memoirer og Breve – Islænderen Jon Olafssons Oplevelser som Ostindiefarer under Christian IV', Anden Del, Gyldendal (1907).
74   'Tranquebar', Arkitekturhistorisk Årsskrift, ARCHITECTURA 9, Copenhagen (1987), p. 89-120.
75   http://videnskab.dk/kultur-samfund/nationalmuseet-udgraver-voldgrav-ved-dansk-koloni-fort-i-indien; The Hindu, 2008
76   The details in this chapter are based on 'The Life of the Icelander Jón Ólafsson', translated from the Icelandic edition of Dr. Sigfús Blöndal, by Dame Bertha Phillpotts, ii, London 1932. The original biography of Jón Ólafsson has not been

found. Sigfús Blöndal was able to find several, slightly differing accounts of Ólafsson's life in Iceland and compiled a biography with consistent recordings. I have made use of both the Danish translation, 'Jon Olafssons oplevelser som ostindiefarer under Christian IV nedskrevne af ham selv – I oversættelse ved S. Bløndal – udgivne af Julius Clausen og P. Fr. Rist '(1907) and the English version translated by Dame Bertha Phillpotts. For the Tamil words, see p. 137 of the English translation from 1932.

77 One gylden was 3/8 rigsdaler: See Bredsdorff, Asta. 'The trials and travels of Willem Leyel' (2009). This is about 15 usd in 2016.
78 Water is perhaps the most important necessity while embarking on such long voyages, and the collection of rainwater for drinking was common. The idea was to put something heavy, such as a lead ball, in the middle of the sheet and place a container under the sheet to collect filtered rainwater. It is also said that later day voyages to India had the benefit of water distillation apparatus on board (Henningsen, Henning 'Sømandens drikkelse', in Handels- og Søfartmuseet på Kronborg, Årbog (1977)).
79 According to 'The life of the Icelander Jón Ólafsson', an Icelandic ell was 21 1/11 inches equivalent to 54 centimeters.
80 Raghunatha Nayak.
81 This custom has been described in Dubois' book, 'Hindu customs, manners and ceremonies', p. 47.
82 பாக்கு
83 வெற்றிலைபாக்கு
84 'The Life of the Icelander Jón Olafsson', loc. cit. p. 139.
85 'The Raj – India and the British 1600-1947', Ed. C. A. Bayly, National Portrait Gallery Publications (1991).
86 தலையர்
87 Baldor comes from the Portuguese Ballador, meaning dancer.
88 This is probably a depiction of a Vishnu incarnation as a fish, see the article by Björn Westerbeek Dahl, 'Omkring et par tidlige kort over Tranquebar' https://tidsskrift.dk/index.php/magasin/article/viewFile/67021/123097.
89 This punishment is known as *strappado* in Portuguese [Dalrymple 2019].
90 பாம்பு
91 அப்பா
92 போ.போ.

3. Inebriety, Intrigue and Slavery

93 Bredsdorff, Asta. 'Willem Leyels liv og farefulde rejse til Indien', Museum Tusculanum (1999); 'The trials and travels of Willem Leyel' Museum Tusculanum (2009). This is the best book available about the life of Willem Leyel.
94 This town is referred to as Masulipatam in the Danish literature. 'Patnam' is a town on the seashore (Chennaipatnam, Nagapatnam etc.) and 'Masuli' or 'Machili' refers to fish.
95 Asta Bredsdorff writes: "Frederik III took pity on him and in recognition of his long and faithful service he was granted such support: 'It is Our gracious will and pleasure

that Our steward shall give our well-beloved Willem Leyel in view of his humble petition from Our victualling store belonging to our Castle in Copenhagen annually until We decide otherwise, to be reckoned from the last St. Philip's and St. James' Day the following victuals, that is rye 3 pounds, barley 4 pounds, butter 1 cask, oatmeal 1 cask, peas 1 cask, dried cod 1,320 pounds. From our Castle in Copenhagen. Haffniæ, 22 Februari Anno 1654'." (From "The trials and travels of Willem Leyel"). See also: RA, Kancelliets Brevbøger, 1654, Copenhagen (2001).

96 The market (or bazaar) was held on the parade grounds; later, it was moved to Setti Street between what is now the Bungalow on the Beach and the Masilanathar Temple.
97 Clarified butter.
98 RA: Danske Kancelli, Rentekammerafdelingen, Willem Leyels Arkiv (Løbenr. B246B).
99 Lauritsen. B, 'Danmarks indiske slaver', Weekendavisen, 10 March 2017.
100 Christensen, Mouritz, 'Mourids Christensen's Skildringer fra et Ophold i Ostindien (begyndte i Tranquebar 16/3 1671), med nogle portugisiske og malebariske Gloser. 95 Bl.', Royal Library, Rostg. 40, folio (1671). Mourids Christensen was a soldier in Tranquebar, spending a year there in 1671, and he proved to be a very shrewd observer of the local society. He commented on everything from the weather and climate, celebration of the Pongal festival, temples and idols, predictions and interpretations by the locals of the eclipses of the sun and the moon, birds and animals, stones and metal, measures and weights, pearl fishing, the death of St. Thomas, how slaves were bought and sold, the income of the king and the extent of his country, yogis and the sexual observances of the Nayak. Commenting on how people were bought and sold like animals, Christensen says that, among the pagans, there were people who were fond of gambling and the rich can gamble away thousands of rigsdaler as well as their house, property, children and wives. No one will sell or purchase goods without first consulting a Brahmin about the best time to do so. Christensen explains in detail how a spinner and weaver, a tailor, shoemaker and fishermen work and how much things cost as well as a thousand other things.
101 Gøbel, E. 'The Danish Slave Trade and its Abolition', Leiden, The Netherlands: Brill (2016).
102 Krieger, M. ' Der Dänische Sklavenhandel auf dem Indischen Ozean im 17. und 18. Jahrhundert', Jahrbuch für Europäische Überseegeschichte, vol. 12 (2012).
103 RA, Asiatisk Kompagni, Afdelingen i Tranquebar, Forfølg af rapport-bøgerne (Løbenr. 1314) p. 188.
104 'Vore Gamle Tropekolonier' vol. 6, ed. Kamma Struwe, Gads forlag, Copenhagen (1966) p. 61.
105 Der Königl. Dänischen Missionarien aus Ost-Indien eingesandter Ausführlichen Berichten, Von dem Werck ihres Amts unter den Heyden, Teil 1, Cont. 11 (1720) p.919.
106 Priesching, Nikole and Grieser, Heike. 'Theologie und Sklaverei von der Antike bis in die frühe Neuzeit', in 'Sklaverei, Knechtschaft, Zwangsarbeit: Unteruchungen zur Sozial-, Rechts- und Kulturgeschichte', Band 14, Georg Olms Verlag, (2016).
107 Svane-Knudsen, A. Private communication.
108 Foster, W. 'The English Factories in India: 1622-1623' Oxford (1908) p.106.

109 Allen, R. B. 'Satisfying the 'want for laboring people': European slave trading in the Indian Ocean, 1500-1850', Journal of World History, 21 (2010) pp. 45-73.
110 Loc. Cit.
111 Larson, P. 'African Diasporas and the Atlantic', in The Atlantic in Global History, 1500-2000, ed. Jorge Cañizares-Esguerra and Erik R. Seeman, Prentice-Hall (2007) pp. 129-147.
112 Senthalir, S. 'Chilling evidence of a slave trade', The Hindu, 18 March 2017.
113 http://www.globalslaveryindex.org/
114 Arockiaraj, Vincent. 'Gaja-hit Tamilnadu parents sold 12-yr-old boy for Rs. 10,000', Times of India, 28 December 2018.
115 Mirasi rights are hereditary rights connected with the possession and cultivation of land. The word 'mirasi' has Arabic origins and means inheritance or heritage. The word 'mirasidar' (mirasdar) or morador is derived from this. (https://en.wikipedia.org › wiki › Mirasi).
116 Hjejle, B. 'Slavery and agricultural bondage in South India in the nineteenth century', Scandinavian Economic History Review, 15 (1967) pp. 71-126.
117 Kaarsholm, Preben. 'From abolition of the slave trade to protection of immigrants: Danish colonialism, German missionaries, and the development of ideas of humanitarian governance from the early eighteenth century to the nineteenth century', Atlantic Studies, vol. 17(3) (2020) pp. 348-374.
118 Rigsarkivet, Chr. Ewalds Samling V-A (Løbenr. 2134).
119 This custom has been described in Dubois' book, 'Hindu customs, manners and ceremonies', (2006) p. 62.
120 Hansen, Thorkild. 'Slavernes Øer', Gyldendal (1970); Rigsarkivet, Højesteret 1797-1805, 'Sophie Magdalena afg. Sørensens enke contra afg. Major Abbesteés Stervboe og arvinger', (Løbenr. 172).

4. Murders, Property Disputes and Caste Conflicts

121 Nielsen, Villiam. 'Lidt om Trankebar og Trankebarmønter', Siegs Forlag (1974).
122 Harding, Georgina. 'Tranquebar – A season in South India', Sceptre (1993).
123 Several of the documents in the National Archivess (RA) refer to the Black Court, stating that it is located at 'Mutiradi'; the house of justice (Town court) was next to the New Jerusalem Church, at what is now a Teachers' Training College.
124 Peter Anker, map from 1798, University of Oslo, photographed by Ann Christine Eek.
125 RA: Det Kgl. Ostindiske Guvernement, Kolonien Trankebar, Sorteretsprotokol (1779-1781) (Løbenr. 1496a).
126 Translation from the Treaty of 19 November 1620 in 'The Life of the Icelander Jón Olafsson', vol. II (1931) p. 23.
127 Brimnes, Niels. 'Constructing the colonial encounter – Right and Left hand castes in early colonial South India', London: Curzon (1999).
128 RA, Kommercekollegiet, Journalsager (1789) (Løbenr. 995) #84.
129 This term probably comes from Tamil 'பிரவர்த்திகர்' [Ramachandran].

130 RA, Asiatisk Kompagni, Afdeling i Trankebar, Byetingsprotokol 1760-1762 (Løbenr. 1476-1479) p. 76.
131 RA: Asiatisk Kompagni, Afdelingen i Trankebar, Tamilske dokument vedr. den Sorte Ret (Løbenr. 20) – 'சத்தியமுள்ளவருமாய் நாசீவதாயாபரருமாயிருக்கிற எக பராபரவஸ்து அறிய அவர் முன்னிலையாக நான் ஞாயத்திலே இந்தச் சம்மதியைத் தொட்டு சொன்னது இப்பொ எனக்கு வாசிச்சு காண்பிச்சபடி பசுவை தான் அதிலெ ஒன்றும் எறவும் இல்லை குறையவுமில்லை அறிஞ்ச செதி சொன்னேன் இதுக்கு ? பாக சத்தியப்பிறகாரமாக என் வலது கையினாலெ எழுதி ஞாயகாறர் கையிலெ குடுத்தேன் – 1763 வருஷம் கார்த்திகை (மாதம்) 8 (தேதி) இப்படிக்கு குருவப்பன் கையெழுத்து'.
132 RA, Asiatisk Kompagni, Afdeling i Trankebar, Byetingsprotokol 1760-1764 (Løbenr. 1476-1479) p. 113. This is referred to in the case of Rudolph Müller contra Iver and Just Bonsach in April 1764. The 'pagode' in this case was in the town of Poraiyar.
133 See note 116, p. 81.
134 RA: Det Kgl. Ostindiske Guvernement – Kolonien Trankebar: Indkomne breve – AsK 1386 (1841) #124: 'அய்யனார் கோவில் வழக்கமான சத்தியம் செய்யும் படி யென் யெதிரியை சுமதலைப்படுத்தவும்'.
135 RA: Asiatisk Kompagni, Afdelingen i Trankebar: Dokumenter angående den sorte ret i Trankebar (1736-1779) (Løbe nr. 1493a) (sadly, this packet is in a poor state and cannot be studied at present); Det Kgl. Ostindiske Guvernement, Kolonien Trankebar, u. d. bog ført på tamulisk, Sorteretsprotokol (Løbenr. 1495a); Det Kgl. Ostindiske Guvernement, Kolonien Trankebar, Sorteretsprotokol 1762-1767 (Løbenr. 1495b); Det Kgl. Ostindiske Guvernement, Kolonien Trankebar, Sorteretssprotokol (Løbenr. 1496a); Det Kgl. Ostindiske Guvernement, Kolonien Trankebar, Forligsprotokol ved sorteretten, (1808) (Løbenr. 1496b); General Toldkammer og Kommercekollegiet, Indiske Kontor, Sager vedr. Sorteretten (1787-1818) (Løbenr. 3304).
136 RA, Asiatisk Kompagni, Afdelingen i Trankebar: Dokumenter angående den sorte ret i Trankebar (1736-1779) Document from 27 September 1768 (Løbe nr. 1493a).
137 RA: Det Kongl. Ostindiske Guvernement, Kolonien Trankebar, Sorteretsprotokol, (Løbenr. 1496a) p. 33.
138 ஒழுகமங்கலம்
139 Proceedings of the Black Court in Tamil for the years 1799-1803 are to be found in the Tamil Nadu Archives.
140 RA: Det Kgl. Ostindiske Guvernement, Kolonien Trankebar, u. d. bog ført på tamulisk, sorteretts protokol, (Løbenr. 1495a) p. 4.
141 RA, Chr. Ewalds samling, V-A (Løbenr. 2134); Chr. Ewalds Samling VI-A (Løbenr. 2137).
142 RA, Chr. Ewalds samling, VI-A (Løbenr. 2137).
143 Sirkazhi (சீர்காழி), a town approximately 30 km north of Tranquebar.
144 RA: Asiatiske Kompagni – Afdeling i Tranquebar, Breve fra Guvernementet i Tranquebar (1758 Feb. 7 – 1761 Sept) (Løbenr. 200).
145 Shamiana.
146 Ellen Margrethe Attrup.
147 Variously called Ravseba and Ratzapa; it probably refers to Rajappa.
148 RA, Asiatisk Kompagni, Afdelingen i Tranquebar, Byetingsprotokoller: Byetingsprotokol fra 12 aug. 1754-19 juli 1756 (Løbenr. 1467-1471).

149 Pial: A raised platform on which people sit, usually under the verandah or on either side of the door of the house (Hobson-Jobson); திண்ணை
150 Dübeck, Inger. 'Herrefolket og Hedningen', Politiken, 26 March 1988.
151 RA, Ostindisk Kompagni, Afdelingen i Trankebar: Engelharts registratur over det kongl. Gouvernements arkiv i Trankebar (Løbenr. 1230-1230A) p. 209. The original document in Persian has been lost, but Engelhart refers to this document in his register; RA, Asiatisk Kompagni, Afdelingen i København, Breve fra Guvernementet 1758 Feb 7 – 1761 Sep. 11 (Løbenr. 200-201).
152 RA: Asiatisk Kompagni, Afdeling i København, Asiatisk Kompagnis Justitsprotokoller, (Løbenr. 257) #297.
153 Dansk Biografisk Leksikon.
154 Ancher, P. Kofod. 'Svar paa nogle spørgsmaale til det juridiske fakultet givne af P. Kofod Ancher, Conferentsraad og Professor Juris ved Kiøbenhavns Universitet', Gyldendal (1779) p. 168.
155 'Et menneskets forsæt er iblant de usynlige ting for andres øjne, uden for saavidt det lader sig at tilsyne ved udvortes gierninger. Det er derfor af gierningen og dens omstændigheder man maa dømme om gierning mandens villie og forsæt'.
156 Dübeck. loc. cit.; RA. Danske Kancelli, Ostindiske Sager (1699-1798) (Løbenr. D34B).
157 RA: Asiatisk Kompagni – Afdeling i København, Breve fra Guvernementet 1758 Feb 7 – 1761 Sep 11 (Løbenr. 200-201).
158 A topas or topaz was an Indian lascar of Portugese descent. A lascar was a militiaman from the Indian subcontinent.
159 RA, Asiatisk Kompagni, Afdelingen i Trankebar, Byetingsprotokol 1762-1764 (Løbenr. 1476-1479). p. 22 of 1765.
160 Small pies.
161 RA, Asiatisk Kompagni, Afdelingen i Trankebar, Bytingsprotokol 1760-1764 (Løbenr. 1476-1479), nov. 1765.
162 RA: Asiatisk Kompagni – Afdeling i København, Asiatisk Kompagnis Justitsprotokoller, (Løbenr. 257) #410.
163 RA: Asiatisk Kompagni, Afdeling i København, Breve fra Guvernementet, 1758 Feb. 7 -1761 Sep. 11 (Løbenr. 200-201) #308.
164 Ramanujam, P. S. 'Tranquebar Registers' (2013); 'Tranquebar Registers – Version 2', Saxo (2016).
165 RA, Asiatisk Kompagni, Afdeling i Trankebar, Byetingsprotokol (1769-1771) (Løbenr. 1481).
166 RA: Asiatisk Kompagni, Afdeling i København, Asiatisk Kompagnis Justitsprotokoller, (Løbenr. 258) #23.
167 See, for example, Niels H. Krogh-Nielsen: 'At have sit liv forbrudt' – Henrettelse på Roskilde-egnen', Historisk Samfund for Roskilde Amt, Årbog 2019, p. 95.
168 RA, Asiatisk Kompagni, Afdeling i Trankebar, Byetingsprotokol (1760-1764) (Løbenr. 1476-1479).
169 RA: Det kgl. Ostindiske Guvernement – Kolonien Trankebar: AsK 1495a: Protokol for sorteretten.

170 RA, Det Kgl. Ostindiske Guvernement, Kolonen Trankebar, Indkomne breve til guvernementet i Tranquebar (Løbenr. 1391B) #290.
171 RA, Det Kgl. Ostindiske Guvernement, Kolonen Trankebar, Indkomne breve til guvernementet i Tranquebar (Løbenr. 1391B) #305.
172 RA, Det Kgl. Ostindiske Guvernement, Kolonen Trankebar, Indkomne breve til guvernementet i Tranquebar (Løbenr. 1391B) #315.
173 RA, Det Kgl. Ostindiske Guvernement, Kolonen Trankebar, Indkomne breve til guvernementet i Tranquebar (Løbenr. 1391B) #375.
174 Dörnbach, Rolf 'Danish East Indies: Once they Existed', The Post Horn, August (2005).

5. Pluripotency, Power and Painting

175 RA: Kommercekollegiet, Journalsager (1786) 1-115 (Løbenr. 982) #82.
176 RA: Kommercekollegiet – Journalsager (1783) (Løbenr. 975) #229.
177 Also known as Thillaiyadi and Thillali (தில்லையாடி).
178 Also known as Poreiar (பொரயார் or பொறையார்).
179 மணியக்காரர்
180 RA: Kommercekollegiet – Journalsager (1791) (Løbenr. 1009) #172.
181 கணக்குப்பிள்ளை
182 மணியக்காரன்
183 According to the Tranquebar Census of 1790, there were at least 45 dubashes in Tranquebar alone.
184 Appadurai, Arjun. 'The right- and left-hand castes in South India', Indian Economic and Social History Review, vol. 11 (1974).
185 வெள்ளாளர்
186 Mackenzie Manuscripts, Summaries of the Historical Manuscripts in the Mackenzie Collection, Vol. 1, Manuscript #23, Ed. T. V. Mahalingam, University of Madras (1972) p. 147.
187 பாஞ்சாலர்
188 சலுப்பன்- ஐணப்பன்
189 The Danish Archives refer to this caste as Chellappa or Chelpa.
190 சணல்
191 Dubois, Abbe J. A. 'Hindu manners, customs and ceremonies', translated by H. K. Beauchamp, Clarendon Press (1906) p. 26.
192 Subramanian, P. 'Social History of the Tamils (1707-1947)', Printworld (P) Ltd., New Delhi (2005).
193 மஹாநாடு தேசத்தர்
194 RA: Kommerce Kollegiet – Journalsager (1788) (Løbenr. 992) # 204, # 206; Journalsager 1789 #236; see also Feldbæk.
195 RA, AsK 1514b, Littra D and E.
196 RA, AsK 1330.
197 RA: Kommercekollegiet – Ostindiske sekr. Journalsager (1789) (Løbenr. 996) #158: 'han er en sort af maadeligt kast, der er begavet med det allerypperligste Genie

for Intriguer. Han har vidst at forene sine medfødde Mallabarske Talenter som skiælmstykker med Europæiske Procurator Kneeb, at han er fuldkommen Mæster af den Kunst at dække de allerværste Handlinger saavel, at intet lovligt Beviis skal fælde ham'.

198 Nielsen, Y. 'General-Major Peter Anker – Guvernør i Trankebar', Historisk Tidsskrift, Vol. 1, Oslo (Kristiania) (1870) p. 313.

199 'Jeg har selv havt dem i min tjeneste; men tyveri og drukkenskab med alle deraf flydende laster forefandtes lige så stærk indprentet i deres natur, som hos deres uomvendte brödre' (op. cit.) p. 314-315.

200 RA: Kommercekollegiet, Ostindiske Sekr., Journalsager (1789) (Løbenr. 997) #254.

201 ஒழுகமங்கலம் [Ramachandran]

202 RA: Kommercekollegiet, Ostindiske Sekr,, Journalsager (1799) (Løbenr. 2020) #284.

203 RA: Kay Larsen's Personal Kartotek (www.ddd.dda.dk).

204 Lord Mornington, Marquis Wellesley, was the eldest of the three Wellesley brothers. He was the Governor General of India, but was recalled to Britain in the wake of his high-handed imperial policies, his exorbitant constructions in Calcutta and his general extravagant behaviour. He died a dejected man on 26 September 1842. For an interesting account of his time in India, see William Dalrymple's 'White Moghuls', Penguin, India (2009).

205 RA: Det kgl. Ostindiske Gouvernement – Kolonien Trankebar (1787-1804): Korrespondence med engelske og franske kolonialembedsmænd. AsK 1378d.

206 The letter sent by Lord Mornington to General Anker can be seen in 'The despatches, minutes and correspondence of the Marquess Wellesley K. G. during his administration in India', Ed. M. Martin, Vol. V (1837).

207 RA: Det kgl. Ostindiske Gouvernement – Kolonien Trankebar (1787-1804): Korrespondence med engelske og franske kolonialembedsmænd. AsK 1378d.

208 RA, Asiatisk Kompagni, Afdeling i København, Breve fra Guvernøren i Tranquebar (1751 sept. 28 – 1756 oct.15) (Løbenr. 199) #25.

209 Christensen, H. 'De danske fremstød i Indien i 1750-erne, Baggrund og Forløb' Thesis, University of Copenhagen (1992).

210 RA, Asiatisk Kompagni, Afdeling i Tranquebar, Kopibog over indkomne breve 1754-1758 (Løbenr. 1356) p. 425.

211 'Der Königliche Missionarien aus Ost-indien eingesandter ausführlichen Berichte' (1765) p. 253.

212 Thillaiyali gains its name from the myth that Vishnu in the shape of the mythical beast, Yali, worshipped Shiva here. 'Thillai' (தில்லை), another name for the town of Chidambaram, is the place where Shiva in the shape of the dancing Nataraja annihilates the Universe. The figure of Yali (யாளி) worshipping a lingam can be seen on the temple's flagpole ('dwajasthambam').

213 George Pigot, 1st Baron Pigot (4 March 1719 – 11 May 1777), was twice over the British President of the British East India Company (India).(https://en.wikipedia.org/wiki/George_Pigot,_1st_Baron_Pigot).

214 RA, Asiatisk Kompagni, Afdeling i Tranquebar, Kopibog over indkomne breve 1754-1758 (Løbenr. 1356) p. 39.

215 Is it the same Perumal Naik? The missionaries report: 'We understand from an old heathen in Tiliali that Perumal Naiken, who had been troubling the Danish Company for several years, has died in Tirukadeiur after a long and terrible illness' ('Weiterhin erfuhr man von einem Tilealischen Einwohner, einem alten Heiden, was man sonst schon von mehreren erfahren, nemlich, dass Peruma Naiken, der sich selbst und dem Dänischen Compagnie-Grund durch seinen unruhigen kopf seit vielen Jahren viele Unruhen gemach, nun endlich in Tirukadeiur, an einer langwierigen schlimmen Krankheit gestorben' Neuere Geschichte der evangelischen Missionsanstalten zu Bekehrung der Heiden in Ost-Indien, 1.1770/1773 Stück 1-6 (1776) p. 726.

216 RA: Det kgl. Ostindiske Gouvernement – Kolonien Trankebar (1787-1804): Korrespondence med engelske og franske kolonialembedsmænd. AsK 1378d.

217 RA: Det kgl. Ostindiske Gouvernement – Kolonien Trankebar (1787-1804): Korrespondence med engelske og franske kolonialembedsmænd. AsK 1378d.

218 According to Webster's Encyclopedic Unabridged Dictionary of the English Language, 'cavil' is 'to raise irritating and trivial objections'; I do not know, whether this was what Lord Mornington meant.

219 RA: Kommercekollegiet, Ostindiske Fags Sekretariat, Journalsager (1811) (Løbenr. 2045) #63.

220 http://www.khm.uio.no/tema/utstillingsarkiv/peteranker

221 RA: Det kgl. Ostindiske Guvernement: Kolonien Trankebar (1789-94) Komm. Protokol og bilag (Løbenr. 1514B).

222 RA: Det kgl. Ostindiske Guvernement, Kolonien Trankebar, Indkomne breve til guvernøren i Tranquebar, 1795-1837 (Løbenr. 1396B2) – Complaints in Tamil.

223 Brimnes, Niels. 'From civil servant to little king: An indigenous construction of colonial authority in early nineteenth-century South India' in 'Engaging Colonial Knowledge', Ricardo Roque and Kim A. Wagner, Editors, London (2012). This article gives a very detailed description of the conflict during the period 1818-1823.

224 RA, Kommercekollegiet, Ostindiske Fags Sekretariat, Journalsager (1822) (Løbenr. 3268).

225 Kay Larsen. 'Guvernører, Residenter, Kommandanter og Chefer', Copenhagen (1940).

226 The Asiatic Journal and Monthly Register for British and Foreign India, China and Australasia, Vol. 9 (1832) p. 145; Rosen, D. 'Erindringer fra mit Ophold paa de Nikobarske Øer', Copenhagen (1839).

227 Kay Larsen, loc. cit.

228 Colbjörnsen, a senior councillor for the government, remarked in 1790 that: 'The Malabarians are a cantankerous people. They are negligent in their accounts, they utter intricate lies to their superiors, and abuse their authority'.

229 1 lakh = 100,000.

230 Fischer, P. R. 'En rejsefærd fra Helsingør til Tranquebar skildret i breve' *Handels- og Søfartsmuseets årbog 1952*, p. 24-78.

6. A Stowaway from Tranquebar

231 RA, Peter Ankers private arkiver (Løbenr. 7392).

232 சின்னய்யனா..

233 RA, Asiatisk Kompagni, Afdelingen i København, Skibsjournaler for Ostindiefarere 'Juliane Maria' (1794-1795) p. 66.
234 Much of the present work is based on Waaben's article.
235 The complaint is not in his handwriting; he obviously had a scribe to do this for him.
236 RA, Kommercekollegiet, Ostindiske Fags Sekretariat, Journalsager (1798) (Løbenr. 2015) #358.
237 RA, Kommercekollegiet, Ostindiske Fags Sekretariat, Journalsager (1798) (Løbenr. 2018) #394.
238 RA, Kommercekollegiet, Ostindiske Forestillinger og Kongelige Resolutioner (1798) (Løbenr. 1976).
239 மஹாநாடு தேசத்தார்
240 RA, Kommercekollegiet, Ostindiske Fags Sekretariat, Journalsager (1799) (Løbenr. 2019) #202.
241 Ærekrænkelse
242 ராமசெயம்
243 https://www.sa.dk/ao-soegesider/da/billedviser?bsid=211786
244 https://www.danishfamilysearch.dk/sogn578/churchbook/source3898/opslag1790458
245 https://www.sa.dk/ao-soegesider/da/billedeviser?bsid=2#2,630 (Child number 335, mother number 330).
246 However, according to the census of 1801, Birgitte was married for the first time (https://www.danishfamilysearch.com/cid968816).
247 RA: Kommercekollegiet, Ostindiske Fags Sekretariat, Journalsager (1801) #200 (Løbenr. 2024).
248 RA: Kommercekollegiet, Ostindiske Fags Sekretariat, Journalsager (1802) #58 (Løbenr. 2025).
249 RA: Kommercekollegiet, Ostindiske Fags Sekretariat, Journalsager (1802) #58 (Løbenr. 2025).
250 RA: Kommercekollegiet, Ostindiske Fags Sekretariat, Journalsager (1804) #135 (Løbenr. 2033).
251 A very detailed article on the churches in Tranquebar during the Danish period 1660-1845, including many construction details, has been published by Karin Kryger in Architectura vol. 29, Copenhagen (2007) pp. 57-90.
252 RA, Kommercekollegiet, Ewalds Papirer VI A 'Regnskab for Zionskirkens ombygning (1778-1779) (Løbenr. 2137).
253 RA, Indkomne breve til guvernementet i Tranquebar (1839), (Løbenr. 1391A). #501.
254 RA, Kommercekollegiet, Journalsager (1797) (Løbenr. 1033) #423.

7. A Forgotten Astronomer – A Forgotten Blessed Soul

255 Halley, E. 'A new method of determining the parallax of the sun, or his distance from the earth', Philosophical Transaction of the Royal Society, vol. 29 (1716) p. 454-464.
256 Kapoor, R. C. 'Indian astronomy and the transits of Venus. 1. The early observations', Journal of Astronomical History and Heritage, vol. 16 (2013) p. 269-286.
257 Dumont, Simone and Gros, Monique, 'The important role of the two French astronomers J. -N. Delisle and J. -J. Lalande in the choice of observing places during

the transits of Venus in 1761 and 1769', The Journal of Astronomical Data, vol. 19 (2013) p. 131.
258   Novi Commentarii MDCCLXV (p. 569).
259   Gentleman's Magazine and Historical Chronicle, Vol. XXXII for the year MDCCLXII., London (1762) p. 177.
260   The Gentleman's and London Magazine, (1764) p. 201-203.
261   Der Königl. Dänischen Missionarien aus Ost-Indien eingesandter Ausführlichen Berichten, Von dem Werck ihres Amts unter den Heyden , Teil 8, Cont. 95 (1761) p. 1155.
262   'Den 6ten Jun: Heute passierte die Venus den Discum Solis. Der Eingang geschahe ohngefähr um sechs Uhr, ein und funfzig Minuten. Der Ausgang aber um ein Uhr, neun and vierzig Minuten. Diese Conjunction der Veneris mit der Sonne ist um so viel seltsamer, weil sie sich seit dem Jahr 1639 nicht zugetragen'.
263   Espenak, Fred. (https://eclipse.gsfc.nasa.gov/transit/catalog/VenusCatalog.html).
264   'So viel wir uns auch angeschickt und bemühet, den Durchgang der Venus durch die Sonne bey den Aufgang derselben zu beobachten, so war es doch eine gänzliche Unmöglichkeit, davon etwas gewahr zu werden, denn der ganze Horizont in Osten war umgezogen, und die Sonne bis um 7 Uhr gar nicht zu sehen; nach 7 Uhr aber könte man zwar den Ort sehen, wo die Sonne stand, allein sie steckte so in Dünsten, dass man die Sonnen-Scheibe nicht völlig deutlich erkennen könte, so wie sie auch den ganzen Tag nicht recht helle geschienen' (Neuere Geschichte der evangelischen Missionsanstalten zu Bekehrung der Heiden in Ost-Indien, 1.1770/1773, Stück 1-6 (1776)) p. 328.
265   The transits of Venus in 1761 and 1769 paved the way for astronomical observations in Indonesia. Reverend J. Mohr, using his wife's inheritance, built a fully equipped observatory in Batavia. See Huib J. Zuivervaart and Rob H. Van Gent, 'A bare outpost of learned European culture on the edge of the jungles of Java', Isis, vol. 95, History of Science Society, University of Chicago Press (2004), pp. 1-33.
266   'Als ich Morgens um vier Uhr unter meinem Zelt hervorkam, und zum Preise Gottes den hell bestirnten Himmel ansahe, erblickte ich im Tauro einem Cometen mit einem ausserordentlich langen Schwanze' (Neuere Geschichte der evangelischen Missionsanstalten zu Bekehrung der Heiden in Ost-Indien, 1.1770/1773, Stück 1-6 (1776) p. 371.
267   'Den 10ten ging er kurz vor 2 Uhr auf und stand in Minoceros, in gleicher linie mit dem Sirius, nordwarts. Sein Schwanz ging durch den Orion bis in den Taurum', Neuere Geschichte der evangelischen Missionsanstalten zu Bekehrung der Heiden in Ost-Indien, 1.1770/1773, Stück 1-6 (1776) p. 455. Very likely, this comet was C/1769, which was discovered by Messier on 8 August 1769.
268   'Vom 8ten bis zum 13ten Januar, haben wir hier einen Cometen gesehen. Er is auch am Madras gesehen worden', Neuere Geschichte der evangelischen Missionsanstalten zu Bekehrung der Heiden in Ost-Indien, 1.1770/1773, Stück 1-6 (1776) p. 763. This was probably the great comet C/1771, also discovered by Messier.
269   Thomas Bugge (1740-1815) was a Danish astronomer, mathematician and surveyor. He was responsible for the triangulation of Denmark from 1768. His instruments are

exhibited at the Kroppedal Museum, situated at the observatory ruins of the famous Danish astronomer and scientist Ole Rømer, close to Copenhagen (www.kroppedal.dk).

270 Jensen, Niklas Thode. 'The Tranquebarian Society: Science, enlightenment and useful knowledge in the Danish-Norwegian East Indies, 1768–1813' (2015) Scandinavian Journal of History, 40, pp. 535-561.

271 ஆத்திச்சூடி

272 கொன்றைவேந்தன்

273 மூதுரை

274 ஔவையார்

275 RA: Håndskriftsamlingen VII E.

276 A transcription of this manuscript together with other important works by Engelhart (including commentary) has just been published. ('Videnskab, Oplysning og Historie i Dansk Ostindien: Udvalgte skrifter af Henning Munch Engelhart. ', Groesmeyer, L., Jensen, N. T., and Ramanujam P. S., Selskabet for udgivelse af Kilder til Dansk Historie (2020)).

277 Engelhart, H. E. 'Tanker om oplysnings udbredelse blandt Indianerne i anledning af det Trankebarske Selskabs Opgave', Det Kongl. Bibl. NKS 425 b folio.

278 The astronomical clock showed both the solar time and the sidereal time.

279 RA: Kommercekollegiet – Ostindiske Sekretariat: Journalsager 1790 (Løbenr. 1001) #292.

280 Engelhart probably refers to the saltiness of the air, as the observatory was situated very close to the seashore.

281 During opposition, the Sun and Jupiter are on opposite sides of the earth.

282 Gøbel, Erik. 'Asiatisk Kompagnis sejlads på Indien 1732-1772', Handels- og Søfartsmuseet på Kronborg, Årbog 1987, pp. 22-86.

283 There is a misunderstanding in the literature that John Goldingham was a Dane (see the URL below). Surely, this must be due to his association with Henning Munch Engelhart's measurements. Saba Risaluddin writes: 'I should like to correct the misconception that John Goldingham was Danish. He was my great-great-grandfather, born in London in 1767, the son of Benjamin Goldingham, a wine merchant of Eastcheap, London, and Elizabeth Williams, also of London, and grandson of John Goldingham, a clothier, of Devizes, and Martha West, also of Devizes. John Goldingham of Madras was a Fellow of the Royal Society, the Royal Geographical Society and the Royal Astronomical Society. He returned to England after a lengthy period of service in Madras as official astronomer, engineer, architect and amateur archaeologist, and died in Worcester in 1849' (http://www.bl.uk/onlinegallery/onlineex/apac/other/019wdz000000962u00002000.html).

284 Rastén, Simon. 'Mødet med den Nicobarernes Klima', Master's Thesis, University of Copenhagen (2012).

285 RA, Kommercekollegiet, Ostindiske fags sekretariat, Sager vedr. Nikobarerne, Journal over Nikobars opmaaling (1791) (Løbenr. 2055).

286 RA: Kommercekollegiet – Ostindiske Sekretariat: Journalsager 1792 (Løbenr. 1005) #30.

287 Udi slutning af May Maaned erfoer vi den ligesaa bedrövelige som uheldige hændelse af præsten Engelhardt, og hofjuncker Lachmans Död paa Nikkobar, begge Döde

om Bord paa Expeditions Fartöyet Ketchen Intengport den 12de Aprill, Lachman om Morgenen og Engelhardt om Eftermiddagen, af de dræbende fölge som det Nikkobarsk Feber med sig förer, naar patienten er særdeles forsigtig i Bruugen af Lægemidlerne hvis misbrug værkede disse mænds precipiterede Död. Efter Skiibsföererens Beretning fandt Engelhardt strax efter ankomsten paa Nikkobar som skeede den 11de Martii, overdreven sin Nidkærhed i forretningen og trodset de fornöden Precautioner i et usund Climat, hvilket snart paaforte ham det Nikkobarske feber og da Præstens helbred forværredes saa skreed man til den Resolution at giöre Virkningen af Soe Lüften en Krydstoeg blev foretaget den 1ste Aprill faae Dage forinden blev Lachman befahldt med Feber dog og hæftig, men den 12de Aprill toeg Hof-Jünkere meget uforsigtigen 1 ½ Dosis Brækpulver og da det ikke strax vilde paabringe Virkningen overvældende(?) Mængde kaaget Vand, saa at denne overordentlige Omgangs Maade bragte ham inden faae Minuter til Graven – Begge disse haabefulde Mænd, hvis överiilede Död ey noksom kand beklages af Fædrenelandets Patrioter, bleve begravat paa öen Taraka med behörige Solemniteter. Beklageligt er det, at man af alle Omstændigheder maae Dömme at begge have selv været skyld i deres hastige Död, og ikke som man maaskee urigtigen vilde formode, Nikkobars berygtede Climat.

288 RA: Kommercekollegiet – Ostindiske Sekretariat: Journalsager 1792 (Løbenr. 1010) #248.

8. Death, Despotism and Destruction.

289 Daniel Pulley's letters are found in RA, Breve fra tolken Daniel i Tanjore ang. indløsning af pantsatte landsbyer (1783 – 1784) (Løbenr. 2183c). Referred to hereafter as RA: AsK2183c.

290 Malleson, G. B. 'The decisive battles of India – 1746 to1849', New Delhi: Asian Educational Services (2007).

291 Pollilur (Pullalur) is a small village north of Kanchipuram in Tamilnadu, India (12.9463648 N,79.7018044,653E). The place has two obelisks in memory of Captain James Hislop and Lieutenant Colonel George Brown from 1781 (http://know-your-heritage.blogspot.in/search/label/Battle%20of%20Pollilur); the battle of Pollilur and its impact has been described vividly by Dalrymple [Dalrymple].

292 Jasanoff, Maya. 'Edge of empire: lives, culture, and conquest in the East, 1750-1850' New York: Knopf (2005).

293 Not a captured hostage like Gowan Harrop, but more as an envoy.

294 Vormbaum, R. 'Evangelische Missionsgeschichte in biographien', Bd. 2,5/6, Düsseldorf (1852). p. 95.

295 RA: Kommercekollegiet, Ostindiske Sekretariat, Journalsager (1783) (Løbenr. 975) #96.

296 RA: Det kgl. Ostindiske Guvernement, Kolonien i Trankebar, Breve fra tolken Daniel (1782)(Løbenr. 2183c) #18.

297 Siyeresthe: Citing from 'Mitteilungen Daniel Pulleys aus dem Lager Haidar Alis, von Klein übersetzt', NGEMA, p. 438, Liebau writes that Mr. Surstädt was the Danish Representative at the court of Heider Ali [Liebau 2001]; According to Kay Larsen's Personkartotek at the National Archives, his name was Bertel Siersted. Larsen

writes further that he became a clerk in Tranquebar 27 Nov. 1780 through a Royal Resolution. Bertel Siersted was born in the town of Ringsted in Denmark. It is likely that his family came from the near-by town of Sigersted. Census records in Denmark indicate that he was born around 1751. He sailed from Copenhagen on board the *Queen Juliane Marie* in January 1781 and arrived in Tranquebar on 28 June 1781. He was an efficient and intelligent man and was therefore given difficult tasks, such as being an envoy in Heider Ali's court. Ironically, he was appointed Public Notary on 2 December 1782, before the news of his death reached Denmark.

298 21 Ani would correspond to 1 July, according to Swamikannu Pillai. However, while Daniel Pulley writes that it was a Friday, according to 'An Indian Ephemeris', 1 July was a Monday. I think the date must be 21 June, which was a Friday – this also fits better with the letters to Klein, mentioned below.

299 Krishna Rayan (or Krishna Rao) was Heider Ali's treasurer.

300 Castarede: Name written in Latin alphabet. 'Jean Martin, a French doctor, deserted from Heider Ali, the ruler of Mysore, to the East India Company at Vaniambadi in 1767. According to him, there were three English doctors with Heider Ali. Jean Castarede served from 1770-1789 under Heider and Tippu, deserted to the British and was made Assistant Surgeon in 1790. He died in Kadalur (Cuddalore) in 1798' [Jain and Murthy].

301 Daniel writes Budono – probably Boudenot – a cavalry officer in the service of Tippu Sultan. I am grateful to Jean Lecloche for this reference.

302 Daniel writes Aas; Hasz was a Dutch official with Heider Ali [Ramaswami].

303 Daniel writes Piporen: Puis Morrin – see letter from Abbestée (Journalsager from 1781 (Løbenr. 969) #76.

304 Daniel writes Kariar: probably Carrière.

305 Daniel writes Dusameng: Duchemin, a French general, famous for the battle fought at Sadraspatnam against the British. He arrived in May 1782.

306 Muhammad Ali: Muhammad Ali Wallajah (1749-1795) was a Nawab of Arcot and an ally of the British East India Company, but he commanded little real power. (see www.princeofarcot.org)

307 Nawab is a term for a ruler; it was used to denote Heider Ali.

308 The period of 8 Chittirai until 24 Ani corresponds to 17 April until 4 July [Swamikannu Pillai].

309 Chennapatnam is synonymous with Chennai (modern day Madras).

310 Dhobigarh and Chembargarh; the two names literally mean the 'house of washermen' and the 'house of cobblers'. They are supposedly located between Vellore and Ambur, close to the town of Pallikonda [see Hayavadana Rao, C. 'History of Mysore 1399-1799', vol. iii (1946).

311 RA: AsK 2183c #68.

312 Daniel writes 'asara nawab' – probably a respectful invocation 'Hazrat nawab', a name for Heider Ali.

313 The name Suffrein is written both in Tamil and Latin letters. <u>Admiral</u> comte Pierre André de Suffrein de Saint Tropez, bailli de Suffrein (17 July 1729 – 8 December 1788) was the third son of the marquis de Saint Tropez, head of a family of nobles of

Provence who claimed to have emigrated from Lucca in the 14th century. He was born in the Château de Saint-Cannat, near Aix-en-Provence in the present département of Bouches-du-Rhône. He became famous for his campaign in the Indian Ocean, in which he inconclusively contended for supremacy against the established British power there, led by Vice-Admiral Sir Edward Hughes. (en.wikipedia.org).

314 ரகசியமா இருக்கிற சேதிகளை தமுழிலி எழுதாமல் பாஷையில் சுருக்கமே எழுதியனுப்பிவிக்க சொன்னார்கள்.
315 RA: AsK 2183c #69.
316 One varahan is approximately 4 g gold.
317 Lally – The elder Lally, comte de Lally, was tried and executed in 1769 in France. The younger Lally stayed in India, he died in approximately 1785.
318 RA: AsK 2183c #16.
319 Ayyangar is a Brahmin caste worshipping Vishnu.
320 Naazhi: one naazhi is equal to 24 minutes. The Nawab was camping 2 hours west of Cuddalore.
321 This could be a mail sent on a Selling.
322 Probably Harper, as is explained in a letter to Klein.
323 Kattumannarkoil is a town north west of Tranquebar and south west of Chidambaram.
324 Pattambakkam: There is a Melpattambakkam and a Kizhpattambakkam. The place is near Panrutti in Cuddalore District, close to Nellikuppam. There was a Leipziger Mission here.
325 RA: AsK 2183c #119.
326 Daniel writes Lonayi: Mons. De Lannoy.
327 Samayya (Shamaiya Iyengar) was the Minister of Post & Police.
328 Guignace Benjamin was 'Substitut du Procureur général and later Agent du roi á Tranquebar avant sou déces'.
329 RA: AsK 2183c #57.
330 Vazhudavur (வழுதவூர்), a place west of Pondichery.
331 Daniel writes 'paather' (பாதர்) . I do not know what he means, but one can guess that it refers to Heider.
332 Col. Braithwaite.
333 வந்தவாசி – Wandiwash.
334 கொள்ளிடம்.
335 Mons. de Bussy.
336 Olevarius.
337 Daniel writes Yoos: Admiral Hughes.
338 Eyre Coote.
339 காமக்கூர் – a place west of Arni.
340 வழுதவூர்; வாழுடவூர் – Vazhudavur, west of Pondichery.
341 பெருமுக்கல் – to the east of Tindivanam.
342 கொடுக்கூர்
343 Surstädt is Siersted
344 வண்ணான்துருவம்
345 Vazhudavur.

346 The Kallar, together with the Maravar and Agamudayar, constitute a united social caste on the basis of parallel professions, although their locations and heritages are entirely separate from one another. *Kallar* is a Tamil word meaning *thief*. Their history has included periods of banditry. Other proposed etymological origins include 'black skinned', 'hero', and 'toddy-tappers' (https://en.wikipedia.org/wiki/Kallar_(caste)).

347 தைலாபுரம் – north of Pondichery.

348 வைரபுரம் – north of Tindivanam.

349 தெல்லர் – தெள்ளாறு

350 சாத்தமங்கலம்; சட்டமங்கலம் – east of Tindivanam.

351 கருங்குழிப்பள்ளம்? – close to Mahabalipuram.

352 பொதி

353 This must be Daniel's elder brother, Peter Rajappen. It is obvious from here that Daniel had at least one younger brother.

354 Sesame oil.

355 Colonel Baillie was captured in the Battle of Pollilur.

356 RA: AsK 2183c #2a.

357 RA: AsK2183c #26a.

358 RA: AsK2183c #29a

359 RA, Kommercekollegiet, Ostindiske Sekretariat, Journalsager (1796) (1-124) (Løbenr. 1025) #124; Journalsager (1796) (216-347), (Løbenr. 1027) #334.

360 RA: AsK 2183c #35.

361 Kurzer Lebenslauf des Daniel Pulley – Erster Königl. Gouvernements Dollmetscher Assessor im Schwarzen oder Tamilischen Gerich und Vorsteher der Christl. Missions Gemeine in Trankebar. Geb. 1740 Gest. 1802.

362 RA: Det kgl. Ostindiske Guvernement : Kolonien Trankebar (1790) mandtal over indbyggere i Trankebar.

363 Krieger, M 'Wohnkultur in Tranquebar um 1800. Auf spurensuche in den Tamilnadu State Archives', in Studia Eurasiatica, S. Conermann and J. Kusber (ed) EB-Verlag (); 'Material culture, knowledge, and European society in colonial India around 1800: Danish Tranquebar', in 'Artistic and cultural exchanges between Europe and Asia 1400-1900', M. North (ed), Ashgate (2010).

364 RA: Det kgl. Ostindiske Guvernement – Kolonien Trankebar (1823-1845) Indkomne breve til guvernøren (Løbenr. 1386).

365 RA: Det kgl. Ostindiske Guvernement – Kolonien Trankebar (1823-1845) Indkomne breve til guvernøren (Løbenr. 1386), #75.

366 மோட்டுக்கண்ணமூலை

367 Grønseth, K. 'The four histories of the village: Landmarks and historical identities', in Fihl and Venkatachalapathy (2014) pp. 50-73.

368 A Muslim saint.

369 Andersen, Peter B. 'Processions and chariot festivals: Cultural markings in Tharangampadi and Vailankanni', in Fihl and Venkatachalapathy (2014) pp. 74-94.

9. Pietism, Printing and Peccadillos

370 Der Königl. Dänischen Missionarien aus Ost-Indien eingesandter Ausführlichen Berichten, Von dem Werck ihres Amts unter den Heyden , Teil 2, Cont. 18 (1724) p. 226.

371 The term 'Malabar' means hill country in Tamil. People living in the south-west corner of India (Kerala today) were therefore referred to as 'Malabarians'. The term is no longer in use, but occurs in various historical texts and documents.

372 The missionaries had also started registering births, marriages and deaths within their congregation. The New Jerusalem Church Register shows the first recordings in German from 1707.

373 Nørgaard, Anders, 'Tranquebarmissionens tidlige historie', Kirke historiske samlinger, Akademiske Forlag, Copenhagen (1977) pp. 81-107.

374 Manual of the Administration of the Madras Presidency, vol. 1 (1885) p. 567.

375 http://192.124.243.55/digbib/hb.htm

376 Forchhammer, Herluf. 'Missionærerne I Tranquebar i 1700-tallet', Master's Thesis, University of Copenhagen (1985).

377 Hallesche Berichte, vol. 1, Cont. 7 (1714) pp. 451-454.

378 நீதிவெண்பா, கொன்றைவேந்தன், உலகநீதி.

379 Jeyaraj, Daniel. 'Bartholomäus Ziegenbalg: The Father of Modern Protestant Mission – An Indian Assessment', Delhi (2006).

380 'Bibliotheca Malabarica: Bartholomaus Ziegenbalg's Tamil Library', Edited and translated by W. Sweetman and R. Ilakkuvan, Institut Francais de Pondichery and Ecole Francaise d'extreme-orient (2012).

381 The dates of birth of the three children can be found in the New Jerusalem Church Register, National Archives, Copenhagen (p. 7, 8 and 9, respectively). The book by Brijraj Singh on Ziegenbalg contains factual errors. He states, *inter alia*, that two of the children died early, which is not correct.

382 J. F. Fenger. 'Den Trankebarske Missions Historie'. Germann, vol. 2 (1868).

383 கருவேப்பிலை

384 இலுப்பை

385 Neuere Geschichte der evangelischen Missionsanstalten zu Bekehrung der Heiden in Ost-Indien : aus d. eigenhändigen Aufsätzen u. Briefen der Missionarien hrsg', Germany: Halle.

386 He could be mistaken for a Singh belonging to the Sikh sect; however, his name was Amarasimhan.

387 Brimnes, Niels (Ed.) 'Danmark og Kolonierne : Indien – Tranquebar, Serampore og Nicobarerne', Gads Forlag (2017) p. 146.

388 Brimnes, N and Jørgensen, H. 'Lokalsamfundet Tranquebar 1630-1750', in Brimnes, N. 'Danmark og Kolonierne: Indien – Tranquebar, Serampore og Nicobarerne', Gads Forlag (2017) p. 155.

389 Rasch, Aage. 'Vore gamle tropekolonier' vol. 7, Fremad (1952) p. 104.

390 RA, Kommercekollegiet, Journalsager (1807) (Løbenr.) #220; RA, Kommercekollegiet, Journaler (1798) (Løbenr. 2000-2001) #276.

391 RA, Christian Ewalds Samlinger VI B-D (Løbenr. 2138).

392 RA, Det Kgl. Ostindiske Gouvernement – Kolonien Trankebar – Indkomne breve til Gouvernement i Trankebar (1837) – (Løbenr. 1389) – #276.
393 Det Kgl. Ostindiske Guvernement – Kolonien Trankebar – Indkomne breve til Guverneuren i Trankebar (1833-1836) (Løbenr. 1384).
394 Det Kgl. Ostindiske Guvernement – Kolonien Trankebar – Guvernements Resolutionprotokol (1838 Dec. 27 – 1845 Okt. 30) (Løbenr. 1350) #6884.
395 'Arrival of the first Moravian missionaries in Tranquebar', Moravian Archives, Bethlehem, Pa., USA, Issue 55, July 2010.
396 See note 395.
397 Grafe, H. 'The first Lutheran Indian Christians in Tranquebar' in 'Halle and the beginning of Protestant Christianity in India', Ed. Gross, Kumaradoss and Liebau, Verlag der Frankeschen Stiftung zu Halle (2006) p. 215.
398 Günther, Henrik. 'Samlingssalen i skolen i Admiralgade' in Tranquebar, Architectura 9 (1987).
399 RA, Kommercekollegiet, Journalsager (1792) (Løbenr. 1009) #172.
400 RA, Kommercekollegiet, Ostindiske Fags Sekretariat, Journalsager (1814) (Løbenr. 2046) Summary of the document #88.
401 RA, Kommercekollegiet, Journalsager (1815) (Løbenr. 2047) #58.
402 That this is possible is evident from the excavation of King Richard III. See 'The last days of Richard III and the fate of his DNA' by John Ashdown-Hill, in which the DNA of the long-dead king is related to that of a recent descendant of his.
403 RA, Kommercekollegiet, Journalsager (1833) (Løbenr. 3279) #219.
404 Architectura vol. 9 (1987).
405 Refer, Maria Rehling. ' Livlinen til Danmark – kvindebreve Tranquebar-Helsingør', Folk og minder fra Nordsjælland, Årg. 71 (2016).

10. Philology comes to Town

406 Jensen, N. T. 'The medical skills of the Malabar doctors in Tranquebar, as recorded by surgeon T. L. F. Folly', Med. Hist. vol. 49 (2005) p. 489.
407 Svane-Knudsen, A. 'Den Arabiske rejse og Asiatisk Kompagni 1763-1766', Danske Magazin, vol. 51, (2012), pp. 483-513.
408 Petersen, Carl S. 'Fra Rasks ungdom', Danske Studier (1909) p. 18.
409 Hansen, Thorkild. 'Arabia Felix: The Danish Expedition of 1761-1767', Beirut: Collins (1964).
410 Rask, Rasmus. 'On the Age and Genuineness of the Zend Language and the Zendavesta', Madras, 1821; tr. 'Om Zendsprogets og Zendavestas Ælde of Ægthed', Copenhagen: 1826; tr. F. H. von der Hagen as Über das Alter und die Echtheit der Zend-Sprache und des Zend-Avesta, und Herstellung des Zend-Alphabets . . . , Berlin, 1826.
411 Kevin J. Cathcart. 'The Earliest Contributions to the Decipherment of Sumerian and Akkadian Cuneiform', Digital library journal, 2011: 1.
412 18th/19th-century misnomer for the Avesta (https://en.wiktionary.org/wiki/Zend-Avesta).

413 Rask, Rasmus. 'Remarks on the Zend language and Zendavesta', Transactions of the Royal Asiatic Society of Great Britain and Ireland' vol. III (1834).
414 This daughter must be Louisa Augusta Fjellerup, who was born on 11 May 1811.
415 Rask, R. 'Remarks on the Zend language and the Zendavesta', Transactions of the Royal Asiatic Society of Great Britain and Ireland, Vol. III, London (1834).
416 Royal Library, NKS 149 c kvart vols. 73 and 74.
417 Læsningen foregaar i Tamul som i de øvrige ind. sprog fra venstre til højre, men er her saare vanskeligere og indviklet, # umulig for den som ikke forstaar sproget, da skriftordningens ufuldkommenhed har gjort det nødvendigt at tillægge samme Bogstaver forskjellig Lyde efter deres forskjellige forbindindelser; og antaget at sammenflette Ordene, saa at Begyndelsesbogstavet af et følgende anbringes paa slutning bogstaver af det foregaaende, eller kastes ind i samme og endelig ofte undladt at skjelne imellem forskjellige mulige udtale ved forskjellig betegnelse. De vigtigste særheder i Skrivning ere følgende
De malebariske Sprog ere vel i så strængt kønløse som finniske; men Könner har dog her en ganske anden Beskaffenhed end i de japetiske Tungemål, og de tamuliske Sproglærde have været så hældige i at udfinde denne beskaffenhed at man ikke kan betænke sig noget Øjeblik på at følge dem. De antage først tvende Hovedkön : det ypperste og det ringeste, eller som vi tydeligere kunne kalde dem der personlige og Sagkönnet, til det første hører alle fornuftige væsener : mennesker, Engle, Guder desl. til det sidste alle øvrige Skæbninger være sig levende eller livløse. Det personlige deles igjen i to, som vi vilde kalde Mandkön og Kvindekön for ikke at forvexle dem med vore Sprogs (Hankön og Hunkön) der også strække sig til Dyrene, ja næsten den hele livløse Natur. De Endelser og Former hvorved de adskilles i Böjningen forholde sig også her ganske anderledes, da de personlige Kön i Ent. altid ligne hinanden og i Fl. have en og samme Form undtagen nogle Ord af sans. Oprindelse hver. Hunkönnet er mere forskjelligt. Sagkönnet derimod er her ligesom enestående og ingenlunde det hvoraf Mandkönsformen er udviklet. Læseren ville derfor ikke anse det som en Modsigelse, eller Forandring af mening at jeg her ordner könnene anderledes her end i min angels. og svenske udg. af den it. Sprogl. Det er n# ikke samme gjenstande og kan Sprogene have her forskjellig Natur og fordre derfor en forskjellig Anordning. Man ser ellers heraf at man i Tam. umulig kan tvivle om noget Ords Kön, når man ved dets Betydning.
(Royal Library, Copenhagen, 'Erasmi Raskii Collectanea & Commentationes argumenti philologici, qvæ continent, præter lineamenta grammatica et indices vocabulorum, etiam apparatum observationum de origine & indole lingvarum scandinavicarum, germanicarum, celticarum aliarumque Europæ occidentalis, slavicarum, fennicarum, caucasiarum, persicarum, indicarum ex utraque Indiæ parte, semiticarum, Asiæque insuper tam borealis quam orientalis', NKS 149 c kvart).
418 Citing Henrichsen, F. Gregersen writes: 'About a year before his death I found him with an – as far as I can recall – Georgian bible in front of him working on such a grammatical topic and when asked how he could do this without a dictionary or any other instrument or preliminary work, he answered 'that he did not need anything else than the Lord's prayer in a particular language in order to build the morphological system of the language'. Such was the expertise he had accomplished'.

419 'Breve fra og til Rasmus Rask', ed. Louis Hjelmslev, København: vol. II (1941) p. 53.
420 RA, Kommercekollegiet, Journalsager (1823) (Løbenr. 3269) #82.
421 This corresponds to more than 3,000 usd in today's money.
422 Det kgl. Bibliotek – Rasmus Rasks Dagbøger: ' ... to Trankebar next day, where I was heartily received by Councillor Rehling and Governor Koefoed; I stayed with the former after receiving his written invitation (...til Trankeb. för næste Dag, hvor jeg blev inderlig vel modtaget af Regjeringsråd Rehling og Guvernør Koefoed; jeg indlogerte mig hos den første efter hans skriftlige Indbydelse)' (entry for september 1822). Rasmus Rask does not mention where he stayed when he first came to Tranquebar, but in all likelihood, he stayed with Rehling. His entry for 28 October says: '...dined with the Lady (of the house) and both Misses Stricker and Miss Sötman and Mr. Rehling (... spiste hjemme med Fruen og begge Frökner Stritter (Stricker) samt Iomfru Sötman og Hr. Rehling)'.
423 Petersen, N. M. 'Bidrag til forfatterens levnet' in 'Samlede tildels forhen utrykte afhandlinger', p. 98.
424 Rask, H. K. 'Samlede tildels forhen utrykte afhandlinger af R. K. Rask', Copenhagen, 3 vols. (1834).
425 Franciska Genoveve von Qualen's effigy was portrayed in the 500 Danish kroner banknote. (http://spinnet.eu/wiki-banknotes/index.php/File:Qualen.den.jpg). The portrait was painted by the famous Danish painter Jens Juel.
426 Wiesener, A. M. 'Slegten Boalth', Bergen (1911).
427 'Peace of mind for God-fearing sailors'.
428 'Fröken Boalth overlod mig V.Kr.Hjorts Gudfrygtige Sømænds Sjælero til ham, hans rette Navn var: Gunvald Rejersen fra Øster-Risør. Læser mest i Corinne. Dans om Aftenen. Slutter den 12. Bog i Corinne. Lodsen. Uendelig skönne Morgner og Aftner'.
429 'Bidrag til R. Kr. Rasks Levnet (Kbh. 1834). – Tilføjelser af H. K. Rask', NKS 389 en oktav, Royal Library, Copenhagen.
430 While it may be true that Hans Kristian Rask destroyed the letters that Rasmus Rask received, it is conceivable that the letters written by Rasmus Rask to 'F. B.' may still exist; the most probable place to look for them would be the Blücher Archives either in Altona or Hamburg.
431 http://dengang.dk/artikler/3659.
432 By Pinnerup – Own work, CC BY-SA 4.0, https://commons.wikimedia.org/w/index.php?curid=72925933
433 There is one other gravestone in Denmark, which has a Sanskrit inscription. Viggo Fausbøll, buried at Gentofte cemetery, has an inscription from Dhammapada. 'Festskrift til Birgit Anette Olsen', Ed. Adam Hyllested, Anders Richardt Jørgensen, Jenny Helena Larsson and Thomas Olander, Copenhagen (2003).
434 आलस्यं हि मनुष्याणां शरीरस्थो महान् रिपुः । नास्त्युद्यमसमो बन्धुः कुर्वाणो नावसीदति ॥

11. Pride, Pomp and Circumstance

435 According to the currency estimates noted in the preface (note 3), this would be approximately 30,000 usd in today's money. This fits with values of between 25,000 and 35,000 USD for the price of an elephant seen on the internet. (www.quora.com)

436 RA, Kommercekollegiet, Ostindiske sekr., Journalsager (1788) (Løbenr. 992) #211.
437 *Macrotyloma uniflorum*, horsegram.
438 Ayyampettai, a small village not far from Tanjore.
439 Thiruvidaikazhi (திருவிடைக்கழி) is a village northwest of Tranquebar, close to Thillaiyali.
440 Thirukkkalacheri (திருக்கலச்சேரி, திருகாலச்சேரி) is a village to the southwest of Tranquebar.
441 https://www.sa.dk/ao-soegesider/da/billedeviser?bsid=157744#157744,26471735 (see also https://www.dis-danmark.dk/forum/read.php?1,291343,291585).
442 Erichsen, John. 'Brødrene Classen', Gyldendal (2017) p. 220.
443 Richards, Annette. 'Carl Philipp Emanuel Bach, Portraits, and the Physiognomy of Music History', Journal of the American Musicological Society, vol.66, nr. 2, (2013) pp. 337-396.
444 A portrait of Walter, drawn by Hadrich in black and colored chalk, can be found in Staatsbibliothek, Preussicher Kulturbesitz, Musikabteilung, Berlin (see Richards, p. 377). I am grateful to BPK-images, Germany, for permission to reproduce the portrait.
445 It is hard to verify these claims. Bertil von Boer asserts that: 'In 1775, however, Walter's public abuse of his wife cause [sic] them to separate, and the composer was sent abroad, first to Italy to hire musicians, then to France as legate, and finally to the Danish colony of Tharangabadi [sic] in India' ('Music in the Classical World: Genre, Culture and History', Routledge (2019)).
446 https://www.sa.dk/ao-soegesider/da/billedeviser?bsid=156082#156082,26129660 (see also https://www.dis-danmark.dk/forum/read.php?1,291343,291585).
447 Brusendorff, Ole. 'Om skuespillerinden Caroline Halle – Lidt personalhistorisk detektiv arbejde', Personal Historisktidskrift (1964) pp. 9-16.
448 '4 nov./10 Nov. 1777 Commerce Secretaire Thomas Christ: Walther søger om at udnævnes til Gouvernements Secretaire i Tranquebar med et lidet Tillæg i den reglementerte Gage, da samme paa et saa kostbart sted ellers vil blive alt for ringe; han har arbeidet udi 12 aar ved det Kongl. Oecon. og Comerce Collegio deels som volontaire, deels som secretaire, i hvilken tiid han har anvendt sine frie Timer paa at dyrke sprogene og videnskaberne. Hans academisk studeringer haver han i aaret 1770 fuldendt med charactere Laudabilis in Examine Juridico Publico, og til sidst har han af hans Mayestæt Kongen nydt et Reyse Stipendium til at dyrke sin Talenter i Musiquen' (RA: Kommercekollegiet, Indisk Kontor, Journaler 1777-1782 (Løbenr.947-949)).
449 Hemingway, F. R. 'Tanjore Gazetteer', vol. 1, Cosmo Publications (2000).
450 Pearson, H. 'Life of Schwartz' (1835).
451 Neuere Geschichte der evangelischen Missionsanstalten zu Bekehrung der Heiden in Ost-Indien : aus d. eigenhändigen Aufsätzen u. Briefen der Missionarien hrsg, Halle, Dritter Band (1782).
452 RA: Kommercekollegiet, Ostindiske Sekr. – Journalsager (1783) (Løbenr. 975) #96.
453 RA. PA 86, pk. 9. P. Anker til Schimmelmann, 26.01.1789, cited from Hodne p. 37.
454 Sriram, V. 'A palace where music echoed', The Hindu, 3 January 2014.
455 Det Classenske Fideicommis, Korrespondence 1787-1788 (Løbenr. I. I. C. -6).
456 Perhaps this was for his daughter, Friderica Charlotte Margrethe.

457 This refers to Johan Frederik Classen and his brother, Peter Hersleb Classen.
458 http://www.nationalbanken.dk/en/publications/Pages/2009/02/Consumer-Prices-in-Denmark-1502-2007.aspx; www.dst.dk/cpi
459 Vore Gamle Tropekolonier, vol. 6, Kamma Struwe, Fremad (1952).
460 Kommercekollegiet, Ostindiske Sekretariat, Journalsager (1794) 166-180 (Løbe nr. 1018). Lists of books in the probates of various officials are found in the above-mentioned packet. There are many such probates in the Archives.
Customs official Faulhagen had the following books: Two Latin Lexica in German, Stookii? Clavis Lingvæ Hebrææ, Den Svendsk Argus Lateius, and an English Bible. J. H. Berner's residence had the following books: Bayles Dictionaire Histor: & Critique 4 vol: folio, Mortimers History of England: 3 vols., A system of geography, a general Atlas containing 40 Maps, Hume's History of England: 6 vols., Cook's voyages: 3 vol., Bolt's India affairs. 2 vol., copies of papers concerning the Restoration of the King of Tanjore: 2 vol, Den Danske Spectator og anti Spectator, Kong F5tes Krigs articles Brev, Lehmes Beskrivelse over Lapperne, latinsk og Dansk, Jónges Beskrivelse over Dannmark og Norge : 2 vols., von Aphelens franskt Dictionaire: 3 vol., Schónnings Norges Riges Historie, Norskes Oprindelse, Suhms Forberedelser i Historien, Suhms Critiske Histor: af Danmark, de fra Norden udvandrede Folk, om Folkenes oprindelse, de Norske folks oprindelse, e Hedenske Gudelære & Norden, Samlinger, The works of Voltaire: 35 vol., The works of Swift: 21 vol., Bagnals European Settlements in East & Westindies: 4 vol., Collections of Voyage & Travels: 6 vols (2 vol. defect), Sir Wm. Temples Works – 4 vols., Bohnbroke's Philospn: Works – 4 vols, Miscellaneous Works – 4 vols, Blackstone on the Laws of England – 4 vols., some(?) vol. of Sterns Works, Memoirs of Sully – 5 vols., La belle assemble in English 4 vol., Bossuet's Historie of France – 4 vols., Entuk's History of London – 4 vols., Locke on human understanding – 2 vol., Vansittar(t)s narrative of Transaction in Bengal : 3 vols., Natuurlyk Histor: der Duren Planten & Mineralien, Youngs Latin & English Dictionary, L'Histoire ancienne par Mikol 4 vols., Nedrus Chronological Lexicon: 2 vol., Bayles English & German Dictionary, Ewalds Prækener, Millot's verdens Historie, Hedegaard's Criminal Rett, Ordqvader, Trefolium Juridicum, Anmærkninger om Danske og Norske Lov. 2 vol., do over James 3 & 4 Bog., Kirkeret, om Tyverie, Foytmans Kongl. Rescripter 4, 5, 6, Decl., Corpus Juris Civilis – 2 vols., Gognet? om Lovenes Oprindelse 3 vol., Hoyers Juridiske Colleg., Don Quixote in Danish 4 vol., Bomares Natur Historie 8 vol., Bibliotec for det Smukke Kion 2 vol., Dansk Musæum – 2 vol., Hinds Dagbog, Tordenskiolds Levnet 3 vol., Prams Starkodder, Leonidas in Danish 2 vol:, Gesners Skrifter og Abels Dód 3 vol:, Stephen om Udsprudende Bierge, Rhodes Laalands Historie, Mallets introduction to Denmark's History, Den Danske Lov, Ankers Danske Jurist, Collect: of voyages 1 vol., 3 vol. of Flags?, les ava(e)ntures de Telemagne, 2 speeches of Malling, Epulets Haandbog, Folkets Róst til Kronprindsen, Om Heikla, Om Tarvelighed, Om Financevæsenet, Reinike Foss, Jacob Bies fabler, Gers fortællinger, Zadig oversadt af Sneedorf, Faddersens Sædelære, 3 Hæfter lærde Tidender, 2 franske Piecer, Peplurs Grammaire, Zenophons History of Greece, Letters to W. Hastings, The Hackney Coach a Novell, The State of Denmark, 5 Týdske og Danske Psalmbóger, 6 Gudelige Piecer, Spanbergs Soe Reiser, Xenophons Cyropædie, en Himmel og 1 Jord Kugle.

Member of the Secret Council, Christian Fibiger Juul's residence contained the following books: The Universal Dictionaires of Trade & Commerce, 2 vol., The Universal Dictionary of Marine, Donglas's proof, The History of Hindustan, 2 vol., Venlets View of Bengal, Hamiltons Proof, Dictionaire Espagno, 2. Vol., Berthelsen English and Danish Dictionary, Rondsom de Werreld, Holbergs Danmarks og Norges Staat, Brochmanns Huus Postill, C 4te Bibel in folio, History of Paraguay, 2 vol., English Dictionary, Fieldings Works – 12 vol., Chrysae 4. Vol., Revere 2. vols., Les Histoires des différente Peuples du Monde, 6. vol., Ouvre de Roussea, 6: vol., Ephraim, Mairs Book keeping, den Patriotiske Tilskuer, 6; vol., 1:dansk Bibel i 2 bind, The Persian Grammar, Wilson's Navigation, Hesselbergs Juridiske Collegium, Hindostan Dictionary, Papes Homero Odyssey, Boyers Dictionary, Routier des Côtes des Indes Orientales et de la Chine, Marmontels Moralische Ertzehlungen, Rothes Samling af Köngelig Rescripter 4 vol, The Scots Magazine, Holbergs Epistler i 3 vol., Universal Historie, Hoyers Juridiske Collegium, an English Bible, Curas french Gramaire, Mathematics Books, 1 bunch of descriptions of Iceland and Bergen, Description of Rome, and Land maps.

461 Claus Kröckel came to Tranquebar in 1704 as an ensign in the Danish East India Company's garrison (see https://ddd.dda.dk/dop/visning_billed.asp?id=3437&sort=e)
462 Winckler, D. 'New Jerusalem Church, Tranquebar 1718-1968', Madras (1968); Eva Fog, 'Ny Jerusalem Kirke', Architectura, vol. 9 (1987).
463 Architectura, vol. 9, Copenhagen (1987).
464 Kryger, Karin. 'The churches of Tranquebar in the Danish period' in 'Halle and the beginning of Protestant Christianity in India', Ed. Gross, Kumaradoss and Liebau, Verlag der Frankeschen Stiftung zu Halle (2006) p. 229.
465 Ramanujam, P. S. 'Tranquebar Registers – Version 2', Saxo (2016) p. 342: 'Tÿdsk kirke Alte Jerusalem'.
466 RA, Ny Jerusalem Kirken & Zionskirken, Eneministerial bog (1707-1808) (Løbenr. EC-777).
467 RA, Det Kgl. Ostindiske Guvernement, Kolonien Trankebar, Indkomne breve til guvernementet I Tranquebar (1840) (Løbenr. 1391B) #280.
468 Ramanujam, P. S. 'Fra skatteopkræver i Serampore til keglespiller i Roskilde – Frederik Emil Elberling og Harriet Anna Fjellerup', Historisk Samfund for Roskilde Amt (2017) pp. 65-80.
469 Elberling, F. E. 'A treatise on inheritance, gift, will, sale and mortgage: With an introduction on the laws of the Bengal presidency', Madras: Higginbotham (1856).
470 Elberling wrote: 'The inhabitants excel in being non-industrious. The majority of them are lazy, and it is distress rather than desire that forces them to carry out their daily duties. As long as castes exist, there will be no industriousness'.

12. The Old Cemetery

471 For an extensive biography and a detailed discussion of Jacob Worm's works, see Sønderholm, cited in the bibliography.
472 Jeg veed en Calot,
En Geistlig at bære, hand nylig har faaet,

Hun sidder paa Toppen hans Hoved saa fast,
Hand kand dend for ingen aftage med Hast,
Hun varmer hans Pande, det giør ham saa got,
At bære Calot.
(Worm, J. 'Satyre over Kingos Kalot', Jacob Worms Skrifter I, Munksgaard (1966)).

473 Karen Bek-Pedersen suggests the following alternative:
'I know of a calotte
Worn by a man of the cloth
As a gift, so fine and new,
It sits so firmly on his caput
He can only remove it at the speed of a sloth,
Oh, and it keeps him warm in the pew,
To him it truly hits the spot
To wear his calotte'

474 Thi Halsen hand fylder med Øl og med Viin
I [Kroeret] hand ligger saa fuld som et Sviin.

475 Og naar du i [Kroeret] har drucket dit Øl,
[Tag vand i Calotten, og Halsen i skiøll,]
Og om du om Natten behøver en Pot,
Da brug din Calot.

476 Hand har ey kræffter til, at skue Indiens soel
Men tienner bedre til den danske prædikestoel.
(Det Kongl. Bibliotek, Uldall 528/40, J. Worms skandskrifter, indlæg, supliker og afskedsvers)
…
Jeg Heller nøyes vil hoss jer med Vand og brød,
End med Ost-indiens den daglige Risengrød.
[Sønderholm, p. 252]

477 Pedersen, Karl Peder. 'Tranquebar', Siden Saxo (1987) p. 26.
478 http://ddd.dda.dk/dop/visning_billede.asp?id=5105&sort=e.
479 Names like Savari or Chavari are derived from the Spanish catholic missionary, Francis Xavier; she must have been a catholic. It is not uncommon even today to find people in Tamilnadu with names beginning with Savari.
480 https://lists.rootsweb.com/hyperkitty/list/india@rootsweb.com/thread/6409943/.
481 Rühde, A. W. F. 'Etablissementet Tranquebars Sundhedstilstand i Almindelighed', Bibliotek for Læger', Classenske Litterurselskab, vol.14 (1831) pp. 229-286.
482 Organist Tannen (see the Tranquebar Registers).
483 This must be where the Tamilnadu Hotel presently is.
484 In 1820, Johan Friederich Sundt was prevented from marrying Anna Maria Köhn as he had leprosy (see P. S. Ramanujam, Tranquebar Registers – Version 2).

13. A Musician and His Tragic Fate

485 Ramanujam, P. S. 'Carl Ludvig Runge – en tragisk skikkelse fra Tranquebar til Roskilde', Historisk Samfund for Roskilde Amt (2017) p. 9.

486 RA: Kommercekollegiet – Ostindiske Sekretariat – Journalsager (1793) (Løbenr. 1011) #68.
487 RA, Det kgl. Ostindiske Guvernement – Kolonien Trankebar – Guvernementets resolutionsprotokol (1778 Aug. 1 – 1781 Okt. 21) (Løbenr. 1266B) #16 Aug. 1779.
488 Ramanujam, P. S. 'Tranquebar Registers – Version 2', Saxo (2016).
489 Det Classenske Fideicommis, Korrespondence 1787-1788 (Løbenr. I. I. C. -6).
490 RA: Kommercekollegiet – Ostindiske Sekretariat – Journalsager (1793) (Løbenr. 1011) #72.
491 RA: Kommercekollegiet – Ostindiske Sekretariat – Journalsager (1793) (Løbenr. 1011) #94.
492 op. cit.
493 Ramanujam, P. S. 'Tranquebar Registers – Version 2', Saxo (2016).
494 RA: Kommercekollegiet – Ostindiske Sekretariat – Journalsager (1798) (Løbenr. 2015) #194.
495 RA, Kommercekollegiet, Journalsager (1803) (Løbenr. 2031) #254.
496 RA, Kommercekollegiet, Ostindiske Fags Sekretariat, Journalsager (1818) (1-120) (Løbenr. 3260).
497 RA, Kommercekollegiet, Ostindiske Fags Sekretariat, Journalsager (1803) (Løbenr. 2031) #254.

14. Plunder in Porto Novo

498 Webster, A. 'Gentlemen Capitalists – British imperialism in south east Asia (1770-1890)', Tauris Academic Studies (1998).
499 RA: Asiatisk Kompagni – Afdelingen i Trankebar: Indkomne breve til rådet III (1773-1775) (Løbenr. 1376).
500 See 'The Governor's residence in Tranquebar', ed. Esther Fihl, Museum Tusculanum Press (2017).
501 Bookkeeper.
502 RA: Det ostindiske Guvernement: Kolonien Trankebar: (Løbenr. AsK 2184a).
503 For more information on Peter Dahl, see the article by Eliassen, referred to in the bibliography.
504 Abdul Kareem was the youngest son of Heider Ali.
505 Mannarkudi.
506 One catty is approximately 600 grams.
507 A corge is a mercantile term for 'a score' (a lot of 20 pieces) ('A glossary of Anglo-Indian colloquial words and phrases and of kindred terms', Henry Yule and Arthur Coke Burnell, London (1866) – commonly known as the Hobson-Jobson dictionary'
508 Plain cotton cloth in long pieces.
509 Brahmin.
510 Chief police officer.
511 Vakil.
512 Pariah – the lowest Hindu caste.
513 Pichavaram forest.
514 Krishnapuram.

515 Vriddhachalam.
516 Tamarind.
517 Kammanallur (கம்மானல்லூர்), Krishnarayapuram Taluk, located between Trichy and Karur, close to Mahadanapuram.
518 Purniah.
519 Purniah.
520 Purniah.
521 Harrop uses this word thrice; I have not been able to find this word in any dictionary.
522 Thirumalai.
523 Haricar – a messenger.
524 Administration office.
525 பறங்கியர்
526 Olai – ஓலை
527 Hoskote.
528 Hoskote.
529 From 'qila' meaning fort: Killedar or Qiladar is thus the man in charge of the fort.
530 Balaji Rao.
531 I have not been able to locate this word in any dictionary; I could imagine that this means 'pleasantries' or 'formalities'?
532 Hoskote.
533 Narsapura.
534 Kolar.
535 Kuppam.
536 Budikote.
537 Krishnagiri.
538 Mettur.
539 Thiruvannamalai.
540 Panruti.
541 Mangalampettai.
542 Krishna Rao or Krishna Rayan.
543 Krishna Rao.
544 From jalabdar from Persian literally meaning 'bridle-holder' (Hobson-Jobson).
545 Myrmidons were soldiers commanded by Achilles in Homer's Iliad.
546 கலசப்பாக்கம்
547 Aarany or Arnee or Arni (ஆரணி)
548 Conjeevaram/Kanchipuram.
549 Rosalia Stevenson (Mrs. Stevenson) and Francois Lange (Mrs. Abbestée) were buried in the same grave in the Catholic churchyard – however, there is no evidence that they were sisters.
550 Bhuvanagiri (புவனகிரி)
551 Already in June 1781, Daniel Pulley knew that Harrop's wife had died. In a letter to Vakil Nagayyen, who was a 'hostage' in Heider Ali's camp, he wrote: 'Madam Harrop is dead. The sum of 10,000 rupies collected by her and her friends can now be paid' (see note 220). But this news was not conveyed to Gowan Harrop.

552 Kanakkupillai/accountant (கணக்குப்பிள்ளை)
553 1 lakh = 100,000
554 சிலம்பு? (cat o' nine tails).
555 More than 2 million US dollars in today's money.
556 RA, Kommercekollegiet, Journalsager (1782) (141-185), (Løbenr. 973) #141.
557 This might be Burhanpur in Madhya Pradesh.
558 Masulipatnam.
559 RA: Kommerce Kollegiet – Ostindiske sekr. Journalsager (1783) (Løbenr. 975) #112.
560 Regional Archives, Copenhagen – Kirkebøger fra Dansk-Ostindien 1767-1845: Trankebar / Zionskirken.
561 http://www.lauritz.com/Item/Item.aspx?LanguageId=2&ItemId=1372780&WI=1.
562 The Asiatic annual register for the year 1800 – Google book.
563 Regional Archives, Copenhagen – Kirkebøger fra Dansk-Ostindien 1767-1845: Trankebar / Zionskirken.
564 This Stevenson was Daniel Stevenson, one of three brothers. Daniel Stevenson was born in 1748, married Metta Margretha Sundt and died in Porto Novo in 1806. One of his brothers was James Daniel Stevenson, a Major-General with the Madras Establishment. He died in the parish of St. Marylebone and was buried on the 21 February 1805. The third brother was Edward Stevenson, who owned the house, which was later bought by Governor Brown, after which it became the governor's residence. Edward was married to Rosalia Fischer née Tournac in 1779, and died in Tranquebar in 1780. He is buried at the Zion Church. It must have been Rosalia Stevenson, who helped Gowan Harrop. Their son Edward William Stevenson married Maria Barbara Mühldorff and had two sons, Edward Boyd Stevenson (born in Porto Novo, 1810, died in Tranquebar in 1872) and Willoughby Carpenter Stevenson (born in 1814 and died in Tranquebar in 1832) [Cotton; Kryger and Gasparski].
565 Regional Archives: '1801 Marts 9de Blev udi den saakaldte Walthers Hauge af Præsten John ægtede Mr. Charles Edding og Jomfrue Elisabeth Harrup…1803 Aug. 10 Blev udi Missionskirke, fordi den danske Kirke var under Reparation, døbt en dreng kaldet John Gowin. Forældrene vare Skibskaptain C. Edding og hustruen Elisabeth Edding (født Harrop)'.
566 James Dalrymple is mentioned in: 'The Anarchy' by William Dalrymple.

Journey's End

567 Neuere Geschichte der Evangelischen Missions-Anstalt zur Bekehrung der Heiden in Ostindien, Halle (http://digital.bibliothek.uni-halle.de/hd/periodical/pageview/602942).
568 By Danes, I mean to include all white people in the colony.
569 Mesler, Hans D. 'Journal på reisen fra Kiøbenhavn til Trankebar med skibet Kronprindsen af Danmark 1708-1711', Det Kongl. Bibliotek, NKS 769 kvart. Transcription of the text can be found in RA, Georg Nørregård, 'Afskrift af manuskript til malabarernes liv i Tranquebar' (Løbenr. 141).
570 My interpretation of 'pagans' is 'hindus'.

571 All this information was also substantiated by Ziegenbalg in 1709 (Der Königl. Dänischen Missionarien aus Ost-Indien eingesandter Ausführlichen Berichten, Von dem Werck ihres Amts unter den Heyden , Teil 1: Cont. 3 (1713) p. 1-43), Teil 1, Cont. 7 (1713)).

572 Der Königl. Dänischen Missionarien aus Ost-Indien eingesandter Ausführlichen Berichten, Von dem Werck ihres Amts unter den Heyden , Teil 4. Cont. 38 (1736) p. 283.

573 Irschick, E. F. 'Conversations in Tarangampadi: Caring for the self in early eighteenth century South India', Comparative Studies of South Asia, Africa and the Middle East, 23:1&2 (2003) p. 254.

574 Muthiah, S. 'Tales of old and new Madras', East-West (2014).

575 The Armenians came to the Coromandel Coast probably in the early part of the 16th century and flourished there in the 17th and 18th centuries. According to 'Armenians in India', 'The most eminent Armenian merchant at Madras in the earlier half of the eighteenth century was Khojah Petrus (Coja Petrus Uskan), son of Khojah Woskan, and a grandson of the famous Khojah Pogose of Julfa ... He was strongly attached to the English. He is first alluded to in the Madras Records, in 1724, as 'Coderjee [Cojah] Petrus, an Armenian lately arrived from Manilla and an inhabitant of this place [Madras]'. At that period, the highly lucrative commerce with Manilla was entirely in the hands of the Armenians, and they were blamed by the President for carrying their merchandise from Europe in Danish ships, and consigning their oriental goods to Pondichery and other foreign ports in India…He (thus) amassed considerable riches, but sustained heavy losses in the troubled days when the French captured Madras in 1746 under Count Lally…Upwards of forty houses belonging to him in the city were levelled with the ground, besides other houses that he had in the Fort. The French, moreover, seized all that he had in the Fort (Fort St. George) and carried the spoil to Pondichery. He took refuge in a Danish town close to Madras, and Count Lally sent him a message to place himself under the protection of the French Government, when the property confiscated by them would be restored. He spurned the overture, replying tersely and sarcastically that whatever riches he had possessed, had been acquired under auspices of the British Government, to whom he would remain loyal…..In November 1749, the Capuchins were ordered by the Government to hand over the church (Church at Vepery – auth) to the Danish Missionaries… Petrus Woskan, protested vehemently against the high-handedness of the English'. He wrote, 'I have no ill will to the Danish Missionaries nor to any Christian Missionaries, and have already wrote the Governor I am willing to contribute something towards building a Church for them: but to let them have Viparee Church is what I can never consent to.' [Seth].

Index

Aalborg 109
Aaron 211, 212
Abbestée, Pauline 91, 229
Abbestée, Franciska Genoveve 90, 91, 229, 231, 400
Abbestée, Johan Ludvig 91
Abbestée, Maria Barbara 90, 229
Abbestée, Peter 91
Abbestée, Peter Hermann 15, 89-91, 152
Abrahamstrupensis 262
achromatic telescope 136
Achton, Abild 261, 262
Achton, Anders Christensen 261
Adler, Johann Gottlieb 194, 195
Admiral Street 30, 151, 187, 213, 251, 398
Agambadaiyar 91
Ahren 165
Aleutian 221
Alexander, the Great 222
Alftafjord – Álftafjörður 41, 52, 53
Altona 90, 229, 230, 400
Amager, Jacob 59
Amarasimhan 397
Amarda Singh (see Amarasimhan) 203, 233
Ambrose 212
amme 27, 37
Ananda Ranga Pillai 151
Anandamangalam 99, 100
Ancher, Peter Kofod 78, 79, 386
Andala 81
Anker, Carsten 16, 86, 103, 114, 115, 118, 120, 122
Anker, Peter 16, 17, 38, 68, 69, 75, 85-87, 89, 93-97, 101, 103-107, 113-115, 117-120, 147, 180, 207, 213, 215, 244, 245, 274, 279, 355, 356, 369, 384, 388, 401
Annagudi 155
anthrax 270
Anundgary 297
Appu Mohammad 160, 161, 163, 165, 167
Appu Setti 106
Arasur Nayken 74
Arcot 77, 78, 154, 170, 197
areca nut 13, 22, 45, 161
Arnachillum Pulle 290, 306, 307, 316
Arnie 339
Arsène 241
arsenic 219, 270
Assyriology 222
astronomical circle 132, 135, 138, 144
astronomical clock 132, 135, 136, 392
Athichudi 131, 200

Athangarai Street 257, 264, 273, 355
Attrup 99, 188, 385
Australia 215
Avalloor 330
Avvaiyar 131, 200
Ayder Chan 75
Ayyanar 49, 72
Bacchus 65
Bach, Carl Philipp Emanuel 236, 241, 370, 401
Bailey, Colonel 322, 326, 339, 353
Bailly, see Bailey
Baillie, see Bailey 178, 396
Balagerow 325
Baldor 46, 382
Balkenborg, Sille 259, 260
Bangalore 154, 279, 327, 367
Benglore, see Bangalore
Banks, Sir Joseph 199
Bantam 26, 56, 57
Bauernfeind 221, 222
Bazaar Street   23, 268, 383
Beauvais 358
Beck, Claus Peter 274, 275
Benares 223
Berggren 221, 222
Berlin, Johann 194
betel leaf 45, 361
Bethlehem Church 82, 99, 207
Bhakti Manjari 182
Bhartrhari 232
Bjerrum, Marie 230
Black Court 15, 67-75, 77, 82, 93, 96, 110, 180, 182, 183, 359, 384, 385
Blåtårn 116

Bliesner 205
Bloch, Marcus Eliezer 199
Blücher, Conrad 90, 229, 400
Blume 115
Boalth, Abigail Catharina 230
Boalth, Christian Tullin 89, 91, 229, 400
Boalth, Fanny 230, 231
Boalth, Jens 229
Boalth, Paulina 230
Boanaventure David 207
Böhme 204, 205
Bommaraja 163
Bonsach 78, 250, 252, 385
Boodapally 330
Boody Cottah 330
Boorhanpoor 351
Borges, Juan 59
Boshouwer, Marcelis de 13, 26, 27, 28
Boschouwer, see Boshouwer
Boschouver, see Boshouwer 378
Bosse, Martin 207
botanical garden 131, 199
Böttger, Gottlieb Friedrich 265
Boudenot 158, 159, 394
Boye, Christopher 42
Brahe-Trolleborg 270
Braithwaite 155, 163, 169, 179, 244, 332
bramney 290, 296, 297, 299, 306, 309, 314, 318, 321, 324, 325, 330, 331, 334, 335, 337, 338, 340, 342, 346
Braun, Carl Wilhelm von 93-95, 216, 352

Braun, Catharina Elizabeth 253, 352
Bredstrup, Svend 132, 207
Brinck-Seidelin 108
Brown, David 85, 279, 280, 407
Brüdergarten 209
Bruuse 75
Buddha 227
Bugge, Thomas 130, 132, 134, 138, 140, 148, 240, 391
Bunares 351
Bungalow on the Beach 67, 69, 83, 383
Bussy 156, 165, 169, 174, 177, 178, 395
Caemmerer, A. F. 206, 207, 274, 275
Caleskpeak 339
calibrating a clock 144
Calicut 49, 50
Calicut (place) 9, 18, 285, 375
Callicut 79
Campbell 234, 340
Cape of Good Hope 27, 62, 129, 188, 194
Carlsen, Carl Wilhelm 115, 116
Carrim Sahib 284, 295-297
Cashmere 351
Castarede 300
castoreum 43
Catholic Church 129, 208, 209, 226, 352, 406
Catmadoo 341
cavalry 161, 163, 176, 339, 394
Cedar 91
Ceniyar 91

Ceylon 13, 17, 26-28, 31, 34, 56, 60, 64, 117, 198, 200, 201, 204, 205, 226, 227, 250, 363, 378
Chambers, William 202
Charlotte Amalie 60
Chavari Ammal 264
Chengamow 330
Chengleput 170, 177
Chennai 7, 9, 82, 159, 240, 242, 356, 375
Chennapatnam, see Chennai 394
Cheringapatnam 350
Cheshire 279
Chetty, Wengidasala 65
Chidambaram 8, 154, 388, 395
China 64, 68, 112, 131, 351, 364, 389
Chingernow Pass 330
Chinnayya Naik 16, 96, 113 - 124
Chola 7, 91, 103, 175, 378
cholera 267
choultry 226, 322-324, 326, 328, 329, 339, 361
Christ Church, Tanjore 204
Christensen, Lauritz 108, 147
Christian IV 13, 22, 23, 26-28, 32, 36, 42, 47, 57, 68, 358, 379, 381, 382
Christian V 262
Christian VIII 104
Christianshavn 42, 43, 47, 56, 58
chubdar 285, 296, 299, 302, 361
Chutta Nabob 284
Classen, Johan Frederik 240, 242, 246, 364, 369, 402
coffee 116, 178, 246, 248

Colar 330
Colaram 179
Colbjørnsen – also Colbjörnsen 89, 95, 96, 126, 232, 389
comets 130, 391
Commenalore 296, 297, 301, 307, 317, 320, 327, 328, 333
complementary altitude 146
complementary declination 146
complementary latitude 146
Conery 81
Congee Varam 342
connakoply, see kanakkupillai 280
Consistory Court 68, 274
Coopom 330
Coote 168, 170, 175, 179
Coote, Eyre 154, 338
Corselitze 240
Courtallam 201
cow dung 271
Crappé, Roelant 13, 14, 21-23, 28, 29, 31, 33-35, 49-52, 55, 377, 378
Cruse, Pastor 120
Cudelur 174, 175, 177, 179
cuneiform 221, 222, 398
Cuppa Chetty 247
curry leaves 199
Curtis, Sir Roger 124
cutchery 300, 322
Cuthia Pullei 74
D.E.M.E.P. 215
da Costa, Andre Botelho 21, 376
Dahl, Peter 282, 346, 347, 364, 405
Dalrymple, Lieutenant 339, 340, 353, 407

Dame, Petrus 152
Daniel Pullei (Daniel Pulley) 15, 16, 73, 75, 89, 95, 96, 151, 152, 154-158, 160-162, 164, 166-168, 170-172, 178, 180-184, 235-238, 335, 336, 350, 380, 393-396, 406
Danish East India Company 16, 26, 27, 40, 42, 52, 55-57, 60, 61, 68, 76, 77, 90, 115, 188, 191, 197, 198, 234, 263, 373, 403
Danish East Indian Establishments 30, 132
Danish-Halle mission 152
Dansborg 14, 29, 36, 38, 40, 41, 43, 55-59, 76, 79, 85, 93, 103, 112, 183, 208, 209, 251, 263, 274, 358, 379
Darius 222
De Close 290
de Lannoy 166, 167, 168, 395
declination 140, 144, 146
Danmark 81, 137
devadasi 92, 361
Devanhalli 153
Dhobikedi, Sambarkedi 160, 162
diabetes mellitus 270, 271
diamonds 17, 28, 117, 118, 147, 165, 167, 171, 175, 246, 288, 314, 350
diarrhoea 158, 197, 265, 267
Diogo 212, 213
dip of the horizon 144
Ditlevsen 276, 277
Dollond telescope 132, 142
dubash 15, 16, 74, 75, 89, 93-96,

114, 151, 152, 182, 235, 236, 243, 244, 290, 298, 304, 340, 343, 361, 387
Dubois, Abbé 92, 364, 382, 384, 387
Duchemin 158, 159, 162, 165, 167, 394
Due, Arabella 252, 255, 258
Duntzfeldt 122, 123
Dutch man of war 124
dysentery 45, 47, 50, 265, 267
dyspepsia 265
Edding, Charles 353, 407
Edding, John Gowin 353
Eibye, Christian Christoffer 207, 208, 257
Elberling, Frederik Emil 112, 254, 255, 403
Elephanten 60
Emmrich 192
Engelhart, Henning Munch 16, 30, 34, 126, 131, 132, 134, 136, 140, 142, 143, 144, 146-148, 187, 200, 207, 208, 359, 364, 366, 379, 380, 386, 392
Epistle to the Philippians 173
Eppert, Jasmin 192
Erukatancheri 38
Fabricius, Johann P. 197, 206
Favart, Charles Simon 241
Fincke, Jonas 194
firangi 33, 64, 361, 366, 379
Fjellerup, Hans Jacob 108, 223, 253, 352,
Fjellerup, Harriet Anna 254, 255, 353, 403
Flaxman 204

Folly, Theodor Ludvig Fredrich 217, 245, 251, 264, 265, 274, 277, 367, 398
Forck, Herman Jacob 78, 152
Forsskål, Peter 221, 222
Forster, Johann Reinhold 199
Fort St. George 7, 370, 408
Fortuna 58
Francis Xavier 209, 479
Francke, August Hermann 188, 191, 195-197, 365
Frederik III 53, 57, 259, 382
Frederik IV 15, 188, 191, 195, 196, 251
Frederik V 78, 215, 221
Frederik VI 221
Frederik's Hospital 116, 270
Frederikshald 86
Frederiksværk 7, 240, 242
Freiberg 86
Friderica Charlotte Margrethe 241, 401
Friis, A. C 116, 118, 122
Früchtenicht, Lambert Christian 207
Fugl 131, 155, 350
Fuglsang, Niels Studsgaard 83, 148, 208
fumigations of sulphur 270
Fyn 270
Galileo 140
Galle 226
Gautier, Jean Jaques 209
Gedde, Ove 13, 27, 28, 29, 31, 33, 34, 36, 38, 40, 42, 187, 376, 378, 379
Gekee 343

Gensichen 148, 365
Gericke 204
Gertie, Henry Montgomery 112
Ginge, Andreas 132
Gingee 196, 201, 330
Giomar, May 59, 60
Glorioso 223
Gnanammal 183, 184
Golconda 56
gold leaf 8, 31, 33, 34
Goldingham, John 140, 142, 365, 392
Goldsmith Street 151, 185, 250
Gopalrow 296, 316
Götting, Lucil 208
Grabow, Adolf Frederik 42
Greenwich 139-141
Greyfriars 261
Grotefend, Georg Friederich 222
Gründler. Johann Ernst 133, 193, 196, 197, 251, 253
Guignace 156, 167, 168, 170, 328
Gulam Muhammad 15, 74
Gurupada Upadesiar 181
Gwalior 223
Haider Ali, se Heider Ali
Halle 15, 31, 38, 110, 129, 152, 182, 188, 190, 192-197, 199, 200, 201, 206, 210, 211, 240, 241, 243, 251, 265, 366, 367, 397, 398, 401, 403, 407
Halle, Caroline 240, 241
Halley, Edmund 127, 255
Hansen, Peder 8, 17, 38, 109-112, 149, 255, 368, 376
Harboue 223, 227
harem 37, 92

Harrison 140
Harrop, Gowan 16, 149, 254, 278, 279, 281, 282, 291-293, 320, 321, 333, 334, 336, 342-345, 350353, 393, 406, 407
Harrup, Elizabeth 353
Hasz 158, 167, 170, 394
Hazrat Nabab 160, 171, 172, 394
Heiberg, Knud 125, 126, 352, 366
Heichon, Anneke 259
Heider Ali 10, 15, 16, 152-157, 162, 168, 169, 172, 175-180, 202, 243, 244, 281, 282, 284-287, 290, 300, 311, 318, 322, 326, 330, 333, 348, 350, 351, 368, 376, 393-395, 406
hemp (jute) 92
Henriksdatter, Anne Katrine 220
Henry Dundas 124
Hermann Rosenkrantz 26
Hermanson 89, 117, 226
Herrnhuter, see Moravian
Herst 299
Hesselberg 75, 76, 79, 99
Hetting 244
Heuss, Johan Christian 116
Hildeman 116
hircar 164, 167
Hjort, V. Kr. 229, 400
Hoddel, Capt. 339, 340
Hof- og Stadsretten 118
Holford, Robert 340-342, 344, 345
Holmsted 62
Hoosare Cottah 322, 330
Houerup, Peder Andersen 79, 80

hour-angle 144, 146
Hudson, Dennis 183
Hughes, Admiral 170, 395
Hull 86
Hystapes 222
Iceland 14, 39, 41, 44, 47, 52, 132, 220, 382, 403
Idaiyar 91
idankai 92, 361
Idola Jeroboami 262
Ihle, A. 8, 253, 263, 367
Indian Civilisation 200
inflexion 220, 223, 225
Irlappa 69, 70
Irlapulle 290, 298, 299, 301, 303, 305-308, 312-316, 326-328, 331, 334, 347, 348
Irschick 357, 408
Irulappa 156, 247
Isle de France 96, 97, 128
Ismael 79, 80
Jamalgan 75, 76, 79
Jan de Willem 26
Janapa 92
Jesuit 35, 129, 208, 209, 211
Johannes van Wijck 23
John, Christoph Samuel 82, 96, 131, 148, 151, 152, 156, 181-183, 199, 200, 201, 207, 213, 217, 226, 249, 275, 359, 407
Jomfru Materna 247
Jón Indíafari 53
Josef 74
Juel, Axel 263
Juel, Jens 90, 91, 400
Juliane Marie 113, 390, 394
Jupiter 49

Jupiter's moons 138, 140
Jylland 204, 275
Kadamba Pullei 74
Kadera, Venkata Rau 236
Kaikolar 91
kallars 168, 176, 396
Kalnein 23, 24, 263
kammalar 15, 92
Kammela 81, 82
Kanabadi Wathiar 211
kanakkupillai 407
Kanchipuram 163, 174, 393, 406
kanji 171
Karaikal 13, 21, 22, 50, 81, 94, 95, 134, 154, 244
Karim Saheb 154, 351
Kariyer 158
Karrier, Charles 245
Karumkurichipalayam 177
Kattucheri 106
Kattumannar 165
Kavaraikomutti 91
Kelso, A. H. 126
Keslow 75, 76, 78
King of France 167, 169
King Street 22, 83, 125, 127, 129, 148, 187, 196, 201, 209, 213, 232, 233, 246, 249, 250, 252, 265, 359
Kingo, Thomas 258-262
Kingree Kotta 297
Kissen(g)row 330, 331, 334-338, 341, 343, 345
Kistna Gurry 330
Kistnaparam 293, 330
Klein, Johann Gottfried 201
Klein, Johann Jacob 178

Knie, Madam 245
Knoll, Samuel Benjamin 265
Kodukur 172
Kohlhoff, John Balthasar 81, 130, 204-206
Kolding 204
Kollidam 169, 378
Kongsbakke, Eskild Andersen 14, 57, 191, 355
König, Johan Friderich 274
König, Johann Gerhard 77, 197
Konraivendan 131, 200
Korsør, Paul Hansen 57
Krishna Rayan 159, 160-163, 167, 394, 406
Krog, Hans Georg 97, 100
Kroger, Captain 347
Kroppedal 136, 392
Kulasekhara Pandian 13, 22
kuli 173
Kumbakonam 112, 235, 245
La Valiere 332, 352
Lala 154, 167
Lally 164, 179, 284, 395, 408
Landporten 22, 215
Lang, Colonel 330, 340
Lange, Francoise 90, 229, 406
Lassen 117
last 27
latitude 56, 137, 138, 140, 143, 144, 146, 365
Lawaetz, Christian 118
Le Gentil 128-130
lead acetate 266
Left hand caste 15, 91-94, 106, 243, 361, 363, 384, 387
Lemming 114

Leyel, Willum 14, 55-59, 209, 363, 377, 382, 383
Lichtenstein, Franz von 16, 89, 94-97, 147, 209, 244, 275
Liebe 155
Lievog, Rasmus 132
Lindam, P. H., se Lindham, P.H.
Lindham, P. H. 115
Linné, Carl von 197
Livland 197
Lollik, Peter 46, 50
longitude 26, 138, 140, 142-146, 365, 371
Lord's Prayer 200, 225, 229, 230, 399
Louis, King of France 169
Lübe, Anne Catherina 147
Lutchmenarain 290, 299, 306, 318, 319, 321, 331, 334, 335, 338, 342, 344, 346, 347
Lütkens, Franz Julius 188
Luxdorph 131
Lyche, Ivar 126
Macassar 56, 57
Mackenzie manuscripts 91, 387
Maderup, Ole 130, 152, 209
Madsen, Jens 59
maha nadu thesattar 93, 95
Mahe 128
Maleiappen, Peter 192, 193
Malvila, Lieutenant 339, 340
Mangalam 330
Manila 128, 129
Manjalkuppam 176
Manosiappa 99
Margrethe II 358
Marianne 124

Mariyammal 184
Markandeya 375
Marsvin, Ellen 27
Martini 275, 276
Masilanathar temple 21-23, 383
Masulipatam, se Masulipatnam
Masulipatnam 8, 18, 26, 36, 56, 375, 382, 407
Matturaja Pulle 75, 95, 96
Mauritius 96, 128, 129
Mayavaram 99, 235, 245
Meersche, Jacob van den 37, 381
mercury 267, 270
Mesler 356, 357, 407
Meyer, Christian Rasmussen 69, 70
Mikkelsen, Einar 358
Minoceros 130, 267
mirasdar 362, 384
Mirza Heider Hossen 322
Mohammad Ali Khan 234
Mohanavelu 10, 71, 368
Möller, Caspar 126
Moors 71, 79, 189, 298, 328
Moota Combra Mudliar 340
morador 75, 362, 384
Moravian Brothers (Brethren) 12, 152, 209, 210, 359, 398
Mornington 97, 388, 389
Mosque Street 151, 185
Mottoor 330
Mourier, Konrad Emil 37, 108, 208, 373
Mucramia 155, 172
Muhammad Ali 77, 158, 394
Mühldorff, Agatha Maria 265
Mühldorff, Mathias Jørgen 89, 96, 101, 117, 155, 213-215, 235, 258, 355, 356, 407
Mundt, Christopher 223
Munro, General 154, 203, 244
Murraya koenigii 199
Mutchliputtun 351
Muthiah 7, 197, 368, 375, 408
Muthurai 200
Muttiappan 213
Muttien 125
Muttradi (see Mutirady) 73
Muturady, se Mutirady 68
naazhi 165, 172, 395
Nadar 68
Nagapatnam 62, 81, 134, 155, 238, 244, 250, 270, 382
Nagaswamy, Ramachandran 10, 31, 34, 368
Nagayyan 159, 161, 406
Nagor 134, 238
Naik, Chinnayya (see Chinnayya)
Nancowri 143, 144, 148
nanjai 108
Nautical Almanac and Astronomical Ephemeris 134, 138, 140, 141
Nawab of Arcot 77, 78, 154, 197, 394
Nayak, Raghunatha 13, 22, 23, 28, 29, 31, 32, 34-38, 44, 50, 68, 358, 359, 379, 381, 382
Nayak, Ramabhadra 32, 35, 37, 381
Nayak, Vijayaraghava 35
Neuere Geschichte der Evangelischen

Missionsanstalten 171, 195, 389, 391, 397, 401, 407
New Jerusalem Church 24, 196, 197, 200, 206, 249, 250, 252, 253, 255, 384, 397, 403
Nicobar Islands 7, 16, 18, 108, 142, 143, 145, 147, 210, 211, 359, 364, 369, 392, 397
Niebuhr, Carsten 221, 222, 246, 358, 369
Nitisataka 232
Nørgaard, Bjørn 358
Novi Commentarii 129, 391
Nursapuram 330
Nygade 14, 17, 213-215, 252, 257, 263, 264, 273, 351
Obelitz, Lieutenant 267
Obuch, Anna Dorothea 201
occultations 140
Odense 218-220, 261, 366, 368
Ohrugamangalam 95, 246
Ólafsson, Jón 9, 14, 30, 39-53, 369, 381, 382, 384
Olai 37, 72, 73, 108, 362, 369, 381, 406
Olivarius 156, 170
opium 18, 266
Øresund 13, 21, 22, 376, 377
Orion, Constellation of 130, 391
Ossetian 221
Ottison, Halkier & Lÿcke 318, 320, 333, 334, 342, 345
Pachaiyappa Mudali 152
Pacheo, Antonio 59
padi 22, 377
pagoda (currency) 62, 121, 155, 172, 180, 183, 207, 214, 234, 235, 237, 246, 247, 275, 280, 287, 288, 290, 301-303, 305, 306, 308-310, 314, 316, 317, 319, 323, 324, 328, 333, 334, 348, 376
pagoda (temple) 99, 100, 227, 268, 294
pagode de Brahe 72
palayakkarar 176, 362
palm leaf 64, 72, 196, 208, 223, 226, 357, 381
pana comprido 247
panchalar 15
Panchanada Iyer, Tharangampadi 358
Panck, Ellen Christine 63, 126
pandel 75, 76
Pandian 9, 369
panniaram 80
Panoratty 330
Pap, Anna Sophie 205
pardau 9, 37, 38, 238, 376
parwannah 301
Passow, Christian Albrekt von 99, 247, 248
Patcheswaram 292
Pattagan 75-79
Pattambakkam 166-168, 395
Pearoya 335, 337, 338, 340, 341
Peer Mohammad 296, 299, 302, 316
Perlen 49, 51, 52
Persepolis 221-223
Perumal Naik 79, 97-102, 389
Perumal Koil 149
Perumuckel 172
Pessart, Bernt 14, 55-57

Pettai 28, 378
Philipp 211-213
philology 91, 217, 398
Philosophical Transactions of the Royal Society 140, 390
pietist 15, 188, 209
Pigot, George 100, 388
Pihl, Abraham 132
Pingel 359
Piragasam Pullei 16, 89, 95, 96, 105, 114, 117, 118, 162, 167, 168, 180, 182, 380
Piveron (Puis Morrin) 158, 160, 161, 164, 167
Plutschau, Heinrich 15, 63, 188, 191, 195
podi 177
poena capitali proxima 79
Poiyatha Pillaiyar Kovil 83, 85
Pollilur 154, 393, 396
polygar, see palayakkarar 100-102, 362
Poltzenhagen, David 152
Pomerania 204
Pondichery 8, 65, 106, 128-130, 162, 164, 168, 171, 172, 174, 175, 197, 211, 226, 358, 395-397, 408
Poreiar 38, 74, 82, 87, 95, 99, 155, 183, 184, 195, 207, 209, 211, 267, 387
Porney Oyan (see Purniah) 296-298
Portbury, Edward Swale 352
Porto Novo 10, 16, 18, 78, 110, 126, 154, 183, 214, 235, 246, 247, 279-283, 286-288, 290, 291, 295, 297-299, 305, 307, 308, 313, 316, 318, 319, 328, 329, 333, 336, 344, 345, 347, 348, 350-353, 376, 405, 407
Portrait of Walter 401
Post Horn 83, 387
Post Office Street 83
poultice 270
Povengerry 343
Prahl, Bendix 74, 75, 147, 369
Pratab Singh (Pratapasimhan) 236
Prince of Migomme 26
Prinsesse Lovisa Augusta 114
Puduchery (see also Pondichery) 8
Pullei, Christian Daniel (see Daniel Pulley)
Pullei, Daniel (see Daniel Pulley)
Pullei, Johan Daniel 183, 184
Pullei, Piragasam (see Piragasam Pullei)
Pulleimuttu 212
Pulsnitz 188
Pungel 29
punjai 108
Purniah 311, 406
quackery 267, 270
Queen Street 125, 149, 151, 183, 185, 187, 252
Raghunathabhyudayam 35
Rajappen, Peter 152
Rajappa 385
Rama Naik 97, 247
Rama Sandra Nayken 74
Ramalinga 75
Ramaseyam 119, 121
Rasch, Niels Christian Hansen 218

Rask, Hans Kristian 220, 229-231, 400
Rask, Kirsten 230, 370
Rask, Rasmus 17, 217-232, 253, 352, 365, 366, 368-370, 398-400
refraction 144
Rehling, Johannes 108, 109, 112, 149, 183, 207, 216, 217, 226, 227, 400
Rehling, Otto 111, 112, 216
Repstorff 95
right hand caste 15, 91-94, 106, 243, 362
Ringsted 155, 394
Rømer, Ole Christian 134, 392
Roselt, Henry 124
Roskilde 11, 31, 254, 276, 386, 403, 404
Rottler, Johan Peter 96, 200, 201, 206, 223, 275
Roxburgh, William 199
Rubella 266
Rühde, Dr. 17, 257, 264, 266-269, 271, 404
Rühde, Magdalena Elizabeth 264
Rühde, Sara Minerva 265
Rulangalappai 34, 379
Rumley, Captain 339, 353
Runge, Carl Ludvig 16, 273-277, 404
Runge, Sophie Magdalene 276, 277
Rurik 221
Rytter, Claus 56
Sadras 313
Sadraspatnam 8, 251, 394
Saeed Saheb 16
Salomon Pillai 180, 181
Saluppan 92, 361
Salzmann, Maria Dorothea 192, 197
Samayya 167, 395
Saminathayyan 167
Samraj, Christian 11, 192
Sarti, G. 240
Sastri, Vedanayagam 213
Sathangudi 74, 210, 211
sati 47, 92, 362
satrum 330
Sattamangalam 169, 170, 176
Saturn 130, 357
Saur, Thomas 240
Sautguru pass 330
Savarimuthu 74, 212
Savary 247
scarlet fever 268
Schlerk, Agatha 79, 80
Schlimmermann 276
Schmidt, Kaj 7
Schönheyder 108
Schulze, Benjamin 195, 197, 200, 201, 375
Schumacher, Peder 260
Schwabe 115
Schwarz, Christian Frederik 179, 182, 201-206, 238, 213, 234, 243, 245, 371, 401
Sehested, Ove 118
Seiyadina Saiyad Sahib Sadat Valiyullah 185
Sela sela Setti 94
Selling 62, 362, 395
semi-diameter of the sun 144
Senapathi 92

Senepa, see Chinnayya
Senopa, see Chinnayya
Serampore 8, 18, 81, 112, 197, 223, 227, 253-255, 364, 375, 397, 403
Serfoji II 38, 203, 204, 206, 213, 233, 234, 239, 245, 381
Setti, Lakshmana 82
Shadanganpadi 13, 21, 22
Shatooraw 290
Sheikh Ismail Sadaat Valiyullah 185
siambue 350
Siersted, Bertil 155-157, 159-163, 393, 394
Simone, David 343
Simone, Isaac 343
Sinay 247
Singalese, Singhalese 225, 226, 229
Singrepelly 330
Sinnacchi 74
Sinnaja, see Chinnayya
Sinnia, see Chinnayya
sipoy or seapoy – also sepoy 89, 94, 101, 159, 168-170, 176, 268, 271, 283, 285, 287, 289, 293-298, 301, 308, 316, 318, 321, 324, 329, 336, 339, 343, 362
Sirius 130, 391
slave house 62
slavery 55, 56, 60, 61, 64, 359, 382, 384
slaves 56, 58, 60-65, 80, 131, 213, 244, 270, 290, 321, 359, 383
Smith, General 322

Smyth, Harriet Maria 112, 149
snake(s) 43, 48, 131, 199
Society for Promoting Christian Knowledge 194
solar parallax 128, 390
solar system, size of 128
Solen 56
Soliman den anden 239, 241
Sønderborg 204
Sophia Hedewig 188
Sørensen, Sophie-Magdalena 65, 384
Sorgenfrey 276
Souffrein, Suffrein, see Suffren
Soyad Sahib 285-291, 294-297, 300, 313
St. Anna 57
St. Laurentius 49
Stahlmann, Georg Johann 209
Stevenson, Edward 85, 342, 344, 407
Storm, Christian Pedersen 14, 57, 58, 209
Strandberg, Elisabeth 9, 371
Stricker 96, 216, 270, 335, 337, 400
Stricker, Otto 96
Strøbel 99
Stuart, Colonel 236
Sturluson, Snorri 220
Suffren, Pierre André de 155, 156, 164-166, 175, 394
Sumatra 26, 211
Sundt, Maria Barbara 215
Sundt, Michael 216
Suppremania Setti 93-95, 105, 180, 235, 244, 245, 247, 352

Surappa Mudali 158
Surinam 270
Suserup 116
Svane-Knudsen, Asger 63, 359, 378, 383, 398
Svarthamar 39, 41
Sweden 26, 27, 56, 57, 221, 227, 241, 262
syntax 220
Talliar 46, 98
tamarin(d) 296
Tambu Chetty 95, 96, 114, 117
Tandatzia Pulle 89
Tannen, Anna Elizabeth 274, 276
Taraxis indica 266
Taurus 130
tea 68, 116, 123, 169, 178, 179, 223, 248, 253
Teilaburam 176
Teler, Harriet 352
temperature 265-267
Texera, Philippa 59
Thaae, Sophia 208
Thestrup 9, 10, 371, 378
Thillaiyali 38, 387, 388, 401
Thirukadiyur 8
Thirumalai Naik 106, 406
Thiruvidaimarudur 245
Thoppila Pillai 181
Thorbjörg Einarsdatter 52
Thors, Pernille 203, 205, 206
Thorsen, Petronella (see Thors, Pernille)
Tiagapen 207
Tiemroth, Christian 108, 184
tiger 169, 176

Tippu Sultan 15, 153-156, 159, 165, 179, 180, 243, 244, 311, 376, 394
Tirumudi Setti 106
Tirunelveli 201, 203
Tiruvidakalli 237
Tistorph, Michael Henrichsen 28, 378
Tomarp (Kvidinge) 27
Tondevory Pulle 347
Tønnesen, see Yding
Topander L. C. 283, 285, 290, 299-301, 303, 305, 307-309, 310, 312, 313-315, 316, 318, 319, 321, 323-329, 331, 334, 337, 338, 353
Topas or Topaz 79, 100, 362, 386
Topping 142
Toshakannah 330
Tranquebar Society 78, 132, 134, 148, 207
transit instrument 132, 136, 140, 144
transit of stars 140
Trellund, Gregers Daa 23, 24, 83, 355, 356, 377
Tremeloya 299
Trenamally 330
Trincomalee 60, 177
Troquedor Street 83
Tulsaji 152
Udbyneder, Niels Andersen 14, 57
Ulandeesu cheneral 33, 34
Ungerhof 197
Uscan, Coja Petrus 358
vakil 89, 121, 159, 162, 163, 362, 405, 406

Vackeel, see vakil
Vakeel, see vakil
valankai 92, 362
van Teylingen 232, 249
Vandhavasi 169
Vanketrow 290
Vannanturuvam 174
Verabadrapulle 299, 307, 314, 321, 327
Verbadro Pulle, Veerabadrepulle, Verabadraopulle see Varabadrapulle
Varadayyangar 82
Varde 379
Vedarasa Chetty 247
vellalar 15, 91, 212, 362
Vellore 159, 163, 168-170, 394
Velur 175
Vengitasala Setti 106
Venkatesu Ayyan 159
Venus transit 127, 128, 129, 130, 211, 390, 391
Vepery mission 200, 201
Vepery press 197
Verdechellom 294
Vereinigte Ostindische Compagnie (VOC) 23
Viborg 259, 261, 262
Villock 290, 293, 294, 307-309, 317, 321, 328, 329
Viraraghava Ayyangar 15, 74
Virinchipuram 169
von Haven, Christian Frederik 221, 222
von Krämer 221, 222
von Qualen, Frederik Carl Ferdinand 90, 229, 400
von Strambow 115
Vridhagirisan 35, 372
Waaben, Knud 114, 118, 372, 390
wahanam 99
Waidy 59
Walter, Edele Margaret 240
Walter, Thomas Christian 11, 16, 93-95, 149, 232, 233, 235, 236, 238-241, 243-247, 273, 274, 335, 338, 350, 353, 401
Walther, C. T. 33
Wandiwash, see Vandhavasi 395
Warhudaur 175
Wendelboe, Andreas 118
whooping cough 268
Willednow herbarium 201
Windfeldt 79
Winter, Lucas 79, 80
Wiraraga Chetty 81
Worm, Jacob 14, 258-263, 371, 404
Worm, Peder Jacobsen 259
Würger, Anton Gunter 249, 250
Xerxes 222
Yding, see Ytting 120, 122
Ytting, Birgitte 120, 121
Zeglin 130, 204, 205
Zend 223, 226, 398, 399
Zendavesta 222, 223, 226, 398, 399
Ziegenbalg, Bartholomäus 15, 63, 76, 187-197, 206, 209, 211-213, 249-251, 253, 356, 397, 408
Ziegenbalg, Bartholomäus Lebrecht 197

Ziegenbalg, Ernst Gottlieb 197
Ziegenbalg, Johan Christian 197
zinc sulphate 266
Zion Church 16, 24, 80, 105, 112, 125-127, 131, 132, 134, 136, 137, 149, 188, 207, 208, 245, 249, 251, 255, 257, 264, 265, 274, 276, 352, 353, 366, 407